Lecture Notes in Computer Science 5340

Commenced Publication in 1973
Founding and Former Series Editors:
Gerhard Goos, Juris Hartmanis, and Jan van Leeuwen

Sandeep Kulkarni   André Schiper (Eds.)

Stabilization, Safety, and Security of Distributed Systems

10th International Symposium, SSS 2008
Detroit, MI, USA, November 21-23, 2008
Proceedings

 Springer

Volume Editors

Sandeep Kulkarni
Department of Computer Science and Engineering
Michigan State University
East Lansing, MI, USA
E-mail: sandeep@cse.msu.edu

André Schiper
École Polytechnique Fédérale de Lausanne (EPFL)
Lausanne, Switzerland
E-mail: andre.schiper@epfl.ch

Library of Congress Control Number: Applied for

CR Subject Classification (1998): C.2.4, C.3, F.1, F.2.2, K.6

LNCS Sublibrary: SL 1 – Theoretical Computer Science and General Issues

ISSN   0302-9743
ISBN-10   3-540-89334-2 Springer Berlin Heidelberg New York
ISBN-13   978-3-540-89334-9 Springer Berlin Heidelberg New York

Springer is a part of Springer Science+Business Media

springer.com

© Springer-Verlag Berlin Heidelberg 2008
Printed in Germany

Typesetting: Camera-ready by author, data conversion by Scientific Publishing Services, Chennai, India
Printed on acid-free paper   SPIN: 12566174   06/3180   5 4 3 2 1 0

Preface

This volume contains the proceedings of the 10th International Symposium on Stabilization, Safety, and Security of Distributed Systems (SSS), held November 21–23, 2008 in Detroit, Michigan USA.

SSS started as the Workshop on Self-Stabilizing Systems (WSS), which was first held at Austin in 1989. From the second WSS in Las Vegas in 1995, the forum was held biennially, at Santa Barbara(1997), Austin (1999), Lisbon (2001), San Francisco (2003) and Barcelona (2005). The title of the forum changed to the Symposium on Self-Stabilizing Systems (SSS) in 2003. Since 2005, SSS was run annually, and in 2006 (Dallas) the scope of the conference was extended to cover all safety and security-related aspects of self-* systems. This extension followed the demand for self-stabilization in various areas of distributed computing including peer-to-peer networks, wireless sensor networks, mobile ad-hoc networks, robotic networks. To reflect this change, the name of the symposium changed to the International Symposium on Stabilization, Safety, and Security of Distributed Systems (SSS).

This year we received 43 submissions from 13 countries. Most submissions were from the USA and France. Each submission was carefully reviewed by three to six Program Committee members with the help of external reviewers. For the first time a rebuttal phase allowed the authors to react to the reviews before the discussion of the papers within the Program Committee. Out of the 43 submissions, 17 excellent papers were selected for presentation at the symposium, which corresponds to an acceptance rate of 40%. It can be noted that the highest acceptance rate was for papers with keywords *sensor networks* (86%), *MANETs* (67%), and *security of sensor and mobile networks protocols* (67%). Interestingly, the best paper award (a recent tradition is SSS) was given to a paper without any of these keywords, namely, to Peter Robinson and Ulrich Schmid for the paper "The Asynchronous Bounded-Cycle Model." In addition to the regular papers, the symposium included three invited keynotes that covered the large spectrum of topics of the symposium: "Primitives for Physical Trust" by Anish Arora, "Distributed Algorithms and VLSI" by Ulrich Schmid, and "Trustworthy Services and the Biological Analogy" by Mike Reiter.

We thank all the members of the Program Committee and their external reviewers for their thorough work and for the time they spent selecting the best papers. Paper submission, selection, and generation in the proceedings was greatly eased by the use of the EasyChair conference system (http://www.easychair.org). We wish to thank the EasyChair creators and maintainers for their commitment to the scientific community. We also thank the members of the Steering Committee for their invaluable advice. We gratefully acknowledge the Organizing

Committee members for their generous contribution to the success of the symposium. Finally, we wish all the participants a fruitful and enjoyable symposium.

November 2008   Sandeep Kulkarni
                                                        André Schiper

Organization

Program Chairs

Sandeep Kulkarni
André Schiper

Program Committee

Anish Arora
Mahesh Arumugam
Levente Buttyan
Wei Chen
Alain Cournier
Ajoy Datta
Xavier Défago
Murat Demirbas
Shlomi Dolev
Felix Freiling
Roy Friedman
Sukumar Ghosh
Mohamed Gouda
Yong Guan
Constance Heitmeyer
Ted Herman
Lisa Higham

Jaap-Henk Hoepman
Martin Hutle
Alex Liu
Jean-Philippe Martin
Achour Mostéfaoui
Mikhail Nesterenko
Guevara Noubir
Rui Oliveira
Fernando Pedone
Ravi Prakash
Ulrich Schmid
Alex Shvartsman
Neeraj Suri
Sébastien Tixeuil
Philippas Tsigas
Tatsuhiro Tsuchyia

Poster Chairs

Doina Bein
Ali Ebnenasir

Local Organization

Hongwei Zhang

External Reviewers

Najla Alam
Murat Ali Bayir
Doina Bein
Martin Biely
Christian Boulinier
Lasaro Camargos
Łukasz Chmielewski
Thomas Clouser
Sylvie Delaët
Dan Dobre
Matthias Függer
Flavio Garcia
Hirotsugu Kakugawa
Jing Li
Zvi Lotker
Xuming Lu
Matthias Majuntke

Amirhossein Malekpour
Toshimitsu Masuzawa
Calvin Newport
Lucia Draque Penso
Maria Potop-Butucaru Gradinariu
Peter Robinson
Lifeng Sang
Nicolas Schiper
Jörg Schwenk
Marco Serafini
Onur Soysal
Mukundan Sridharan
Vincent Villain
Josef Widder
Reuven Yagel
Wenjie Zeng

Table of Contents

Stabilizing Algorithms II

Wireless Networks II

Security and System Models

Tutorial Abstract

Keynote: Primitives for Physical Trust

Anish Arora

Department of Computer Science and Engineering
The Ohio State University
Columbus Ohio 43210, USA
anish@cse.ohio-state.edu

Abstract. This talk explores the question of whether wireless communication can achieve security - confidentiality (unicast and broadcast), authentication, non-repudiation, anonymity - without assuming any shared secrets and using only low-cost computation primitives. The key idea is to exploit physical characteristics of the network medium to develop a basis of physical primitives that suffice for rethinking a security protocol suite.

S. Kulkarni and A. Schiper (Eds.): SSS 2008, LNCS 5340, p. 1, 2008.
© Springer-Verlag Berlin Heidelberg 2008

Keynote: Trustworthy Services and the Biological Analogy

Michael Reiter

Department of Computer Science
University of North Carolina at Chapel Hill
Campus Box 3175, Sitterson Hall
Chapel Hill, North Carolina 27599-3175, USA
reiter@cs.unc.edu

Abstract. Biological systems survive through a combination of redundancy, diversity and modularity. It has been argued that these principles can also be applied to construct information services that survive a variety of hostile attacks, including even the compromise of computers that help implement the service. Despite nearly 30 years of research to advance these principles and to apply them to the construction of trustworthy services, each remains an active and fruitful topic of research. In this talk we will describe recent progress in achieving redundancy, diversity and modularity, and in using these to implement trustworthy services. This progress, we will argue, is paving the way to next-generation services that are significantly more resilient than todays. We will also discuss challenges that remain in achieving this goal.

S. Kulkarni and A. Schiper (Eds.): SSS 2008, LNCS 5340, p. 2, 2008.

Keynote: Distributed Algorithms and VLSI

Ulrich Schmid*

Technische Universität Wien
Embedded Computing Systems Group (E182/2)
Treitlstrasse 1-3, A-1040 Vienna (Austria)
s@ecs.tuwien.ac.at

Abstract. Shrinking feature sizes and increasing clock speeds are the most visible signs of the tremendous advances in VLSI (Very Large Scale Integration). Modern VLSI chips can no longer be viewed as monolithic blocks of synchronous hardware, where all state transitions occur simultaneously. Moreover, the reduced voltage swing needed for high clock speeds and low power consumption dramatically increases the adverse effects of particle hits, crosstalk and ground bouncing, and, hence, leads to much higher failure rates. As a consequence, modern VLSI devices have much in common with the loosely-coupled distributed systems that have been studied by the fault-tolerant distributed algorithms community for decades. This keynote will address ways of utilizing some of the existing research in the VLSI context, and identify new and challenging distributed computing research problems emanating from this important application domain.

* This work is supported by the bm:vit FIT-IT project DARTS (proj. no. 809456-SCK/SAI) and the Austrian Science Foundation (FWF) projects P17757 and P20529.

S. Kulkarni and A. Schiper (Eds.): SSS 2008, LNCS 5340, p. 3, 2008.

A Distributed and Deterministic TDMA Algorithm for Write-All-With-Collision Model

Mahesh Arumugam

Cisco Systems, Inc.,
San Jose, CA 95134
maarumug@cisco.com

Abstract. Several self-stabilizing time division multiple access (TDMA) algorithms are proposed for sensor networks. Such algorithms enable the transformation of programs written in abstract models considered in distributed computing literature into a model consistent with sensor networks, i.e., write all with collision (WAC) model. Existing TDMA slot assignment algorithms have one or more of the following properties: (i) compute slots using a randomized algorithm, (ii) assume that the topology is known upfront, and/or (iii) assign slots sequentially. If these algorithms are used to transform abstract programs into programs in WAC model then the transformed programs are probabilistically correct, do not allow the addition of new sensors, and/or converge in a sequential fashion. In this paper, we propose a self-stabilizing deterministic TDMA algorithm where a sensor is aware of only its neighbors. We show that the slots are assigned to the sensors in a concurrent fashion and starting from arbitrary initial states, the algorithm converges to states where collision-free communication among the sensors is restored. Moreover, this algorithm facilitates the transformation of abstract programs into programs in WAC model that are deterministically correct.

1 Introduction

One of the important concerns in programming distributed computing platforms is the model of computation used to specify programs. Programs written for platforms such as sensor networks and embedded systems often have to deal with several low level challenges of the platform (e.g., communication, message collision, race conditions among different processes, etc). Therefore, to simplify programming, it is important to abstract such low level issues. In other words, the ability to specify programs in an abstract model and later transform them into a concrete model that is appropriate to the platform is crucial.

Transformation of programs has been studied extensively (e.g., [1,2,3,4,5,6]). These transformations cannot be applied for sensor networks as the model of computation in sensor networks is *write all with collision* (WAC) model. In WAC model, whenever a sensor executes an *action*, it writes the state of all its neighbors in one atomic step. However, if two neighbors j and k of a sensor (say i) try to execute their write actions at the same time then, due to collision,

S. Kulkarni and A. Schiper (Eds.): SSS 2008, LNCS 5340, pp. 4–18, 2008.
© Springer-Verlag Berlin Heidelberg 2008

state of i will remain unchanged. The actions of j and k may update the state of their other neighbors successfully.

Recently, several approaches have been proposed to transform programs written in abstract models considered in distributed computing literature into programs in WAC model [7,8,9,10]. In [7], the author proposes a transformation to correctly simulate an abstract program in sensor networks. This algorithm uses carrier sensor multiple access (CSMA) to broadcast the state of a sensor and, hence, the transformed program is randomized. And, the algorithm in [9] uses time division multiple access (TDMA) that ensures collision-free write actions. In this approach, in WAC model, each sensor executes the *enabled* actions in the TDMA slots assigned to that sensor. And, the sensor writes the state of all its neighbors in its TDMA slots. If the TDMA algorithm in [11], a self-stabilizing and deterministic algorithm designed for grid-based topologies, is used with [9] then the transformed program in WAC model is self-stabilizing and deterministically correct for grid-based topologies. And, if randomized TDMA algorithms proposed in [8,12] are used with [9] then the transformed program is probabilistically correct. Finally, the algorithm in [10], a self-stabilizing and deterministic TDMA algorithm for arbitrary topologies, allows one to obtain programs in WAC model that are deterministically correct for arbitrary topologies.

In this paper, we are interested in stabilization preserving deterministic transformation for WAC model. As mentioned above, a self-stabilizing deterministic TDMA algorithm enables such a transformation. One of the drawbacks of existing self-stabilizing deterministic TDMA algorithms (e.g., [10]) is that the recovery is sequential. Specifically, in [10], whenever the network is perturbed to arbitrary states (e.g., slots are not collision-free), a distinguished sensor (e.g., base station) initiates recovery and each sensor recomputes its slots one by one. However, it is desirable that the network self-stabilizes in a distributed and concurrent manner (without the assistance of distinguished sensors).

To redress this deficiency, in this paper, we propose a self-stabilizing deterministic TDMA algorithm that provides concurrent recovery. In this algorithm, whenever a sensor observes that the slots assigned to its neighbors are not collision-free, it initiates a recovery. As a result, its neighbors recover to legitimate states (i.e., the slots are collision-free) and the network as a whole self-stabilizes concurrently. We show that the algorithm supports addition or removal of sensors in the network. While a removal of a sensor does not affect the normal operation of the network, our algorithm ensures that the slots assigned to removed sensors are reused. And, our algorithm supports *controlled* addition of new sensors in the network.

Organization of the paper. The rest of the paper is organized as follows. In Section 2, we introduce the models of computation considered in distributed computing platforms and formally state the problem definition of TDMA. In Section 3, we present our distributed self-stabilizing TDMA slot assignment algorithm. And, in Section 4, we discuss extensions to our algorithm. Subsequently, in Section 5, we compare our algorithm with related work. Finally, in Section 6, we provide concluding remarks.

2 Preliminaries

In this section, we define the write all with collision model, formally state the problem, and list the assumptions made in this paper.

2.1 Write-All-With-Collision (WAC) Model and Collision Detectors

A computation model limits the variables that a program can read and write. Program actions are split into a set of processes (i.e., sensors). Each action is associated with one of the processes in the program.

In WAC model, each sensor consists of write actions (to be precise, write-all actions). In one atomic step, a sensor can update its own state and the state of all its neighbors. However, if two or more sensors simultaneously try to update the state of a sensor, say, k, then the state of k remains unchanged. Thus, WAC model captures the fact that a message sent by a sensor is broadcast. But, if multiple messages are sent to a sensor simultaneously then, due to collision, it receives none.

It is clear that WAC model does not provide any indication of collision. However, the physical layer of the communication stack may be required to expose state of the communication medium (e.g., collision information) to the higher layers of the stack. To enable such notifications, collision detectors are proposed in [13]. Collision detectors provide receiver-based notifications when message loss is detected. In [13], the authors identify 6 classes of collision detectors based on completeness and accuracy. In the context of this paper, we integrate *eventually accurate collision detector* to our model. In an eventually accurate collision detector, there exists a *frame*, say f_r, such that if k detects a collision in $f_{r'} \geq f_r$ then k does not receive some messages that were broadcast in $f_{r'}$.

2.2 Problem Statement

Distributed TDMA slot assignment. TDMA is the problem of assigning communication time slots to each sensor. Two sensors j and k cannot transmit in the same slot if their communication interferes with each other. In other words, j and k cannot transmit in the same slot if the communication distance between them is less than or equal to 2. To model this requirement, we consider the sensor network as a graph $G = (V, E)$ where V is the set of all sensors and E is the communication topology of the network. More precisely, if sensors $u \in V$ and $v \in V$ can communicate with each other then the edge $(u, v) \in E$. Finally, $distance_G(u, v)$ identifies the communication distance between u and v in G. The communication distance is the number of links in the shortest path between the two sensors. Thus, the problem statement of TDMA is shown in Figure 1.

Definition 1. *(TDMA frame) In TDMA, time is partitioned into fixed sized frames. Each TDMA frame is divided into fixed sized slots. In this paper, we ensure uniform bandwidth allocation among sensors. Therefore, each sensor is assigned one slot in every TDMA frame. A sensor is allowed to transmit in the slots assigned to it.*

Problem Statement: Distributed TDMA Slot Assignment
Consider the communication graph $G = (V, E)$; Given a sensor $j \in V$, assign time slots to j such that the following condition is satisfied:
$k \in V \wedge k \neq j \wedge distance_G(j, k) \leq 2 \implies slot.j \cap slot.k = \emptyset$
where $slot.i$ identifies the slots assigned to sensor i.

Fig. 1. Problem statement of distributed TDMA slot assignment

Definition 2. *(TDMA period) The length of the TDMA frame is called the TDMA period. More specifically, it is the interval between the slots assigned to a sensor in consecutive frames.*

Distance 2 coloring. The problem statement of TDMA is similar to the problem of distance 2 coloring. Distance 2 coloring algorithm assigns colors to all the sensors in the network such that the colors assigned to distance 2 neighborhood of a sensor are unique. The color assigned to a sensor identifies the initial TDMA slot of that sensor. The sensor can compute its subsequent TDMA slots using TDMA period. Ideally, TDMA period $P = (d^2 + 1)$, where d is the maximum degree of the network. (We refer the reader to [10] for a proof that the number of colors required to obtain distance 2 coloring is at most $d^2 + 1$.) Thus, Figure 2 states the problem definition of distance 2 coloring.

Self-stabilization. An algorithm is self-stabilizing iff starting from an arbitrary state, it: (a) recovers to legitimate state and (b) upon recovery continues to be in legitimate states forever [14,15]. Extending this definition, we have the problem statement of a self-stabilizing TDMA slot assignment algorithm as shown in Figure 3.

2.3   Assumptions

In this paper, we do not assume the presence of a base station. In our algorithm, the sensors collaborate among themselves to obtain distance 2 coloring and TDMA slot assignments. We assume that each sensor knows the IDs of the sensors that it can communicate with. This assumption is reasonable since the sensors collaborate among their neighbors when an event occurs. To simplify the presentation of the algorithm, we assume that frame numbers are not corruptible. However, we note that relaxing this assumption does not affect the correctness of the algorithm. Moreover, we can extend the algorithm to make

---

Problem Statement: Distance 2 Coloring
Consider the communication graph $G = (V, E)$; Given a sensor $j \in V$, assign a color to j such that the following condition is satisfied:
$k \in V \wedge k \neq j \wedge distance_G(j, k) \leq 2 \implies color.j \neq color.k$
where $color.i$ identifies the color assigned to sensor i.

Fig. 2. Problem statement of distance 2 coloring

Problem Statement: Self-Stabilizing TDMA Slot Assignment
Consider the communication graph $G = (V, E)$; A TDMA slot assignment algorithm is self-stabilizing iff starting from arbitrary initial states, the algorithm recovers to the following state:
$$j \in V \wedge k \in V \wedge k \neq j \wedge distance_G(j, k) \leq 2 \implies slot.j \cap slot.k = \emptyset$$
and continues to remain in this state forever.

Fig. 3. Problem statement of self-stabilizing TDMA slot assignment

frame numbers bounded. We assume that the maximum degree of the graph does not exceed a certain threshold, say d. This can be ensured by having the deployment follow a certain geometric distribution or using a predetermined topology. Finally, we assume that the clocks of the sensors are synchronized. We can adopt the approach discussed in [10] to synchronize the clocks of the sensors.

3 TDMA Slot Assignment Algorithm

In this section, we present our distributed and deterministic TDMA algorithm. In Section 3.1, we give an outline of the algorithm. Then, in Section 3.2, we present the algorithm in detail. We discuss how the network self-stabilizes starting from arbitrary states to states where the slots are assigned as identified in Figure 3. Subsequently, in Section 3.3, we illustrate our algorithm with an example.

3.1 Outline of the Algorithm

Initially, the colors assigned to the sensors may be arbitrary. As a result, the communication among the sensors may not be collision-free. To achieve collision-free communication among the sensors, we adopt *distributed reset* (e.g., [16,17]) approach. More specifically, whenever *collisions are detected* for a particular slot (i.e., color) for a threshold number of consecutive TDMA frames (say, at j), the algorithm resets the colors of appropriate sensor(s) in the neighborhood of j. In other words, a reset computation is used to update the colors assigned to the sensors such that the sensors in distance 2 neighborhood of j have unique colors and, thus, ensure that slots assigned to them are collision-free at j.

Towards this end, j schedules a reset computation in its current TDMA slots. It schedules the reset such that the following requirements are satisfied: (i) reset computations of others sensors in the distance 2 neighborhood of j do not interfere with each other and (ii) when j initiates reset, the sensors in the distance 3 neighborhood of j have stopped transmitting. The first requirement ensures that only one reset computation is active in a given neighborhood at any instant. Otherwise, simultaneous resets in a distance 2 neighborhood may result in collisions and/or sensors choosing conflicting colors. The second requirement ensures that the reset messages and update messages are communicated in a collision-free manner.

Whenever a sensor, say k, receives the reset message from j, first, it updates the color information it maintains about its distance 1 and distance 2 neighbors.

Next, it checks if it has to change the color in response to the reset. If k needs to update its color, it chooses a non-conflicting color among the sensors in its distance 2 neighborhood. And, subsequently, k broadcasts change color message in its newly computed slots.

Now, whenever a sensor, say l, receives the change color message from k, first, it cancels any scheduled reset computations. Subsequently, l updates the color information it maintains about its distance 1 and distance 2 neighbors. When j receives change color message, it sends restart message to signal its distance 3 neighborhood to restart application communication. Thus, the algorithm resets the neighborhood of j to deal with a collision at j. However, note that one reset computation may not be sufficient to restore the state of the entire network.

3.2   Reset Computation and Slot/Color Assignment

In this section, we discuss the algorithm in detail. This is a 5-step algorithm: (1) observe collision and schedule reset computation, (2) send reset message, (3) update color, (4) notify color, and (5) restart communication. These steps may be repeated until the network self-stabilizes to legitimate states. (For reasons of space, we do not include a pseudo code for the proposed algorithm.)

Step 1: Observe collision and schedule reset computation. If a sensor, say j, observes collision at slot c_x (i.e., color c_x) for a threshold number of consecutive frames then it schedules a reset computation. Towards this end, first, j appends c_x to *collisions.j*, the list of collision slots it has observed so far. Also, it adds $(f_c.j, c_x)$ to *timestamp.j*, where $f_c.j$ is the frame in which j observed the collision at slot c_x. If j observed a collision for the first time then j determines the slot in which it can send a reset message. Sensor j schedules a reset computation such that requirements identified in Section 3.1 are met.

Requirement 1: Ensure only one active reset in the neighborhood.   To satisfy this requirement, j schedules the reset computation in TDMA frame $f_{reset}.j = f_c.j + ID.j + D3_{timeout}$, where $ID.j$ is the ID of sensor j and $D3_{timeout}$ is defined below. This ensures that if two sensors observe a collision simultaneously, then their resets are scheduled in unique frames. On the other hand, if the sensors observe a collision in different frames, it is possible that their resets are scheduled in the same frame. However, before a sensor initiates a reset, requirement 2 ensures that the distance 3 neighborhood has stopped. As a result, the sensor that observed a collision earlier will be able to proceed.

Requirement 2: Ensure distance 3 neighborhood has stopped.   Suppose j has scheduled reset in $f_{reset}.j$. Before j initiates reset, it has to wait until its distance 3 neighborhood stops transmitting messages. Towards this end, j stops transmitting for *at least* $D3_{timeout}$ frames before it fires the reset. $D3_{timeout}$ is the number of TDMA frames required for distance 3 neighborhood of j to stop transmitting messages. Specifically, when j stops, its neighbors will notice that j has stopped. As a result, distance 1 neighbors of j stop. Likewise, distance 2 and distance 3 neighbors of j stop. To prevent false positives, neighbor, say $l \in N.j$, stops only after it detects that j has stopped for a threshold number of consecutive frames, $stop_{timeout}$. Therefore, in order to ensure that distance 3 neighborhood of a sensor has stopped, $D3_{timeout} \geq 3 \times stop_{timeout}$.

Step 2: Send reset message.   Each sensor, say j, maintains the state of its distance 2 neighborhood: $nbrClr.j$ (contains the state of distance 1 neighbors of j) and $dist2Clr.j$ (contains the state of distance 2 neighbors of j). Each entry in $nbrClr.j$ contains color assignment and the last frame in which j or its neighbors received a message from the corresponding sensor. Likewise, each entry in $dist2Clr.j$ contains color assignment and the last frame in which one of the neighbors of j received a message from the corresponding sensor. Initially, $nbrClr.j$ and $dist2Clr.j$ contain arbitrary color assignments that may not reflect the accurate state of its distance 2 neighborhood.

Notation. An entry in $nbrClr.j$ is denoted as (k, c_k, f_k); this indicates that j last received a message from k in frame f_k and in slot (i.e., color) c_k. Entries in $dist2Clr.j$ are denoted similarly. Additionally, we use "-" to wildcard or *ignore* a field in an entry. For example, $(-, c_x, -)$ indicates that we are interested in entries that have the color c_x. Additionally, we denote the current frame at j as $f_{current}.j$.

Sensor j initiates a reset in $f_{reset}.j$ only if it has not stopped transmitting in response to another reset. From Step 1, we note that j sends the reset message to its distance 1 neighbors in a collision-free manner. The reset message format is shown in Figure 4. This includes the state of distance 1 neighbors that j knows currently, list of collisions and their timestamps, the sensor that should update its color in response to this reset, and the initiator of the reset (i.e., j). Sensor j selects the sensor that should update its color based on IDs of the neighbors that j did not hear for a threshold number of consecutive frames.

Theorem 1. *Reset computation initiated by any sensor executes in a collision-free manner.*

Proof. Suppose two reset computations execute simultaneously in a distance 2 neighborhood. Let k and l be two unique sensors that have initiated the reset such that $distance_G(k, l) \leq 2$. Both k and l should have observed a collision in the same frame and scheduled resets to start at the same frame. Otherwise, either one of them would have observed that the neighbors have stopped in

	neighbor	color	lastReceived
$rm_j.neighborState$	j	$color.j$	$f_{current}.j$
			$nbrClr.j$
$rm_j.collisionInfo$			$collisions.j$
$rm_j.resetTimestamp$			$timestamp.j$
$rm_j.sensorToChange$	l, where $l \in N.j$ is the sensor with lowest ID for which j did not hear any thing for a threshold number of frames		
$rm_j.initiator$			j

Fig. 4. Reset message of j, rm_j

---

if $(j = rm_j.initiator \wedge (j, c_j, -) \in rm_j.neighborState)$
$\quad nbrClr.k = \{nbrClr.k - (j, -, -)\} \cup (j, c_j, f_{current}.k)$
if $(p \in N.k \wedge (p, c_p, f_1) \in rm_j.neighborState \wedge (p, -, f_2) \in nbrClr.k \wedge f_2 < f_1)$
$\quad nbrClr.k = \{nbrClr.k - (p, -, -)\} \cup (p, c_p, f_1)$
else if $(p \notin N.k \wedge (p, c_p, f_1) \in rm_j.neighborState \wedge (p, -, f_2) \in dist2Clr.k \wedge f_2 < f_1)$
$\quad dist2Clr.k = \{dist2Clr.k - (p, -, -)\} \cup (p, c_p, f_1)$
// addition/removal of sensors are updated in $nbrClr.k$ and $dist2Clr.k$ as
$\quad$ discussed in Section 4

Fig. 5. Updating $nbrClr.k$ and $dist2Clr.k$ of sensor k

response to a reset of the other and, hence, it would have stopped as well. Therefore, we have, $f_{reset}.k = f_{reset}.l$. In other words, $f_c.k + ID.k + D3_{timeout} = f_c.l + ID.l + D3_{timeout}$. Without loss of generality, assume that $ID.k < ID.l$. Now, we have $f_c.k > f_c.l$. More specifically, l observed the collision before k did. This is a contradiction. $\square$

Step 3: Update color. Whenever a sensor, say k, receives the reset message rm_j, first, it cancels any scheduled reset. Next, it updates its neighbor state using the information in rm_j as shown in Figure 5. (Note that k updates an entry in $nbrClr.k$ or $dist2Clr.k$ only if the initiator j had received a message from the corresponding sensor most recently than that of k.)

Sensor k then checks if it has to update its color. If $k = rm_j.sensorToChange$ then j requires k to update its color. Sensor k updates its color as shown in Figure 6. Specifically, if $color.k$ is in $rm_j.collisionInfo$, k chooses a color c from K (i.e., the set of all available colors) such that there is no collision in slot c at j and is unique among its distance 2 neighborhood.

Step 4: Notify color. If $k = rm_j.sensorToChange$, it sends *change color message* cm_k to all its neighbors as shown in Figure 7 (regardless of whether it changed its color or not). Specifically, k sends its color information, $nbrClr.k$, and the initiator of the reset. Whenever a sensor receives change color message, first, it cancels any scheduled resets. Next, it updates its $nbrClr$ and $dist2Clr$ similar to the discussion shown in Figure 5. Specifically, if l receives cm_k, it updates $nbrClr.l$ with $(k, c_k, f_{current}.l)$, where $(k, c_k, -) \in cm_k.neighborState$. Similarly, l updates $nbrClr.l$ and $dist2Clr.l$ based on cm_k.

Theorem 2. *If a sensor updates its color in response to a reset then the change color message of that sensor is communicated in a collision-free manner.*

---

if $(k = rm_j.sensorToChange \wedge color.k \in rm_j.collisionInfo)$ {
$\quad potentialColors = \{c | c \in K \wedge c \notin rm_j.collisionInfo \wedge (-, c, -) \notin nbrClr.k$
$\quad\quad\quad\quad \wedge (-, c, -) \notin dist2Clr.k\}$
$\quad color.k = min(potentialColors)$
}

Fig. 6. Updating color assignment of sensor k

	neighbor	color	lastReceived
$cm_k.neighborState$	k	$color.k$	$f_{current} \cdot k$
		$nbrClr.k$	
$cm_k.initiator$		j	

Fig. 7. Change color message of k, cm_k

Proof. Let j be the initiator of the reset. And, $l \in N.j$ updates its color in response to the reset of j. When j initiates the reset (rm_j), distance 3 neighbors of j have stopped transmitting. Therefore, when l sends change color message cm_l, neighbors of l will receive it successfully. Hence, all neighbors of l will get the latest color assigned to l.   □

Step 5: Restart communication. Whenever j initiates a reset, it expects to receive a change color message from $rm_j.sensorToChange$ before its next allotted slot in $f_{current} \cdot j + 1$ frame. If j receives the change color message from the sensor that changed the color in response to reset of j, j cleans *collisions.j* and *timestamp.j*. Then, it signals its neighbors to restart application communication. Specifically, it sends restart message, sm_j; the format of sm_j is the same as change color message (cf. Figure 7). Once a sensor receives sm_j, it updates $nbrClr$ and *dist2Clr* and starts application communication in its slots. Continuing in this fashion, the distance 3 neighborhood of j restarts. Note that the restart operation updates the color assignment of $l = rm_j.sensorToChange$ at distance 2 neighborhood of l, potentially causing collisions at some distance 2 neighbors of l. When a sensor hears a restart message or collision, it restarts communication.

On the other hand, if $l = rm_j.sensorToChange$ did not send change color message (possibly, due to failure of l) then j marks l as *potentially failed*. And, it cleans *collisions.j* and *timestamp.j*. Also, it sends a restart message. In future resets at j, j will not set l in $rm_j.sensorToChange$. If l has not failed, j will remove l from the list of potentially failed sensors when j hears from l.

Theorem 3. *If a sensor updates its color in response to a reset, eventually, the distance 2 neighborhood of that sensor learns the state of the sensor.*

Proof. Suppose $k \in N.j$ updates its color in response to a reset initiated by j. Distance 3 neighborhood of j have stopped transmitting in response to the reset of j. Therefore, we can conclude that sensors in distance 2 neighborhood of k have stopped transmitting. Now, when k sends change color message cm_k, distance 1 neighbors of k receive it successfully. When j sends restart message, distance 2 neighbors of k are updated. Note that it is possible that when distance 1 neighbors of k forward this restart, collisions may prevent some distance 2 neighbors of k to not receive the update. Future resets will restore the state of the neighborhood of k (cf. Figure 8 for illustration). Hence, eventually, state of k will be updated at all sensors in its distance 2 neighborhood.   □

We note that in this algorithm at most one neighbor is recovered in any reset. Therefore, if j observes collisions at two or more colors/slots then j may observe

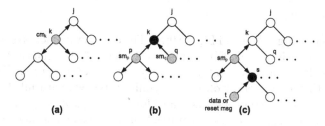

Fig. 8. Illustration of Theorem 3. (a) sensor k sends change color message cm_k to all its distance 1 neighbors. (b) sensor k forwards restart message sm_k to all its distance 1 neighbors. However, $p, q \in N.k$ may have the same color. As a result, when p and q forward sm_p and sm_q, some distance 2 neighbors of k may not be updated. This collision is detected by k and it will schedule a future reset. (c) sensor p forwards sm_p to its neighbors. However, sensor t such that $distance_G(p, t) = 2 \land distance_G(j, t) > 3$ may be assigned the same color as p. Future resets at s that detected this collision will restore the neighborhood. Note that (b) is a special case of (c).

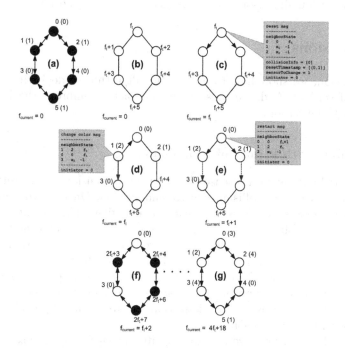

Fig. 9. Illustration of the TDMA slot assignment algorithm

collisions after this reset. Subsequent resets at j or at other sensors will eventually restore collision-free communication at j. Thus, we have

Theorem 4. *Eventually, the network self-stabilizes to the states where collision-free communication among the sensors is restored.*   □

3.3 Illustration

Consider the topology shown in Figure 9(a). The color assignments of each sensor is specified along with its ID. For example, 2(1) denotes that sensor 2 is assigned color 1. Initially, we assume that $f_{current} = 0$ at all sensors. From Figure 9(a), we can note that every sensor observes a collision (shown with filled circles).

Each sensor, say j, determines the frame for reset: $f_{reset}.j = f_{current} + ID.j + f_t$, where $f_t = D3_{timeout}$ (cf. Figure 9(b)). Sensor 0 sets $rm_0.sensorToChange = 1$. As a result, sensor 1 changes its color to 2. Then, it sends a change color message, cm_1 (cf. Figure 9(d)). Once sensor 0 receives cm_1, it updates its state and sends restart message, sm_0 (cf. Figure 9(e)). Once sensors 1 and 2 receive sm_0, they restart their communication. Continuing in this fashion, distance 3 neighborhood of sensor 0 restart communication. As we can observe from Figure 9(f), message communication is still not collision free. Sensors then schedule subsequent resets and, finally, as shown in Figure 9(g), collision-free communication is restored. In this example, the network converges in $4f_t + 18$ frames. (Note that in this illustration all sensors are within distance 3 of each other.)

4 Extensions

In this section, we show how to extend the algorithm to deal with addition/removal of sensors. And, we present an approach to improve the bandwidth allocation of the sensors.

4.1 Dealing with Failure of Neighbors

In our algorithm, whenever a sensor (say j) hears a collision, it schedules a reset computation to restore collision-free communication. On the other hand, if j does not hear a message or observe a collision in a given slot, it could be because of the one of the following factors: (i) suppose $k \in N.j$ is the neighbor that is assigned the corresponding color; k may have failed, (ii) k may have stopped in response to a reset, or (iii) k does not have any data to send. If a sensor fails, the TDMA slots assigned to other sensors are still collision-free and, hence, normal operation of the network is not affected. However, the slots assigned to the failed sensors are wasted. In this section, we discuss an approach to reclaim slots assigned to failed sensors.

Towards this end, first, we introduce control message. Each sensor transmits a control message once in every $T_{control}$ frames. This message includes the color assignment of the sensor and its $nbrClr$. And, $T_{control}$ is determined when the network is deployed and is chosen based on how frequently the network changes. If topology changes are common, a smaller $T_{control}$ lets the sensors to quickly learn the state of their neighbors. On the other hand, a larger $T_{control}$ is more appropriate for a network that changes only occasionally.

To reclaim the slots, we proceed as follows. Sensor j concludes that $k \in N.j$ has failed if $f_{current}.j - lastReceived_k > T_{control}$, where $(k, -, lastReceived_k) \in$

nbrClr.j. In other words, if j sees that it did not receive any message from k for more than $T_{control}$ frames, it concludes that k has failed.

When j concludes k has failed, it sets $(k, -, failed)$ in *nbrClr.j*. And, sends control message, $control_j$. Whenever a sensor observes that $(k, -, failed)$ is present in *control_j.neighborState*, it marks k as failed. The active neighbors of j remove $(k, -, -)$ from *nbrClr* or *dist2Clr*. This allows the sensors to reuse the color assigned to k to other sensors (in case of dynamic addition of new sensors or during reset computations). However, if k has not failed, it announces its presences in its current TDMA slots by sending $control_k$. When neighbors of k receive this message they update their *nbrClr* values. Subsequently, distance 2 neighbors of k also restore the state of k.

4.2   Dealing with Addition of Sensors

In this section, we discuss an approach to dynamically add new sensors in the network. This approach is similar to [10]. Suppose a sensor (say p) is added to the network such that the maximum degree of the network is not changed. Before p starts transmitting application messages, it listens to the message communication of its neighbors. To let p learn the colors used in its distance 2 neighborhood, we extend our algorithm as follows.

Sensor p waits for $T_{control}$ frames before it participates in the network. This allows p to learn distance 1 and distance 2 neighbors and their color assignments (from control messages of its neighbors). After $T_{control}$, p chooses a color. Next, p announces its presence to its neighbors by sending a control message in its newly computed slot. When a sensor receives a control message from p, it adds p to its neighbor list and updates *nbrClr*. Subsequently, distance 2 neighbors of p also learn its presence and update their *dist2Clr* values.

Thus, this approach allows the addition of new sensors in a neighborhood such that it does not violate the maximum degree assumption. However, if two or more sensors are added simultaneously, it is possible that they may choose the same color. Since our algorithm is self-stabilizing, the network will eventually self-stabilize to states where the color assignments are collision-free.

4.3   Improving the Bandwidth Allocation

In this section, we discuss an approach that allows the sensors to reduce the TDMA period and, hence, get better bandwidth allocation. The intuition behind this extension is that if c_x is the maximum color used in the network, the ideal TDMA period should be $c_x + 1$.

Each sensor (say j) maintains *maxColor.j* that denotes the maximum color used in its distance 2 neighborhood. It also maintains *controlMax.j* that denotes the maximum color used in the network. Note that j may not yet have the accurate information about the maximum color used in the network.

To improve the bandwidth allocation of the sensors, we extend the control message (discussed in Section 4.1) as follows. Any sensor in the network may decide to improve bandwidth allocation in the network. Let j decides to improve bandwidth allocation. It sends a control message, $control_j$ that includes

$$controlMax.k = \max(controlMax.k, control_j.maxColorInfo)$$
$$f_{switchOn}.k = \max(f_{switchOn}.k, control_j.switchOn)$$

Fig. 10. Receiving control message with $maxColorInfo$

$control_j.maxColorInfo = \max(controlMax.j, maxColor.j)$. Sensor j also indicates when the sensors can switch to new TDMA period, i.e., $control_j.switchOn = f_{switchOn}.j$, where $f_{switchOn}.j \geq f_{current}.j + 2 \times T_{control}$. (We discuss why this is necessary below.)

Whenever k receives $control_j$ with $maxColorInfo$, k sets $controlMax.k$ and the frame in which it can switch to the new TDMA period as shown in Figure 10. Sensor k includes this information in its control messages. Thus, continuing in this fashion, each sensor will eventually learn the maximum color used in the network, i.e., $controlMax$. And, each sensor also knows the ideal TDMA period (i.e., $controlMax + 1$).

Once the sensors have learned the maximum color used in the network, they can update their TDMA period. However, this operation should occur synchronously. In other words, all the sensors should update their TDMA period at the same time. Otherwise, collisions may occur. To address this issue, first, we note the following. If the TDMA slots assigned to the sensors are consistent then all the sensors learn the maximum color used in the network in at most $2 \times T_{control}$ frames, where $T_{control}$ is the period between two successive control messages (cf. Section 4.1). Since the initiator of this operation includes the frame in which new TDMA period is effective, each sensor knows exactly when to switch. Thus, the TDMA period can be updated to reflect the ideal value.

5   Related Work

Related work that deals with self-stabilizing deterministic slot assignment algorithms include [10, 11, 18]. In [11], Kulkarni and Arumugam proposed self-stabilizing TDMA (SS-TDMA). In this algorithm, the topology of the network is known upfront and remains static. Also, a base station is responsible for periodic diffusing computations to revalidate the slots. In [10], Arumugam and Kulkarni proposed self-stabilizing deterministic TDMA algorithm. Again, this algorithm assumes the presence of a base station that is responsible for token circulation. And, the slots are assigned in a sequential fashion.

In [18], Danturi et al proposed a self-stabilizing solution to dining philosophers problem where a process cannot share the critical section (CS) with non-neighboring processes also. This problem has application in distance-k coloring, where k is the distance up to which a process cannot share CS. This algorithm requires each process p to maintain a tree rooted at itself that spans the processes with whom p cannot share CS.

Related work that deals with randomized algorithms for TDMA slot assignment include [8, 12]. In [8], Herman and Tixeuil proposed a probabilistic fast clustering technique for TDMA slot assignment. In this algorithm, first, a maximal independent set that identifies the leaders is computed. These leaders are then responsible for distance 2 coloring. In [12], Busch et al proposed a randomized algorithm for slot assignment. The algorithm operates in two phases: (1) to compute the slots and (2) to determine the ideal TDMA period. Both these phases are self-stabilizing and can be interleaved.

6   Conclusion

In this paper, we presented a self-stabilizing deterministic TDMA slot assignment algorithm for write all with collision (WAC) model. We showed that the algorithm allows sensors to recover concurrently and self-stabilize starting from arbitrary states. While the convergence time of the proposed algorithm is expected to be reasonable (since concurrent recoveries initiated by sensors that are sufficiently far apart are allowed), it can be improved further by integrating *neighborhood unique naming* scheme from [8] that assigns unique IDs for sensors within any distance 3 neighborhood.

Additionally, as discussed in [9], our algorithm is applicable in transforming existing programs in abstract models considered in distributed computing literature into programs in WAC model that are deterministically correct. This allows one to reuse existing solutions in distributed computing for problems such as routing, data dissemination, synchronization, and leader election in the context of sensor networks. Thus, the algorithm proposed in this paper allows one to transform such solutions and evaluate them in sensor networks. (We refer the reader to [19] for examples of such transformations, prototype implementations of the transformed programs, and their evaluations.)

References

1. Antonoiu, G., Srimani, P.K.: Mutual exclusion between neighboring nodes in an arbitrary system graph tree that stabilizes using read/write atomicity. In: Amestoy, P.R., Berger, P., Daydé, M., Duff, I.S., Frayssé, V., Giraud, L., Ruiz, D. (eds.) Euro-Par 1999. LNCS, vol. 1685, pp. 824–830. Springer, Heidelberg (1999)
2. Gouda, M., Haddix, F.: The linear alternator. In: Proceedings of the Third Workshop on Self-stabilizing Systems, pp. 31–47 (1997)
3. Gouda, M., Haddix, F.: The alternator. In: Proceedings of the Fourth Workshop on Self-stabilizing Systems, pp. 48–53 (1999)
4. Ioannidou, K.: Transformations of self-stabilizing algorithms. In: Malkhi, D. (ed.) DISC 2002. LNCS, vol. 2508, pp. 103–117. Springer, Heidelberg (2002)
5. Kakugawa, H., Yamashita, M.: Self-stabilizing local mutual exclusion on networks in which process identifiers are not distinct. In: Proceedings of the 21st Symposium on Reliable Distributed Systems (SRDS), pp. 202–211 (2002)
6. Nesterenko, M., Arora, A.: Stabilization-preserving atomicity refinement. Journal of Parallel and Distributed Computing 62(5), 766–791 (2002)
7. Herman, T.: Models of self-stabilization and sensor networks. In: IWDC 2003. LNCS, vol. 2918, pp. 205–214. Springer, Heidelberg (2003)

8. Herman, T., Tixeuil, S.: A distributed TDMA slot assignment algorithm for wireless sensor networks. In: Nikoletseas, S.E., Rolim, J.D.P. (eds.) ALGOSENSORS 2004. LNCS, vol. 3121, pp. 45–58. Springer, Heidelberg (2004)

9. Kulkarni, S.S., Arumugam, M.: Transformations for write-all-with-collision model. Computer Communications 29(2), 183–199 (2006)

10. Arumugam, M., Kulkarni, S.S.: Self-stabilizing deterministic time division multiple access for sensor networks. AIAA Journal of Aerospace Computing, Information, and Communication (JACIC) 3, 403–419 (2006)

11. Kulkarni, S.S., Arumugam, M.: SS-TDMA: A self-stabilizing mac for sensor networks. In: Sensor Network Operations. Wiley, IEEE Press (2006)

12. Busch, C., M-Ismail, M., Sivrikaya, F., Yener, B.: Contention-free MAC protocols for wireless sensor networks. In: Proceedings of the 18th Annual Conference on Distributed Computing, DISC (2004)

13. Chockler, G., Demirbas, M., Gilbert, S., Lynch, N., Newport, C., Nolte, T.: Consensus and collision detectors in wireless ad hoc networks. Distributed Computing 21(1), 55–84 (2008)

14. Dijkstra, E.W.: Self-stabilizing systems in spite of distributed control. Communications of the ACM 17(11) (1974)

15. Dolev, S.: Self-Stabilization. MIT Press, Cambridge (2000)

16. Arora, A., Gouda, M.: Distributed reset. IEEE Transactions on Computers 43(9), 1026–1038 (1994)

17. Varghese, G., Arora, A., Gouda, M.G.: Self-stabilization by tree correction. Chicago Journal of Theoretical Computer Science 3 (1997)

18. Danturi, P., Nesterenko, M., Tixeuil, S.: Self-stabilizing philosophers with generic conflicts. In: Proceedings of the Eighth International Symposium on Stabilization, Safety, and Security of Distributed Systems (November 2006)

19. Arumugam, M.: Rapid prototyping and quick deployment of sensor networks. PhD thesis, Michigan State University (2006)

Distance-2 Self-stabilizing Algorithm for a b-Coloring of Graphs

Lyes Dekar[1] and Hamamache Kheddouci[2]

[1] Université de Lyon
Lab. LIESP, Université Lyon 1, IUTA, Département Informatique
71 rue Peter Fink, F-01000 Bourg en Bresse, France
ldekar@bat710.univ-lyon1.fr
[2] Université de Lyon
Laboratoire LIESP, Université Lyon 1
Bât. Nautibus, 43 bd du 11 Novembre 1918
69622 Villeurbanne Cedex, France
hkheddou@bat710.univ-lyon1.fr

Abstract. A b-coloring of a graph G is a proper k-coloring of G such that for each color i, $1 \leq i \leq k$, at least one vertex colored with i is adjacent to every color j, with $1 \leq j \neq i \leq k$. This kind of coloring is useful to decompose any system into communities, where each community contains a vertex adjacent to all the other communities. This kind of organization can provide improving in many fields, especially in the data clustering. In this paper we propose a new self-stabilizing algorithm for finding a b-coloring of arbitrary undirected connected graphs. Because the characteristics of the b-coloring problem, the proposed self-stabilizing algorithm use a distance-2 knowledge.

Keywords: b-coloring, self-stabilizing algorithm, clustering, data mining, graphs.

1 Introduction

A coloring is called a proper k-coloring if it uses k colors such that two adjacent vertices have different colors. Then, a b-coloring is a proper k-coloring where for each color i, $1 \leq i \leq k$, there exists a vertex x with color i, adjacent to vertices colored with every color j, $1 \leq j \neq i \leq k$. Such vertices are called *dominating vertices*.

The b-coloring was introduced by Irving and Manlove [16] where they presented the b-chromatic number, denoted $\varphi(G)$, as the maximum integer k such that G admits a b-coloring with k colors. Thus, the aim in the b-coloring problem is to color a graph with the largest number of colors, by considering the b-coloring constraints given above. Irving and Manlove [16] also proved that finding the b-chromatic number of any graph is a NP-hard problem and they gave a polynomial-time algorithm for finding the b-chromatic number of trees. This parameter was also studied for other classes of graphs like cartesian product of graphs [17], bipartite graphs [18], power graphs of paths and cycles [6].

S. Kulkarni and A. Schiper (Eds.): SSS 2008, LNCS 5340, pp. 19–31, 2008.
© Springer-Verlag Berlin Heidelberg 2008

More recently, Corteel et *al.* [4] proved that the b-chromatic number problem is not approximative within 120/133- ϵ for any $\epsilon > 0$, unless P=NP. Effantin and Kheddouci [7] proposed a distributed algorithm for a b-coloring of graphs. The b-coloring is useful to decompose any system into communities, where each community contains a vertex adjacent to all the other communities. This kind of organization can provide improving in many topics such as clustering and fault localization.

A distributed system can be modelled by a simple connected undirected graph $G = (V, E)$, where V is the set of vertices and E is the set of edges representing communications links between vertices. Its state is divided into two categories: *legitimate state* and *illegitimate state*. The distributed system should remain in a legitimate state to work correctly. However, perturbations and faults can bring it to an illegitimate state, and it is desirable that the system be automatically brought back to a desirable legitimate state. This is called *self stabilization* [5]. A system is said to be self-stabilizing if (1) it can converge to a legitimate state starting form any illegitimate state without the intervention of an external agent, and (2) when it is in a legitimate state, the system remains henceforth. We note that the system must converge to a legitimate state in a finite time.

In a self-stabilizing model, each vertex has only a partial view of the system, called the *local state*. The vertex's local state include the state of the vertex itself and the state of its neighborhood. The union of the local states of all the vertices gives the *global state* of the system. Based on its local state, a vertex can decide to make *a move*. Then, self-stabilizing algorithms are given as a set of rules of the form "**if** $p(i)$ **then** M, where $p(i)$ is a predicate and M is a move. $p(i)$ is true when state of the vertex i is locally illegitimate. In this case, the vertex i is called a *privileged/active* vertex. We assume that a vertex executes the algorithm as long as it is active (at least one predicate is true). Each vertex makes its decision independently, so more than one vertex may be selected at the same time. Then, we assume the existence of a *central daemon* [5], which arbitrarily selects only one of these active vertices to make a move. If two or more vertices are privileged, we cannot predict which vertex will move next. Our algorithm uses a composite read/write atomicity. Several distributed protocols (transformers) [3, 2, 19] exist that provide such a scheduler, which enable central daemon-based self-stabilizing algorithms to be executed in any distributed system. Our algorithm can be easily combined with any of these protocols to work under different schedulers as well.

Many self-stabilizing algorithms were proposed in graph theory such as self-stabilizing algorithms for finding spanning tree, matchings and independent set [1, 14, 20]. Graph coloring is also a very attractive field in which self-stabilizing algorithms are studied. In 1993, Ghosh ana Karaata [10] proposed a self-stabilizing algorithm to color planar graphs with six colors by transforming it in a direct acyclic graph. Sur and Srimani [22] presented a vertex coloring algorithm for bipartite graphs. Shukla et *al.* [21] exhibit a randomized self-stabilizing coloring of several classes of bipartite graphs and trees. In 2000,

Gradinariu and Tixeuil [12] showed algorithms to color the arbitrary networks. Their algorithms use at most $\Delta + 1$ colors and stabilize in $O(n\Delta)$. More recently, Hedetniemi et al. [13] presented two self-stabilizing algorithms which use at most $\Delta + 1$ colors. The first algorithm they proposed gives a Grundy coloring of a graph. In 2005, Huang et al. [15] give a self-stabilizing algorithm to color planar graphs with six colors, but in comparison to [10], they do not construct a directed acyclic graph and decrease the quantity of memory required for the algorithm.

Our paper is organized as follow: the next section introduces the distance-k self-stabilizing algorithms and justifies the need of more than distance-1 information to perform the b-coloring. In Section 3 we give a distance-2 self-stabilizing algorithm for a b-coloring of graphs. We also give an execution example, as well as correctness and convergence proofs of the algorithm. Then, in Section 4, we highlight the use of a b-coloring self-stabilizing algorithm in the data mining for data clustering. Finally, Section 5 outlines the main conclusions and future works.

2   Distance-k Self-stabilizing Algorithms

In the usual self-stabilizing model, each vertex i can read only the variables of its neighbors, that is, those vertices which are within distance 1 from i. Then, the local state of a vertex is its sate and the state of its adjacent vertices. However, as it was observed in [9] certain algorithmic problems can be solved more easily and more efficiently on an extended model in which each vertex can instantly see all state information of vertices that are within distance $k > 1$. In [9], the authors gives a model where each vertex has information about vertices within distance two. This model was extended in [11] and a general model is proposed to transform any distance-k knowledge self-stabilizing algorithm to distance-1 self-stabilizing algorithm. Thus, they define a new class of self-stabilizing model called *distance-k self-stabilizing model*. In the distance-k self-stabilizing model, each vertex i can instantly see its distance-k ball, along with all state information of these vertices. The proposed transformation model has a time and space overhead equal to $n^{o \log(k)}$. As application, the authors give polynomial time self-stabilizing algorithm for finding maximal irredundant sets, problem which seems to require distance-4 information.

In the b-coloring problem, the distance-1 knowledge seems to be not sufficient. Indeed, if we assume a distance-1 model in Figure 1, every vertex should be Dominating for its color since the coloring is proper and a vertex can not see if there is another dominating vertex for its color beyond its immediate neighborhood. Then, the vertex v dominates the colors $\{1, 2, 3\}$, while the vertex u dominates the color $\{4\}$ only. This implies that the vertex u is not dominating. It is clear that it should have at least distance-2 information to decide if it is dominating or not. Therefore, a distance-k information with $k \geq 2$ are required to perform the b-coloring well.

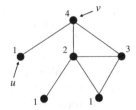

Fig. 1. The distance-2 information requirements of the b-coloring

3   A Distance-2 Self-stabilizing Algorithm for a b-Coloring of Graphs

In this section, we give a self-stabilizing algorithm for a b-coloring of graphs that requires distance-two information at each vertex. Our algorithm provides a b-coloring (not necessarily maximum) of any graph. Finding a b-coloring (not necessarily maximum) of a graph can be solved in polynomial time. The number of colors $w(G)$ generated by our algorithm represents a lower bound of the b-chromatic number of the graph G. Then, we have $\chi(G) \leq w(G) \leq \varphi(G) \leq \Delta + 1$.

Our strategy is to construct a b-coloring locally and lead to a general b-coloring of the graph G. To achieve this aim, we try to color the graph G such that the maximum color c_{max} in the graph G appears on dominating vertices, and every dominating vertex of color c_{max} is adjacent to a dominating vertex of every color less than c_{max}. This enables to restrict the required information to construct the b-coloring of G to the 2-neighborhood of every vertex. Since every vertex has only information about its 2-neighborhood, then the color c_{max} is relative to the 2-neighborhood of every vertex.

First, we start by giving some notations and definitions used in this section: We note $N(v)$ and $N_c(v)$ respectively the set of vertices adjacent to the vertex v and the set of colors that appear on them. We note $N^2(v)$ and $N_c^2(v)$ respectively the set of vertices in the 2-neighborhood of v and the set of colors that appear on them. We also note $N^2[v]$ and $N_c^2[v]$ respectively the set of vertices that includes v and its 2-neighborhood, and the set of colors that appear on them.

A vertex u is considered as a *maximum dominating vertex* by a vertex v, with $u \in N^2[v]$, if u is dominating and has the maximum color in $N_c^2[v]$. Moreover, we say that a vertex v makes an *increasing* move if $c(v)$ increases. Otherwise, we say that it makes a *decreasing* move.

In order to determine if a vertex v is dominating or not according to a set of colors S, we define the function *Dominating(v,S)*. The function return true if the vertex is dominating, and false otherwise. A vertex v is dominating according to a set of colors S if it is adjacent to all the colors in S except its own color, and has the minimum color not appearing in its neighborhood.

---

bool Dominating(v,S)
Begin
   If $S \setminus \{c(v)\} \subseteq N_c(v)$ AND $c(v) = \min\{c : c \notin N_c(v)\}$ Then return True.
   Else return False.
End

3.1 The Rules of Our Algorithm

In this subsection, we give the different rules that compose our self-stabilizing algorithm, and the conditions required to execute them. Our self-stabilizing algorithm is composed of two rules.

Rule 1: The rule R_1 enables to maintain a proper coloring. If two adjacent vertices u and v have the same color, then v takes the minimum color not appearing in its neighborhood.

R1:
BEGIN
   If $\exists u \in N(v)$ $c(v) = c(u)$ THEN $c(v) = \min\{c : c \notin N_c(v)\}$
END

Rule 2: The rule R_2 enables to delete not dominating colors from the graph G, starting from the largest one. The rule is performed locally such that every vertex decides if it is dominating according to the colors in its 2-neighborhood, and if it should change its color accordingly. A vertex v changes its color by executing the rule R_2 if it is not dominating and there is an adjacent maximum dominating vertex u that has not a dominating vertex colored $c(v)$ in its neighborhood. Indeed, by this move, the vertex v aims to make u not maximum dominating and obliges it to make a decreasing move. Then, we ensure that at the end of our algorithm execution, all the maximum dominating vertices colored c_{max} are adjacent to dominating vertices of all the other colors c, with $c < c_{max}$.

Before giving the rule R_2, we define three predicates that we use in this rule.

The predicate $P_1(v)$ is true if all the vertices in the two neighborhood of v are properly colored.

$$P_1(v) = \neg \exists u \in N^2[v] \ c(u) \in N_c(u)$$

The predicate $P_2(v)$ is true in two cases:

1. There exists at least one maximum dominating vertex u in the neighborhood of v that is not adjacent to a dominating vertex colored $c(v)$. This is shown in Figure 2.
2. There is no maximum dominating vertices in the neighborhood of v.

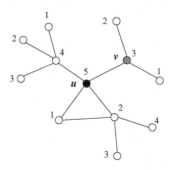

Fig. 2. The maximum dominating vertex u is not adjacent to a dominating vertex colored $c(v) = 3$

$P_2(v) = (\exists u, u \in N(v)$ AND $c(u) = \max\{c : c \in N_c^2[v]\}$ AND $Dominating(u, N_c^2[v])$
AND $\neg \exists w \in N(u)\ c(w) = c(v)$ AND $Dominating(w, N_c^2[v]))$

OR

$(\neg \exists u, u \in N(v)$ AND $c(u) = \max\{c : c \in N_c^2[v]\}$ AND $Dominating(u, N_c^2[v]))$

The predicate $P_3(v)$ is true in the same conditions as the case 1 of the predicate $P_2(v)$.

$P_3(v) = \exists u, u \in N(v)$ AND $c(u) = \max\{c : c \in N_c^2[v]\}$ AND $Dominating(u, N_c^2[v])$
AND $\neg \exists w \in N(u)\ c(w) = c(v)$ AND $Dominating(w, N_c^2[v])$

Let c_1 be the minimum color not appearing in the immediate neighborhood of a vertex v:

$c_1 = \min\{c' :\ c' \notin N_c(v)\}.$

Let c_2 be the minimum color c, such that for every maximum dominating vertex u adjacent to v, there exists in its neighborhood a dominating vertex w colored c.

$c_2 = \min\{c : \forall u, u \in N(v)$ AND $c(u) = \max\{c' : c' \in N_c^2[v]\}$ AND $Dominating(u, N_c^2[v])$
$\exists w \in N(u)\ c(w) = c$ AND $Dominating(w, N_c^2[v])$ AND $c(w) \notin N_c(v)\}.$

Then, the rule R_2 is executed by a vertex v if the following conditions are verified:

- All the vertices in the 2-neighborhood of v are properly colored ($P_1(v) = true$).
- If $c_1 < c(v)$, and either there exists an adjacent maximum dominating vertex u that has not a dominating vertex w colored $c(v)$ in its neighborhood, or there is simply no maximum dominating vertices in the neighborhood of v ($P_2(v) = True$).
- if $c_1 > c(v)$, v is not dominating and there exists a maximum dominating vertex u, adjacent to v, that has not a dominating vertex w colored $c(v)$ in its neighborhood ($P_3(v) = True$).

We note that if $c_1 < c(v)$ then we consider necessarily that the vertex v is not dominating. If more than one vertex verify the conditions above, then the vertex having the largest color executes the rule R_2 first.

R2:
BEGIN

$P_4 = P_1(v)$ AND $[(c_1 < c(v)$ AND $P_2(v))$ OR $(c_1 > c(v)$ AND $Dominating(v, N_c^2[v]) = False$ AND $P_3(v))]$.

If $P_4(v)$ AND $c(v) = \max\{c(x) : x \in N^2[v]$ and $P_4(x)\}$ Then

If $c_1 < c(v)$ Then $c(v) = c_1$
Else $c(v) = c_2$

End

3.2   Execution Example

We give in Figure 3 an execution example of our distance-two self-stabilizing algorithm for a b-coloring of graphs.

(a) First, the coloring of the graph is not a b-coloring. The selected vertex has not a proper coloring, and then the predicate of the rule R_1 is true. (b) The selected vertex executes the rule R_1 and takes a proper color 1. (c) A new active vertex v is selected to execute the algorithm. The vertex has the largest color in its 2-neighborhood and is not dominating. Then, there exists a color $c_1 < c(v)$ and we have $P_2(v) = True$. (d) The selected vertex v executes the rule R_2 and get the color 4. It also becomes maximum dominating. (e) A new active vertex is selected. It is not dominating and is not adjacent to a maximum dominating vertex. Then, the predicate $P_2(v)$ is true. (f) The selected vertex executes the rule R_2 and takes the minimum color not appearing in its neighborhood. (g) A new active vertex v is selected. The selected vertex is adjacent to a maximum dominating vertex u, which has not a dominating vertex colored $c(v)$ in its neighborhood. Then, the predicate $P_3(v)$ is true. Moreover, there exists a color $c_2 > c(v)$ that appears on a dominating vertex in the neighborhood of u. (h) The vertex v takes the color $c_2 = 3$ by executing the rule R_2. (i) A new active vertex is selected that is not adjacent to a maximum dominating vertex and is not dominating. Then, we have $P_2(v)$ is true. (j) The selected vertex executes the rule R_2 and takes the minimum color not appearing in its neighborhood. (k) The obtained coloring is a b-coloring. The black vertices represent the dominating vertices. The grey vertices are those not dominating, but having dominating vertices with their color in the neighborhood of all their adjacent maximum dominating vertices.

3.3   Convergence and Correctness of the Algorithm

In this section, we prove the correctness and the convergence of our self-stabilizing algorithm.

Lemma 1. *Each vertex can execute the rule R_1 at most once.*

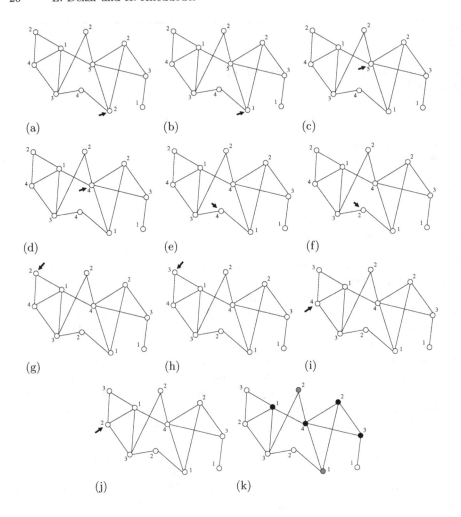

Fig. 3. An execution example of the algorithm

Proof. After executing the rule R_1, a vertex becomes properly colored. Since no vertex can destroy the proper coloring of another vertex, then the rule R_1 is executed at most once.   ∎

Lemma 2. *A vertex v can make at most 2 moves, when there exists a maximum dominating vertex in its neighborhood that is not adjacent to a dominating vertex with a color $c(v)$.*

Proof. If a vertex v has a maximum dominating vertex in its neighborhood that is not adjacent to a dominating vertex with a color $c(v)$, then v is active. Hence, in a first step, if v has not the minimum color c_1 not appearing in its neighborhood, then the predicate $P_2(v)$ is true and then it executes the rule R_2 to take this color. Once colored with c_1, the vertex v checks if there is a maximum dominating vertex in its neighborhood that is not adjacent to a dominating vertex with a color c. If yes, the predicate $P_3(v)$ is true and v executes R_2 a second time to take the color c_2. The color c_2 is the minimum color such that each maximum dominating vertex in the neighborhood of v has an adjacent dominating vertex colored c_2. Such color always exists as proved in Lemma 7. Therefore, the vertex v makes at most 2 moves. ∎

Lemma 3. *If a maximum dominating vertex of color c_{max} is not adjacent to a dominating vertex of color $c < c_{max}$, then it will make a decreasing move and becomes eventually not maximum dominating vertex.*

Proof. When a maximum dominating vertex u colored c_{max} is not adjacent to a dominating vertex of color $c < c_{max}$, then all the vertices adjacent to u and colored with c execute the rule R_2 and move to change their color. Hence, the vertex u will not have the color c in its neighborhood, which means that it has not the minimum color not appearing in its neighborhood and is not maximum dominating too. In this case, the predicate $P_2(v)$ is true and the vertex u executes the rule R_2 and takes the color c ∎.

Lemma 4. *Let S be a set of the maximum dominating vertices adjacent to v and colored c_{max}. A vertex v can make at most 2Δ moves, when there is no dominating vertices colored $c(v)$ in the neighborhoods of the S's vertices*

Proof. A vertex v can have at most Δ maximum dominating vertices with a color c_{max} in its neighborhood. Moreover, a vertex v can make at most 2 moves if a maximum dominating vertex in its neighborhood u is not adjacent to a dominating vertex with a color $c(v)$, according to Lemma 2. The moves of v causes a move of u that becomes not maximum dominating as proved in Lemma 3. Then, from these statements, we can deduce that a vertex can make at most 2Δ moves when there is no dominating vertices with its color in the neighborhoods of its adjacent maximum dominating vertices ∎.

Lemma 5. *A maximum dominating vertex or a vertex that is not adjacent to a maximum dominating vertex can make only decreasing moves, and at most $\Delta(G)$.*

Proof. If a vertex v is not adjacent to a maximum dominating vertex, then the predicate $P_3(v)$ is false. This implies that the vertex v can only make a decreasing move when executing R_2. ∎

Lemma 6. *A vertex can make at most $2\Delta^2 + 1$ moves.*

Proof. As proved in Lemma 4, a vertex v can make at most 2Δ moves when there is no dominating vertices colored $c(v)$ in the neighborhoods of its adjacent maximum dominating vertices colored with c_{max}. In this case, all the maximum dominating vertices with color c_{max} disappear, according to Lemma 3, whereas the new maximum dominating vertices have at most the color $c_{max} - 1$. Then, the vertices adjacent to these vertices can make another 2Δ moves. Hence, we can deduce that the maximum color c_{max} can only decrease during the execution of our algorithm, and for every value of c_{max}, $2 \leq c_{max} \leq \Delta(G) + 1$, the vertices adjacent to the maximum dominating vertices make at most 2Δ moves. By considering the execution of the rule R_1, we deduce that a vertex can make at most $2\Delta^2 + 1$ moves.

We note that a vertex v that is maximum dominating or not adjacent to a maximum dominating vertex makes only decreasing moves until one of its neighbors become maximum dominating. This happens when c_{max} decreases and becomes equal to the color of this neighbor. Then, such vertex makes also a number of moves that does not exceed $2\Delta^2 + 1$. ∎

Lemma 7. *Let v be a not dominating vertex colored with $c_{max} - x$ and having the minimum color not appearing in its neighborhood. Let $S = \{u_1, u_2, ..., u_q\}$ be maximum dominating vertices adjacent to v. Then, when the vertex v executes the rule R_2, every maximum dominating vertex u_i, $1 \leq i \leq q$, is adjacent to dominating vertices colored with every color c, for $c = c_{max} - x + 1$ to $c_{max} - 1$.*

Proof. We give a proof by contradiction. We assume that there exists a maximum dominating vertex u_i in S that is not adjacent to a dominating vertex colored with c, with $c_{max} - x + 1 \leq c \leq c_{max} - 1$, when v executes the rule R_2. Since $c(u_i) > c > c(v)$, then according to Lemma 3, the vertex u_i makes a decreasing move and become not maximum dominating before the vertex v executes the rule R_2. Thus, the vertex u_i will not belong to S when v executes R_2, which gives a contradiction. ∎

Lemma 8. *Our self-stabilizing algorithm gives a b-coloring of any graph G.*

Proof. Let v be a not dominating vertex colored with $c_{max} - x$ and $u_1, u_2,..., u_q$ be the maximum dominating vertices adjacent to v and colored c_{max}. In our proof, we distinguish four different cases:

In the first two cases, we assume the vertex v has not the minimum color not appearing in its neighborhood.

- **Case 1:** All the vertices u_i, $1 \leq i \leq q$, are adjacent to a dominating vertex of color $c(v) = c - x$. Then, the vertex v keeps its color and does not make a move. We observe then that a dominating vertex colored $c - x$ exists in the graph.
- **Case 2:** There exists a vertex u_i, $1 \leq i \leq q$, not adjacent to a dominating vertex of color $c(v)$. In this case, the predicate $P_2(v)$ is true and the vertex v takes the minimum color not appearing in its neighborhood. By Lemma 3, the dominating vertex u_i makes a decreasing move and takes the color $c - x$ by executing R_2. Then, two scenarios can happen: 1- All the maximum dominating vertices of color c_{max} in G are not adjacent to a dominating vertex of color $c - x$. Thus, they all make the same operation as u_i and become dominating for the color $c - x$. 2- There exists a maximum dominating vertex of color c_{max} in G that is adjacent to a dominating vertex v' of color $c - x$. Thus, the color $c - x$ has a dominating vertex in G that is v'.

In the two scenarios, we observe that we have always a dominating vertex of the color $c - x$ by decreasing the number of colors or by maintaining it.

In the following two cases, we suppose that the color of the vertex v is the minimum not appearing in its neighborhood.

- **Case 3:** All the vertices u_i, $1 \leq i \leq q$, are adjacent to a dominating vertex of color $c(v)$. Then, the vertex v keeps its color as in Case 1.
- **Case 4:** There exists a vertex u_i, $1 \leq i \leq q$, not adjacent to a dominating vertex of color $c(v)$. In this case, the predicate $P_3(v)$ is true and the vertex v executes R_2 and takes a color $c' > c(v)$, such that every maximum dominating vertex u_i is adjacent to a dominating vertex colored c. We note that the color c' always exists according to Lemma 7. Hence, by Lemma 3, the dominating vertex u_i makes a decreasing move. The same two scenarios as Case 2 can be identified with the same observations.

Now, according to these four cases, we can deduce that if a dominating vertex with a color $c - x$, $c - x < c_{max}$, exists in the graph, then the number of colors (expressed by c_{max}) is maintained. Otherwise, a dominating vertex colored with $c - x$ is obtained by decreasing the number of colors.

Therefore, we obtain necessarily a b-coloring of the graph, since at the end, every color will have a dominating vertex. ∎

Theorem 9. *Our self-stabilizing algorithm gives a b-coloring of any graph G on $O(\Delta^2)$.*

Proof. This is a direct consequence of 6 and 8. ∎

4   The Application of the b-Coloring Self-stabilizing Algorithm in Distributed Data Mining

A clustering is a fundamental data mining process that aims to classify observation into categories, such that all the objects in the same category share a same property. Clustering plays an important role in data mining applications such as Web analysis, information retrieval and many other domains. The b-coloring of graphs is a useful way to partition data set into several clusters. Our previous works [8] introduced this approach and showed its efficiency. Among the most interesting features of the b-coloring for the data clustering, we cite the identification of each cluster by one dominating object which guarantee the disparity between clusters. A b-coloring self-stabilizing algorithm can be interesting to cluster data objets in dynamic distributed systems (e.g. peer-to-peer networks), where data objects join and leave the system continuously. Then, we can assume that the data objects are distributed on several peers, and every data object is considered autonomous. Then, the system can be modelled by a graph where vertices are the data objects and the edges are the relation between them. Thus, the data clustering is performed and maintained through the maintenance of a b-coloring, by using a self-stabilizing algorithm.

5 Conclusion

In this paper, we propose a distance-two self-stabilizing algorithm for a b-coloring of a connected undirected graph G. The algorithm converge on $O(\Delta^2)$. As future works, we aims to use our algorithm for data clustering in distributed systems.

References

[1] Antonoiu, G., Srimani, P.K.: A self-stabilizing distributed algorithm for moinimal spanning tree problem in a symmetric graph. Computer and Mathematics with Application 35(10), 15–23 (1998)

[2] Antonoiu, G., Srimani, P.K.: Mutual exclusion between neighboring nodes in an arbitrary system graph tree that stabilizes using read/write atomicity. In: Amestoy, P.R., Berger, P., Daydé, M., Duff, I.S., Fraysseé, V., Giraud, L., Ruiz, D. (eds.) Euro-Par 1999. LNCS, vol. 1685, pp. 823–830. Springer, Heidelberg (1999)

[3] Beauquier, J., Datta, A.K., Gradinariu, M., Magniette, F.: Self-stabilizing local mutual exclusion and daemon refinement. In: Herlihy, M.P. (ed.) DISC 2000. LNCS, vol. 1914. Springer, Heidelberg (2000)

[4] Corteel, S., Valencia-Pabon, M., Vera, J.: On approximating the b-chromatic number. Discrete Applied Mathematics 146, 106–110 (2005)

[5] Dijkstra, E.W.: Self-stabilizing systems in spite of distributed control. ACM 17(11), 643–644 (1974)

[6] Effantin, B., Kheddouci, H.: The b-chromatic number of some power graphs. Discrete Mathematics and Theoretical Computer Science 6, 45–54 (2003)

[7] Effantin, B., Kheddouci, H.: A distributed algorithm for a b-coloring of a graph. In: Guo, M., Yang, L.T., Di Martino, B., Zima, H.P., Dongarra, J., Tang, F. (eds.) ISPA 2006. LNCS, vol. 4330, pp. 430–438. Springer, Heidelberg (2006)

[8] Elghazel, H., Kheddouci, H., Deslandres, V., Dussauchoy, A.: A new graph-based clustering approach: Application to pmsi data. In: IEEE International Conference on Services Systems and Services Management (ICSSSM 2006), France (2006)

[9] Gairing, M., Goddard, W., Hedetniemi, S.T., Kristiansen, P., McRae, A.A.: Distance-two information in self-stabilizing algorithms. Parallel. Process. Lett. 14, 387–398 (2004)

[10] Ghoch, S., Karaata, S.: A self-stabilizing algorithm for coloring planar graph. Distributed Computing 71, 55–59 (1993)

[11] Goddard, W., Hedetniemi, S.T., Jacobs, D.P., Trevisan, V.: Distance-k knowledge in self-stabilizing algorithms. Theoretical Computer Science 399, 118–127 (2008)

[12] Gradinariu, M., Tixeuil, S.: Self-stabilizing vertex coloring of arbitrary graphs. In: Proceedings of the International Conference on Principles of Distributed Systems OPODIS 2000, pp. 55–70 (2000)

[13] Hedetniemi, S.T., Jacobs, D.P., Srimani, P.K.: Linear time self-stabilizing colorings. Information Processings Letters 87, 251–255 (2003)

[14] Hsi, S.-C., Huang, S.-T.: A self-stabilizing algorithm for maximal matching. Information Processing Letters 43(2), 77–81 (1992)

[15] Huang, S.-T., Hung, S.-S., Tzeng, C.-H.: Self-stabilizing coloration in anonymous planar networks. Information Processing Letters 95, 307–312 (2005)

[16] Irving, R.W., Manlove, D.F.: The b-chromatique number of a graph. Discrete Applied Mathematics 91, 127–141 (1999)

[17] Kouider, M., Maheo, M.: Some bounds for the b-chromatic number of a graph. Discrete Mathematics 256(1-2), 267–277 (2002)

[18] Kratochvil, J., Tuza, Z., Voigt, M.: On the b-chromatic number of graphs. In: Kučera, L. (ed.) WG 2002. LNCS, vol. 2573, pp. 310–320. Springer, Heidelberg (2002)

[19] Nesterenko, M., Arora, A.: Stabilization-preserving atomicity refinement. In: Jayanti, P. (ed.) DISC 1999. LNCS, vol. 1693, pp. 254–268. Springer, Heidelberg (1999)

[20] Shi, Z., Goddard, W., Hedetniemi, S.T.: An anonymous self-stabilizing algorithm for 1-maximal independent set in trees. Information Processing Letters 91, 77–83 (2004)

[21] Shukla, S., Rosenkrantz, D., Ravi, S.: Developement self-stabilizing coloring algorithms via systematic randomization. In: Proceedings of the International Workshop on Parallel Processing, pp. 668–673 (1994)

[22] Sur, S., Srimiani, P.K.: A self-stabilizing algorithm for coloring bipartite graphs. Information Science 69, 217–219 (1993)

Duty Cycle Stabilization in Semi-mobile Wireless Networks

Jing Li and Anish Arora

Department of Computer Science and Engineering
The Ohio State University, Columbus, OH 43210
{ljing,anish}@cse.ohio-state.edu

Abstract. Coordinating the duty cycles of nodes in low power wireless networks raises challenging stabilization issues. In this paper, we show how to maintain duty-cycle coordination across the partitions of a static network of nodes. The idea is to synchronize the wakeup times of the nodes based on information carried by mobile "token" nodes between the otherwise disconnected partitions; the stabilization challenge is to deal with the corruption of state in both the static nodes and the mobile tokens. Our basic protocol assumes zero or more token nodes traversing disconnected static nodes in a circular order without overtaking each other. Refinements of our protocol accommodate richer patterns of token traversal and speeds.

1 Introduction

Energy-efficient operation is a basic requirement for battery powered wireless sensor networking. Almost-always-off operation of sensor nodes is thus the norm in any wireless sensor network application whose lifetime has to be nontrivial. In synchronous architectures, almost-always-off operation is achieved via ultra-low duty cycle processing. (By way of contrast, in asynchronous architectures, it is achieved via wake-up-on-event based processing.) 1% to 0.1% duty cycling is characteristic of the state-of-the-art in mote-scale wireless sensor networks.

Duty cycling entails two inter-related issues: one is the maintenance of coordination between the nodes so that they are repeatedly simultaneously up in order to communicate with each other when need be; and the other is choosing the appropriate rate of cycling so that nodes are neither contending excessively for the communication medium nor are they waking up excessively and performing wasteful idle listening. In some cases, coordination may be needed globally across the network while in others it may be needed only with respect to node neighborhoods. Analogously, the same duty cycle may be chosen at all nodes in the network or, should the load across the nodes vary, different rates may be chosen in each locality.

Stabilization of both the coordination and the rate selection aspects of duty cycling is an unavoidable consideration, not only for initializing wireless sensor networks, but also for dealing with faults, clock drift, configuration or environment change, traffic or application mode changes, etc. For the case of static,

S. Kulkarni and A. Schiper (Eds.): SSS 2008, LNCS 5340, pp. 32–46, 2008.

connected networks, the stabilization problem has received significant attention; see for instance the work on stabilizing time synchronization in wireless sensor networks [1]. In this paper, we focus on the less studied but no less important case of mobile or partially mobile networks. We motivate the problem at hand via a case study.

1.1   Duty Cycling for Elevator Sensing

PeopleNet is a wireless sensor network currently deployed in Dreese Labs, our department building on the Ohio State campus. As the name suggests, PeopleNet is about people-centric sensing; it comprises scenarios that involve sensing for the people, by the people, and of the people.

A realized PeopleNet scenario involves communicating the location of all the elevators in the building to a server, which in turn makes this information available in real-time via the web or, more usefully for the residents of the building, via a multi-hop low-power wireless network involving mobile hand-held devices.

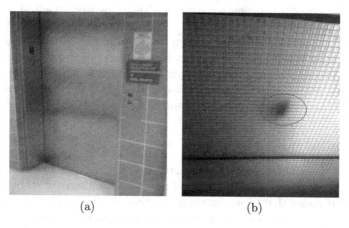

(a)   (b)

Fig. 1. (a) A Dreese Labs Elevator   (b) TelosB Mote Deployed in Elevator

As shown in Figure 1, each elevator car has a battery powered mote sensor embedded in its false ceiling which sends a radio beacon every time the elevator door opens at any floor. Beacons from an elevator mote are heard by a static battery-powered "relay" mote which is mounted nearby the elevator egress at the corresponding floor. In turn, the relay communicates the beacon information to a wired infrastructure network that respectively forwards the beacons to a base station server. The base station in turn makes the elevator location available to the local cellphone network upon demand as well as to the web continuously, see Figure 2.

Note that this scenario involves both mobile sensor nodes (on each elevator) and static relay nodes (on each floor). Duty cycling involves having both mobile and static nodes simultaneously up. When elevators do not move at all, i.e., at night, the rate of duty cycling should decrease to suit energy-efficient operation; conversely, when elevators use increases, the rate of duty cycling should increase.

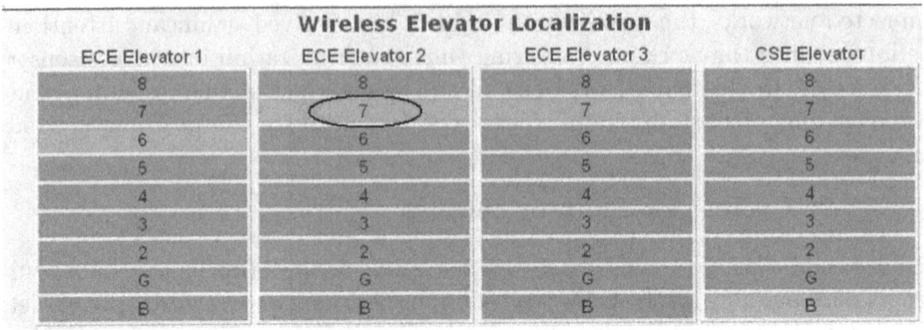

Fig. 2. PeopleNet Elevator Localization Webpage

In the particular case of our building, a static relay node cannot communicate directly with relay nodes on neighboring floors. The static relay nodes thus comprise a network of singleton node partitions. Achieving stabilization of almost-always-off operation within the wireless network itself –i.e., without resorting to using the out-of-band wired infrastructure network— thus needs the elevator to serve as a token carrying the coordination information between the floor relays. When elevators do not move at all, for instance at night, the network is disconnected and its partitions can gradually fall out of sync. When the elevators resume functioning, stabilization is needed to regain the duty cycle coordination across the relay and elevator motes.

1.2   Contributions

We abstract the problem of energy-efficient duty cycling as achieving stabilizing wakeup coordination across a network of partitioned clusters of static nodes via mobile token nodes that move between the clusters. To begin with, we further abstract each cluster as a single static node and consider the special case where the tokens traverse the static nodes in a unidirectional ring fashion without overtaking each other.

For this "unidirectional ring" model, where the static nodes cannot communicate with other static nodes but only via the mobile tokens, we design a stabilizing protocol by which all nodes converge to being simultaneously up according to a pre-selected global duty cycle.

We also present refinements of the basic protocol whereby: (1) tokens may not individually traverse the entire ring, but the set of all tokens cumulatively traverse the ring; (2) the ring topology is generalized to an arbitrary graph consisting of zero or more pre-specified unidirectional rings, each of which has the group token traversal criterion; and (3) the duty cycle is adapted depending upon the token traffic rates.

1.3   Organization of the Paper

Section 2 formulates the system model and the basic ring duty-cycling problem. Section 3 presents our stabilizing program for the basic ring, and its proof of correctness. Section 4 discusses extensions of the program to accommodate a richer token mobility model, underlying graph model, and traffic adaptivity. Section 5 discusses related work. Finally, concluding remarks are in Section 6.

2   System Model and Problem Statement

The system consists of up to N static nodes and 0 or more mobile tokens. Each static node and token has a unique integer identifier (Id); we assume that token identifiers are smaller than node identifiers. Note that our use of tokens is in contrast to the standard notion of tokens in the stabilization literature, in which tokens refer to state at nodes (or state relationships between nodes); tokens here refer to independent computing entities.

For convenience, we henceforth refer to a static node as simply a node. Nodes are all isolated, in the sense that their communications cannot be heard by other nodes. In contrast, tokens are never isolated: at each point in time, each token can communicate with some one static node and, vice versa, that node can always communicate with that token. Communications are half-duplex, so at a given time a token can communicate with a node or vice versa, but both cannot simultaneously. Note that multiple tokens may be in the vicinity of a given static node at any time. It is thus possible that tokens may hear each others' messages.

To begin with, we assume that tokens move such that they visit all nodes according to a fixed unidirectional ring ordering of the nodes; we may thus regard the nodes as being organized in a virtual ring. We assume that there is a lower bound on the amount of time that a token may be in the vicinity of a node; informally speaking, this lower bound will imply that each token is able to exchange a synchronization message to and from with the node in question even when synchronization between the node and the token is lost. There is no upper bound on the time that a token visits with the node. So tokens may stop moving or move arbitrarily slow. However, tokens cannot overtake other tokens as they move around the ring. (We will generalize the mobility model in Section 4.)

A "slot" is a unit of time in which a node may send or receive a message, and/or perform some local computation. A "frame" is a contiguous sequence of some large number, m, of slots. The time sequence at each node is divided into a sequence of frames. The ratio of the number of slots in which a node is awake in each frame to the number of slots in each frame is the duty cycle of the node. We assume the network is synchronous at the level of "slots". (The assumption is readily removed, and is introduced only for ease of exposition.) If properly initialized, nodes and tokens are synchronous even at the level of frames.

Fault Model. Tokens may leave or join the system spontaneously. Nodes may leave or join the ring as well, subject to the upper bound of the node number not exceeding N. The state of the tokens and the nodes may be arbitrarily corrupted. Nodes and tokens may become desynchronized at the level of frames. As a result of these faults, the starting state for the protocol may be thus arbitrary. Also, the clocks of individual nodes may exhibit skew during the operation of the system and this should ideally be tolerated without much overhead.

Problem Statement. Required is a stabilizing protocol whereby the frames of each token and node are synchronized so that visiting tokens and nodes can mutually communicate at one or more well known moments during the frame.

3   Duty-Cycle Coordination in a Multi-token Ring

Coarsely speaking, the central idea of our protocol is to let a leader token dictate the frame schedule to all nodes and tokens in the system. This is programmed as follows: When the leader token visits a node, the node directly synchronizes its frame schedule to be consistent with that of the leader. In turn, when a non-leader token visits a node which has more recently synchronized with the leader, the non-leader is indirectly resynchronized with the leader via the more recent information at the node. And so on: When a non-leader token that has been indirectly synchronized with the leader visits with a node which has less recently synchronized with the leader, the node may indirectly resynchronize itself with the leader. Thus, as long as tokens are moving around the ring, all tokens and nodes become globally synchronized.

We refer to the information exchange between a token and a node to synchronize the frame as a "synchronization-exchange". In our protocol, synchronization-exchange is programmed as follows. We let each node wake up in the first slot of their frame. Each token sends its overall state in a message to the node which it is visiting by waking up in the first slot of the frame. A node that receives a message from the token sends its response in the next slot. Note that the token may not receive a response, however, if the frames of the token-node pair are not synchronized or if a collision occurs with another token message during its original send.

Two basic issues now need to be addressed: (1) how to complete a synchronization-exchange between a token and a node when their frames are out of sync or when message collisions occur when multiple tokens are in the vicinity of a node; and (2) how to stabilize the synchronization information system-wide after faults happen.

The protocol deals with the first issue as follows. To regain communication should frames be out of sync, each node randomly beacons during one or more other slots in its frame. When a token does not receive its anticipated response, it remains awake until it hears the node beacon. Upon receiving the node beacon, the token can adjust the time for its next communication so as to ensure that the node is then awake and, by using random backoffs over the set of possible send times, to avoid collision with other visiting tokens. The next subsection explains how the protocol deals with the second issue.

3.1   Synchronization-Exchange Protocol Design

The protocol consists of four main components: leader election, continuous frame synchronization, false leader detection, and global reset, which are described next.

Leader Election. A leader token is elected so that its frame schedule serves as a global reference to synchronize the frames of all nodes and tokens in the system, which may initially be arbitrarily staggered. Stabilizing leader election is achieved as follows. The up token with lowest Id is prioritized to win the election; a variable l is maintained at each node and token to store the lowest Id known.

Continuous Frame Synchronization. Each node and token maintains a recency/staleness time estimate of the number of frames since it last received synchronization information about the leader frame schedule, either directly from the leader token or indirectly from some other token/node.

This count is maintained using an integer variable c. The c value is assumed to be (implicitly) incremented at the end of every frame in which no new synchronization information is received. A special case is that the c value of a leader token is always zero. When a node encounters a token with the same l, whichever has the smaller c dominates their pairwise synchronization of the frame schedule, since the smaller c represents a more recent and therefore more accurate schedule. In other words, when a node and token agree on the leader Id, the one with the larger c value will adjust its frame schedule to conform to that of the one with the smaller c value.

Since non-leader tokens and nodes propagate frame synchronization information, they may introduce errors because of their local clock skew. Tokens and nodes therefore make adjustments to compensate for their skew. Figure 3 illustrates the schedule adjustment and skew calculation. Node j measures the relative difference between its clock time as well as c and the corresponding values at i, namely T_{Err} and d_c, respectively. Since i has a smaller c, j adjusts its frame schedule. By way of compensation for skew, it calculates the T_{Err}/d_c to be the average clock shift compared with the leader and incorporates T_{Err}/d_c to its skew estimate.

False-Leader Detection. Tokens are responsible for detecting whether the current leader is no longer up, i.e., has left the system. Each token maintains the total number of nodes visited by the token that have its $\langle l, c \rangle$ value, in a variable cc. Thus, if a token propagates its $\langle l, c \rangle$ to a node or the node already has the same value, the token increments cc; likewise, if a node has smaller $\langle l, c \rangle$ value than a token, the token copies the value of the node and resets its cc to 1.

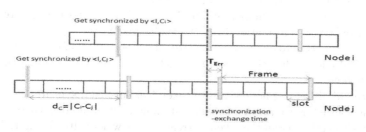

Fig. 3. Illustration of Continuous Synchronization

If the current leader is not up, the lowest $\langle l, c \rangle$ value in the system is propagated to other nodes in the ring because none of them would have met the corresponding leader more recently. One or more tokens would thus eventually detect that their cc value has increased to N, where N is an upper bound on the number of nodes in the ring, thereby detecting that the leader is false. Should tokens and nodes become desynchronized before a false leader is detected, we let nodes temporarily follow the tokens' schedule.

Global Reset.   Once a false leader is detected, the detecting node launches a new round of leader election in the ring. This objective could be simply realized using an integer sequence number, which is incremented to launch the new round. Upon seeing the higher sequence number, other nodes would reset their status and then participate in electing a new leader. Since the previous lowest Id has left the ring, a new lowest Id will succeed in the competition.

We bound this sequence number in size by using instead a two-valued (green and red) state variable s to reset the ring. "Green" represents a normal state. In an ideal initial state, tokens and nodes would both be green. When a token detects that leader l is not up, it updates s to red, which indicates that their $\langle l, c \rangle$ information is outdated. Note that when a token changes its s to red, it must be the case that the entire ring has the same $\langle l, c \rangle$. Therefore, if a node meets a red token, since both have the same $\langle l, c \rangle$, the node can follow the token and change into red. Only when all nodes and tokens have changed to the red state will a token reset itself into green, and thereby trigger other red nodes to reset themselves. The $\langle l, c \rangle$ value after reset cannot equal a false leader's $\langle l, c \rangle$, therefore, when a red node or token encounters a different $\langle l, c \rangle$, the red node has to reset itself. Thus, the entire ring will be reset to a green state again. A new round of leader election is then started, having cleaned that false leader from the system. The state transition is implemented by actions P_2 and P_3 in next subsection and proof of convergence is presented in Lemma 4 in Appendix.

3.2   Synchronization-Exchange Protocol Variables

Each node and token maintains variables l, c, s; each token additionally maintainss variables p and cc. The associated semantics are summarized below:

- l is the lowest Id currently known to the token/node. Recall that token Ids are lower than node Ids, hence l at any node need never be higher than its node Id. Upon reset, l is set to the local Id.
- c is a count of the number of frames in which a node has not received synchronization information from the leader token.
- s is the state of a token/node: 1 denotes the green state, and 0 the red state where false leader has been detected. 1 is the ideal initial state for both nodes and tokens.
- p is the Id of the last node that the token has finished a synchronization exchange with. Since a token may visit with a node indefinitely, p is used to distinguish whether or not the token has reached a new node. Its ideal initial value is -1 which means that the token has not yet synchronized with any node.

- cc is, when $s = 1$, the count of nodes that a token has synchronized with that have the same $\langle l, c \rangle$ value; when $s = 0$, cc is the count of nodes that a token has synchronized with that have the same $\langle l, c, s \rangle$ value.
- $token.i$ is true iff i is a token.
- $Up.i$ is true iff the token i is currently up.

The statement $reset\ i$ is defined to restore the initial value for token/node i:

$$reset\ i \ \triangleq \ l.i, c.i, s.i := i, 0, 1; \ (\ \textbf{if}\ token.i\ \textbf{then}\ p.i, cc.i := -1, 0)$$

3.3 Synchronization-Exchange Protocol Actions

In this subsection, we present the actions of our stabilizing program at token (respectively, node) i by which i synchronizes with a node (respectively, token).

P_1: $token.i \ \wedge \ (\langle l, c, s \rangle.i = \langle l, c, s \rangle.j \ \vee \ (\langle l, c \rangle.i = \langle l, c \rangle.j \wedge s.i > s.j)) \ \wedge \ l.i \neq i \ \wedge \ p.i \neq j \ \wedge cc.i < N$
     $\rightarrow \quad cc.i := cc.i + 1; \ p.i := j$

[]

P_2: $(\langle l, c \rangle.i = \langle l, c \rangle.j \ \wedge \ s.j < s.i \ \wedge \ token.j) \ \vee \ (\langle l, c \rangle.j < \langle l, c \rangle.i \ \wedge \ s.i = s.j = 1)$
     $\rightarrow \quad \langle l, c, s \rangle.i := \langle l, c, s \rangle.j; \ if\ token.i\ then\ cc.i := 0$

[]

P_3: $token.i \wedge cc.i = N$
     $\rightarrow \quad s.i := s.i +_2 1; \ cc.i := 0; \ p.i := -1; if\ s.i = 1\ then\ reset\ i$

[]

P_4: $l.i > i \ \vee \ (l.i = i \wedge (c.i \neq 0 \vee s.i \neq 1 \vee cc.i \neq 0)) \ \vee \ (\langle l, c \rangle.i \neq \langle l, c \rangle.j \wedge s.i = 0) \ \vee \ cc.i > N$
     $\rightarrow \quad reset\ i$

3.4 Synchronization-Exchange Protocol Correctness

As is standard in proofs of correctness of stabilizing programs, we: (i) identify an invariant predicate, i.e., a predicate that is closed in the program and is such that all the computations of the program starting from any state where the predicate is true satisfy the specification of the program, and (ii) show convergence from arbitrary states to the invariant, i.e., upon starting from an arbitrary state, every computation of the program eventually reaches a state where the invariant predicate holds.

Invariant. An invariant of our program, S, is a conjunction of the predicates $S.1$, $S.2$, $S.3$, $S.4$ and $S.5$, defined below. Let T denote the set of tokens, Z denote the set of nodes in the ring, $T \cup Z = U$. Also, let $d(i, j)$ be the clockwise distance between nodes i and j, i.e., the number of nodes between node i and node j (we are assuming here that tokens move in a clockwise order.)

$S.1$ $(\forall i, j \in U :: l.i \leq i)$

$S.2$ $(\forall i \in U :: l.i = i \Rightarrow (c.i = 0 \wedge s.i = 1 \wedge (token.i \Rightarrow cc.i = 0)))$

$S.3$ $(\forall i \notin T :: (s.i = 1 \wedge p.i \neq -1) \Rightarrow (\exists j \in Z :: \langle l, c \rangle.j \neq \langle l, c \rangle.i \Rightarrow d(p.i, j) \leq N - cc.i))$

$S.4$ $(\forall i \in T :: (s.i = 1 \wedge cc.i = N) \Rightarrow (\forall j \in U : \langle l, c \rangle.i = \langle l, c \rangle.j))$

$S.5$ $(\forall i, j \in U :: s.i = s.j = 0 \Rightarrow \langle l, c \rangle.i = \langle l, c \rangle.j = \min(\langle l, c \rangle.k | k \in U))$

The structure of the proof is as follows (details of individual sub-proofs are in the Appendix).

Lemma 1. *S is closed in the synchronization-exchange protocol.*

The following progress proofs assume that the token do not all stop moving. Let $H.1 = (S.1 \land S.2 \land S.3)$.

Lemma 2. *true converges to H.1 in the synchronization-exchange protocol.*

Lemma 3. *H.1 converges to S in the synchronization-exchange protocol.*

Theorem 1. *The synchronization-exchange protocol is stabilizing with respect to the predicate S.*

Let R denote the stable states upon starting from any state where the invariant S holds where the up token with least Id is known as the new leader to the entire system. Let $k = \min(i | i \in T \land Up.i)$.
$R = (\forall i \in U :: l.i = k \land s.i = 1 \land (token.i \Rightarrow cc.i < N))$

Lemma 4. *S converges to R in the synchronization-exchange protocol.*

3.5 Synchronization-Exchange Protocol Analysis

First, we note that the synchronization time is equal to the leader election time. When a leader is acknowledged by all tokens and nodes in the ring, global synchronization is achieved, after which the synchronization is maintained by the movement of the leader.

Leader election happens within a constant number of rounds of each token circulating around the ring, in the model where no overtaking is allowed. From the proof of Theorem 1, upon starting from an arbitrary state, every token has the correct cc and p values within one round of circulating around the ring. If there is no "maximum" false leader (as defined in the proof), the system converges to R within the time taken by that lowest ID token to circulate around the ring. Otherwise, the maximum false leader will first be detected by a non-leader token within one round time. After the detectors second round of circulation, all tokens and nodes change state to "red". Thus, after each token traverses around the ring and before at most 2 rounds each, global reset is completed, i.e., no false leader exists any more. Finally, the system converges to R after the true leader circulates the ring. Thus, the system converges to a state in R in 4 rounds of circulation, where "round" is defined as the time for the lowest token to traverse the ring.

4 Model Extensions and Protocol Refinements

In this section, we refine the basic protocol to accommodate three extensions to the system model.

Token mobility patterns. While mobility in many operational settings is often predictable, tokens may not traverse across all nodes (let alone in order and without overtaking other tokens). In our elevator setting, for instance, elevator tokens go back and forth across contiguous –but not necessarily all– nodes.

We therefore extend the model to assume that cumulatively some set of tokens repeatedly traverse the ring in a given direction, even though individual tokens may stop or reverse course.

To accommodate this mobility pattern, in which the elected leader token may not itself visit each node in the ring, we refine the basic protocol so that in addition to tokens carrying information about how many nodes have copied their potentially false $\langle l, c \rangle$ value (via the variable cc), nodes also play the role of relaying this information to other tokens that pass by. Specifically, we let each node maintain the cc variable and update it during its synchronization-exchanges. Subsequent tokens that visit the node may inherit and propagate this value to other nodes. Thus tokens and nodes can continue to cooperate to detect false leaders.

More general topologies. The virtual ring is readily generalized to any graph that is the superposition of multiple rings, assuming that each ring has a set of tokens that collectively traverse it repeatedly. Note that the token sets of abutting (and, more generally, connected) rings may share tokens. Thus the individual token traversal pattern may be arbitrary.

To accommodate this generalization, we refine the protocol so that each node maintains independent state for each of the rings it participates in. Its frame schedule is thus effectively the union of the frame schedules of the respective rings; in other words, its duty cycle is the sum of the duty cycles for the respective rings.

Global/local adaptivity of duty cycle to the rate of token arrival. For each ring, its leader token may take on the responsibility for choosing the frame length m, and accordingly globally changing the frame length when it visits (or other tokens on its behalf visit) all nodes. To achieve global adaptivity, we refine the protocol with memory of the previous and the new frame length at tokens/nodes.

A complementary approach is for each node to estimate/predict the local rate of token arrival, and to correspondingly adapt the number of times it wakes up in each frame to receive messages from tokens. This local approach relates to the issue (1) discussion in Section 3 regarding collisions during local synchronization-exchanges, and is useful when the arrival rate across the network is spatially variable. In particular, when the number of tokens visiting a node changes, the node should accordingly adapt the number of slots per frame that it wakes up in (in other words, adapt its local duty cycle).

To achieve local adaptivity, we refine the protocol so that instead of being up to receive a message from a token in the first slot of each frame, each node broadcasts a beacon in the first slot of the frame. The beacon advertises its wakeup schedule for the current frame. (The beacon may be randomly reiterated during the frame to deal with frame resynchronization between visiting tokens and the node.) Tokens can then choose which wakeup slots to contend in, thereby decreasing the probability of collision. Conceivably, the beacon may even indicate slot assignments for the tokens which the node knows are visiting it.

5   Related Work

Power management in wireless networks has been deeply studied in recent years, particularly for the radio because radio communication is a dominant power consumer among all components at sensor node. Power management is, broadly speaking, coarse-grain or fine-grain. Coarse grain duty-cycling is exploited in [2]. By way of contrast, fine grain duty-cycling focuses on scheduling sleep and wakeup time for each node, and is the focus of this paper.

MAC. Duty cycling impacts the MAC layer, in that coordination between potential communicators is necessary. MACs are, broadly speaking, synchronous or asynchronous. A number of synchronous MACs have been proposed for static networks, such as [9] and [10], but few have dealt with the stabilization issues associated with loss of coordination or mobility. OMAC in [7] is an exemplar which has: It is a receiver-centric MAC protocol which implements a locally exclusive receiver wakeup schedule. The setting in this paper is different: there is an asymmetry between tokens and nodes which does not exist in OMAC, as a result of which only the tokens need to discover the node; thus, neither the optimal unidirectional or bidirectional schedules of OMAC apply in this setting. Asynchronous MAC approaches are considered more appropriate for mobile sensor networks for the reason that the neighborhood may change periodically [11]. However, continuously sending out long preamble for each send is a very energy inefficient way of avoiding neighborhood discovery.

Stabilizing coordination and mobility. The literature on stabilization has considered synchronization and mobility in a number of ways, of which we recall a few. In [1], a stabilizing converge-to-max protocol is presented that deals with clock skew of nodes and uses on bounded size variables, but does not explicitly consider stabilization of duty-cycling. Earlier work of Herman achieved time synchronization by disseminating the leader value across a stabilizing spanning tree. [3] provides a constant time clock synchronization algorithm for synchronous and partially synchronous systems for the special case of initial synchronization. Under a virtual ring model similar to ours, [4] presents a self-stabilizing solution to a mobile philosophers problem. [5] studies location management and routing in mobile ad-hoc networks using external "leader" information to achieve stabilization. [6] maintains a stabilizing structure rooted at a "leader" token whose mobility is controlled for exfiltrating data efficiently.

Duty-cycle adaptivity. Adaptivity of duty-cycles in the presence of traffic changes is important, since if the duty cycle is lower than required, collisions or sender buffer overflow result; but, if the duty cycle is higher than required, energy is wasted on idle listening. [8] discusses a local technique for stabilizing adaptation of the duty cycle to optimize energy-efficiency.

6   Conclusions

In this paper, we addressed an abstract duty-cycling problem for low-power wireless networks in terms of stabilizing maintenance of coordinated awake slots across isolated static nodes. The result could be as substantial as increasing the battery life of the network from a couple of weeks to several years.

Mobile tokens provided the information flow for achieving the desired coordination in our solution. But since token mobility is largely independent of the system, achieving stabilization involved a nontrivial consideration of a potentially cyclic dependency between token information and node information. Our solution works largely for networks comprising one or more rings; the problem of stabilizing to a common duty cycle globally across an arbitrary graph that is connected by mobile tokens deserves further attention.

We also presented global and local methods for adapting the duty cycle to avoid collision and idle listening. Our solution of node discovery by keeping tokens continuously awake until they hear node beacons exploited the asymmetry between tokens and nodes in semi-mobile wireless networks, but is not necessarily optimal, and would be another topic for further consideration.

References

1. Herman, T., Zhang, C.: Best Paper: Stabilizing Clock Synchronization for Wireless Sensor Networks. In: SSS 2006, pp. 335–349 (2006)
2. Gouda, M.G., Choi, Y.-r., Arora, A.: Sentries and Sleepers in Sensor Networks. In: OPODIS 2004, pp. 384–399 (2004)
3. Widder, J., Schmid, U.: Booting clock synchronization in partially synchronous systems with hybrid process and link failures. Distributed Computing 20(2), 115–140 (2007)
4. Datta, A.K., Gradinariu, M., Raynal, M.: Stabilizing mobile philosophers. Inf. Process. Lett. 95(1), 299–306 (2005)
5. Dolev, S., Lahiani, L., Lynch, N.A., Nolte, T.: Self-stabilizing Mobile Node Location Management and Message Routing. Self-Stabilizing Systems, 96–112 (2005)
6. Demirbas, M., Soysal, O., Tosun, A.S.: Data Salmon: A Greedy Mobile Basestation Protocol for Efficient Data Collection in Wireless Sensor Networks. In: DCOSS 2007, pp. 267–280 (2007)
7. Cao, H., Parker, K.W., Arora, A.: O-MAC: a receiver centric power management protocol. In: ICNP 2006 (2006)
8. Cao, H., Arora, A., Parker, K.W., Lai, T.H.: Continuous Asynchronous Discovery with Efficient Synchronous Communication for Mobile Networks. 12 pp. OSU-CSE Technical Report OSU-CISRC-4/07–TR34 (2007)
9. Ye, W., Heidemann, J., Estrin, D.: An energy-efficient MAC protocol for wireless sensor networks. In: INFOCOM 2002 (2002)
10. van Dam, T., Langendoen, K.: An adaptive energy-efficient mac protocol for wireless sensor networks. In: SenSys 2003, pp. 171–180 (2003)
11. Polastre, J., Hill, J., Culler, D.: Versatile low power media access for wireless sensor networks. In: SenSys 2004 (2004)

Appendix

Closure of the Program

Lemma 1: S is closed in the synchronization-exchange protocol.

Proof. Predicates $S.1$ and $S.2$ are closed under the program trivially. If $S.3$ holds before P_1 is executed and $cc.i < N - 1$, the distance to possible lower $\langle l, c \rangle$ value should be decreased by 1 since $\langle l, c \rangle.i = \langle l, c \rangle.j$; if $cc.i = N - 1$ before P_1 is executed, P_2 and P_4 are closed under $S.3$ trivially. After P_3 is enabled, if $s.i$ changes to 0, $S.3$ holds obviously; if $s.i$ changes to 1 by reset, $p.i$ becomes -1, thereby $S.3$ still holds. $S.4$ holds for P_1, P_2 and P_3 because $\langle l, c \rangle$ doesn't change after execution. P_4 holds for $S.4$ trivially. Similar to $S.4$, $S.5$ is closed under the protocol.

Convergence of the Program

Lemma 2: *true* converges to $H.1$ in the synchronization-exchange protocol, where $H_1 = (S.1 \wedge S.2 \wedge S.3)$.

Proof. By fairness, state predicates $S.1$ and $S.2$ would be satisfied by executing action P_4 continuously, which are purely local stabilization.

Variable p at token may have an arbitrary value in state *true*, however, we argue that this value will become correct after the token moves forward and communicates with the next node, because p will be updated to the Id of the next node.

The cc value at each token could also be an arbitrary value between 0 and N. Nevertheless, it only remains in finite illegal states because later on the token would either change its $\langle l, c \rangle$ or s so that cc would be decreased to 0, also, becomes a correct value from this moment. In particular, if a token's $\langle l, c \rangle$ is replaced by other node, cc is set to 0; otherwise, if it encounters larger or the same $\langle l, c \rangle$ at a node, cc keeps increasing by 1 each time. Since previous cc is arbitrary, it would reach N quickly. However, whenever it equals N, it will be set to 0 according to P_3, which is a correct value with respect to the new state s or $\langle l, c \rangle$.

$S.3$ is satisfied obviously if token resets. Otherwise, when the token's value is replaced by other lower $\langle l, c \rangle$, cc becomes 1 because it is the first node that has the value met by the token. If a token copies its own value to a node or the node already has the same $\langle l, c \rangle$, cc keeps increasing by 1. It indicates that a relatively lowest value has been copied to number of cc nodes. Therefore, if there exists a token who carries a lower leader information, it must stay somewhere outside the sequence of nodes with same $\langle l, c \rangle$, which is equivalent to the predicate $S.3$. Hence, $S.3$ would be satisfied when cc becomes correct.

Thus, token and node would eventually converge to state H_1, where the first 3 predicates are satisfied and variables cc, p are correct with respect to $\langle l, c \rangle$ and s.

Lemma 3: $H.1$ converges to S in the synchronization-exchange protocol.

Proof. We define the state that false leader exists in the ring as $S_{FL} = (\exists i \in U : token.l.i \wedge \neg Up.l.i)$ and the set of false leaders is defined as $FL = \{l.i \mid i \in U : token.l.i \wedge \neg Up.l.i\}$.

1. $H_1 \wedge \neg S_{FL}$ converges to S.

   Let $l_0 = \min(l.i | i \in U)$. Since token l_0 is up, the lowest value of $\langle l, c \rangle$ in the system is $\langle l_0, 0 \rangle$. No matter what type of nodes token l_0 meets, nodes will copy the leader's $\langle l, c, s \rangle$. There might be some tokens or nodes previously in state 0, however, when l_0 visits them, nodes must change to state 1 by reset. Since true leader always provides fresher c values to visited nodes, According to $S.3$, the clockwise distance between token and the true leader cannot be decreased to 0, indicating that all nodes have copied the same value. Therefore, no token in state 1 will increase its cc to N. $S.4$ is satisfied. Since no token changes s from 1 to 0, hence, $S.5$ is satisfied.

2. $H_1 \wedge S_{FL}$ converges to S.

   We define the "maximum false leader" as the token who carries the false leader information with the highest priority. In particular, $\langle l_0, c_0, s = 1, cc = 0 \rangle$ is the maximum false leader, where $\langle l_0, c_0 \rangle = \min(\langle l, c \rangle.i | i \in U)$, $s = 1$ and cc is the lowest value.

   According to program actions, the maximum false leader will copy this value to all nodes it has visited unless they are the same. After each action performed, cc increases by 1. Thus, the maximum false leader is reduced by increasing its cc. Eventually, it will reach N and according to $S.3$, there would be no lower leader in the system, therefore, $S.4$ is satisfied when all nodes have copied this value. Subsequently, the maximum false leader will change its state to 0, and propagate state 0 to all nodes it has visited. During this procedure, the maximum false leader decreases itself from $\langle l_0, c_0, s = 0, cc = 0 \rangle$ by increasing cc again. Eventually, it will reach N again because all nodes kept value $\langle l_0, c_0, s = 1 \rangle$, therefore, they may only change to state 0 after seeing the maximum false leader in state 0. Before the maximum false leader resets (decreases) itself again, it has propagated state 0 to N nodes. Since tokens do not overtake each other, at the moment that maximum false leader encounters 2N nodes with same $\langle l_0, c_0 \rangle$ (at the end of first round, change from 1 to 0; at the end of second round from 0 to 1), all other tokens must have met at least N nodes with the same value. Therefore, all nodes and tokens who remain in state 0 would have the same value where $S.5$ is satisfied.

Theorem 1: The synchronization-exchange protocol is stabilizing with respect to the predicate S.

Proof. *ture* leads to H_1, H_1 leads to S, therefore *true* leads to S.

Lemma 4: S converges to R in the synchronization-exchange protocol.

Proof. We define R as a stable state where starting from a state at S eventually an alive token with minimum Id is known as the new leader among the entire system, while cleaning previous false leader information if there is any. $R = (\forall i : k = \min(i | i \in T \wedge Up.i) : l.i = k \wedge s.i = 1 \wedge (token.i \Rightarrow cc.i < N))$

1. $S \wedge R$ is closed.

   $\{S \wedge R\}P_1\{R\}$: Assume that $cc.i$ equals N-1 and the guard of P_1 is enabled. We argue that this claim cannot be true under $S \wedge R$. Because when $cc.i =$

$N - 1$ the same $\langle l, c \rangle$ has already been copied to N-1 nodes. According to $S.3$, the clockwise distance between last visited node $p.i$ and the live leader is within one node. If $\langle l, c \rangle$ at this node is the same again, where P_1 is enabled, there cannot be a live leader k who has a lower c (0). Hence, $\langle l, c \rangle$ value at the rest node should not be the same, and P_1's guard will not be satisfied. Therefore, the claim above is false. If $cc.i$ is less than N-1, R still holds after execution. Obviously, R is held under P_2, P_3 and P_4.

2. S leads to R.

There are two phases. In the first phase, neither token nor node is in state 0. Let $l_0 = \min(l.i | i \in U)$. A variant function is provided as follows.

$$F_1 = \left\langle \sum_{i \in U} |l.i - l_0|, \sum_{i \in U} |s.i|, \sum_{i \in T} |N - cc.i| \right\rangle$$

The first element decreases until all nodes have acknowledged leader l_0. If l_0 equals k, then R is reached when the first element of function F_1 reduces to 0. Otherwise, the third element will decrease till the second element becomes less than $|U|$, the second phase is reached where state 0 appears in the system.

In the second phase, all nodes in state 0 have the lowest $\langle l, c \rangle$ by $S.5$, therefore, we provide the variant function which decreases till R is reached. Let $\langle l_0, c_0 \rangle$ indicate the lowest value in the system.

$$F_2 = \left\langle |i \mid i \in U : l.i = l_0|, \sum_{i \in U} |s.i|, \sum_{i \in U} |l.i - k|, |\sum_{i \in T} |N - cc.i| \right\rangle$$

When false leader information $\langle l_0, c_0, s = 0 \rangle$ is in propagation, the second and last element keeps decreasing. Because when some token has detected the false leader, it will decrease its $s.i$ and also trigger nodes to decrease their $s.i$. After all tokens and nodes turn to state 0, the first detector starts reset so that the first element of F_2 is reduced. When F becomes $\langle 0, |U|, 0, |T| \rangle$, which means that k is considered as the new leader in the system, state R is reached again.

DISH: Distributed Self-Healing
(In Unattended Sensor Networks)

Di Ma and Gene Tsudik*

Computer Science Department
University of California, Irvine
{dma1,gts}@ics.uci.edu

Abstract. Unattended wireless sensor networks (UWSNs) operating in hostile environments face the risk of compromise. Unable to off-load collected data to a sink or some other trusted external entity, sensors must protect themselves by attempting to mitigate potential compromise and safeguarding their data. In this paper, we focus on techniques that allow unattended sensors to recover from intrusions by soliciting help from peer sensors. We define a realistic adversarial model and show how certain simple defense methods can result in sensors re-gaining secrecy and authenticity of collected data, despite adversary's efforts to the contrary. We present an extensive analysis and a set of simulation results that support our observations and demonstrate the effectiveness of proposed techniques.

1 Introduction

Sensors and sensor networks are deployed and utilized for various applications in both civilian and military settings. One of the most attractive properties of sensors is their alleged ease of deployment. Because of the low cost of individual sensors and commensurately meager resources, security in sensor networks presents a number of formidable and unique challenges. A large body of research has been accumulated in recent years, dealing with various aspects of sensor network security, such as key management, data authentication/privacy, secure aggregation, secure routing as well as attack detection and mitigation.

Recently, unattended sensors and unattended sensor networks (UWSN) have become subject of attention in the security research community [1,2]. In the unattended setting, a sensor is unable to communicate to a sink at will or in real time. Instead, it collects data and waits for an explicit signal (or for some pre-determined time) to upload accumulated data to a sink. In other words, there is no real-time reporting of sensed data. The inability to off-load it in real time exposes the potentially sensitive data accumulated on unattended sensors to certain risks. This is quite different from prior sensor security research where there is an assumption of an on-line sink collecting data in a more-or-less real-time fashion.

---

* This research was supported in part by an award from the US Army Research Office (ARO) under contract W911NF0410280.

S. Kulkarni and A. Schiper (Eds.): SSS 2008, LNCS 5340, pp. 47–62, 2008.

Unattended sensors deployed in a hostile environment represent an attractive attack target. Without external connectivity, sensors can be compromised with impunity and collected data can be altered, erased or substituted. Sensor compromise is a realistic threat since sensors are often mass-produced commodity devices with no secure hardware or tamper-resistance components. Prior security work typically assumed that some number of sensors can be compromised during the entire operation of the network and the main goal is to detect such compromise. This is a reasonable goal, since given a constantly present sink, attacks can be detected and isolated. The sink can then immediately take appropriate actions to prevent compromise of more sensors.

In our case, in contrast, the adversary can compromise a number of sensors within a particular interval. This interval can be much shorter than the time between successive visits of the sink. Thus, given enough intervals, the adversary can subvert the entire network as it moves between sets of compromised sensors, gradually undermining security. Generally speaking, this type of adversary is well-known in the cryptographic literature as the *mobile adversary* [3].[1]

Consequently, the main security challenge in the UWSN scenario is: *How can a disconnected sensor network protect itself from a mobile adversary?* Here, "protect", means: "maintain secrecy of collected information", i.e., can a sensor keep the adversary from learning sensed data even though the adversary might eventually break into that sensor and learn all of its secrets. We view this as an important problem because there are many scenarios where sensors are used to collect critical or high-value data. Once a sensor is compromised and the adversary learns its secrets, collected data – even if encrypted – becomes exposed. This holds regardless of where encrypted data is stored: on the sensor that produced it or elsewhere. Some recent work [2] has analyzed and confirmed the futility of hiding data by moving it around the network.

We now zoom in further onto the problem of data secrecy. Considering that compromise of a given sensor has a certain duration, data collected by the said sensor can be partitioned into three categories, based on the time of compromise: (1) before compromise, (2) during compromise, and (3) after compromise. Obviously, nothing can be done about secrecy of data that falls into category (2) since the adversary is fully in control. The challenge thus becomes two-fold:

- **Forward** Secrecy: the term *forward* means that, category (1) data remains secret as time goes forward.
- **Backward** Secrecy: the term *backward* means that, category (3) data remains secret even though a compromise occurred before it was collected.

We are interested in the **confidentiality of data** collected when sensors are not under direct control of the adversary. In the cryptographic literature, notions of *intrusion-resilience* [6] and *key insulation* [7][2] refer to techniques of providing both forward and backward security to mitigate the effect of exposure of

---

[1] The mobile adversary model is used to justify proactive cryptographic primitives, such as signatures and decryption [4,5].

[2] Both extend the notion of *forward security* [8].

Table 1. Notation Summary

v	number of rounds between successive sink visits
n	number of sensor nodes in the network
r, r'	collection round (interval) indices, $0 < r, r' \leq T$
s_i	sensor i, $0 < i \leq n$
d_i^r	data collected by s_i at round r
E_i^r	encrypted version of d_i^r
$\mathcal{H}()$	one-way, collision-resistant hash (e.g. SHA-2)
$Enc(X, Y)$	randomized encryption of Y under key X
$Dec(X, Y)$	decryption of Y under key X
O^r	set of *compromised* sensors at round r
H^r	set of *healthy* sensors at round r
S^r	set of *sick* sensors at round r
$|U|$	number of elements in set U

decryption keys. However, these techniques are unsuitable for solving the problem at hand, as discussed in Section 3.2.

Data integrity is an equally important issue which is normally considered in tandem with data secrecy. However, in this paper, we ignore data integrity. This is because we distinguish between **read-only** and **read-write** adversaries. The former is assumed to compromise sensors and leave no evidence behind: it merely reads all memory and storage. In contrast, a read-write adversary can delete or modify existing – and/or introduce its own fraudulent – data.[3] We consider a read-only adversary to be more realistic, especially since it aims to remain stealthy. A stealthy adversary has an incentive (and the ability) to visit the UWSN again and again, while a non-stealthy one might be unable to do so as corresponding measurements are taken once an attack is detected.

Contributions: In this paper we propose DISH (**D**istributed **S**elf-**H**ealing), a scheme where unattended sensors collectively attempt to recover from compromise and maintain secrecy of collected data. DISH does not absolutely guarantee data secrecy; instead, it offers probabilistic tunable degree of secrecy which depends on variables such as: adversarial capability (number of nodes it can compromise at a given time interval), amount of inter-node communication the UWSNs can support, and number of data collection intervals between successive sink visits. We believe that this work represents the first attempt to cope with the powerful mobile adversary in UWSNs. Consequently, it might open up a new line of research.

Organization: We state our assumptions about the network and the mobile adversary in Section 2. We examine public key-based schemes and NON-cooperative symmetric key based-schemes in Sections 3 and 4 respectively. (These schemes not

---

[3] In the security literature, read-only is often referred to as a *passive* adversary. We do not use the term "passive" as it does not fit an adversary who is assumed capable of compromising sensors. Whereas, read-write is called an *active* adversary.

only serve as our security yard-stick but also represent the entire solution space for the unattended WSN compromise problem described in this paper.) We present the cooperative symmetric key-based DISH scheme in Sections 5. We analyze the effectiveness of DISH in Section 6. We discuss drawbacks of DISH as well as possible ways to mitigate them in Section 7. We conclude the paper in Section 8. Due to paper size restrictions, simulation results as well as overview of related work are deferred to the extended version of this paper [9].

2   Assumptions

We now state our network assumptions and present our model of the adversary. Table 1 summarizes the notation used in the rest of the paper. Note that the terms *round* and *interval* are used interchangeably.

2.1   Sensor Network Assumptions

We envisage a homogeneous network consisting of peer sensors uniformly distributed over a certain region. The network operates as follows:

- Sensors are programmed to collect data periodically. [4] Each sensor obtains a single fixed-size data unit in each collection interval. v denotes the maximum number of collection intervals between successive sink visits.
- Sensors are unattended. Each sensor waits for either a signal or for some pre-determined time to upload accumulated data to the sink.
- The network is connected at all times. Any two sensors can communicate either directly or indirectly, via other sensors.
- Sensors are capable of conducting certain cryptographic computations, such as one-way hashing, symmetric encryption and – optionally – public key encryption (but not decryption). However sensors are not able to run IDS on their own.
- Regardless of its type, encryption is always **randomized** [10]. Informally speaking, randomized encryption means that, given two encryptions under the same key, it is unfeasible to determine whether the corresponding plaintexts are the same.
- There is enough storage on a sensor to contain $O(v)$ sensed (encrypted) data items between successive sink visits.
- Each time a sink visits the network, the security "state" of all sensors is securely re-initialized. This includes all cryptographic keys as well as initial seeds for PRNGs. All sensors maintain loosely synchronized clocks.
- There are no power constraints. Although we try to minimize both computation and communication costs, we assume that security has a much higher priority than power conservation.

---

[4] Event-driven sensing is also possible in the unattended setting; however, we do not consider it for the time being.

We make no assumptions about the **richness** of sensed data: the set of possible sensor readings might be very large or very small. It clearly depends on the specific sensor application. In some cases, sensed data can vary widely, e.g., for complex chemical sensors. Whereas, a simple light sensor might only collect 1-bit values (i.e., 0 or 1).

2.2 Adversarial Model

We now describe the anticipated adversary. We refer to it as ADV from here on. Our adversary model resembles that in [2], albeit with somewhat different operations and goals.

- Compromise power: ADV can compromise at most $k < n$ sensors during any single collection interval. When ADV compromises a node, and for as long as it remains in control of that node, it reads all of memory/storage contents and monitors all incoming and outgoing communication.
- Network knowledge: ADV knows the composition and topology of the network. It is capable of compromising any node it chooses.
- Key-centric: ADV is only interested in learning the secrets (keys) of sensors it compromises (since knowledge of keys allows it to decrypt data).
- No interference: ADV does not interfere with any communications of any sensor and does not modify any data sensed by, or stored on sensors it compromises. In other words, ADV is *read-only*, as discussed above.
- Stealthy operation: ADV's movements are unpredictable and untraceable. Specifically, it is infeasible to detect when and if the adversary ever compromised (or intends to compromise) a particular sensor.
- Atomic movement: ADV moves monolithically, i.e., at the end of each interval ADV selects at most k nodes to compromise in the next interval and migrates to them in a single action.
- Strictly local eavesdropping: ADV is unable to monitor and record **all** communication. It can only monitor incoming and outgoing traffic on currently compromised nodes.

ADV's main goal is to learn data collected by sensors. However, this does not imply that ADV can not *guess* that data. Since there might be only a few possible values a sensor could obtain, ADV might know well in advance the entire range of all such possible values as discussed at the end of Section 3.1. Instead, ADV is interested in knowing exactly which value is being sensed. In the extreme case, this might correspond to a 1-bit flag.

3 Public Key-Based Schemes

Although, for usual performance reasons, we prefer a scheme based on symmetric cryptography, for the sake of completeness we start with a simple public key-based approach and examine its advantages and limitations.

3.1   A Simple Public Key Scheme

The main features of the simple public key-based scheme are as follows:

- The sink has a long-term public key, PK_{sink}, known to all sensors.
- As soon as a sensor collects data d_i^r at round r, s_i encrypts it to produce: $E_i^r = Enc(PK_{sink}, R_i^r, d_i^r, r, s_i, \cdots)$ where R_i^r refers to a one-time random number included in each randomized encryption operation, as specified in the OAEP+ quasi-standard [10].
- When the sink finally visits the UWSN and gathers encrypted data from all sensors, it can easily decrypt it with its private key SK_{sink}.

Note that a sensor has no secret (private) key of its own – it merely uses the sink's public key to encrypt data. Since ADV does not know the sink's private key (SK_{sink}), the only way it can determine cleartext data is by guessing and trying to encrypt it with the sink's public key, PK_{sink}. In other words, given a ciphertext E_i^r (which conceals data d_i^r), ADV cycles through all possible data values d' and compares $Enc(PK_{sink}, d')$ to E_i^r. If they match, ADV learns that d' is the encrypted value. However, as discussed in Section 2.1, we use randomized encryption and each E_i^r is computed as: $Enc(PK_{sink}, R_i^r, d_i^r, ...)$ where R_i^r is a one-time random value produced by the sensor for each encryption operation. Assuming that bit-length of R_i^r is sufficient (e.g., 160 or more), the guessing attack becomes computationally infeasible.

There is, however, a crucial security distinction based on the source of random number R_i^r used in randomized encryption. If random numbers are obtained from a strong physical source of randomness, then we can trivially achieve both forward and backward secrecy. To argue this claim informally, we observe that a true random number generator (TRNG) generates statistically independent values. That is, given an arbitrarily long sequence of consecutive TRNG-generated numbers, removing any one number from the sequence makes any guess of the missing number equally likely. Let us suppose that ADV compromises a sensor s_i at round r' and releases it at round $r'' > r'$. Encrypted data from any round $r < r'$ remains secret, since it has the form: $Enc(PK_{sink}, R_i^r, d_i^r, ...)$ and all the random numbers that ADV learns while in control of s_i are statistically independent from R_i^r. Thus, we have forward secrecy. Similarly, any data encrypted after round r'' (after ADV releases s_i) also remains secret, because all random numbers ADV learns while in control of s_i are statistically independent from those generated later. Thus, we have backward secrecy.

On the other hand, if *random* numbers are obtained from a pseudo-random number generator (PRNG), the resulting security is much lower. This is because a typical PRNG produces "random" numbers by starting with a (secret) seed value and repeatedly applying a suitably strong one-way function $\mathcal{H}()$ as: $R_i^{r+1} = \mathcal{H}(R_i^r)$. Therefore, again assuming that s_i is compromised at round r' and released at r'', data $E_i^r = Enc(PK_{sink}, R_i^r, d_i^r, ...)$ for $r < r'$ remains secret since computing R_i^r from $R_i^{r'}$ is computationally infeasible (even if $r' = r + 1$) due to the one-way property of function $\mathcal{H}()$. This implies that forward secrecy is preserved. However, for $r > r''$, encrypted data is easily decrypted by ADV since it is easy to compute R_i^r from $R_i^{r''}$ by repeatedly applying ($r - r''$ times) the function $\mathcal{H}()$. Therefore, backward secrecy is lost.

3.2 Key-Insulated and Intrusion-Resilient Schemes

We now consider more complex – and seemingly relevant – cryptographic techniques that provide both forward and backward secrecy. They include key-insulated [7] and intrusion-resilient [11,12] encryption schemes. In both models, time is divided into fixed intervals. The public key remains fixed throughout the entire system lifetime, whereas, the private key is updated in each interval. When it is time to update the private key, the *user* contacts the *base*, a separate secure entity typically in the form of a remote trusted server or a local tamper-resistant hardware, for help in updating its key. This way, without simultaneously compromising both the *user* and the *base*, ADV is unable to learn future keys (thus backward security is achieved).

However, all such schemes are completely useless in our scenario since nodes (sensors) do not possess any decryption keys. They only use the sink's public key to encrypt data. Therefore, a key-insulated or an intrusion-resilient scheme can only help against sink's private key compromise – a problem irrelevant in our context.

3.3 Public Key Summary

To summarize our discussion thus far, simple public key encryption can help in achieving both backward and forward secrecy (our *"holy grail"* in this paper) only if each sensor is equipped with a physical source of randomness, i.e., a TRNG. Simple public key encryption with PRNG-equipped sensors achieves forward secrecy but fails with regard to backward secrecy. More exotic key-insulated and intrusion-resilient schemes are geared for digital signatures and decryption. They are unsuitable for the problem at hand.

4   A Simple Symmetric Key Scheme

We now construct a scheme based on symmetric cryptography and discuss its benefits and shortcomings.

We assume that, after each sink visit, each s_i shares an initial and unique secret key K_i^1 with the sink. (This is in line with our assumptions in Section 2.1.) Then, at round $r \geq 1$, as it collects data, s_i produces $E_i^r = Enc(K_i^r, d_i^r, ...)$. If the encryption key does not change as rounds go by, all encrypted data can be trivially read by ADV. It only needs to compromise the sensor once, obtain its key and decrypt any encrypted data, whether generated before or after the compromise period. Instead, we require that, at the end of each round, each sensor evolve its key using a one-way hash function $\mathcal{H}()$, thus achieving forward secrecy. Specifically, round r (for $1 < r \leq T$) key is computed as: $K_i^r = \mathcal{H}(K_i^{r-1})$.

If ADV breaks in at round r, it learns K_i^r but can not obtain K_i^{r-1} (which was used to encrypt d_i^{r-1}) due to the one-way property of $\mathcal{H}()$.

Unfortunately, backward secrecy is lacking. This is because ADV who breaks in at round r learns K_i^r. Then, by mimicking the key evolution process, it can obtain any future key $K_i^{r'}$ ($r' > r$) as: $K_i^{r'} = \mathcal{H}^{r'-r}(K_i^r)$.[5] Armed with $K_i^{r'}$, it can decrypt any data (that it might find later) encrypted with $K_i^{r'}$. Hence, there is no backward secrecy. Worse still, after $\frac{n}{k}$ rounds, ADV reaches a *steady state*, whereby all data collected and encrypted by all sensors is easily readable.

Based on our discussion in Section 3.1, it might seem that, if all sensors had TRNGs, both backward and forward secrecy are achievable. This intuition is wrong due to the following *paradox*: if s_i uses each random number R_i^r as a one-time symmetric encryption key to produce $E_i^r = Enc(R_i^r, d_i^r)$, there is no way for the sink to later decrypt it. This is because R_i^r, as a *true* random number, is unpredictable, unique to s_i and irreproducible by anyone, including the sink. So, there is no other way for s_i to communicate R_i^r to the sink.

Summary: Having reviewed simple public key and symmetric approaches, we observe that – except for the public key scheme used in conjunction with all sensors equipped with TRNGs – neither achieves the desired level of security: forward and backward secrecy of encrypted data. We believe that the combination of public key encryption and per-sensor TRNG is not realistic for many current and emerging sensor networks. Public key encryption requires more computation and consumes higher storage and bandwidth than symmetric encryption. Similarly, node-specific TRNGs are not always realistic, at least not on the scale in envisaged UWSNs. Therefore, below we focus on symmetric key techniques which do not assume any strong source of randomness on individual sensors.

5   DISH: Distributed Self-Healing

We now describe DISH: **D**istributed **S**elf-**H**ealing scheme providing probabilistic key-insulated data secrecy. We first describe the general idea and then present protocol details.

5.1   General Idea

Each sensor s_i shares an initial unique secret key K_i^1 with the sink, as in Section 2.1. At the start, none of these keys are known to ADV. As soon as the sink collects data and leaves the network unattended, ADV starts compromising sets of nodes, at most k per round. We observe that, at round 1, when ADV first compromises k sensors in O^1, there are still $n - k$ sensors that have not been compromised. We call such sensors *healthy* and the currently compromised sensors – *occupied*. While ADV moves to the next compromised set O^2 in round 2, nodes in O^1 remain *sick*. That is, O^1 becomes S^2. The term *sick* refers to the ADV's ability to compute their secret keys for round 2 (and later), even though it no longer occupies them.

---

[5] The notation $\mathcal{H}^p()$ means p repeated applications of $\mathcal{H}()$.

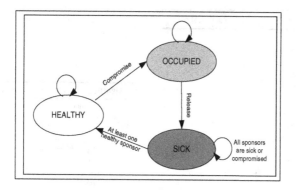

Fig. 1. DISH sensor state transition diagram

Our main idea is very simple: we let healthy sensors *cure* sick sensors to become healthy. A healthy sensor is the one that has either never been compromised yet or regained its security through DISH. Specifically, sick sensors ask for contributions from healthy sensors and the latter contribute secret values to sick sensors. A healthy sensor generates each contribution share - a random number - using its PRNG. This random number is secret to ADV since learning it requires knowledge of the healthy sensor's current PRNG state. A sick sensor uses contribution shares from healthy sensors – along with its current key – as input to a one-way function to generate its next round key. As long as there is at least one contribution from a healthy sensor, ADV is unable to learn the new key (unless it compromises the same sensor again in the future). Consequently, a previously sick sensor becomes healthy after a key update. We call a sensor a *sponsor* of another sensor if it furnishes the latter with a contribution in the latter's key update process. A sick sensor asks a set of t sponsors for their contribution shares at the end of every round.

To better illustrate the process, refer to Figure 1 which shows the sensor state transition diagram. Our approach can be characterized by the following axioms:

- Axiom 1: A healthy sensor remains healthy until ADV compromises it.
- Axiom 2: An occupied sensor can not become healthy. (For it to have a chance of becoming healthy, ADV has to release it).
- Axiom 3: A sick sensor can become healthy in next round if and only if at least one healthy sensor contributes input to the computation of its (sick sensor's) key for round $r + 1$.

5.2   DISH Details

Within each round, each sensor runs two separate processes: main and sponsor. The main process is shown in Algorithm 1 and the sponsor process in Algorithm 2. As in Section 4, at every sink visit, each s_i is securely re-initialized with K_i^1 – a unique secret generated by the sink (details of this process are out of scope of the present work). All sensors are thus *healthy* at the initial stage.

Algorithm 1: DISH: sensor s_i main process at round r

/* **start round r** */
1 collect new sensed data d_i^r
2 compute $E_i^r = Enc(K_i^r, d_i^r, r, \cdots)$
3 store E_i^r on local storage
4 set $HELP[1..t] = \emptyset$
5 **for** $(p - 1$ to $t)$ **do**
5.1   set $j = PRNG()$ mod n
5.2   send $REQUEST$ to s_j
5.3   set $HELP[p] = REPLY(s_j)$
6 set $K_i^{r+1} = \mathcal{H}(K_i^r, HELP[1], ..., HELP[t])$
7 erase K_i^r and $\{HELP[1], ..., HELP[t]\}$
/* **end round r** */

Algorithm 2: DISH: sensor s_i helper process at round r

/* **start round r** */
while $(;;)$ **DO do**
1   receive $REQUEST$ from s_j
2   set $HELP = PRNG()$
3   compose $REPLY$ using $HELP$
4   send $REPLY$ to s_j
5   erase $HELP$
/* **end round r** */

The main process (loop at line 5) shows how s_i selects a set of t sponsors and obtains a random contribution $HELP[p]$ from each. All collected contributions, in addition to the current key, are then used to derive the next key K_i^{r+1}. The one-way property of $\mathcal{H}()$ ensures that it is infeasible for ADV to compute this key as long as at least one input out of: $\{K_i^r, HELP[1], ..., HELP[t]\}$ is unknown. As shown in Algorithm 1 and 2, each sensor node uses its local PRNG for both sponsor nodes selection and contribution share generation (as a sponsor). As mentioned earlier, a PRNG is often realized as a one-way function (such as our $\mathcal{H}()$). This allows ADV to compromise s_i at round r, copy the PRNG state, release s_i by round $r + 1$, and still be able to compute the set of sponsors that s_i will ask for help and the set of contribution values that s_i will generate as a sponsor in round $r + 1$. Thus, ADV knows the entire set of sponsors of each sick sensor and also all the contribution values the sick sensor will generate for each sponsoring request. Because the sink knows all initial secrets and can compute all intermediate states of all sensors; therefore, it can also re-generate all sensor keys by mimicking the main and sponsoring processes in each round. That is, the proposed key update process does not affect the sink's knowledge of sensors' round keys and ability to eventually decrypt data encrypted with these keys.

Communication and Computation Overhead. In DISH, each sensor needs to contact t sponsors for help and also serve as a sponsor for t other sensors in every key update. This incurs a total of $2t$ messages traversing the UWSN in the end of each round. Each node needs to conduct $2t + 1$ hash operations per round: t for sponsor selection, t for contribution generation and 1 for key generation.

6 Analysis

In this section, we present some adversarial strategies, followed by analytical results demonstrating how DISH fares against these strategies. We also developed a UWSN simulator which we used to support our analysis. However due to length restrictions, we refer to the extended version of this paper [9] for detailed simulation results.

6.1 ADV Migration Strategies

The goal of ADV is to minimize the set of healthy sensors - H^r (or maximize S^r). To achieve this goal, its best strategy is to always choose k healthy sensors to compromise in the next round. We distinguish between two varieties of ADV, based on its O^r selection strategy: *Trivial Adversary* (T.ADV for short) and *Smart Adversary* (S.ADV for short).

T.ADV's strategy is to select and compromise k sensors from H^r randomly. T.ADV estimates current sensor states by maintaining a network state map which records IDs of sensors compromised and also the compromise time. Each round, T.ADV either chooses to compromise sensors that have not yet been compromised - these are absolutely healthy sensors - or those have ever been compromised a long time ago - there is higher probability that these sensors have regained their security through DISH.

S.ADV's strategy is to select k healthy sponsors of some sick sensors, such that the latter remain sick in the next round. S.ADV learns PRNG states of currently sick sensors; therefore, it can determine the entire set of sponsors for each sick sensor.

6.2 Analytical Results

We analyze the performance of DISH against T.ADV in terms of the number of healthy nodes at any round. Recall that a sick node becomes healthy if at least one of its healthy contributions is not intercepted by T.ADV. Let $p(i)$ denote the probability that i out of t sponsors for a given sensor are healthy and $pp(i)$ – the probability that at least one (out of i) replies is not routed through any occupied nodes. The probability that a sick sensor with t sponsors becomes healthy after the r-th round key update can be expressed as:

$$p^r(t) = \sum_{i=1}^{t} p(i) * pp(i) \tag{1}$$

where $p(i) = \dfrac{\binom{|H^r|}{i} * \binom{n-|H^r|-1}{t-i}}{\binom{n-1}{t}}$. Note that $pp(i)$ is influenced by the routing algorithm and UWSN topology. To make our analysis independent from these parameters, we define p as the probability of any contribution from a sponsor to a recipient being intercepted (eavesdropped on) by T.ADV. We then have: $pp(i) = 1 - p^i$. Therefore, expected number of healthy sensors at round $r+1$ can be expressed as:

$$|H^{r+1}| = |H^r| + |S^r| * p^r(t) - k \tag{2}$$

From this we see that $|H^r|$ depends on k, p and t. More specifically, $|H^r|$ is proportional to t, and, inversely proportional to k and p. We now plot Equation 2 varying these three parameters. In this and all other plots in this paper, we fix UWSN size at $n = 400$.

Figure 2 illustrates the influence of k and p on the number of healthy nodes with t fixed at 6. When T.ADV can intercept 20% of all traffic (e.g. $p = 0.2$

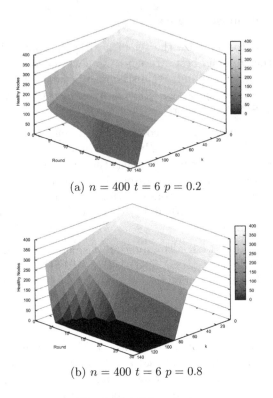

(a) $n = 400 \ t = 6 \ p = 0.2$

(b) $n = 400 \ t = 6 \ p = 0.8$

Fig. 2. T.ADV analysis

as shown in Figure 2(a)), for $k \leq 127$, the number of healthy nodes decreases in the first several rounds and then remains steady afterwards. That is, there are enough healthy nodes for the UWSN to successfully defend against T.ADV. However, when the compromise power of T.ADV increases above the threshold value of $k = 127$, healthy nodes eventually dwindle to none, as T.ADV controls all nodes' secrets from that round onwards. If T.ADV can intercept 80% of traffic (as shown in Figure 2(b)), the threshold k value decreases to 68.

Figure 3 shows the effect of t on the number of healthy nodes when T.ADV compromises $k = 80$ nodes at each round. We identify two critical t values and denote them as t_r and t_o ($t_o > t_r$), respectively. t_r determines whether the network can successfully defend against T.ADV. If $t < t_r$, T.ADV eventually learns all secrets and wins. It is easy to see that a higher t brings better security with more healthy nodes when the network reaches stable state. However, it also incurs higher communication overhead. We note that there is a value t_o such that: when $t < t_o$, the number of healthy nodes (after the network reaches stable state) increases quickly with the increase in t. If $t > t_o$, increasing t brings little extra security. Since DISH is not designed to achieve guaranteed (deterministic) security, t_o represents a balance between security and performance. It also determines the communication overhead. As shown in Figure 3(a), if T.ADV intercepts 20% of all traffic, $t_r = 1$ and $t_o = 4$.

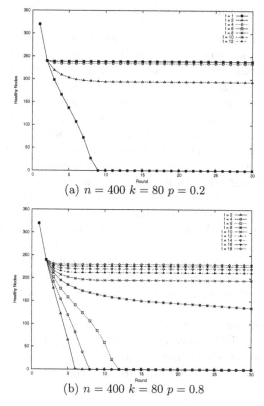

(a) $n = 400$ $k = 80$ $p = 0.2$

(b) $n = 400$ $k = 80$ $p = 0.8$

Fig. 3. Analysis of the effect of t

Whereas, if T.ADV intercepts 80% of all traffic (Figure 3(b)), $t_r = 9$ and $t_o = 14$.

In contrast with T.ADV, S.ADV strategically selects k healthy sponsor nodes from a subset of the sick sensor set S^r, such that sensors in this subset are unable to re-gain security through the key update process, since their sponsors are now controlled by S.ADV. To maximize its advantage, S.ADV must also maximize the number of sick sensors. It turns out, that this problem is reducible to the well-known *Subset Cover Problem* which is **NP**. Since we consider a polynomial-time S.ADV, the size of the covered subset is determined by the specific O^r selection algorithm used by S.ADV. However, it is safe to say that there should be at least $\frac{k}{t}$ more sick sensors with S.ADV than with T.ADV, under the same set of parameters. This hypothesis is validated by simulation results demonstrated in the extended version of this paper [9].

7   Discussion

In this section, we discuss some limitations of the proposed technique and consider ways to mitigate them.

7.1 Attack Model Limitations

In this paper, we considered a relatively simple single-minded adversary who is only interested in learning secret keys of compromised sensors by reading all storage and eavesdropping on all traffic traversing these sensors. The proposed DISH scheme defends against such attacks, as discussed in Section 6.

However, it is not difficult to image other types of attacks that could be mounted by a more sophisticated ADV. For example, ADV can remain stealthy if it deletes existing measurements and replaces them with (the same number of) fraudulent measurements. Fraudulent data may change overall sensing statistics and affect sink's actions. Therefore, data integrity might be as important as data secrecy. We acknowledge that DISH cannot be applied directly to address data integrity since more issues (such as storage and bandwidth overheads) incurred by authentication need to be studied further.

Although it is in ADV's interest to be subtle, subtlety is not always possible. If ADV's goal is denial-of-service, by introducing fraudulent data, erasing existing measurements or interfering with legitimate communication, ADV cannot possibly avoid detection. In addition, nothing prevents ADV from physically destroying or damaging sensors, especially, since the network is unattended most of the time.

In summary, ADV can disrupt and attack the network in many other ways that are unaddressed by DISH. However, at least initially, we focused on the basic read-only type of adversarial behavior, since its successful mitigation will allow us to address more advanced (and perhaps more realistic) adversarial models in the future.

7.2 Communication and Sensor Model Limitations

We considered DISH in an *idealized* network model where no message is lost and no sensor fails. In this model, the sink can mimic the entire key evolution process for all sensors and re-generate all secret keys. However, message loss and/or sensor failures complicate this process.

Unreliable Communication & Reliable Sensors: If communication is unreliable but no sensor failures occur, a sensor might receive $< t$ contributions in a given round. It then considers the rest to be lost and records the ID-s of sensors whose it did not receive. This incurs additional storage and communication overhead of $O(p_l * t)$ per sensor per round, where p_l is message loss rate.

Unreliable Communication & Sensors: If both communication and sensors themselves are faulty, the sink cannot (later) mimic the correct key update process and is thus unable to decrypt all sensor data. It seems that no symmetric key-based approach (such as DISH) can fully address this problem, i.e., public key techniques are needed. There are two basic approaches of using public key cryptography in this context. In the first, each node encrypts its data with the sink's public key and uses K_i^r as input input to the randomized public key encryption function. In the second approach, each node encrypts sensed data with

K_i^r and then uses the sink's public key to encrypt K_i^r. The security of the two approaches is the same. However, the latter is preferable if the size of sensed data exceeds the public key block size (e.g., 320 bits for Elliptic Curve ElGamal or 1024 bits for RSA).

7.3 Drawbacks of Reactive Sponsoring

The proposed DISH scheme is reactive in nature: a sensor selects its sponsors based on local pseudo-randomness and each sponsor generates a contribution to the next-round key. Reactive sponsoring has two drawbacks: First, it allows ADV to learn the sponsors of a sick sensor, thereby allowing more powerful S.ADV attacks. Second, it incurs the overhead of two messages for each contribution. An intuitive alternative is *proactive sponsoring*, whereby, in each round, every sensor unilaterally selects t sensors to sponsor. This simple change precludes ADV from learning the sponsor set of a sick sensor; thus, S.ADV attacks become ineffective. Also, without explicit sponsorship request messages, bandwidth overhead is reduced by half. We are currently conducting a detailed analysis and comparison of the two (proactive and reactive) approaches and hope to report on our findings in the near future.

8 Conclusion

In this paper, we explored techniques for intrusion-resilient data secrecy in UWSNs. We proposed DISH, a symmetric key-based self-healing scheme that achieves both forward and (probabilistically) backward secrecy. DISH successfully mitigates the effect of sensor compromise. Our simulation results clearly demonstrate the efficacy of DISH against a stealthy mobile adversary.

Acknowledgments

The authors are grateful to Claudio Soriente and Roberto Di Pietro for comments and discussions pertaining to this paper.

References

1. Ma, D., Tsudik, G.: Forward-secure sequential aggregate authentication. In: IEEE Symposium on Security and Privacy 2007 (May 2007)
2. Pietro, R.D., et al.: Catch me (if you can): data survival in unattended sensor networks. In: IEEE PERCOM 2008 (2008)
3. Ostrovsky, R., Yung, M.: How to withstand mobile virus attacks. In: ACM PODC 1991, Montreal, Quebec, Canada, August 19-21 (1991)
4. Herzberg, A., Jakobsson, M., Jarecki, S., Krawczyk, H., Yung, M.: Proactive public key and signature systems. In: ACM CCS 1997 (1997)
5. Frankel, Y., Gemmel, P., MacKenzie, P., Yung, M.: Proactive rsa. In: Kaliski Jr., B.S. (ed.) CRYPTO 1997. LNCS, vol. 1294, pp. 440–454. Springer, Heidelberg (1997)

6. Itkis, G., Reyzin, L.: Sibir: signer-base intrusion-resilient signatures. In: Yung, M. (ed.) CRYPTO 2002. LNCS, vol. 2442. Springer, Heidelberg (2002)
7. Dodis, Y., Katz, J., Xu, S., Yung, M.: Key-insulated public key cryptosystems. In: Knudsen, L.R. (ed.) EUROCRYPT 2002. LNCS, vol. 2332. Springer, Heidelberg (2002)
8. Bellare, M., Miner, S.K.: A forward-secure digital signature scheme. In: Wiener, M. (ed.) CRYPTO 1999. LNCS, vol. 1666, pp. 431–448. Springer, Heidelberg (1999)
9. Ma, D., Tsudik, G.: DISH: Distributed Self-Healing (in Unattended Sensor Networks). Cryptology ePrint Archive, Report 2008/158 (2008)
10. Shoup, V.: OAEP reconsidered. In: Kilian, J. (ed.) CRYPTO 2001. LNCS, vol. 2139. Springer, Heidelberg (2001)
11. Dodis, Y., Franklin, M., Katz, J., Miyaji, A., Yung, M.: Intrusion-resilient public-key encryption. In: Joye, M. (ed.) CT-RSA 2003. LNCS, vol. 2612. Springer, Heidelberg (2003)
12. Dodis, Y., Franklin, M., Katz, J., Miyaji, A., Yung, M.: A generic construction for intrusion-resilient public-key encryption. In: Okamoto, T. (ed.) CT-RSA 2004. LNCS, vol. 2964. Springer, Heidelberg (2004)

Universe Detectors for Sybil Defense in Ad Hoc Wireless Networks

Adnan Vora[1], Mikhail Nesterenko[1,*], Sébastien Tixeuil[2,**],
and Sylvie Delaët[3,**]

[1] Kent State University
{avora,mikhail}@cs.kent.edu
[2] Université Pierre et Marie Curie - Paris 6
sebastien.tixeuil@lip6.fr
[3] Université Paris Sud 11
sylvie.delaet@lri.fr

Abstract. The Sybil attack in unknown port networks such as wireless is not considered tractable. A wireless node is not capable of independently differentiating the universe of real nodes from the universe of arbitrary non-existent fictitious nodes created by the attacker. Similar to failure detectors, we propose to use *universe detectors* to help nodes determine which universe is real. In this paper, we (i) define several variants of the neighborhood discovery problem under Sybil attack (ii) propose a set of matching universe detectors (iii) demonstrate the necessity of additional topological constraints for the problems to be solvable: node density and communication range; (iv) present $\mathcal{SAND}$ — an algorithm that solves these problems with the help of appropriate universe detectors, this solution demonstrates that the proposed universe detectors are the weakest detectors possible for each problem.

1 Introduction

A Sybil attack, formulated by Douceur [1], is intriguing in its simplicity. However, such an attack can incur substantial damage to the computer system. In a Sybil attack, the adversary is able to compromise the system by creating an arbitrary number of identities that the system perceives as separate. If the attack is successful, the adversary may either overwhelm the system resources, thus channeling the attack into denial-of-service [2], or create more sophisticated problems, e.g. routing infrastructure breakdown [3].

Ad hoc wireless networks, such as a sensor networks, are a potential Sybil attack target. The ad hoc nature of such networks may result in scenarios where each node starts its operation without the knowledge of even its immediate neighborhood let alone the complete network topology. Yet, the broadcast nature of the wireless communication prevents each node from recognizing whether

* This research is supported in part by NSF Career award CNS-0347485. Part of the research was done while this author was visiting University of Paris-Sud 11.
** This research is supported in part by the ANR grant SOGEA and by the INRIA ARC FRACAS.

S. Kulkarni and A. Schiper (Eds.): SSS 2008, LNCS 5340, pp. 63–78, 2008.
© Springer-Verlag Berlin Heidelberg 2008

the messages that it receives are sent by the same or different senders. Thus, an attacker may be free to either create an arbitrary number of fictitious identities or impersonate already existing real nodes. The problem straddles the security and fault tolerance domains as the attacker may be either a malicious intruder or a node experiencing Byzantine fault. A fault is Byzantine [4] if the faulty node disregards the program code and behaves arbitrarily. For convenience, in this paper we assume that the attacker is a faulty node rather than intruder. We view the Sybil attack as a convenient way to study elementary ability of a wireless node to ascertain who its neighbors are. As such, the capability to counter the Sybil attack is a fundamental building block for constructing a dependable wireless network.

Problem Motivation. A standard way of establishing trust between communicating parties is by employing cryptography. There is a number of publications addressing the Sybil attack in this manner [5,6,7,8,9,10,11]. For example, if each node has access to verified certificates and every sender digitally signs its messages, then the receiver can unambiguously determine the sender and discard superfluous identities created by the faulty node by checking the digital signature of the message against the certificates. However, there are several reasons for this approach to be inappropriate. A cryptography-based solution pre-supposes a key-based infrastructure which requires its maintenance and update and thus limits its applicability. Moreover, resource constrained devices, such as nodes in sensor networks, may not be able to handle cryptographic operations altogether.

Another approach is intrusion detection based on *reputation* [12,13,14]. Due to the broadcast nature of wireless communication, the messages from each node are observed by its neighbors. A fault is detected if the node deviates from the protocol. It is unclear how reputation-based schemes would fare if the messages cannot be matched to the sender: the faulty node may impersonate other nodes or create an arbitrary number of fictitious nodes and set up its own alternative reputation verification network.

However, there are two unique features of wireless communication that make defense against the Sybil attack feasible. The wireless communication is broadcast. Thus, the message transmission of a faulty node is received by all nodes in its vicinity. In addition, the nodes can estimate the *received signal strength* (RSS) of the message and make judgments of the location of the sender on its basis. Note that the latter is not straightforward as the faulty node can change its *transmission signal strength* (TSS). In this paper we investigate the approaches to Sybil defense using this property of wireless communication.

Related Literature. Newsome et al [15] as well as Shi and Perrig [16] survey various defenses against the Sybil attack. They stress the promise of the type of technique we consider. Demirbas and Song [17] consider using the RSS for Sybil defense.

A line of inquiry that is related to Sybil defense is secure location identification [18,19,20,21,22]. In this case, a set of trusted nodes attempt to verify the location of a possibly malicious or faulty node. However, the establishment of such trusted network is not addressed. Hence, this approach may not be useful for Sybil defense.

Delaët et al [23], and Hwang et al [24] consider the problem where the faulty node operates synchronously with the other nodes. Delaët et al [23] provides examples of positioning of faulty nodes and their strategies that lead to neighborhood discovery compromise. Note that the synchrony assumption places a bound on the number of distinct identities that the faulty node can assume before the correct nodes begin to counter its activities. Even though the faulty node may potentially create an infinite number of fictitious identities, the correct nodes only have to deal with a finite number of them at a time. However, this approach simplifies the problem as it limits the power of the faulty node and the strength of the attack.

Nesterenko and Tixeuil [25] describe how, despite Byzantine faults, every node can determine the complete topology of the network once each node recognizes its immediate neighbors. Thus, to defend against the Sybil attack it is sufficient to locally solve Byzantine-robust neighborhood discovery.

Note that the problem is trivial when the ports are known. In this case, the receiver may not know the identity of the transmitter of the message but can match the same transmitter across messages. This prohibits the faulty node from creating more than a single fictitious identity or impersonating other real nodes and allows a simple solution.

Our Approach and Contribution. We consider the problem of neighbor identification in the presence of Byzantine nodes. The nodes are embedded in a geometric plane and know their location. They do not have access to cryptographic operations. The nodes can exchange arbitrary messages, but the only information about the message that the receiver can reliably obtain is its RSS. We consider the asynchronous model of execution. That is, the execution speed of any pair of nodes in the network can differ arbitrarily. This enables the faulty node to create an arbitrary number of fictitious identities or impersonate the correct nodes in an arbitrary way. Moreover, in this model, the only unique identities that the nodes have are their coordinates. Hence, the objective of each node is to collect the coordinates of its neighbors. We focus on local solutions to the neighborhood discovery. That is, each node only processes messages from the correct neighbors within a certain fixed distance. We do not consider a denial-of-service attack or jamming attack [2], where the faulty nodes just overwhelm resources of the system by continuously transmitting arbitrary messages. We assume that the network has sufficient bandwidth for message exchanges and the nodes have sufficient memory and computing resources to process them. In our model selection we intentionally abstracted from the complexity of radio signal propagation. For example, we do not consider hidden terminal effect, unreliable message delivery, intricate message propagation patterns [26]. Instead, we focus on two specific aspects of wireless sensor networks that give rise to Sybil attacks: asynchrony and the inability of the receiver to determine the sender of the message.

In Section 2 we provide details for our execution model and formally state several variants of the neighborhood discovery problem. Sections 3, 4, 5, and 6 outline the boundaries of the achievable. In Section 3, we formally prove that this problem is not solvable without outside help. Intuitively, the faulty node may create a *universe* of an arbitrary number of fictitious identities whose messages are internally consistent and the correct node has no way of differentiating those from the universe of correct nodes. In Section 4, we introduce *universe detectors* as a way to help nodes select the correct universe. The idea is patterned after failure detectors [27]. Just like failure detectors, universe detectors are not implementable in asynchronous systems. However, they provide a convenient abstraction that separates the concerns of algorithm design and implementation of the necessary synchrony and other details that enable the solution to Sybil defense. However, unlike failure detectors, universe detectors alone are insufficient to allow a solution to the neighborhood discovery problem. If the density of the network is too sparse, the faulty nodes may introduce a fictitious identity such that the detector is rendered unable to help the correct nodes. In Section 5, we prove the necessary condition for the location of the correct nodes to enable a solution to the neighborhood discovery problem. However, the faulty node may still be able to compromise the operation of correct nodes. For that, a faulty node may assume the identity of a correct node and discredit it by sending incorrect messages to other nodes. In Section 6 we prove another necessary condition for the minimum transmission range of correct nodes that eliminates this problem.

In Section 7 we present a Sybil-attack resilient neighborhood discovery algorithm $\mathcal{SAND}$ that uses the universe detectors to solve the neighborhood discovery problem provided that the necessary conditions are met. In their study of failure detectors Chandra et al [28] defined the weakest failure detector as the necessary detector to solve the specified problem. With the introduction of $\mathcal{SAND}$, we show that the employed detectors are the weakest detectors necessary to solve the neighborhood discovery problem. In Section 8, we conclude the paper by discussing the implementation details of the algorithm and the attendant universe detectors.

2   Computation Model Description, Assumptions, Notation and Definitions

A computer network consists of nodes embedded in a geometric plane. Each node is aware of its own coordinates. A (*node*) *layout* is a particular set of nodes and their locations on the plane. Unless explicitly restricted, we assume that the node layout can be arbitrary. Any specific point in the plane can be occupied by at most one node. Thus, the node's coordinates in the plane uniquely identify it. The nodes have no other identifiers. For ease of exposition, we use identifiers at the end of the alphabet such as u or v to refer to the particular locations or non-faulty nodes occupying them. We use f and k respectively to refer to a faulty node and a location where the faulty node may pretend to be located. The distance between u and v is $|uv|$. The *neighborhood set* or just *neighborhood* of a node u is a set of nodes whose distance to u is less than a certain fixed distance d_n.

Program Model. We assume the asynchronous model of algorithm execution. That is, the difference between the execution speed of any pair of nodes can be arbitrarily large. Note that this asynchrony assumption allows any node, including a faulty one, to send an arbitrary number of messages before other nodes are able to respond. The nodes run a distributed algorithm. The algorithm consists of variables and actions. A (*global*) *state* of the algorithm is an assignment of values to all its variables. An action is *enabled* in a state if it can be executed at this state. A *computation* is a maximal fair sequence of algorithm states starting from a certain prescribed initial state s_0 such that for each state s_i, the next state s_{i+1} is obtained by atomically executing an action that is enabled in s_i. Maximality of a computation means that the computation is either infinite or terminates where none of the actions are enabled. In other words, a computation cannot be a proper prefix of another computation. Fairness means that if an action is enabled in all but finitely many states of an infinite computation then this action is executed infinitely often. That is, we assume *weak fairness* of action execution. During a single computation, the node layout is fixed.

Nodes can be either correct or faulty (Byzantine). A faulty node does not have to follow the steps of the algorithm and can behave arbitrarily throughout the computation.

Node Communication. Nodes communicate by broadcasting messages. As the distance to the sender increases, the signal fades. We assume the free space model [29] of signal propagation. The antennas are omnidirectional. The received signal strength (RSS) changes as follows:

$$R = cT/r^2 \tag{1}$$

where R is the RSS, c is a constant, T is the transmitted (or sent) signal strength (TSS), and r is the distance from the sender to the receiver. We assume that r cannot be arbitrarily small. Thus, R is always finite. There is a minimum signal strength R_{min} at which the message can still be received. There is no message loss. That is, if a message is sent with TSS — T', then every node within distance $r' = \sqrt{cT'/R_{min}}$ of the sender receives the message. We assume that every correct node always broadcasts with a certain fixed strength T_r. A *range* r_t is defined as $\sqrt{cT_r/R_{min}}$. The relation between range r_t and neighborhood distance d_n is, in general, arbitrary. A faulty node may select arbitrary TSS. That is, a faulty node is capable of broadcasting with unlimited signal strength. If a node receives a message (i.e. if the RSS is greater than R_{min}), then the node can accurately measure the RSS.

To simplify the exposition we assume that the nodes transmit three types of messages: (i) u transmits *announce*, this message has only the information about u and carries u's coordinates; the purpose of an announcement is for u to advertise its presence to its neighbors; (ii) u transmits *confirm* of another node v's transmission; (iii) u transmits *conflict* with another node v's transmission if its observations do not match the location or the contents of v's message. The original message is attached in *confirm* and *conflict*. Every message contains the coordinates of the sender.

Fictitious Nodes and Conflicts. Since the only way to unambiguously differentiate the nodes is by their location, the objective of every node is to determine the coordinates of its neighbors. Faulty nodes may try to disrupt this process by making the correct node assume that it has a non-existent neighbor. Such a non-existent neighbor is *fictitious*. A node that indeed exists in the layout is *real.* Note that a real node can still be either correct or faulty. Faulty nodes may try to tune their TSS and otherwise transmit messages such that it appears to the correct nodes that the message comes from a fictitious node. Moreover, the faulty nodes may try to make their transmissions appear to have come from correct nodes.

As a node receives messages, due to the actions of a faulty node, the collected information may be contradictory. A *conflict* consists of a message of any type purportedly coming from node k, yet the received signal strength at node u does not match $|uk|$ provided that the signal were broadcast from k with the TSS of T_r. A conflict is *explicit* if u receives this conflicting message. Note that the RSS may be so low that u is unable to receive the message altogether, even though the RSS at u should be greater than R_{min} in case the message indeed come from k and is broadcast at T_r. In this case the conflict is *implicit*. To discover the implicit conflict u has to consult other nodes that received the conflicting message. If u detects a conflict it sends a conflict message.

A *universe* is a subset of neighbors that do not conflict. That is, a universe at node u contains nodes v and w whose announcements u received such that u did not receive a conflict from v about w or from w about v. Note that due to conflicts the information collected by a single node may result in several different universes. A universe is *real* if all nodes in it are real. A universe is *complete* for a node u if it contains all of u's correct neighbors. Note that even though a faulty node is real, it can evade being added to universes by not sending any messages. Hence, a complete universe is not required to contain all the real nodes, just correct ones. To put another way, two complete universes may differ only in faulty nodes.

Program Locality. To preserve the locality of a solution to the neighborhood discovery problem, we introduce the following requirement. Each node ignores information from the nodes outside the range r_t and about the nodes outside the neighborhood distance d_n. Observe that this prevents a node from obtaining information about faulty neighborhood nodes from the nodes outside the neighborhood via multiple-hop transmissions.

Problem Statement. We define several variants of the problem. The *strong neighborhood discovery problem* $\mathcal{SNDP}$ requires each correct node u to output its neighborhood set according to the following properties:

safety — if the neighborhood set of u is output, the set contains only all correct nodes and no fictitious nodes of u's neighborhood;

liveness — every computation has a suffix in whose every state u outputs a neighborhood set that contains all correct neighbors of u. In other words, u eventually outputs its complete neighborhood set.

This problem definition may be too strict. Some correct nodes may be slow in announcing their presence. However, the safety property of $\mathcal{SNDP}$ requires each node to wait for its slow neighbors before outputting the neighborhood set. Hence, we define the *weak neighborhood discovery problem* $\mathcal{WNDP}$. This problem relaxes the safety property to allow the output neighborhood set to contain a subset of correct neighbors of u. Note that the presence of the fictitious nodes in the output is still prohibited. Also note that the liveness property requires that the neighborhood set of u in $\mathcal{WNDP}$ eventually contains all correct neighbors. Further relaxation of the safety property yields the *eventual neighborhood discovery problem* $\diamond\mathcal{NDP}$. It requires that the safety of $\mathcal{SNDP}$ be satisfied only in the suffix of a computation. That is $\diamond\mathcal{NDP}$ allows the correct nodes to output incorrect information arbitrarily long before providing correct output. Observe that any solution to $\mathcal{SNDP}$ is also a solution to $\mathcal{WNDP}$, and any solution to $\mathcal{WNDP}$ is also a solution to $\diamond\mathcal{NDP}$.

3 Impossibility of Standalone Solution to Neighborhood Discovery

In this section we demonstrate that in the asynchronous system any correct node is incapable of discovering its neighborhood if a faulty node is present. The intuition for this result is as follows. Since a faulty node is not restricted in the number of messages that it generates, it can send an arbitrary number of announcements introducing fictitious nodes. The faulty node can then imitate arbitrary message traffic between these non-existent nodes. On its own, a correct node is not able to differentiate these fictitious nodes from the real ones.

Theorem 1. *In an asynchronous system, none of the three variants of the neighborhood discovery problem are deterministically solvable in the presence of a single Byzantine fault.*

Proof: We provide the proof for the eventual neighborhood discovery problem. Since this problem is the weakest of the three that we defined, the impossibility of its solution implies similar impossibility for the other two.

Assume the opposite. Let $\mathcal{A}$ be a deterministic algorithm that solves $\diamond\mathcal{NDP}$ in the presence of a faulty node. Let us consider an arbitrary layout L_1 that contains a faulty node f. Let us consider another layout L_2 containing f such that the neighborhood U_1 in layout L_1 of at least one correct node u differs from its neighborhood U_2 in L_2 and this difference includes at least one correct node. Without loss of generality we can assume that there exists a correct node v such that $v \in U_1$ and $v \notin U_2$.

We construct two computations of $\mathcal{A}$: σ_1 on layout L_1 and σ_2 on layout L_2. The construction proceeds by iteratively enlarging the prefixes of the two computations. In each iteration, we consider the last state of the prefix of σ_1 constructed so far and find the action that was enabled for the longest number of consequent steps. If there are several such actions, we choose one arbitrarily. We attach the execution of this action to the prefix of σ_1. If this action is a message transmission of a node w such that $w \in U_1$, we also attach the following action execution to the prefix of σ_2: node f sends exactly the same message as w in σ_1 with the TSS selected as $T = T_r |uf|^2/|uw|^2$. Observe that u receives the same message and with the same RSS in this step of σ_2 as in the step added to σ_1. If the new action attached to σ_1 prefix is not by a node in U_1, or it is not a message transmission, no action is attached to the prefix of σ_1. We perform similar operations to the prefix of σ_2.

We continue this iterative process until maximal computations σ_1 and σ_2 are obtained. Observe that by construction, both computations are weakly fair computations of $\mathcal{A}$. Moreover, in both cases u receives exactly the same messages with exactly the same RSS.

By assumption, $\mathcal{A}$ is a solution to $\diamond\mathcal{NDP}$. According to the liveness property of the problem, σ_1 has a suffix where u outputs its neighborhood in every state and, due to the liveness property, σ_1 contains a suffix where u's neighborhood set contains all correct nodes. In layout L_1 of σ_1, v is u's correct neighbor. Hence, v has to be included in this set. That is, there is a suffix of σ_1 where u outputs a neighborhood set that contains v. However, u receives the same messages in σ_2. Since $\mathcal{A}$ is deterministic, u has to output exactly the same set in σ_2 as well. That is, σ_2 contains a suffix where the neighborhood set also contains v. However, v is fictitious in layout L_2 of σ_2. According to the safety property of $\diamond\mathcal{NDP}$, every computation should contain a suffix where the neighborhood set of u excludes fictitious nodes. That is, σ_2 of $\mathcal{A}$ violates the safety of $\diamond\mathcal{NDP}$. Hence, our assumption that $\mathcal{A}$ is a solution to the weak neighborhood discovery problem is incorrect. The theorem follows. $\qquad\square$

4   Abstract Universe Detectors

Definitions. The negative result of Theorem 1 hinges on the ability of a faulty node to introduce an arbitrary number of fictitious nodes. A correct node cannot distinguish them from its real neighbors. Still, a correct node may be able to detect conflicts between nodes and separate them into universes. However, it needs help deciding which universe is real. This leads us to introduce the concept of a universe detector that enables the solution to the neighborhood discovery problem in the asynchronous computation model. A *universe detector* indicates to each correct node which universe is real. It takes the universes collected by the node as input and outputs which universe contains only real nodes. That is, a universe detector *points* to the real universe. Note that the algorithm still has to collect the neighborhood information and separate them into universes such that at least one of them is real. If the algorithm does not provide a real universe, the detector does not help.

Depending on the quality of the output, we define the following detector classes. For each node u, a *strongly perfect universe detector* $\mathcal{SPU}$ has the following properties:

completeness — if a computation contains a suffix where in every state, u outputs a real and complete universe, then this computation also contains a suffix where $\mathcal{SPU}$ at u points to it;

accuracy — if $\mathcal{SPU}$ points to a universe, this universe is real and complete.

The strongly perfect universe detector may be too restrictive or too difficult to implement. Unlike $\mathcal{SPU}$, a *weakly perfect universe detector* $\mathcal{WPU}$ may point to a real universe even if it is not complete. That is, the definition of accuracy is relaxed to allow the detector to point to a real universe that is not complete. Note that $\mathcal{WPU}$ still satisfies the completeness property and has to eventually point to the real universe if it is available. A further relaxation of completeness and accuracy yields an *eventually perfect universe detector* $\Diamond \mathcal{PU}$ which satisfies both properties in a suffix of every computation. Observe that the relationship between these detector classes is as follows: $\mathcal{SPU} \subset \mathcal{WPU} \subset \Diamond \mathcal{PU}$.

Observe that these universe detectors enable a trivial solution to the neighborhood discovery problems: each node composes a universe for every possible combination of the nodes that claim to be in its neighborhood. Naturally, as the node receives announcements from all its correct neighbors, one of these universes is bound to be real and complete. Hence, the detector can point to it. However, such an approach essentially shifts the burden of separating fictitious and real nodes to the detector while we are interested in minimizing the detector's involvement. This leads us to introduce an additional property of the algorithms that we consider. An algorithm that solves the neighborhood discovery problem that uses detectors is *conflict-aware* if for each universe U of node u, if nodes v and w do not have a conflict and v belongs to U then w also belongs to U. That is, the algorithm does not gratuitously separate non-conflicting neighbors into different universes. In what follows we focus on conflict-aware solutions.

5   Necessary Node Density

Theorem 1 demonstrates that to solve the neighborhood discovery problem, any algorithm requires outside help from a construct like a universe detector. However, the availability of a universe detector may not be sufficient. Faulty nodes may take advantage of a layout to announce a fictitious node without generating conflicts. Then, a correct node running a conflict-aware algorithm never removes this fictitious node from the real universe. A universe detector then cannot point to such a universe.

5.1   Snare

A faulty node may affect the correct nodes around it. A set E_f of correct nodes is *retinue* of a faulty node f if the following holds: if a correct node u belongs to E_f, then every correct node v such that $|vf| \leq |uf|$, also belongs to E_f. The faulty node is the *leader* of the retinue. For example, assume there are two faulty nodes f_1 and f_2 and three correct nodes u, v and w such that $|f_1 u| < |f_1 v| < |f_1 w|$ and $|f_2 w| < |f_2 v| < |f_2 u|$. The companion technical report [30] contains extensive illustrations of this concept. All three correct nodes can be either in the retinue E_{f1} of f_1 or E_{f2} of f_2. However, if v belongs of E_{f1}, so does u, and if u belongs to E_{f2}, so do v and w.

A *deception field* for a retinue of a faulty node f is the area such that for each point k of the field there exists a TSS that the leader of the retinue can use to transmit a message. The message so transmitted generates the RSS at each member of the retinue as if the message was sent from k with transmission strength T_r. Intuitively, a deception field is the area where f can place fictitious nodes without generating conflicts at its retinue members.

A point k in a neighborhood of a correct node u is a (*simple*) *snare* for u if there exists a set of faulty nodes and a retinue assignment for them such that: u is in one of the retinues and the intersection of the deception fields of the retinues includes k. Note that the nodes in range of k are either in the retinues or not. Intuitively, a snare is a point where faulty nodes can jointly place a fictitious node without generating explicit conflicts at any of the correct neighbors of u. Note that some of the nodes may have implicit conflicts with k. That is, they are within range r_t of k and u but not in one of the retinues. That is, they should receive a message from a node at k but they do not. Note that a snare transmission from faulty nodes may still generate conflicts outside the range of u. However, due to the locality assumption, u ignores this conflict.

A point k is a *perfect snare* for u if it is a snare and all nodes within the transmission range of u and k are in the retinues of the faulty nodes participating in the snare. That is, if faulty nodes broadcast in a perfect snare, neither explicit nor implicit conflicts are generated at the neighbors of u.

5.2   Necessary Node Density Condition

Having described the required instruments, we now demonstrate that the availability of the universe detectors alone is not sufficient to enable a solution to any of the neighborhood discovery problems if the node layout is too sparse (i.e. if the nodes are not properly positioned in the plane).

To simplify the proof we consider solutions that are *well-formed*. An algorithm is well-formed if (i) the action that transmits *announcement* is always enabled until executed; (ii) the receipt of a message may enable either *confirm* or *conflict*, this action stays enabled until executed.

Theorem 2. *There is no conflict-aware well-formed deterministic solution to any of the neighborhood discovery problems despite the availability of the universe detectors if one of the considered layouts contains a perfect snare.*

Proof: In the proof, we focus again on the weakest of the problems: the eventual neighborhood discovery. Assume the opposite: there is a conflict-aware well-formed algorithm $\mathcal{A}$ that uses a detector and solves the problem even though in one of the layouts L_1, the neighborhood of a correct node u contains a perfect snare k.

Consider a layout L_2 that is identical to L_1 except that there is a correct node at location k in L_2. We construct a computation σ_2 of $\mathcal{A}$ on L_2 as follows. Faulty nodes do not send any messages in σ_2. We arrange the neighbors of u, including u itself, into an arbitrary sequence Q. We then build the prefix of σ_2 by iterating over this sequence. Since $\mathcal{A}$ is well-formed, each node in the sequence has *announcement* enabled. We add the action execution that transmits *announcement* to σ_2 in the order of nodes in Q. Since $\mathcal{A}$ is well-formed, these transmissions may enable *confirm* actions at the neighbors of u. Note that since v is correct, *conflict* actions are not enabled by these transmissions. We now iterate over the nodes in Q. For each node v we add the execution of these *confirm* actions at v to σ_2 in arbitrary fixed order, for example in the order that the original senders the appear in Q. We proceed in this manner until the sequence Q is exhausted. Note that these transmissions may potentially generate another round of *confirm* messages at the nodes in Q. We continue iterating over Q until no more messages are generated. We then complete σ_2

by executing the actions of nodes in an arbitrary fair manner. Note that the remaining messages deal with the nodes outside u's neighborhood. Therefore, u ignores them.

Now, the liveness property of all the detectors states that a detector points to a universe if it is output for a suffix of the computation. Since $\mathcal{A}$ is a solution of $\diamond\mathcal{NDP}$ and σ_2 is a computation of $\mathcal{A}$, σ_2 has to contain a suffix where u outputs a real universe in every state. Since k is a correct neighbor of u, k is included in the real universe.

Recall that in layout L_1, point k is a perfect snare. This means that there is an arrangement of retinues and the TSS for the faulty nodes, such that when the faulty nodes transmit, each node in the neighborhood of u in the distance d from k receives a message with the same RSS as if a node at k broadcast with T_d. Moreover, none of the nodes in the neighborhood of u detect conflicts.

We construct a computation σ_1 of $\mathcal{A}$ on layout L_1 as follows. We iterate over the same sequence Q as in σ_2. Note that k is also present in the sequence even though it is fictitious in σ_1. To build the prefix of σ_1 we execute similar actions as for σ_2. The only difference is that when node k broadcasts in σ_2, in σ_1 we have the faulty nodes that constitute the snare broadcast at the appropriate TSS. Note that in the computation thus formed, the correct neighbors of u receive messages at the same RSS and with the same content from the faulty nodes as in σ_2 from k. Thus, these transmissions do not generate conflicts. Observe that this means that node u receives the same messages with the same RSS, and in the same sequence in σ_1 and σ_2. Since $\mathcal{A}$ is deterministic, u has to output the same universes in σ_1 and σ_2. Note also, that this means that u does not record conflicts. Since $\mathcal{A}$ is conflict aware, all u's universes of $\mathcal{A}$ include k together with the correct neighbors.

However, k is a fictitious node in L_1. This means that σ_1 contains a suffix where u does not output a real universe. According to the safety property of the detectors, none of them provides output in a suffix of σ_1. Which means that $\mathcal{A}$ does not output a neighborhood set in a suffix of σ_1. This violates the liveness property of a solution to $\diamond\mathcal{NDP}$. Therefore, our assumption that $\mathcal{A}$ is a solution to $\diamond\mathcal{NDP}$ is incorrect. The theorem follows. $\square$

6   Necessary Transmission Range

In this section we provide another required condition for the existence of a solution to the neighborhood discovery problem. Essentially, if the nodes in the same neighborhood are out of range, the faulty node may introduce a conflict between them. This forces the algorithm to mistakenly split the correct nodes into separate universes and renders the failure detector powerless.

Theorem 3. *There is no conflict-aware deterministic solution for any of the neighborhood discovery problems despite the availability of universe detectors and lack of snares if the node transmission range r_t is less than double the neighborhood distance d_n.*

Proof: Consider the eventual neighborhood discovery and assume that there is an algorithm $\mathcal{A}$ that solves the problem in the presence of detectors on any layout without snares yet the transmission range of the correct nodes r_t is less than $2d_n$. Consider the layout L_1 where the neighborhood of a correct node u contains two nodes v and f_1 as well as a point k with the following properties. As usual, v is correct, f_1 is faulty and there is no node at point k. Even though point k is in the neighborhood of u, it is out of range of v. That is, $r_t < |vk|$. Recall that this is possible since, by assumption, $r_t < 2d_n$. Node f_1 is such that $|uf_1| = |uk|$ and $r_t > |vf_1|$. The rest of the correct nodes in range of u are located such that, with the exception of v, k forms a perfect snare for u. That is, if f_1 sends a message from a fictitious node k, the only node that generates conflict is v. Certainly, with the presence of v, k is not a snare so the assumptions of the theorem apply.

Consider that f_1 indeed sends *announcement* pretending to be a fictitious node at k. Nodes f_1 and k are equidistant from u. Thus, if f_1 does not want u to detect a conflict, f_1 has to send the signal with the TSS of T_r. However, with such TSS, v is in range of f_1 but out of range of k. This means that v receives the announcement ostensibly coming from k and detects a conflict. The RSS at v is $cT_r/|vf_1|^2$. Since $\mathcal{A}$ is a solution to the neighborhood discovery problem and v is the only node that is aware of the conflict, v has to send *conflict* to u which removes the fictitious node k from the real universe of u.

Consider a different layout L_2 which is similar to L_1, only point k is occupied by a correct node and there is a faulty node f_2 near v. Specifically, the distance $|vf_2|$ is such that there are no correct nodes within the following range of f_2:

$$\frac{|vf_2|}{|vf_1|} \sqrt{\frac{c}{R_{min}}}$$

This ensures that when f_2 is going to imitate node k, none of the nodes besides v receive the messages from f_2. Note that f_2 and k still do not form a snare because v is aware of the conflict. Note also, that such location of f_2 can always be found if the faulty node can be placed arbitrarily close to v.

Assume that if the node k in L_2 sends a message, f_2 replicates this message with TSS

$$\frac{T_r |vf_2|^2}{|vf_1|^2}$$

Observe that in this case all nodes, including v and u, receive exactly the same messages as in layout L_1. Since $\mathcal{A}$ is deterministic, the nodes have to act exactly as in the previous case. That is, v has to issue a conflict with the message of node k. However, after receiving this conflict, k is separated from u's real universe. Recall that k is correct in layout L_2. Note that in this case k is never going to be added to the output of $\mathcal{A}$ at u. However, this violates the liveness property of the neighborhood discovery problem since k is a correct neighbor of u. Thus, $\mathcal{A}$ is not a solution to this problem as we initially assumed. $\square$

7   The Sybil Attack Resilient Neighborhood Discovery Algorithm $\mathcal{SAND}$

Our description of the algorithm proceeds as follows. We first motivate the need to frugally encode the universes to be passed to the universes detectors. We then describe the operation of the neighborhood detection algorithm itself. Then, we define the concrete implementations of the abstract detectors specified in Section 4. These concrete detectors should operate with our algorithm. On the basis of the algorithm and detector description we state the theorem of algorithm correctness and detector optimality.

Encoding universes. Observe that a naïve solution for representing universes by the algorithm results in an exponential number of universes. Indeed, assume that node u compiled a set of nodes U that do not conflict with two nodes v and w. Suppose now that u records a conflict between the two nodes. They thus have to be placed in separate universes: $U \cup \{v\}$ and $U \cup \{w\}$. Let us consider another pair of conflicting nodes x and y that are different from v and w. Then, there are four possible universes: $U \cup \{vx\}$, $U \cup \{vy\}$, $U \cup \{wx\}$, and $U \cup \{wy\}$. Hence, if there are N nodes in the neighborhood of u, the potential number of conflicting pairs is $\lfloor N/2 \rfloor$ and the number of universes is $2^{\lfloor N/2 \rfloor}$.

Therefore, our algorithm encodes the universes in the conflicts that are passed to the detector. That is, the algorithm passes a set of conflicts for the detector to generate the appropriate universe on its own. Recall also that in an asynchronous radio network the receiving node can not distinguish one sender from another or decide if the two messages were sent by the same node. This task has to be handled by the detector.

Algorithm Description. We assume that the necessary conditions for the existence of a solution to the neighborhood discovery problem are satisfied: the layout does not contain a (simple) snare and transmission range is at least twice as large as the neighborhood distance d_n.

The $\mathcal{SAND}$ algorithm operates as follows. Every message transmitted by the node contains its coordinates. Each node sends *announce*. After receiving an *announce*, a node replies with a *confirm* message. Each *confirm* contains the information of the announcement. If a node receives a message whose coordinates do not match the received signal strength, the node replies with a *conflict* message. The *conflict* also contains the information of the message that generated the conflict. Observe that *confirm* can only be generated by *announce* while *conflict* can be generated by an arbitrary message. Note that according to the locality assumption every node ignores messages from the nodes outside of its neighborhood distance d_n.

Each node u builds a message dependency directed graph DEP. For each *confirm*, u finds a matching *announce*; for each *conflict* — a matching message that caused the conflict. Note that this message dependence may not be unique. For example a faulty node may send a message identical to a message sent by a correct node. Since a node cannot differentiate senders in asynchronous radio networks, identical messages are merged in DEP. Note also, that a match may not be found because the faulty node may send a spurious conflict message or the conflict message is in reply to the faulty node message that u does not receive. Node u removes the unmatched message. Also, u removes the cycles and sinks of DEP that are not *announce*. Observe that DEP may grow indefinitely as faulty nodes can continue to send arbitrary messages.

Due to no-snare and transmission range assumptions, for every correct process u the following is guaranteed about DEP:

- Eventually, u receives an announcement from every correct node in its neighborhood. An announcement from each correct node will be confirmed by every correct node. There will be no messages from the correct nodes that conflict with any other messages from the correct nodes.
- Eventually, every message from a fictitious node will be followed up by at least one *conflict* message sent by one of the correct nodes from the neighborhood of u.

Concrete Universe Detectors. We define the *concrete* detectors $cSPU$, $cWPU$ and $\diamond cPU$ as the detectors that accept the DEP provided by $SAND$ as input and whose output satisfies the specification of the corresponding abstract detectors described in Section 4. That is, for each correct node u, $cSPU$ only outputs complete and real universe, $cWPU$ may output a real universe that is not complete, while $\diamond cPU$ may provide arbitrary output for a fixed number of computation states. However, all three detectors eventually output the complete and real universe for u. Observe that the detectors have to comply with the specification even though DEP may grow infinitely large.

In $SAND$, each process u observes the output of the detector and immediately outputs the universe presented by the detector without further modification. By the construction of $SAND$ proves the following theorem.

Theorem 4. *Considering layouts without simple snares and assuming that the transmission range is at least twice as large as the neighborhood distance, the Sybil Attack Neighborhood Detection Algorithm $SAND$ provides a conflict-aware deterministic solution to the Neighborhood Discovery Problem as follows: $SNDP$ if $cSPU$ detector is used; $WNDP$ if $cWPU$ is used; and $\diamond NDP$ if $\diamond cPU$ is used.*

Similar to Chandra et al [28] we can introduce the concept of a weakest universe detector needed to solve a certain problem. A universe detector $\mathcal{U}$ is the *weakest* detector required to solve a problem $\mathcal{P}$ if the following two properties hold:

- there is an algorithm $\mathcal{A}$ that uses $\mathcal{U}$ to solve $\mathcal{P}$;
- there is another algorithm $\mathcal{B}$ that uses the input of an arbitrary solution S of $\mathcal{P}$ to implement $\mathcal{U}$.

That is, $\mathcal{B}$ uses the output of S and provides the computations expected of $\mathcal{U}$. The intuition is that if any solution can be used to implement $\mathcal{U}$, then every solution needs the strength of at least $\mathcal{U}$. Hence, the idea that $\mathcal{U}$ is the weakest detector.

Observe that $SAND$ provides the solutions using these detectors to the respective problems. Note also that the outputs of the neighborhood discovery problems that we defined $SNDP$, $WNDP$ and $\diamond NDP$ can be used as the respective universe detectors SPU, WPU and $\diamond PU$. For example, if a process u in $SNDP$ outputs its neighborhood set, this neighborhood set can be used to point to the real universe. Hence the following proposition.

Proposition 1. *Concrete universe detectors $cSPU$, $cWPU$ and $\diamond cPU$ are the weakest detectors required to solve $SNDP$, $WNDP$ and $\diamond NDP$ respectively.*

8 Detector Implementation and Future Research

Detector Implementation. According to Theorem 1, the universe detectors employed by our solution to the neighborhood discovery problem are not themselves implementable in asynchronous systems. The actual implementation of the detectors can depend on the particular properties of the application. Here are a few possible ways of constructing the detectors. The nodes may be aware of the bounds on faulty nodes speed. That is, the detectors will know the maximum number of fictitious nodes they have to deal with. The nodes may contain some topological knowledge of the network. For example, the nodes may know that the network is a grid. Alternatively, the nodes may have secure communication with several trusted neighbors to ensure their presence in the selected universe.

Future Research. We conclude the paper by outlining several interesting areas of research that our study suggests. Even though the concrete detectors we describe in the paper are minimal from the application perspective, it is unclear if the input that $\mathcal{SAND}$ provides is optimal. That is, is there any other information that can be gathered in the asynchronous model that can help the detector decide if a certain universe is real. We suspect that $\mathcal{SAND}$ provides the maximum possible information but we would like to rigorously prove it.

In this study, we assume completely reliable communication within a certain radius of the transmitting node R_{min}. However, in practice the propagation patterns of low-power wireless radios used in sensor and other ad hoc networks are highly irregular. See for example Zhou et al [26]. The problem of adapting a more realistic communication model is left open. Similarly, it is not clear how our analysis fairs against a model where nodes are allowed to move.

Another question is the true relationship between the universe and fault detectors. Observe that unlike fault detectors, the universe detectors require additional layout properties to enable the solution to the neighborhood discovery. It would be interesting to research if there is a complete analogue to fault detectors for this problem.

References

1. Douceur, J.: The sybil attack. In: IPTPS, Cambridge, MA, March 2002, vol. 1, pp. 251–260 (2002)
2. Wood, A., Stankovic, J.: Denial of service in sensor networks. IEEE Computer 35(10), 54–62 (2002)
3. Karlof, C., Wagner, D.: Secure routing in wireless sensor networks: attacks and countermeasures. Ad Hoc Networks 1(2-3), 293–315 (2003)
4. Lamport, L., Shostak, R., Pease, M.: The byzantine generals problem. ACM Transactions on Programming Languages and Systems 4(3), 382–401 (1982)
5. Deng, J., Han, R., Mishra, S.: Security support for in-network processing in wireless sensor networks. In: SASN, pp. 83–93 (October 2003)
6. Martucci, L., Kohlweiss, M., Andersson, C., Panchenko, A.: Self-certified sybil-free pseudonyms. In: The first ACM conference on Wireless network security WiSec, pp. 154–159. ACM, New York (2008)
7. Parno, B., Perrig, A., Gligor, V.: Distributed detection of node replication attacks in sensor networks. In: IEEE Symposium on Security and Privacy, pp. 49–63 (May 2005)

8. Theodorakopoulos, G., Baras, J.: On trust models and trust evaluation metrics for ad hoc networks. IEEE Journal on Selected Areas in Communications 24(2), 318–328 (2006)

9. Yang, H., Ye, F., Yuan, Y., Lu, S., Arbaugh, W.: Toward resilient security in wireless sensor networks. In: MobiHoc, pp. 34–45 (May 2005)

10. Zhang, Q., Wang, P., Reeves, D., Ning, P.: Defending against sybil attacks in sensor networks. In: Second International Workshop on Security in Distributed Computing Systems, pp. 185–191 (June 2005)

11. Zhu, S., Setia, S., Jajodia, S.: LEAP - efficient security mechanisms for large-scale distributed sensor networks. In: SenSys., pp. 308–309 (November 2003)

12. Buchegger, S., Boudec, J.L.: A robust reputation system for mobile ad-hoc. Technical Report EPFL-IC-LCA-50, EPFL, Lausanne, Switzerland (November 11, 2003)

13. Cheng, A., Friedman, E.: Sybilproof reputation mechanisms. In: P2PENCON, pp. 128–132 (2005)

14. Jelasity, M., Montresor, A., Babaoglu, O.: Towards secure epidemics: Detection and removal of malicious peers in epidemic-style protocols. Technical Report UBLCS-2003-14, University of Bologna (December 11, 2003)

15. Newsome, J., Shi, E., Song, D., Perrig, A.: The sybil attack in sensor networks: analysis and defenses. In: IPSN, pp. 259–268 (April 2004)

16. Shi, E., Perrig, A.: Designing secure sensor networks. IEEE Wireless Communications 11(6) (December 2004)

17. Demirbas, M., Song, Y.: An RSSI-based scheme for sybil attack detection in wireless sensor networks. In: WOWMOM, pp. 564–570 (June 2006)

18. Capkun, S., Hubaux, J.P.: Secure positioning in wireless networks. IEEE Journal on Selected Areas in Communications 24(2), 221–232 (2006)

19. Kindberg, T., Zhang, K.: Validating and securing spontaneous associations between wireless devices. In: ISW: International Workshop on Information Security, Bristol, UK, pp. 44–53 (October 2003)

20. Lazos, L., Poovendran, R., Čapkun, S.: ROPE: Robust position estimation in wireless sensor networks. In: IPSN, Los Angeles, CA, pp. 324–331 (April 2005)

21. Sastry, N., Shankar, U., Wagner, D.: Secure verification of location claims. In: Proceedings of the ACM workshop on Wireless security, San Diego, CA, pp. 1–10 (2003)

22. Vora, A., Nesterenko, M.: Secure location verification using radio broadcast. IEEE Transactions on Dependable and Secure Computing 3(4), 369–383 (2006)

23. Delat, S., Mandal, P.S., Rokicki, M., Tixeuil, S.: Deterministic Secure Positioning in Wireless Sensor Networks. In: DCOSS (June 2008) (to appear)

24. Hwang, J., He, T., Kim, Y.: Detecting phantom nodes in wireless sensor networks. In: 26th IEEE Conference on Computer Communications InfoCom, pp. 2391–2395 (2007)

25. Nesterenko, M., Tixeuil, S.: Discovering network topology in the presence of byzantine faults. In: Flocchini, P., Gasieniec, L. (eds.) SIROCCO 2006. LNCS, vol. 4056, pp. 212–226. Springer, Heidelberg (2006)

26. Zhou, G., He, T., Krishnamurthy, S., Stankovic, J.: Impact of radio irregularity on wireless sensor networks. In: The 2nd International Conference on Mobile Systems, Applications, and Services MobiSys, pp. 125–138 (June 2004)

27. Chandra, T., Toueg, S.: Unreliable failure detectors for reliable distributed systems. Communications of the ACM 43(2), 225–267 (1996)

28. Chandra, T., Hadzilacos, V., Toueg, S.: The weakest failure detector for solving consensus. Journal of the ACM 43(4), 685–722 (1996)

29. Rappaport, T.: Wireless communications - Principles and Practice. Prentice-Hall, Englewood Cliffs (2002)

30. Vora, A., Nesterenko, M., Tixeuil, S., Delaet, S.: Universe detectors for sybil defense in ad hoc wireless networks. Technical Report No 6529, INRIA (May 2008)

Self-stabilizing Numerical Iterative Computation

Ezra N. Hoch[1], Danny Bickson[2], and Danny Dolev[1],[*]

[1] School of Computer Science and Engineering
The Hebrew University of Jerusalem
Jerusalem 91904, Israel
[2] IBM Haifa Research Lab
Mount Carmel
Haifa 31905, Israel

Abstract. Many challenging tasks in sensor networks, including sensor calibration, ranking of nodes, monitoring, event region detection, collaborative filtering, collaborative signal processing, *etc.*, can be formulated as a problem of solving a linear system of equations. Several recent works propose different distributed algorithms for solving these problems, usually by using linear iterative numerical methods.

In this work, we extend the settings of the above approaches, by adding another dimension to the problem. Specifically, we are interested in *self-stabilizing* algorithms, that continuously run and converge to a solution from any initial state. This aspect of the problem is highly important due to the dynamic nature of the network and the frequent changes in the measured environment.

In this paper, we link together algorithms from two different domains. On the one hand, we use the rich linear algebra literature of linear iterative methods for solving systems of linear equations, which are naturally distributed with rapid convergence properties. On the other hand, we are interested in self-stabilizing algorithms, where the input to the computation is constantly changing, and we would like the algorithms to converge from any initial state. We propose a simple novel method called SS-ITERATIVE as a self-stabilizing variant of the linear iterative methods. We prove that under mild conditions the self-stabilizing algorithm converges to a desired result. We further extend these results to handle the asynchronous case.

As a case study, we discuss the sensor calibration problem and provide simulation results to support the applicability of our approach.

1 Introduction

Many challenging tasks in sensor networks, for example distributed ranking algorithms of nodes and data items [3], collaborative filtering [1], localization [10], collaborative signal processing [12], region detection [9], etc., can be formulated as a problem of solving a linear system of equations. Several recent works [10],

---

[*] Part of the work was done while the author visited Cornell university. The work was funded in part by ISF.

S. Kulkarni and A. Schiper (Eds.): SSS 2008, LNCS 5340, pp. 79–93, 2008.
© Springer-Verlag Berlin Heidelberg 2008

[12],[9] propose different distributed algorithms for solving these problems, usually by linear iterative numerical methods.

In this work, we extend the settings of the above approaches by adding another dimension to the problem. Specifically, we are interested in *self-stabilizing* algorithms, that continuously run and converge to a solution from any initial state. This aspect of the problem is highly important due to the dynamic nature of the network and the frequent changes in the measured environment.

As a case study, we show that the calibration of local sensors' readings can be formulated as a linear system of equations $A\mathbf{x} = \mathbf{b}$, where $\mathbf{x}$ represents the calibrated output reading, $\mathbf{b}$ represents the local reading, and A represents a weighted communication graph. However, our work is general and can be applied to any problem that can be formulated as a distributed solution to a linear system of equations, including the previous works mentioned above.

Consider a distributed system of sensors measuring real-world data. Sensors are located in different areas; for example, the senors are spread throughout a building and they measure the temperature to adjust the heating or cooling. We would like the collected data to be as reliable as possible, reflecting closely the changing environmental conditions. One of the obstacles we face when designing algorithms that collect data from a sensor network are measurement errors. There are two main types of inaccuracies of sensors' measurements: noisy environment and sensing equipment which is not calibrated. It is desirable that sensors could execute a distributed algorithm for calibrating their environmental readings. In this setting sensors are allowed to communicate among themselves, using data from other nodes to affect their reported individual reading. Furthermore, we would like our calibration algorithm to have fault-tolerance properties. Specifically, we are interested in self-stabilizing algorithms [7] which converge to an optimal solution from any initial state. Observe that self-stabilization helps also in deploying the sensors. There is no need to explicitly synchronize the sensors, once enough of them are deployed and begin functioning the results will converge to the expected value.

The main challenge we have faced in this work, is that in the classical linear algebra literature, $\mathbf{b}$ is assumed to be constant. In our settings, the environment is constantly changing and the computed algorithm never terminates, leading to constantly changing values of $\mathbf{b}$. In this paper, we ask the following question: "Is it possible to devise a self-stabilizing numerical iterative method?" We answer affirmatively, and show that under minor conditions it is possible to devise a self-stabilizing algorithm that solves a dynamic system of linear equations, where the input to the system is constantly changing.

To the best of our knowledge, this is the first work tackling this challenging problem. We believe that our approach can have numerous applications in the field of distributed self-stabilizing computation.

Other works discuss fault tolerance aspects of distributed computation. For example, overcoming faults in sensors by averaging the input was investigated in [11] providing a centralized algorithm. Quantifying faulty nodes' effect on the system's output is discussed in [8] and [5]. These papers consider bounded input paths and their effect on the stability of the output. In [6] infinite input paths are considered under the assumption that only specific sensors' input may change. All three papers consider discrete input values, as opposed to a continuous set of input values discussed in this paper.

The paper is constructed as follows. Section 2 defines the model and problem definition. Section 3 presents our novel algorithm SS-ITERATIVE. Section 4 analyzes our algorithm and gives bounds on the convergence rate. Section 5 presents experimental results of running SS-ITERATIVE using sample topologies. Section 6 extends our construction to the asynchronous case. We conclude in Section 7.

2   Model and Problem Definition

We model the sensor calibration problem as follows. Given a directed communication graph $G = (V, E)$, V is the set of nodes $V = \{p_1, \ldots, p_n\}$, E is the set of weighted edges connecting them (weights can be negative) and $N(p_i)$ denotes p_i's neighbors. Edge weights are used to model the directional dependence between nodes' outputs; i.e., if $w_{p_i,p_j} = 0$ then there is no edge between p_i and p_j and their output is not directly dependent on each other. In addition, we require a non-zero self connected edge, $w_{p_i,p_i} \neq 0$, which represents the weight of p_i's own input.

Initially, we assume a synchronous system: during a single round of communication, any pair of connected nodes may send a single message on each directed edge. Each round r, each node p_i has a scalar input value $I_{p_i}(r)$, which represents the local reading of the sensor.[1] In addition, p_i outputs its output value, which is denoted by $O_{p_i}(r)$; both inputs and outputs are from the domain of real numbers. Denote by $I(r)$ the input vector of the entire system at round r, and by $O(r)$ the output vector of the system at the end of round r. In Section 6 we relax the assumption of synchronous rounds and provide a variant of the algorithm which works in asynchronous settings.

The schematic operation of each node p_i at round r is composed of the following steps: (a) read the value of $I_{p_i}(r)$; (b) send messages; (c) receive messages; and (d) do some processing and output $O_{p_i}(r)$. Then a new round is started, and the nodes continue so forever.

Definition 1. *A* **configuration** *C of the system at round r consists of the state of each node prior to performing any operation at round r; this configuration is denoted by $C(r)$.*

Definition 2. *An* **input sequence** *$\mathcal{I}$ of length ℓ is a list of ℓ vectors such that each $\mathbf{v} \in \mathcal{I}$ is a possible input vector of the system (i.e., $\mathbf{v} \in \mathfrak{D}$, the domain of allowed values). An* **output sequence** *$\mathcal{O}$ of length ℓ is a list such that each $\mathbf{v} \in \mathcal{O}$ can potentially be an output vector of the system.*

---

[1] For simplicity of notations we use scalar variables in the paper. An extension to the vector case (where each sensor measures a set of measurements) is immediate.

Definition 3. *A step from configuration C to configuration C' on input vector $\mathbf{v}$ is* **legal** *if C' is reached from C by the system when having $\mathbf{v}$ as the input vector. $\mathbf{u}$ is* **produced** *by a legal step if $\mathbf{u}$ is the output vector of the system resulting from such a legal step.*

Definition 4. *A* **run** *of a system on input sequence $\mathcal{I} = \{\mathbf{v}(1), \ldots, \mathbf{v}(\ell)\}$ starting from configuration $C(r)$ is the sequence $C(r), O(r), C(r+1), O(r+1), \ldots$ s.t. for any $i \geq 0$: the step from $C(r+i)$ to $C(r+i+1)$ on input vector $\mathbf{v}(i+1)$ is legal, and $O(r+i)$ is produced by that legal step. The system is said to produce the output sequence $\mathcal{O} = \{O(r), \ldots, O(r+\ell-1)\}$.*

In the special case when the sensor observations (the input to the system) are fixed, the output decision of the sensors should converge to a solution that preserves the linear relations among node inputs and outputs. More formally, consider an input sequence $\mathcal{I}$ of identical input vectors; *i.e.*, $\mathcal{I} = \{\mathbf{v}, \mathbf{v}, \mathbf{v}, \ldots\}$. It is desired that for such an input a run from any configuration C on $\mathcal{I}$ would end up producing an output sequence $\mathcal{O} = \{\mathbf{u}(1), \mathbf{u}(2), \ldots\}$ such that $\|\mathbf{u}(i) - \mathbf{u}\| \to 0$ as $i \to \infty$, for a $\mathbf{u}$ that solves the following linear system of equations:

$$\mathbf{u}_i = w_{p_i,p_i} \cdot \mathbf{v}_i + \sum_{p_j \in N(p_i)} w_{p_i,p_j} \cdot \mathbf{u}_j . \tag{1}$$

We assume that the above equations are uniquely solvable, denoting $\mathbf{u}$ as the solution to $\mathbf{v}$.

One of the most efficient distributed approaches for solving a set of linear equations of the type $A\mathbf{x} = \mathbf{b}$ is by using linear iterative algorithms. Unlike Gaussian elimination, which has a cost of $O(n^3)$, where n is the number of variables, an iterative algorithm usually solves a system of linear equations in time of $O(n^2 r,)$ where r is the number of iterations, which is typically logarithmic in n. These algorithms are naturally distributed and work well in asynchronous settings. Furthermore, when converging, the algorithms converge to a solution from *any* initial state. An excellent survey of such methods is found in [2].

The main novel contribution of this paper is in analyzing the self-stabilizing properties of algorithms from the linear iterative methods domain. In a practical setting, it is highly unreasonable to assume that sensor readings do not change over time. However, it is reasonable to assume that at steady state the change in sensor readings is bounded. Informally, in this work we show that once the input readings are bounded, the output solution is bounded as well. This useful observation enables us to tie together numerical iterative methods and dynamically changing environments in a self-stabilizing manner.

The following definition bounds the change in sensor observations:

Definition 5. *An input sequence $\mathcal{I} = \{\mathbf{v}(1), \mathbf{v}(2), \ldots, \mathbf{v}(\ell)\}$ is δ-bounded around $\mathbf{v}$ if for every i, $1 \leq i \leq \ell$, it holds that $\|\mathbf{v}(i) - \mathbf{v}\|_\infty \leq \delta$.[2]*

Definition 5 states that a sequence $\mathcal{I}$ is δ-bounded if all the vectors in $\mathcal{I}$ are bounded within an n dimensional hypercube with an edge 2δ, centered around a

---

[2] $\|\mathbf{x}\|_\infty = \max_i\{|\mathbf{x}_i|\}$.

point **v**. We note that once changes in the input are not bounded, then no efficient algorithm (especially in a network that is sparsely connected) can calculate the output fast enough. For example, if the diameter of the communication graph is $\mathcal{D}$, for some system of equations it would take at least $\mathcal{D}$ rounds for the information exchange for input readings at one side of the network to propagate to the other side of the network.

Definition 6. *Let $\mathcal{I}$ be an input sequence that is δ-bounded around **v** and let **u** be the solution to input **v**. A run from configuration $\mathcal{C}$ on input sequence $\mathcal{I}$ ϵ-**converges** to its solution if the produced output sequence $\mathcal{O} = \{\mathbf{u}(1), \mathbf{u}(2), \ldots \mathbf{u}(\Delta t)\}$ satisfies that $\|\mathbf{u}(\Delta t) - \mathbf{u})\|_\infty \leq \epsilon(\Delta t, \delta, \mathcal{C})$; where ϵ is a function of $\Delta t, \delta$ and $\mathcal{C}$.*

Definition 6 requires that if - starting from configuration $\mathcal{C}$ - the inputs are in an n dimensional hypercube of radius δ around **v** then the output at time Δt is bounded within some n dimensional hypercube around **u** with radius $\epsilon(\Delta t, \delta, \mathcal{C})$. We aim at an $\epsilon(\Delta t, \delta, \mathcal{C})$ that decreases as Δt increases, as long as the inputs are bounded by the same **v**-centered, δ-radius hypercube. Clearly, for $\delta > 0$, $\epsilon(\Delta t, \delta, \mathcal{C}) > 0$ for any Δt. That is, there is some minimal radius $\delta' > 0$ around **u** s.t. we cannot ensure a tighter bound.

The above definition considers a single initial configuration, and a single input sequence $\mathcal{I}$. We are interested in an algorithm that works for all initial configurations and all input sequences.

Definition 7. *An algorithm $\mathcal{A}$ ϵ-**converges** for δ-bounded input sequence $\mathcal{I}$ if every run (from any configuration) on $\mathcal{I}$, ϵ-converges to its solution. An algorithm $\mathcal{A}$ ϵ-**always** **converges** if for every δ-bounded input sequence $\mathcal{I}$, $\mathcal{A}$ ϵ-converges.*

Definition 7 formally defines the problem at hand, as an algorithm $\mathcal{A}$ that *always converges* has the desired self-stabilizing property: for any system state, once the sensors' readings changes are bounded, the change in output of the entire system is bounded as well.

Our goal is to find an algorithm $\mathcal{A}$ that is ϵ-always converging for a provably "good" ϵ. Moreover, we aim at having $\mathcal{A}$ efficient also in its message complexity and simplicity of code, allowing lightweight sensors to actually implement it.

3   Our Proposed Solution

An equivalent formulation of the update rule Eq. (1) is

$$\mathbf{u}_i = w_{p_i, p_i} \cdot \mathbf{v}_i + \sum_{j \neq i} w_{p_i, p_j} \cdot \mathbf{u}_j .$$

The above equation states a condition on p_i's output, in regard to p_i's inputs and p_i's neighbors' output. Thus, it encapsulates the requirement that different nodes influence each other's reported readings, while taking into consideration their local readings as well.

Since $w_{p_i,p_i} \neq 0$, the above equation can be stated as:

$$\frac{1}{w_{p_i,p_i}} \mathbf{u}_i - \sum_{j \neq i} \frac{w_{p_i,p_j}}{w_{p_i,p_i}} \cdot \mathbf{u}_j = \mathbf{v}_i .$$

By denoting $w_{i,j} = -\frac{w_{p_i,p_j}}{w_{p_i,p_i}}$ (for $i \neq j$) and $w_{i,i} = \frac{1}{w_{p_i,p_i}}$ we get:

$$\sum_j w_{i,j} \cdot \mathbf{u}_j = \mathbf{v}_i . \tag{2}$$

Let W be the matrix that has $w_{i,j}$ as entries, Eq. (2) can be written in linear algebra notation, (s.t. it applies to all nodes simultaneously):

$$W\mathbf{u} = \mathbf{v} . \tag{3}$$

If we consider a non-self-stabilizing system in which the inputs do not change (that is, the input is fixed to $\mathbf{v}$), then Eq. (3) can be seen as $A\mathbf{x} = \mathbf{b}$, where A and $\mathbf{b}$ are given. In such a case, we are interested in finding the value of $\mathbf{x}$, which is a vector of n unknown variables. However, we are interested in the case where $\mathbf{v}$ changes over time, and thus Eq. (3) does not describe the problem properly, but rather helps in understanding the motivation for our solution.

We use a modified update rule (relative to Eq. (1)):

$$O_{p_i}(r+1) = w_{p_i,p_i} \cdot I_{p_i}(r+1) + \sum_{j \neq i} w_{p_i,p_j} \cdot O_{p_j}(r) . \tag{4}$$

Clearly, for the case of $\delta = 0$, a 0-bounded input sequence $\mathcal{I}$, if $(O_{p_i}(r+1) - O_{p_i}(r)) \longrightarrow 0$ as $r \to \infty$ then Eq. (4) converges to the solution of Eq. (1). Thus, if the update rule of Eq. (4) is executed simultaneously by all nodes, and for all of the nodes $(O_{p_i}(r+1) - O_{p_i}(r)) \longrightarrow 0$, then it also solves Eq. (3). That is, if each node locally executes Eq. (4) then the global solution is reached. This observation motivates algorithm SS-ITERATIVE in Figure 1.

Remark 1. In SS-ITERATIVE there is no notion of the "current round number r". That is, p_i reads and writes to the variables I_{p_i} and O_{p_i} without being "aware" of r. When we discuss the algorithm "from the outside", we will consider $I_{p_i}(r)$ and $O_{p_i}(r)$ instead of just I_{p_i}, O_{p_i}.

Consider p_i is running at round $r+1$. When p_i performs Line 03, it sends the value of O_{p_i}. The last time O_{p_i} was updated was at Line 04 and Line 06 of round r. Thus, the value sent by p_i at round $r+1$ is actually $O_{p_i}(r)$. Therefore, the values received from p_j by p_i and used to update $O_{p_i}(r+1)$ are $O_{p_j}(r)$. However, the value read by p_i in Line 04 is the value of $I_{p_i}(r+1)$. Concluding that p_i updates $O_{p_i}(r+1)$ exactly according to Eq. (4).

Remark 2. Each node p_i must know the values of w_{p_i,p_j} as "part of the code". Thus, these values cannot be subject to transient faults.

Algorithm SS-ITERATIVE

01: Each round **do**:   /* *executed on node p_i* */

    /* *send current value of O_{p_i} to all neighbors* */
02:    **for** each $p_j \in N(p_i)$
03:        **send** O_{p_i} to p_j;

    /* *update O_{p_i} according to values sent by neighbors* */
04:    **set** $O_{p_i} := w_{p_i,p_i} \cdot I_{p_i}$;
05:    **for** each value O_{p_j} received:
06:        **update** $O_{p_i} := O_{p_i} + w_{p_i,p_j} \cdot O_{p_j}$;

07: **od**.

Fig. 1. A self-stabilizing iterative algorithm

4 Analysis of SS-Iterative

[2] shows that the update rule Eq. (4) can be written in linear algebra form as

$$O(r+1) = AI(r+1) + BO(r) , \tag{5}$$

where A is a diagonal matrix with w_{p_i,p_i} in the main diagonal, and $B_{ij} = w_{p_i,p_j}$ for $i \neq j$

$$A \triangleq (diag\{W\})^{-1} , \quad B \triangleq -(AW - I_{n \times n}) \tag{6}$$

where $I_{n \times n}$ is the identity matrix. Using this update rule to solve a set of linear equations iteratively is known as the Jacobi algorithm.

As noted in Section 2, when the input sequence is constant (*i.e.*, $I(r) = \mathbf{v}$ for all r) the iterative execution of the above equations converges to $\mathbf{u} = A\mathbf{v} + B\mathbf{u}$, which is the same as $\mathbf{u} = W^{-1}\mathbf{v}$, thus solving Eq. (3). Following, we analyze the result of iteratively applying these equations for δ-bounded input sequences.

Let $\mathcal{I}$ be an input sequence of length ℓ that is δ-bounded around vector $\mathbf{v}$. That is, $\mathcal{I} = I(r), I(r+1), \ldots, I(r+\ell-1)$ for some round r. Note that SS-ITERATIVE saves a single scalar variable at each node, and thus the configuration of round $r+1$ can be defined by the value of $O(r)$ at round r. Consider SS-ITERATIVE's run, starting from an arbitrary configuration at round r. We aim at showing that $O(r + \Delta t)$ is bounded by a hypercube centered at $\mathbf{u}$. Denote by $\mathbf{c}(\Delta t) \triangleq O(r + \Delta t) - \mathbf{u}$. If we show that $\|\mathbf{c}(\Delta t)\|_\infty$ is bounded (as Δt increases), then $O(r + \Delta t)$ is within a bounded hypercube centered at $\mathbf{u}$. Consider $\mathbf{c}(1)$:

$$\begin{aligned}
\mathbf{c}(1) &= O(r+1) - \mathbf{u} \\
&= AI(r+1) + BO(r) - (A\mathbf{v} + B\mathbf{u}) \\
&= A(I(r+1) - \mathbf{v}) + B(O(r) - \mathbf{u}) \\
&= A(I(r+1) - \mathbf{v}) + B\mathbf{c}(0) .
\end{aligned} \tag{7}$$

Since $\mathcal{I}$ is a δ-bounded input sequence around $\mathbf{v}$, each $I(r + \Delta t)$ can be denoted as $\mathbf{v} + \mathcal{D}(r + \Delta t)$ s.t. $\mathcal{D}(r + \Delta t) \in \mathbb{R}^n$ is a vector, and $||\mathcal{D}(r + \Delta t)||_\infty \leq \delta$. That is, $\mathcal{D}(r + \Delta t) = I(r + \Delta t) - \mathbf{v}$.

Claim. At round $r + \Delta t$, it holds that $\mathbf{c}(\Delta t) = \sum_{j=0}^{\Delta t - 1} B^j A \mathcal{D}(r + \Delta t - j) + B^{\Delta t} \mathbf{c}(0)$.

Proof. Proof by induction. The base of the induction was shown for $\mathbf{c}(1)$; see Eq. (7). Assume that the claim holds for $\Delta t = k$. Thus, $\mathbf{c}(k) = \sum_{j=0}^{k-1} B^j A \mathcal{D}(r + k - j) + B^k \mathbf{c}(0)$. By the update rule in Eq. (5), we have that $O(r + k + 1) = AI(r + k + 1) + BO(r + k)$. Combining the two equations implies

$$
\begin{aligned}
\mathbf{c}(k+1) &= O(r + k + 1) - \mathbf{u} \\
&= AI(r + k + 1) + BO(r + k) - (A\mathbf{v} + B\mathbf{u}) \\
&= A(I(r + k + 1) - \mathbf{v}) + B(O(r + k) - \mathbf{u}) \\
&= A\mathcal{D}(r + k + 1) + B\mathbf{c}(k) \\
&= A\mathcal{D}(r + k + 1) + \sum_{j=0}^{k-1} B^{j+1} A \mathcal{D}(r + k - j) + B^{k+1} \mathbf{c}(0) \\
&= A\mathcal{D}(r + k + 1) + \sum_{j=1}^{k} B^{j} A \mathcal{D}(r + k + 1 - j) + B^{k+1} \mathbf{c}(0) \\
&= \sum_{j=0}^{k} B^{j} A \mathcal{D}(r + k + 1 - j) + B^{k+1} \mathbf{c}(0) .
\end{aligned}
$$

Thus, if the claim holds for $\Delta t = k$ it also holds for $\Delta t = k + 1$; and we have that the claim holds for all $\Delta t \geq 0$. $\qquad\square$

Definition 8. *A matrix $M_{n \times n}$ is **diagonally dominant** if $|M_{ii}| > \sum_{j \neq i}^n |M_{ij}|$. A matrix $M_{n \times n}$ is **normalized** diagonally dominant (normalized, for short) if M is diagonally dominant, and $|M_{ii}| \geq 1$.*

Lemma 1. *For a normalized diagonally dominant matrix W, it holds that $||A||_\infty \leq 1$ and $||B||_\infty < 1$, where A, B are defined in Eq. (6) and $||A||_\infty \triangleq \max_{x \neq 0} \frac{||Ax||_\infty}{||x||_\infty}$.*

Proof. A is zero except for its main diagonal for which $A_{i,i} = w_{p_i,p_i} = \frac{1}{w_{i,i}}$. Since $|W_{ii}| \geq 1$, we have that $|A_{i,i}| \leq 1$. Thus, it holds that $||Ax||_\infty \leq ||x||_\infty$. Furthermore, $\max_{x \neq 0} \frac{||Ax||_\infty}{||x||_\infty} \leq 1$, i.e., $||A||_\infty \leq 1$. Regarding B, $B_{i,j} = w_{p_i,p_j}$ for $i \neq j$ and 0 for $i = j$. Since W is assumed to be normalized diagonally dominant, we have that $\sum_{j \neq i} |W_{i,j}| < |W_{i,i}|$, thus $\sum_{j \neq i} |w_{p_i,p_i}| < 1$. Therefore, $\sum_j |B_{i,j}| = \sum_{j \neq i} |w_{p_i,p_j}| < 1$ for all i. In total, for any $\mathbf{x}$ we have $||B\mathbf{x}||_\infty < ||\mathbf{x}||_\infty$, leading to $||B||_\infty < 1$. $\qquad\square$

If W is a diagonally dominant matrix then node p_i's own input effects p_i's output more than the sum of all of p_i's neighbors outputs. That is, the weight of p_i's input is at least the sum of weights of p_i's neighbors outputs.

Theorem 1. *Given a normalized diagonally dominant and invertible W, there are constants c_1, c_2, where $c_1 > 0$, and $1 > c_2 > 0$, such that* SS-ITERATIVE *ϵ-always converges with $\epsilon(\Delta t, \delta, \mathcal{C}) = \delta \cdot c_1 + (c_2)^{\Delta t} \cdot ||O(r) - \mathbf{u}||_\infty$.*

Proof. By Lemma 1 it holds that $||A||_\infty \leq 1$ and $||B||_\infty < 1$. Consider a δ-bounded input sequence $\mathcal{I}$ around $\mathbf{v}$, and SS-ITERATIVE's run starting from an arbitrary state $O(r)$. We are interested in the behavior of $||\mathbf{c}(\Delta t)||_\infty$:

$$
\begin{aligned}
||\mathbf{c}(\Delta t)||_\infty &= \left\| \sum_{j=0}^{\Delta t-1} B^j A \mathcal{D}(r + \Delta t - j) + B^{\Delta t} \mathbf{c}(0) \right\|_\infty \\
&\leq \left\| \sum_{j=0}^{\Delta t-1} B^j A \mathcal{D}(r + \Delta t - j) \right\|_\infty + ||B^{\Delta t} \mathbf{c}(0)||_\infty \\
&\leq \sum_{j=0}^{\Delta t-1} ||B||_\infty^j \, ||A\mathcal{D}(r + \Delta t - j)||_\infty + ||B||_\infty^{\Delta t} ||\mathbf{c}(0)||_\infty \\
&\leq \delta \cdot ||A||_\infty \sum_{j=0}^{\Delta t-1} ||B||_\infty^j + ||B||_\infty^{\Delta t} ||\mathbf{c}(0)||_\infty \\
&= \delta \cdot ||A||_\infty \frac{1 - ||B||_\infty^{\Delta t}}{1 - ||B||_\infty} + ||B||_\infty^{\Delta t} ||\mathbf{c}(0)||_\infty \ .
\end{aligned}
\tag{8}
$$

For an input sequence $\mathcal{I}$ that is δ-bounded around $\mathbf{v}$, denote by $\mathbf{u}$ the solution to the original system of equations $W\mathbf{u} = \mathbf{v}$. By Eq. (8),

$$
||O(r + \Delta t) - \mathbf{u}||_\infty \leq \delta \cdot ||A||_\infty \frac{1 - ||B||_\infty^{\Delta t}}{1 - ||B||_\infty} + ||B||_\infty^{\Delta t} ||\mathbf{c}(0)||_\infty \ .
$$

Since $||B||_\infty < 1$, we have that $\frac{1-||B||_\infty^{\Delta t}}{1-||B||_\infty} \leq \frac{1}{1-||B||_\infty}$ and by setting $c_1 = \frac{||A||_\infty}{1-||B||_\infty}$ it holds that $||A||_\infty \frac{1-||B||_\infty^{\Delta t}}{1-||B||_\infty} \leq c_1$. By setting $c_2 = ||B||_\infty$ and recalling that $\mathbf{c}(0) = O(r) - \mathbf{u}$ we are done.   □

Theorem 1 states sufficient conditions s.t. SS-ITERATIVE ϵ-always converges. Moreover, the algorithm SS-ITERATIVE is lightweight, as it requires nodes to send only a single value to every neighbor on each round.

5   Experimental Results

For illustrating the behavior of our proposed algorithm, we have simulated SS-ITERATIVE using two sample topologies of one hundred nodes. Figure 2 depicts a circular topology where each node is connected to its left and right neighbors. Figure 3 shows a random unit disc graph, where nodes are randomly spread on a plane, and each node is connected to the nodes that are within a distance of

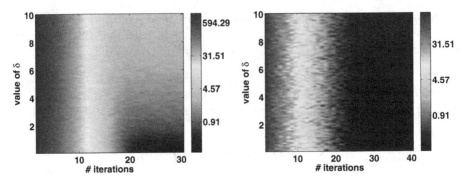

Fig. 2. Sim. of a Circle graph   Fig. 3. Sim. of a Unit-Disc graph

1. The X-axis shows the number of iterations, and the Y-axis shows the value of δ. Area colors in the heatmap depict the average of the following procedure: randomly select a vector $\mathbf{v}$ and a δ-bounded sequence around $\mathbf{v}$, run the simulation for the randomly selected values and return the L_∞ distance between the last output vector and $\mathbf{u}$ (calculated as $\mathbf{u} = W^{-1}\mathbf{v}$). The heatmap uses a log log scale. Both graphs clearly show that as δ decreases and the number of iterations increases, the output of SS-ITERATIVE converges to be bounded by a small hypercube around $\mathbf{u}$.

Note that the unit disc weighted topology matrix is characterized by $||A||_\infty = 0.02, ||B||_\infty = 0.97$ while the circle graph is characterized by $||A||_\infty = 0.33$, $||B||_\infty = 0.66$. As expected, using unit disc topology requires a larger number of iterations for convergence (depends on $||B||_\infty$). In addition, in the unit disc topology the value of δ has a lesser effect on the convergence, due to the value of $||A||_\infty$, which affects the minimal radius around the output. Since $||A||_\infty$ is smaller in the unit disc topology, increasing δ does not significantly affect the convergence.

6   Extension to the Asynchronous Model

Our second novel contribution is in extending our model to support asynchronous communications. In a large sensor network, it is unreasonable to assume that the sensors operate in synchronous rounds. Furthermore, as known from the linear iterative algorithms literature, algorithms usually converge in less asynchronous rounds (when compared to synchronous rounds).

When considering the asynchronous model, it is more convenient to discuss shared-memory as means of communication.[3] Thus, assume that for each directed edge between p_i, p_j there is a read-write register R_{p_i,p_j} that is written by p_i and read by p_j.

An asynchronous run is an infinite sequence of configurations $\mathcal{C}_0 \rightarrow \mathcal{C}_1 \rightarrow \ldots$ such that some process p performs an atomic step between configuration $\mathcal{C}_i$ and

---

[3] In [7] it is shown how to convert an algorithm based on shared-memory to a message-passing algorithm with links of bounded capacity.

C_{i+1}. An atomic step consists of reading or writing from a single register. Notice that in the current model a configuration consists of all of the registers and of the local variables at the different nodes.

In this section we again prove that starting from an arbitrary configuration, when the inputs are bounded, the outputs are bounded as well. We consider each configuration C_r to be assigned a vector input $I(r)$ such that if node p_i reads the input when performing an atomic step on C_r it reads the value of $I_{p_i}(r)$. Equivalently, the output vector of configuration C_r is $O(r)$.

Figure 4 outlines ASYNC-SS-ITERATIVE which is a direct translation of SS-ITERATIVE to the shared-memory model.

Algorithm ASYNC-SS-ITERATIVE

01: Forever **do**:   /* *executed on node p_i* */

        /* *write current value of O_{p_i} to all neighbors* */
02:     **for** each $p_j \in N(p_i)$
03:        **write** O_{p_i} to R_{p_i,p_j};

        /* *update O_{p_i} according to values of neighbors* */
04:     **set** $O_{p_i} := w_{p_i,p_i} \cdot I_{p_i}$;
05:     **for** each $p_j \in N(p_i)$:
06:        **read** R_{p_j,p_i} into *temp*;
07:        **update** $O_{p_i} := O_{p_i} + w_{p_i,p_j} \cdot temp$;

08: **od.**

Fig. 4. A self-stabilizing iterative algorithm for asynchronous networks

ASYNC-SS-ITERATIVE consists of two phases: in the first, the previous value of O_{p_i} is written to all its neighbors. In the second phase p_i calculates its new value of O_{p_i} by reading the registers of all its neighbors.

We consider only "fair" runs, in which each node performs an atomic step infinitely many times. Thus, each node performs both phases infinitely many times. A round is defined to be the shortest prefix of a run such that each node has performed lines 02-07 in the algorithm. We number each atomic step and each round. Note that a round consists of many atomic steps.

We model a fair run as follows. Each node p_i performs infinitely many atomic steps, and participates in infinitely many rounds. Notice that the registers p_i reads in round $k+1$ have all been last written to, no earlier than during round k. Since a round consists of each node performing all the steps in the algorithm, each node p_i manages to read all of its neighboring registers and write to all of its neighboring registers every round. Thus, there is some atomic step r (during round $k+1$) such that:

$$O_{p_i}(r) = w_{p_i,p_i} \cdot I_{p_i}(r') + \sum_{j \neq i} w_{p_i,p_j} \cdot O_{p_j}(r'_j) ,$$

where r', r'_j (for all $p_j \neq p_i$) are smaller than r and are from at least round k.

Let $\mathbf{u}$ be such that $\mathbf{u} = A\mathbf{v} + B\mathbf{u}$, and let the inputs be from a δ-bounded input sequence around $\mathbf{v}$. Denote $\mathbf{c}(r) = O(r) - \mathbf{u}$ and $z = \max_i |\mathbf{c}_{p_i}(0)|$.

Theorem 2. *Given a normalized diagonally dominant and invertible W, and while considering only fair runs, there are constants c_1, c_2, where $c_1 > 0$, and $1 > c_2 > 0$, such that* ASYNC-SS-ITERATIVE *ϵ-always converges with $\epsilon(\Delta t, \delta, C) = \delta \cdot c_1 + (c_2)^{\Delta t} \cdot z$; where Δt counts the asynchronous rounds of a fair run.*

Proof. Notice that if p_i did not perform the rth atomic step then $O_{p_i}(r) = O_{p_i}(r-1)$ and therefore $\mathbf{c}_{p_i}(r) = \mathbf{c}_{p_i}(r-1)$. Consider the value of $\mathbf{c}_{p_i}(r)$ when p_i did perform the rth atomic step (during round $k+1$).

$$
\begin{aligned}
\mathbf{c}_{p_i}(r) &= O_{p_i}(r) - \mathbf{u}_{p_i} \\
&= w_{p_i,p_i} \cdot I_{p_i}(r') + \sum_{j \neq i} w_{p_i,p_j} \cdot O_{p_j}(r'_j) - w_{p_i,p_i} \cdot \mathbf{v}_{p_i} - \sum_{j \neq i} w_{p_i,p_j} \cdot \mathbf{u}_{p_i} \\
&= w_{p_i,p_i} \cdot (I_{p_i}(r') - \mathbf{v}_{p_i}) + \sum_{j \neq i} w_{p_i,p_j} \cdot (O_{p_j}(r'_j) - \mathbf{u}_{p_i}) \\
&= w_{p_i,p_i} \cdot (I_{p_i}(r') - \mathbf{v}_{p_i}) + \sum_{j \neq i} w_{p_i,p_j} \cdot \mathbf{c}_{p_j}(r'_j) \,,
\end{aligned}
$$

where r' and the different r'_j are smaller than r and are all from round k or round $k+1$.

By using Lemma 1 we get:

$$
\begin{aligned}
|\mathbf{c}_{p_i}(r)| &\leq |w_{p_i,p_i} \cdot (I_{p_i}(r') - \mathbf{v}_{p_i})| + \max_{p_j} |\mathbf{c}_{p_j}(r'_j)| \sum_{j \neq i} |w_{p_i,p_j}| \\
&\leq |w_{p_i,p_i} \cdot (I_{p_i}(r') - \mathbf{v}_{p_i})| + ||B||_\infty |\mathbf{c}_{p_{max}}(r_{max})| \\
&\leq \delta + ||B||_\infty |\mathbf{c}_{p_{max}}(r_{max})| \,,
\end{aligned}
$$

for some p_{max} and $r_{max} \leq r$ that is from round k or $k+1$.

Therefore, for any p_i during round $k+1$ there is a list of length $\ell \geq k$ of nodes $p_1, p_2, \ldots, p_\ell$ and a sequence of length ℓ of atomic steps $r_1 > r_2 > \cdots > r_\ell = 0$, such that

$$
\begin{aligned}
|\mathbf{c}_{p_i}(r)| &\leq \delta + ||B||_\infty |\mathbf{c}_{p_1}(r_1)| \\
&\leq \delta + ||B||_\infty (\delta + ||B||_\infty |\mathbf{c}_{p_2}(r_2)|) \\
&= \delta \cdot (1 + ||B||_\infty) + ||B||_\infty^2 |\mathbf{c}_{p_2}(r_2)| \\
&\leq \delta \cdot \sum_{z=0}^{\ell-1} ||B||_\infty^z + ||B||_\infty^\ell |\mathbf{c}_{p_\ell}(r_\ell)| \\
&= \delta \cdot \frac{1 - ||B||_\infty^\ell}{1 - ||B||_\infty} + ||B||_\infty^\ell |\mathbf{c}_{p_\ell}(0)| \,.
\end{aligned}
$$

Denote by $c_1 \triangleq \frac{1}{1 - ||B||_\infty}$, and $c_2 \triangleq ||B||_\infty$. We have that for node p_i performing the rth atomic step during round k it holds that $|\mathbf{c}_{p_i}(r)| \leq \delta \cdot c_1 + c_2^z \cdot z \leq \delta \cdot c_1 + c_2^k \cdot z$. $\qquad\square$

In fair runs, there are infinitely many rounds k, thus, as l and r go to infinity, we have that $\|O(r)\|_\infty$ is bounded by a hypercube of length $\delta \cdot c_1$ around $\mathbf{u}$.

7   Discussion

We have shown that the algorithm SS-ITERATIVE is a modification of the Jacobi iterative method to solve a set of equations $A\mathbf{x} = \mathbf{b}$, where A is given and $\mathbf{b}$ is dynamically changing but bounded. Moreover, Theorem 1 is a generalization of previous analysis of Jacobi's convergence. Our motivation for SS-ITERATIVE originates from the sensor calibration problem where sensors need to calibrate their noisy readings. Unlike previous approaches to this problem, we assume a dynamic system with an infinite execution of the algorithm. In this setting the readings of the sensors continuously change. Under the assumption that the readings' changes are bounded, we have shown that the calibrated output is bounded as well.

Further application for SS-ITERATIVE can be found in any setting where it is desired to solve $A\mathbf{x} = \mathbf{b}$ in a converging and self-stabilizing manner, while A is given, and $\mathbf{b}$ may change slightly from one round to the next. Notice that the analysis given in Section 4 holds in such a system.

As noted in Remark 2 the matrix A is "part of the code". An optional alternative to the current solution is to compute A^{-1} (the inverted matrix of A) beforehand and include it "as part of the code". Thus, each node could locally solve $\mathbf{x} = A^{-1}\mathbf{b}$, and it can be shown that $\mathbf{x}$ will be bounded (as long as $\mathbf{b}$ is bounded). The main problem with such a solution is the connectivity requirements it incurs. In our solution, scalar values are sent in the network only between direct neighbors. The matrix W represents a weighted adjacency graph. Once inverted, the matrix W^{-1} might not be sparse. A non-zero entry $w_{ij}^{-1} \in W^{-1}$ means that node p_i needs to communicate with node p_j. This extra communication might cause the algorithm to lose its self-stabilizing properties, as non-neighboring nodes would require a self-stabilizing overlay network for their communication.

The assumption of a predefined A is suitable for static networks in which the communication graph is predetermined. For dynamic networks, it would be interesting to adjust SS-ITERATIVE to discover the connectivity of the network, inferring the optimal weights dynamically. We assume that after the weights are calculated, the topology of the sensor network remains stable, thus the convergence analysis of Section 4 should hold.

7.1   Relation to Perturbation Theory

A large amount of research focused on the problem of solving $A\mathbf{x} = \mathbf{b}$ when A and $\mathbf{b}$ are not exactly known. That is, let $\hat{A} = A + \delta A$ and $\hat{\mathbf{b}} = \mathbf{b} + \delta\mathbf{b}$, and consider the equation $\hat{A}\hat{\mathbf{x}} = \hat{\mathbf{b}}$; what can be said about $\mathbf{x}$ in relation to $\hat{\mathbf{x}}$?

Our setting is "easier" in one sense, and "harder" in a different sense. In our setting A is known, *i.e.*, $\delta A = 0$. However, $\hat{\mathbf{b}}$ is not well defined. That is, the input vector - which is described by $\hat{\mathbf{b}}$ - changes over time. When solving $\hat{A}\hat{\mathbf{x}} = \hat{\mathbf{b}}$ it is assumed that there is some $\mathbf{b}$ that is *constant* but it was measured with an error. In our case, **b** is not constant as it changes over time, while it represents the measurements correctly.

As a future research, it would be interesting to consider the implications of adding inaccuracy to the measurements. The vast body of knowledge regarding perturbation theory would definitely aid in this extension to our model.

7.2   Relation to Convex Optimization

Many practical optimization problems are given in the quadratic form $f(x) = 1/2\mathbf{x}A\mathbf{x} - \mathbf{b}^T\mathbf{x}$, where the task is to compute $\min_{\mathbf{x}} f(\mathbf{x})$ distributively over a communication network. A survey showing several applications can be found in [3]. Example applications are monitoring, distributed computation of trust and ranking of nodes and data items.

A standard way for solving $\min_{\mathbf{x}} f(\mathbf{x})$ is by computing the derivative and comparing it to zero to get the global optimum. When the matrix A is symmetric, $f'(\mathbf{x}) = A\mathbf{x} - \mathbf{b} = 0$, and we get a linear system of equations $A\mathbf{x} = \mathbf{b}$. In other words, the convex optimization problem is reduced into a solution of a linear system of equations.

Interior point methods [4, Ch. 11] solve linear programming problems by applying Newton method iteratively. Each computation of the Newton step involves a solution of a linear systems of equations. An area of future work is to examine the applications of our self-stabilizing algorithm to these methods. The difficulties arise from the fact that the matrix A needs to be recomputed between iterations, so nodes need to be synchronized and aware of the current iteration taking place.

Acknowledgements

The authors would like to thank Golan Pundak for assisting with the simulations, and the anonymous reviewers for their helpful comments.

References

1. Bell, R.M., Koren, Y.: Scalable collaborative filtering with jointly derived neighborhood interpolation weights. In: ICDM 2007 (2007)
2. Bertsekas, D.P., Tsitsiklis, J.N.: Parallel and Distributed Calculation. Numerical Methods. Prentice Hall, Englewood Cliffs (1989)
3. Bickson, D., Malkhi, D.: A unifying framework for rating users and data items in peer-to-peer and social networks. Peer-to-Peer Networking and Applications (PPNA) Journal (2008)
4. Boyd, S., Vandenberghe, L.: Convex Optimization. Cambridge University Press, Cambridge (2004)
5. Davidovitch, L., Dolev, S., Rajsbaum, S.: Stability of multivalued continuous consensus. SIAM Journal on Computing 37(4), 1057–1076 (2007)
6. Dolev, D., Hoch, E.N.: Ocd: Obsessive consensus disorder (or repetitive consensus). In: Proc. of the 27st Int. Symposium on Principles of Distributed Computing (PODC 2008), Tornoto, Canada (August 2008)

7. Dolev, S.: Self-Stabilization. MIT Press, Cambridge (2000)
8. Dolev, S., Rajsbaum, S.: Stability of long-lived consensus. J. Comput. Syst. Sci. 67(1), 26–45 (2003)
9. Fang, J., Li, H.: Distributed event-region detection in wireless sensor networks. In: EURASIP J. Adv. Signal Process, New York, NY, United States, vol. 2008, pp. 1–10. Hindawi Publishing Corp. (January 2008)
10. Langendoen, K., Reijers, N.: Distributed localization in wireless sensor networks: a quantitative comparison. In: Comput. Networks, New York, NY, USA, November 2003, vol. 43, pp. 499–518. Elsevier North-Holland, Inc., Amsterdam (2003)
11. Marzullo, K.: Tolerating failures of continuous-valued sensors. ACM Trans. Comput. Syst. 8(4), 284–304 (1990)
12. Olfati-Saber, R.: Distributed Kalman Filtering for Sensor Networks. In: Proc. of the 46th IEEE Conference on Decision and Control (December 2007)

A Self-stabilizing $\frac{2}{3}$-Approximation Algorithm for the Maximum Matching Problem

Fredrik Manne[1], Morten Mjelde[1], Laurence Pilard[2], and Sébastien Tixeuil[3,*]

[1] University of Bergen, Norway
{fredrikm,mortenm}@ii.uib.no
[2] University of Franche Comté, France
laurence.pilard@iut-bm.univ-fcomte.fr
[3] LIP6 & INRIA Grand Large, Université Pierre et Marie Curie - Paris 6, France
tixeuil@lri.fr

Abstract. The matching problem asks for a large set of disjoint edges in a graph. It is a problem that has received considerable attention in both the sequential and self-stabilizing literature. Previous work has resulted in self-stabilizing algorithms for computing a maximal ($\frac{1}{2}$-approximation) matching in a general graph, as well as computing a $\frac{2}{3}$-approximation on more specific graph types. In the following we present the first self-stabilizing algorithm for finding a $\frac{2}{3}$-approximation to the maximum matching problem in a general graph. We show that our new algorithm stabilizes in at most exponential time under a distributed adversarial daemon, and $O(n^2)$ rounds under a distributed fair daemon, where n is the number of nodes in the graph.

Keywords: Self-stabilizing algorithm, $\frac{2}{3}$-Approximation, Maximum matching.

1 Introduction

A *matching* in a graph $G = (V, E)$ is a subset M of E such that no pair of edges in M have common endpoints. We say that two nodes v and w are matched if the edge (v, w) is in M. A matching M is *maximal* if no proper superset of M is also a matching. A matching M is *maximum* if there does not exists any matching with cardinality larger than $|M|$. While there exists sequential algorithms for computing a maximum matching in polynomial time, the complexity of such algorithms renders them impractical in many settings when applied to large graphs. Thus, approximation algorithms are often used to rapidly provide matchings that are within an acceptable margin of error. A maximal matching can be computed in linear time over the size of the graph, and it is well known that this results in a $\frac{1}{2}$-approximation to the maximum matching. In order to compute matchings with approximation ratios better than $\frac{1}{2}$, *augmenting paths*

---

* Support for this work was given by the Aurora program for collaboration between France and Norway.

S. Kulkarni and A. Schiper (Eds.): SSS 2008, LNCS 5340, pp. 94–108, 2008.

are often used. An augmenting path is a path in the graph, starting and ending in an unmatched node and where every other edge is either unmatched or matched, i.e. for each consecutive pair of edges exactly one of them must belong to the matching. Once an augmenting path p has been identified one can increase the size of M by performing an augmenting step. This consists of removing each matched edge of p from M and including every unmatched edge of p in M. This way the cardinality of the matching is increased by one. Hopcroft and Karp [12] show that given a graph $G = (V, E)$ and a matching $M \subseteq E$ then if there does not exist an augmenting path of length at most three in G, then M is a $\frac{2}{3}$-approximation to the maximum matching.

The matching problem is often used to model several real world situations. Examples include the problem of assigning tasks to workers or creating pairs of entities. The latter lends itself well to a distributed network, since processes in the network may need to choose exactly one neighbor to communicate with.

In this paper we use augmenting paths and present a self-stabilizing algorithm that computes a $\frac{2}{3}$-approximation to the maximum matching problem in a general, unweighted graph. Our algorithm is based on using an existing maximal matching, and then identifying augmenting paths of length three. These are then used to improve the cardinality of the matching.

1.1   Self-stabilizing Algorithms

Self-stabilizing algorithms [3,4] are distributed algorithms that permit forward failure recovery by means of an attractive property: starting from any arbitrary initial state, the system autonomously resumes correct behavior within finite time. Self-stabilization allows failure detection to be bypassed, yet does not make any assumptions about the nature or the span of those failures. Central to the theory of self-stabilization is the notion of *daemon*, an abstraction for the scheduling of nodes in the system to execute their local code. A daemon is often viewed as an adversary to the algorithm that tries to prevent stabilization by scheduling the worst possible nodes for execution. The weakest possible requirement is that the daemon is *proper*, i.e. only nodes whose scheduling would change the system state are actually scheduled (these nodes are *privileged*). Variants of daemons can be defined along two axis: *(i)* a daemon may be *sequential* (meaning that no two privileged nodes may be selected by the daemon simultaneously) or *distributed* (in which case any number of privileged nodes may be selected at the same time), and *(ii)* a daemon may also be *fair* (which ensures that every privileged node will be allowed to move eventually) or *adversarial* (meaning that a privileged node may have to wait indefinitely, yet always scheduling *some* privileged node for execution). Intuitively, distributed is a more general property than sequential, and adversarial is a more general property than fair. Thus among these daemons, the most general is the distributed adversarial, and the least general is the sequential fair daemon. As a result, an algorithm that tolerates the most general adversary also tolerates the least general one, but the converse is not true.

Time complexity is measured differently depending on the daemon used: for any fair daemon time complexity is measured in *rounds*, where a round is the smallest sub-sequence of an execution in which every node privileged for at least one move at the start of a round has either executed one of these moves during the round, or has become ineligible to do so. For the adversarial sequential daemon, complexity is measured in single node moves, while for the adversarial distributed daemon it is measured in time steps, where a time step is one step in the execution during which at least one privileged node executes one move.

When no nodes in the graph are privileged, we say that the algorithm is *stable*, or has reached a *stable configuration*.

1.2   Related Work

The first self-stabilizing algorithm for computing a maximal matching was given by Hsu and Huang [13]. The authors showed a stabilization time of $O(n^3)$ moves under a sequential adversarial daemon. This analysis was later improved to $O(n^2)$ by Tel [15] and to $O(m)$ by Hedetniemi et al. [11], where m is the number of edges in the graph. The algorithm assumes an anonymous graph and the sequential daemon is used to break symmetry. By means of randomization Gradinariu and Johnen [9] gave a method for assigning identifiers that are unique within distance two. This was then used to transform the algorithm by Hsu and Huang so that it stabilizes under a distributed adversarial daemon, albeit with an unbounded stabilization time.

Goddard et al. [6] gave a synchronous variant of Hsu and Huangs algorithm and showed that it stabilizes in $O(n)$ rounds. While not explicitly proved in the paper, it can be shown that this algorithm stabilizes in $\theta(n^2)$ time steps under an adversarial distributed daemon. Gradinariu and Tixeuil [10] provide a general scheme to transform an algorithm written for the sequential adversarial daemon into an algorithm that can cope with the distributed adversarial daemon. Using this scheme with the Hsu and Huang algorithm yields a time step complexity of $O(\Delta \cdot m)$, where Δ denotes the maximum degree of the graph. Manne et al. [14] later gave an algorithm for finding a maximal matching that stabilizes in $O(m)$ time step under the distributed adversarial daemon, and $O(n)$ rounds when using the distributed fair daemon. The aforementioned protocols of [6,10,14] assume that the nodes are provided with unique identifiers (either globally, or within a certain distance), as [14] points out that deterministic protocols require symmetry breaking to deal with the adversarial daemon.

When it comes to improving the $\frac{1}{2}$-approximation induced by the maximal matching property, only a few works investigate this issue in a self-stabilizing setting. Ghosh et al. [5] and Blair and Manne [1] presented a framework that can be used for computing a maximum matching in a tree under a distributed adversarial daemon using $O(n^2)$ moves, while Goddard et al. [8] gave a self-stabilizing algorithm for computing a $\frac{2}{3}$-approximation in anonymous rings of length not divisible by three using $O(n^4)$ moves, under a sequential adversarial daemon. The polynomial complexity results mainly from the fact that only strongly constrained topologies are investigated.

The case of general graphs is more intricate and is the topic of this paper. It is possible to compute a $\frac{2}{3}$-approximation (or even an optimal solution) for the maximum matching problem by collecting the entire graph topology on each node using a self-stabilizing topology update protocol, and then run a deterministic sequential algorithm on each node. This would yield a self-stabilizing algorithm for the matching problem, but at the expense of having to duplicate the system graph on each node. This approach is not very practical in most settings, due to its considerable memory usage.

As far as feasibility is concerned, it would be possible to use a generic scheme such as [7,2] that prevents nodes at distance k or less of a particular node u to execute code until further notice from u. Such a scheme would permit to devise a protocol that essentially tries to find and then to integrate augmenting paths starting at a node u. Unfortunately, both schemes suffer from severe drawbacks for this purpose. First, both [7] and [2] make use of a large amount of memory at each node (typically, an exponential number of states with respect to k). Second, the complexity of a $\frac{2}{3}$-approximation scheme using [7] would be unbounded. Third, a scheme based on [2] would require operating under a fair daemon, and may not stabilize under an adversarial one.

1.3 Our Contribution

In this paper we present the first self-stabilizing algorithm for computing a $\frac{2}{3}$-approximation to the maximum matching in a general, non-anonymous graph, that performs under any daemon. Complexity-wise, we show that our algorithm stabilizes in $O(2^{n+2} \cdot \Delta \cdot n)$ time steps under the distributed adversarial daemon, and in $O(n^2)$ rounds under the distributed fair daemon. The memory used at each node by our protocol is low: we use three pointers to neighbors and one boolean variables. The rest of the paper is organized as follows. The algorithm is presented in Section 2. In Section 3 we show the correctness of the algorithm, while the stabilization time for the algorithm is shown in Section 4. Finally, we conclude in Section 5.

2 The Algorithm

In this section we present our new algorithm. The algorithm assumes that there exists an underlying maximal matching algorithm, which has reached a stable configuration. In Section 4.3 we will explain how the algorithm works when this algorithm is not in a stable configuration. The new algorithm functions by identifying augmenting paths of length three, and then rearranging the matching accordingly. This is done in several steps. First every pair of matched nodes v, w will try to find unmatched neighbors to which they can rematch. Then one of v and w will first attempt to match with one of its candidates. Only when the first node succeeds, will the second node also attempt to match with one of its candidates. If this also succeeds the rematching is considered complete. The algorithm will stabilize when there are no such augmenting paths left.

2.1 Predicates and Variables

Given an undirected graph $G = (V, E)$ where each node v has a unique identifier. We assume that these can be ordered, and in the following we do not distinguish between a node and its identifier. By definition $v < null$ for every node $v \in V$.

The set of neighbors of v in G is denoted by $N(v)$. In the following, we refer to M' as the set of edges in the underlying maximal matching. If v is matched in M', then m_v denotes the node that v is matched with in M', i.e. $(v, m_v) \in M'$. Note that if v is unmatched in M' then $m_v = null$. For a set of nodes A, we define $\mu(A)$ and $\sigma(A)$ as the set of matched and unmatched nodes in A, respectively, in the maximal matching M'. Since we assume that the underlying maximal matching is stable, a nodes membership in $\mu(V)$ or $\sigma(V)$ will not change, and each node v can use the value of m_v to determine which set it belongs to.

In order to facilitate the rematching, each node $v \in V$ maintains three pointers and one boolean variable. The pointer p_v refers to a neighbor of v that v is trying to (re)match with. If $p_v = null$ then the matching of v has not changed from the maximal matching (we define $p_{null} = null$). Thus two neighboring nodes v, w are matched if and only if either $p_v = w$ and $p_w = v$, or if $p_v = null$, $p_w = null$ and $(v, w) \in M'$.

For a node $v \in \mu(V)$, the pointers α_v and β_v refer to two nodes in $\sigma(N(v))$ that are candidates for a possible rematching with v. Also, s_v is a boolean variable that indicates if v has performed a successful rematching or not.

2.2 Rules and Functions

The following section gives the rules and functions of the algorithm. Each rule is executed on a node $v \in V$. We divide the rules into two sets, one for nodes in $\sigma(V)$ and one for nodes in $\mu(V)$. If more than one rule is privileged for a node in $\mu(V)$, the rules are executed in the order presented here. For a set of nodes A, *Unique(A)* returns the number of unique elements in the set[1], and *Lowest(A)* returns the node in A with the lowest identifier, or $null$ if $A = \emptyset$.

SingleNode
    if $(p_v = null \wedge Lowest\{w \in N(v) \mid p_w = v\} \neq null) \vee$
        $p_v \notin (\mu(N(v)) \cup \{null\}) \vee (p_v \neq null \wedge p_{p_v} \neq v)$
    then $p_v := Lowest\{w \in N(v) \mid p_w = v\}$

Algorithm 1 - Rule for nodes in $\sigma(V)$

Motivation. We now give a brief motivation for each rule in Algorithm 1.

The purpose of the *SingleNode* rule is to ensure that a node $v \in \sigma(V)$ is pointing to a neighbor in $\mu(N(v))$ that points back to v. In doing so, v and p_v will be matched. If there exists more than one candidate, the rule will select the one with the smallest identifier. If no node in $\mu(N(v))$ points to v, the rule ensures that v points to $null$, thereby informing v's neighbors that v is unmatched.

---

[1] Note that $Unique(A) = |A|$. However for the sake of clarity we use $Unique(A)$.

Update
  if $(\alpha_v > \beta_v) \vee (\alpha_v, \beta_v \notin \sigma(N(v)) \cup \{null\}) \vee$
     $(\alpha_v = \beta_v \wedge \alpha_v \neq null) \vee p_v \notin (\sigma(N(v)) \cup \{null\}) \vee$
     $((\alpha_v, \beta_v) \neq BestRematch(v) \wedge (p_v = null \vee p_{p_v} \notin \{v, null\}))$
  then $(\alpha_v, \beta_v) := BestRematch(v)$
       $(p_v, s_v) := (null, false)$

MatchFirst
  if $(AskFirst(v) \neq null) \wedge (p_v \neq AskFirst(v) \vee s_v \neq (p_{p_v} = v))$
  then $p_v := AskFirst(v)$
       $s_v := (p_{p_v} = v)$

MatchSecond
  if $(AskSecond(v) \neq null) \wedge (s_{m_v} = true) \wedge (p_v \neq AskSecond(v))$
  then $p_v := AskSecond(v)$

ResetMatch
  if $(AskFirst(v) = AskSecond(v) = null) \wedge ((p_v, s_v) \neq (null, false))$
  then $(p_v, s_v) := (null, false)$

Algorithm 1 - Rules for nodes in $\mu(V)$.

BestRematch(v)
  $a = Lowest \{u \in \sigma(N(v)) \wedge (p_u = null \vee p_u = v)\}$
  $b = Lowest \{u \in \sigma(N(v)) \setminus \{a\} \wedge (p_u = null \vee p_u = v)\}$
  return (a, b)

AskFirst(v)
  if $\alpha_v \neq null \wedge \alpha_{m_v} \neq null \wedge 2 \leq Unique(\{\alpha_v, \beta_v, \alpha_{m_v}, \beta_{m_v}\}) \leq 4$
    then if $\alpha_v < \alpha_{m_v} \vee (\alpha_v = \alpha_{m_v} \wedge \beta_v = null) \vee (\alpha_v = \alpha_{m_v} \wedge \beta_{m_v} \neq null \wedge v < m_v)$
      then return α_v
  else return $null$

AskSecond(v)
  if $AskFirst(m_v) \neq null$
    then return $Lowest(\{\alpha_v, \beta_v\} \setminus \{\alpha_{m_v}\})$
  else return $null$

Algorithm 1 - Functions

The *Update* rule is used to ensure that a node $v \in \mu(V)$ has α_v and β_v set to two neighbors that v can try to match with. Note that the rule is executed if any one of the current α-, β-, or p-value is not pointing to a node in $\sigma(N(v))$ or to *null*, or if the values of α and β are incorrect, relative to each other. If this is not the case, the rule is executed only if v is not already involved in a rematch attempt. The values of α_v and β_v are returned by the *BestRematch* function, which returns the two unmatched neighbors in $\sigma(N(v))$ with the smallest identifiers.

The *MatchFirst* rule is executed by a node $v \in \mu(V)$ in order to initiate a rematch attempt. The *AskFirst* function returns the neighbor of v that v should attempt to rematch with. If this succeeds, then the node m_v may become privileged for a *MatchSecond* move, which employs the *AskSecond* function in the same way that *MatchFirst* uses *AskFirst*. The *AskFirst* function has two consecutive predicates, both which must evaluate to true in order for the calling node v to become privileged for a *MatchFirst* move. The first predicate (the first *if* statement) checks that v and m_v each have at least one possible unique neighbor to rematch with. The second predicate decides whether v or m_v should initiate the rematch attempt.

If a node $v \in \mu(V)$ becomes unable to participate in a rematch attempt, it may be privileged for a *ResetMatch* move, in order to reset its p- and s-value.

Example. We now give a possible execution of Algorithm 1 under a distributed adversarial daemon. Figure 1 presents a graph, consisting of the four nodes x, v, w, and y, where $v < w$ and $x < y$. Nodes v and w are matched in the underlying maximal matching. This is shown by the double line joining them. In the figure we illustrate one node pointing to a neighbor by an arrow (the absence of an arrow means that the node in question is pointing to *null*), and if the s-value is true for a node we show this by a double border. The values of the α- and β-variables are not shown in the figure.

Figure 1a shows the initial state of the graph. We assume that at this point $(\alpha_v, \beta_v) = (x, null)$ and $(\alpha_w, \beta_w) = (x, z)$, where $z \notin N(w)$. Also note that $s_v = false$. Observe that both v and w are pointing to x, which implies that x is privileged for a *SingleNode* move. Since $\beta_w \notin N(w)$, w is privileged for an *Update* move. In Figure 1b x has executed its *SingleNode* move, and v has executed a subsequent *MatchFirst* move and set $s_v = true$. At this point, w may execute an *Update* move, while no other nodes are privileged. This move will set $(p_w, s_w) = (null, false)$ and, since w has no neighbors that are eligible candidates for a rematch attempt, $(\alpha_w, \beta_w) = (null, null)$. However, this gives $AskFirst(v) = null$, and v can now execute a *ResetMatch* move, which is followed by a *SingleNode* move by x. The result of these moves is shown in Figure 1c.

At this point, both v and w have, combined, at least two unique candidates for a rematching, namely x and y. Thus both nodes will execute *Update* moves, after which $AskFirst(w) = x$ (which implies that $AskFirst(v) = null$), and w may execute a *MatchFirst* move, and point to x, as seen in Figure 1d. Following this

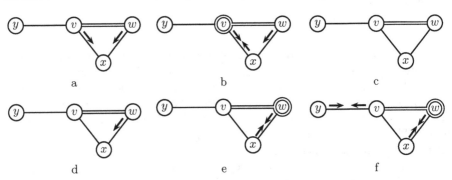

Fig. 1. Execution example of Algorithm 1

move, x executes a *SingleNode* move and points to w after which w will set $s_w = true$ through a *MatchFirst* move (Figure 1e). Since w has successfully established a rematching, v may now attempt the same by executing a *MatchSecond* move and point to y. This will cause y to point back to v (note however that v is not privileged to set $s_v = true$) (Figure 1f). At this point the system has reached a stable configuration, and the augmenting path that existed in Figure 1a has been identified and used to improve the matching.

3   Correct Stabilization

In this section we show that when Algorithm 1 is stable it has computed a $\frac{2}{3}$-approximation to the maximum cardinality matching problem. Due to page constraints we omit some of the proofs.

We first need the following definition.

Definition 1. A node $v \in \mu(V)$ is a *pioneer* if and only if $AskFirst(v) \neq null$.

We define the short hand notation

$$R(v) \equiv \alpha_v \neq null \wedge \alpha_{m_v} \neq null \wedge 2 \leq Unique(\{\alpha_v, \beta_v, \alpha_{m_v}, \beta_{m_v}\}) \leq 4$$

Thus $R(v)$ is equal to the outcome of the first if-statement of the *AskFirst* function. $R(v) = true$ states that v and m_w each have at least one candidate for a rematch, and together they have at least two unique candidates. Note that $R(v) = R(m_v)$. We now make the following observation about Algorithm 1.

Lemma 1. *For a node $v \in \mu(V)$ in a stable configuration where $R(v) = true$ then either $AskFirst(v) \neq null$ or $AskFirst(m_v) \neq null$.*

Next we show the following connection between $AskFirst(v)$ and $AskSecond(m_v)$.

Lemma 2. *If $v \in \mu(V)$ then $AskFirst(v) \neq null$ if and only if $AskSecond(m_v) \neq null$.*

We now proceed to show that in a stable configuration whenever a node v has $p_v \neq null$ then we must have $p_v \in N(v)$ and $p_{p_v} = v$. To do so we look at three different cases. The first case is $v \in \sigma(V)$. For $v \in \mu(V)$ we distinguish if v is a pioneer or not.

Lemma 3. *Let $v \in \sigma(V)$ in a stable configuration. Then $p_v \neq null$ implies that $p_v \in \mu(N(v))$ and that $p_{p_v} = v$.*

To show that the equivalent of Lemma 3 also holds for $v \in \mu(V)$ we first need to show the following two intermediate results.

Lemma 4. *Let $v \in \mu(V)$. Then we cannot have $p_v \neq null$, $p_{p_v} \neq v$, and $(\alpha_v, \beta_v) \neq BestRematch(v)$ in a stable configuration.*

Corollary 1. *Let $v \in \mu(V)$. Then we cannot have $p_v \neq null$, $p_{p_v} \neq v$, and $p_v \in \{\alpha_v, \beta_v\}$ in a stable configuration.*

We can now show that the equivalent of Lemma 3 also holds for $v \in \mu(V)$.

Lemma 5. *Let* $v \in \mu(V)$ *in a stable configuration. If* $AskFirst(v) \neq null$ *then (i)* $p_v \neq null$, *(ii)* $p_v \in \sigma(N(v))$, *(iii)* $p_{p_v} = v$, *and (iv)* $s_v = true$.

Lemma 6. *Let* $v \in \mu(V)$ *in a stable configuration. If* $AskSecond(v) \neq null$ *then (i)* $p_v \neq null$, *(ii)* $p_v \in \sigma(N(v))$, *and (iii)* $p_{p_v} = v$.

We have now established for any node $v \in V$ that if $p_v \neq null$ then $p_{p_v} = v$. We next show that if $v \in \mu(V)$ is matched to a node other than m_v in a stable configuration, then m_v is also matched to a node other than v.

Lemma 7. *If* $v \in \mu(V)$ *in stable configuration then* $p_v \neq null \Leftrightarrow p_{m_v} \neq null$.

Next we show that when Algorithm 1 is stable the original matching M' and the p values define an unambiguous matching. Recall that two neighboring nodes v and w are matched if either $(v, w) \in M'$, $p_v = null$, and $p_w = null$ or if $p_v = w$ and $p_w = v$. Similarly, a node v is unmatched if $v \in \sigma(V)$ and if $p_v = null$.

Lemma 8. *In a stable configuration every node is either matched or unmatched.*

We can now finally show that a stable configuration of Algorithm 1 is a $\frac{2}{3}$-approximation to the maximum cardinality matching problem.

Theorem 1. *A stable configuration of Algorithm 1 is a* $\frac{2}{3}$-*approximation to the maximum matching problem.*

Proof. We first note from Lemma 8 that a stable matching is well defined, meaning that every node is either matched or unmatched. Next, from Hopcroft and Karp [12], we have that for a graph G with a matching M, if there does not exists an augmenting path of length three or less then M is a $\frac{2}{3}$-approximation to the maximum matching in G.

From the definition of an augmenting path it follows that any node in $\mu(V)$ will also be a member of the final matching. Consequently, an augmenting path in a stable configuration must both start and end with nodes from $\sigma(V)$. Due to the underlying maximal matching we know that there does not exist an augmenting path in M' of length one, i.e. two unmatched nodes cannot be neighbors. It is therefore sufficient to show that there does not exist an augmenting path x, v, w, y in a stable configuration where x and y are distinct unmatched nodes and v and w are matched.

Assume that such a path exists in a stable configuration, then $v, w \in \mu(V)$, otherwise two adjacent nodes would be in $\sigma(V)$. Since v and w are matched in the final matching then either *(i)* $p_v = w$ and $p_w = v$ or *(ii)* $p_v = p_w = null$ and $(v, w) \in M'$.

Note that in *Case (i)* $p_v \in \mu(V)$ (and similarly for p_w), which would trigger an *Update* move, contradicting that the configuration is stable.

For *Case (ii)* first note that since x and y are unmatched, $p_x = p_y = null$. Thus, if $Unique(\{\alpha_v, \beta_v\}) = 0$ then v is privileged for an *Update* move (and similarly for w). However, if both $\{\alpha_v, \beta_v\} \neq \emptyset$ and $\{\alpha_w, \beta_w\} \neq \emptyset$ we see from Lemma 1 that either $AskFirst(v) \neq null$ or $AskSecond(v) \neq null$. From lemmas 5 and 6 this implies that the configuration is not stable. □

4 Stabilization Time

We now progress to bound the time needed for the algorithm to stabilize, both for the distributed adversarial and for the distributed fair daemon. For these analysis we assume that the underlying maximal matching is stable. We address the interaction between the maximal matching and Algorithm 1 in Section 4.3. Note that due to page constraints we omit some of the proofs.

4.1 Distributed Adversarial Daemon

In this section we bound the number of time steps needed for Algorithm 1 to stabilize with the distributed adversarial daemon. Recall that one time step is one step in the execution during which at least one node privileged at the start of the time step has executed exactly one move.

We say that a node $v \in \mu(V)$ has executed a *forced Update* move if an *Update* move was executed due to one of the following conditions: *(i)* $\alpha_v > \beta_v$, *(ii)* $\alpha_v, \beta_v \notin \sigma(N(v))$, or *(iii)* $\alpha_v = \beta_v$ while $\alpha_v \neq null$. Since neither of these states can occur as a result of an executed move they must occur as a result of incorrect initial values. Thus, each node $v \in \mu(V)$ can execute at most one forced *Update* move, and this will be the first move that v executes, if it was initially privileged to do so. We now make the following observation about Algorithm 1.

Lemma 9. *Let* $v \in \mu(V)$. *Then* $AskFirst(v) \neq null$ *if and only* $AskSecond(v) = null$.

Lemma 10. *For every nodes* $v \in \mu(V)$, *if neither* v *nor* m_v *is privileged for a forced Update move and* $AskFirst(v) \neq null$ *then* $AskFirst(v) < AskSecond(m_v)$.

The following result shows that once a successful rematching has been established, then if the involved nodes in $\mu(V)$ are not privileged for a forced *Update* move, the involved nodes in $\sigma(V)$ will not move again.

Lemma 11. *Given nodes* $v, w, x,$ *and* y *where* $(v, w) \in M'$, $x \in \sigma(N(v))$ *and* $y \in \sigma(N(w))$. *If* $p_v = x$, $p_w = y$, $p_x = v$, $p_y = w$, $AskFirst(v) = x$, *and* $AskSecond(w) = y$, *then if neither* v *nor* w *is privileged for a forced Update move, neither* x *nor* y *will move again.*

Next we show that the nodes in $\mu(V)$ will stabilize rapidly if no node in $\sigma(V)$ executes a move.

Lemma 12. *A node* $v \in \mu(V)$ *can make* $O(1)$ *moves between each time step that includes a move by a node in* $\sigma(N(v))$

Proof. Let $v \in \mu(V)$ and consider a maximal sequence S of time steps where no node in $\sigma(N(v))$ makes a move. Let a, b be the initial values of α_v, β_v and a', b' their values after the first (if any) *Update* move by v in S. Then from the *BestRematch* function we have that $a', b' \in \sigma(N(v)) \cup \{null\}$. Since the values of α_v and β_v are only changed by the *Update* rule they will remain in

$\sigma(N(v)) \cup \{null\}$ for the duration of S while $(\alpha_v, \beta_v) = BestRematch(v)$ also remains true.

The *Update* rule sets $p_v = null$ and any value subsequently assigned to p_v must be taken from the set $\{\alpha_v, \beta_v, null\}$. It follows that $p_v \in \sigma(N(v)) \cup \{null\}$ will remain true throughout S after the first *Update* move. From these observations it follows that there can at most be one *Update* move in S.

The remaining rules can only be triggered by changes in the values of $\alpha_v, \beta_v,$ $\alpha_{m_v}, \beta_{m_v}, p_v,$ and p_{p_v}. From the above observation we know that there can only be four configurations of $\alpha_v, \beta_v, \alpha_{m_v}, \beta_{m_v}$ in S since each α, β pair can only change value once in S. It follows from Lemma 9 that for fixed $\alpha_v, \beta_v, \alpha_{m_v}, \beta_{m_v}$ values we must have one of the following configurations: *(i)* $AskFirst(v) \neq null$ and $AskSecond(v) = null$, *(ii)* $AskFirst(v) = null$ and $AskSecond(v) \neq null$, or *(iii)* $AskFirst(v) = null$ and $AskSecond(v) = null$. Thus only one of the rules *MatchFirst*, *MatchSecond*, and *ResetMatch* can be privileged before at least one of $\alpha_v, \beta_v, \alpha_{m_v}, \beta_{m_v}, p_v$ changes value. For each of these rules it is straightforward to see that the assignment to p_v or s_v cannot make the same rule become privileged again. The only assignment that can cause a new move is if p_{p_v} changes value which could result in *MatchFirst* to be executed consecutively more than once. But if $p_v \in \sigma(N(v))$ then p_{p_v} will not change in S. Also, if $p_v = null$ then p_{p_v} cannot change and if $p_v \notin \sigma(N(v)) \cup \{null\}$ then the next move executed by v will be an *Update* move. It follows that v can at most execute one move between each time that at least one of $\alpha_v, \beta_v, \alpha_{m_v}, \beta_{m_v}, p_v$ changes value in S and the result follows.   □

In order to reason about *SingleNode* moves and the cause of these, we use the following definitions: Given a node $x \in \sigma(V)$ and a node $v \in \mu(V)$, we refer to x as being *asked first* in a rematch attempt if $AskFirst(v) = x$ and p_v is set to x. Similarly, we refer to x as being *asked second* if $AskSecond(v) = x$ and p_v is set to x. We say that x *accepts* the matching attempt if following either of the above cases it sets $p_x = v$. If x sets $p_x \neq v$ then x *rejects* the matching attempt by v.

Lemma 13. *The node y with the highest identifier in $\sigma(V)$ can execute moves during at most $O(\delta_y)$ time steps where δ_y is the degree of y.*

We now bound the total number of moves executed by nodes in $\sigma(V)$.

Lemma 14. *Each node in $\sigma(V)$ can execute moves during at most $O(2^{n+2} \cdot \Delta)$ time steps, where Δ is the maximum degree in the graph.*

Proof. Order the nodes in $\sigma(V)$ as $x_0, x_1, ..., x_{t-1}$ where $t = |\sigma(V)|$ such that $x_0 > x_1 > ... > x_t$. We denote the number of moves that a node x_i can execute as $L(i)$, and show by induction that $L(i) \leq \sum_{e=0}^{i-1} L(e) + O(\Delta)$.

The base case is $i = 0$. It was shown in Lemma 13 that the single node with the highest identifier in $\sigma(V)$ can execute at most $O(\Delta)$ moves. Thus $L(0) = O(\Delta)$.

For the induction step we assume that the bound holds for every node $x_0, x_1,$ $..., x_{i-1}$ and prove that this implies that it also holds for x_i. We show this by considering the instances where x_i is asked second separately from where x_i is asked first.

The case where x_i is asked second is similar to the base case, and will thus result in $O(\Delta)$ moves.

For the case where x_i is asked first by some node v we first observe that if v is initially privileged for a forced *Update* move, then following this move x_i may become privileged to set $p_{x_i} \neq v$. However, if x_i is again asked first by v, we know that there exists a node $w = m_v$ where $k = AskSecond(w)$ and $k \neq null$. We now consider two cases: *(i)* $k \in \sigma(N(w))$ or *(ii)* $k \notin \sigma(N(w))$.

In Case *(i)* it follows that there exists a node $x_j \in \sigma(V)$ such that $x_j = k$. If $x_j < x_i$ then $\alpha_w \geq \beta_w$, which must be due to an incorrect initialization. Thus, w is privileged to execute a forced *Update* move, after which x_i may again become privileged. Subsequently, if x_i is again asked first by v, then Case *(i)* is again true, but now with $x_j > x_i$.

We will now show that x_i may only become privileged again due to moves made by x_j. At this point, both v and w must have executed any forced *Update* move, if they were privileged to do so. Obviously x_i will not become privileged while $p_v = x_i$, and from the predicate of the *Update* move we see that v will not become privileged for an *Update* move while $p_{x_i} = v$. From the *ResetMatch* predicate it follows that v may only become privileged if $AskSecond(w) = null$, which implies that x_j has made a move. Furthermore, from Lemma 11 we know that if x_j accepts the rematch attempt from w, x_i will not move again. Hence, when $k \in \sigma(N(w))$, the number of moves by x_i is bounded by $\sum_{k=0}^{i-1} L(k)$.

For Case *(ii)* note first that $k \notin \sigma(N(w))$ can only occur once initially due to incorrect initialization. In this case w is privileged for an *Update* move, and x_i may only become privileged again following this move. Since x_i has at most Δ neighbors, it follows that Case *(ii)* may at most cause $O(\Delta)$ additional moves for x_i. Combining the case where x_i is asked second with *(i)* and *(ii)* we get $L(i) \leq L(i-1) + L(i-2) + ... + L(0) + O(\Delta) \leq 2^{i+2} \cdot O(\Delta)$ and the result follows. $\qquad\square$

Based on lemmas 12 and 14 we get the following bound on the step complexity of Algorithm 1 when using a distributed adversarial daemon.

Theorem 2. *Algorithm 1 will stabilize in $O(2^{n+2} \cdot \Delta \cdot n)$ time steps.*

4.2 Distributed Fair Daemon

In this section we consider the complexity of Algorithm 1 when run with a distributed fair daemon. Due to page constraints we only give an outline of the analysis.

We first note that following the first round, for any node $z \in V$ $p_z \in N(z) \cup \{null\}$, and additionally, for any node $v \in \mu(V)$, if $AskFirst(v) \neq null$ then $\alpha_v, \beta_v \in \sigma(N(v))$ and $AskFirst(v) < AskSecond(m_v)$. Consequently, if there exists an augmenting path of length three in the graph, then within $O(1)$ rounds, at least one node $v \in \mu(V)$ must have $p_v = x \neq null$ (possibly as a result of a *MatchFirst* move), where $x \in \sigma(V)$. Thus, within the end of the subsequent round, $p_x = w \neq null$ (note that w may be equal to v). If x was asked second by

w we know that a rematch attempt has succeeded. If x was asked first, we know that there exists a node y where $x < y$ that is asked second by m_w. Thus we can repeat the above argument, creating a chain of nodes in $\sigma(V)$ with increasing identifiers that must eventually lead to two edges joining the matching. Observe that the length of this chain is at most $O(n)$.

Thus we see that after at most $O(n)$ rounds at least two edges must join the matching, and since the cardinality of the matching is at most $O(n)$, we get the following result.

Theorem 3. *Algorithm 1 will stabilize in $O(n^2)$ rounds under a distributed fair daemon.*

4.3   Interaction with the Maximal Matching

While the previous two sections show that Algorithm 1 stabilizes when the underlying maximal matching is stable, we need to consider how Algorithm 1 functions on a non-stable maximal matching. We assume a maximal matching algorithm such as the one given by Manne et al. [14] and denote this as Algorithm 0. This algorithm has the property that if an edge becomes part of the matching then it will remain so for the remainder of the execution. We enforce that no rule in Algorithm 1 will become privileged on a node z if a rule in Algorithm 0 is privileged for the same node. Furthermore, if a node z in Algorithm 0 has made a bid to establish a new matching, then no rule in Algorithm 1 will become privileged for z until the attempt has either succeeded or failed (note that z is not necessarily privileged). This may for example occur if z is attempting to match with a neighbor, but has not yet received a response (for details of Algorithm 0, see [14]). Finally, we assume that Algorithm 0 does not use any variables from Algorithm 1.

Given the above, then at any point during the execution of the combined algorithm, there exists a (possibly empty or disconnected) subgraph of G where Algorithm 0 is stable. Since the non-stable nodes that border on this subgraph will not become privileged for Algorithm 1, it follows that any execution of Algorithm 1 will stabilize on G. Due to page restraints we omit further details.

The algorithm given in [14] has a complexity of $O(m)$ and $O(n)$ for the distributed adversarial and distributed fair daemon respectively, and thus the combined complexity of algorithms 0 and 1 is $O(2^{n+2} \cdot \Delta \cdot n \cdot m)$ for the distributed adversarial daemon and $O(n^2)$ for the distributed fair daemon.

5   Conclusion

We have presented the first self-stabilizing algorithm for computing a $\frac{2}{3}$- approximation to the maximum cardinality matching problem in a general graph. The algorithm uses only constant number of variables for each node, and stabilizes in $O(2^{n+2} \cdot \Delta \cdot n)$ time steps and $O(n^2)$ rounds for the distributed adversarial and distributed fair daemon, respectively, when assuming a stable underlying maximal matching.

It is worth noting that it would have been possible to design an algorithm such that through the use of identifiers, the eventual solution is deterministic, i.e. unaffected by the initial state of the graph and the order in which rules are executed. This algorithm would conceivably be both shorter and have a better complexity than the one presented here, but at the cost of robustness. That is, in the presented algorithm, adding or removing a node in a stable solution would have little or no effect on the majority of the graph, while the hypothetical strict algorithm would possibly have to redo the entire stabilization process.

A possible area for future research is to investigate how better approximation ratios than $\frac{2}{3}$ could be achieved with complexity efficient self-stabilizing algorithms. Furthermore, it would be of interest to see if the algorithm given here could be generalized for weighted instances of the matching problem, or if the stabilization time can be improved.

References

1. Blair, J.R.S., Manne, F.: Efficient self-stabilizing algorithms for tree networks. In: ICDCS 2003: Proceedings of the 23rd International Conference on Distributed Computing Systems, Washington, DC, USA, pp. 20–26. IEEE Computer Society Press, Los Alamitos (2003)
2. Danturi, P., Nesterenko, M., Tixeuil, S.: Self-stabilizing philosophers with generic conflicts. In: Datta, A.K., Gradinariu, M. (eds.) SSS 2006. LNCS, vol. 4280, pp. 214–230. Springer, Heidelberg (2006)
3. Dijkstra, E.W.: Self-stabilizing systems in spite of distributed control. Commun. ACM 17(11), 643–644 (1974)
4. Dolev, S.: Self-Stabilization. MIT Press, Cambridge (2000)
5. Ghosh, S., Gupta, A., Karaata, M.H., Pemmaraju, S.V.: Self-stabilizing dynamic programming algorithms on trees. In: Proceedings of the Second Workshop on Self-Stabilizing Systems (WSSS 1995), Las Vegas, pp. 11.1–11.15 (1995)
6. Goddard, W., Hedetniemi, S.T., Jacobs, D.P., Srimani, P.K.: Self-stabilizing protocols for maximal matching and maximal independent sets for ad hoc networks. In: IPDPS 2003: Proceedings of the 17th International Symposium on Parallel and Distributed Processing, Washington, DC, USA, p. 162.2. IEEE Computer Society Press, Los Alamitos (2003)
7. Goddard, W., Hedetniemi, S.T., Jacobs, D.P., Trevisan, V.: Distance-k knowledge in self-stabilizing algorithms. Theor. Comput. Sci. 399(1-2), 118–127 (2008)
8. Goddard, W., Hedetniemi, S.T., Shi, Z.: An anonymous self-stabilizing algorithm for 1-maximal matching in trees. In: PDPTA 2006: Proceedings of the International Conference on Parallel and Distributed Processing Techniques and Applications & Conference on Real-Time Computing Systems and Applications, vol. 2, pp. 797–803. CSREA Press (2006)
9. Gradinariu, M., Johnen, C.: Self-stabilizing neighborhood unique naming under unfair scheduler. In: Sakellariou, R., Keane, J.A., Gurd, J.R., Freeman, L. (eds.) Euro-Par 2001, vol. 2150, pp. 458–465. Springer, Heidelberg (2001)
10. Gradinariu, M., Tixeuil, S.: Conflict managers for self-stabilization without fairness assumption. In: ICDCS 2007: Proceedings of the International Conference on Distributed Computing Systems. IEEE Computer Society Press, Los Alamitos (2007)

11. Hedetniemi, S.T., Jacobs, D.P., Srimani, P.K.: Maximal matching stabilizes in time $O(m)$. Inf. Process. Lett. 80(5), 221–223 (2001)
12. Hopcroft, J.E., Karp, R.M.: An $n^{5/2}$ algorithm for maximum matchings in bipartite graphs. SIAM J. Comput. 2(4), 225–231 (1973)
13. Hsu, S.-C., Huang, S.-T.: A self-stabilizing algorithm for maximal matching. Inf. Process. Lett. 43(2), 77–81 (1992)
14. Manne, F., Mjelde, M., Pilard, L., Tixeuil, S.: A new self-stabilizing maximal matching algorithm. In: Prencipe, G., Zaks, S. (eds.) SIROCCO 2007. LNCS, vol. 4474, pp. 96–108. Springer, Heidelberg (2007)
15. Tel, G.: Maximal matching stabilizes in quadratic time. Inf. Process. Lett. 49(6), 271–272 (1994)

Self-Stabilizing Leader Election in Optimal Space

Ajoy K. Datta, Lawrence L. Larmore, and Priyanka Vemula

School of Computer Science, University of Nevada Las Vegas

Abstract. A silent self-stabilizing asynchronous distributed algorithm, SSLE, for the leader election problem, in a connected unoriented network with unique IDs, is given. SSLE uses $O(\log n)$ space per process and stabilizes in $O(n)$ rounds, where n is the number of processes in the network.

Keywords: Distributed algorithm, leader election, self-stabilization.

1 Introduction

In this paper, we give a self-stabilizing silent asynchronous distributed algorithm for the *leader election problem*, where all process in a network must agree on which one of them is the leader. A self-stabilizing system, regardless of the initial states of the processes and initial messages in the links, is guaranteed to converge to the intended behavior in finite time; the algorithm is also called *silent* if eventually all execution halts [4,5].

1.1 Related Work

Arora and Gouda [2] present a silent leader election algorithm in the shared memory model. Their algorithm requires $O(N)$ rounds and $O(\log N)$ space, where N is a given upper bound on n, the size of the network. Dolev and Herman [6] give a non-silent leader election algorithm in the shared memory model. This algorithm takes $O(diam)$ rounds, where $diam$ is the diameter of the network, and uses $O(N \log N)$ space. Awerbuch *et al.*[3] solve the leader election problem in the message passing model. Their algorithm takes $O(diam)$ rounds and uses $O(\log D \log N)$ space, where D is a given upper bound on the diameter.

Afek and Bremler [1] introduce the concept of *power supply* which they use to construct an algorithm for the leader election problem in the message passing model. Their algorithm takes $O(n)$ time and uses $O(\log n)$ bits per process. Our algorithm SSLE is partially inspired by Afek and Bremler's algorithm.

1.2 Contributions

We present a self-stabilizing algorithm, SSLE, for the leader election algorithm, in the composite atomicity model of computation. The space complexity of our algorithm is $O(\log n)$ bits per process, and the time complexity is $O(n)$. SSLE does not require knowledge of any upper bounds on n or $diam$.

More precisely. The time complexity of SSLE is actually $O(simp)$, where $simp$ is defined to be the length of the longest simple path in the network; hence $simp \leq n - 1$. Afek and Bremler's algorithm [1] also takes $O(simp)$ rounds.

S. Kulkarni and A. Schiper (Eds.): SSS 2008, LNCS 5340, pp. 109–123, 2008.

1.3   Outline of Paper

In Section 2, we describe our model of computation. In Section 3, we give our self-stabilizing algorithm, SSLE. In Section 4, we give a sketch of the proof of the correctness and time complexity of SSLE. Section 5 concludes the paper.

2   Preliminaries

We are given a connected undirected network, $G = (V, E)$ of $|V| = n$ processes, where $n \geq 2$. Each process P has a unique ID, $P.id$, of ID type, which could be any ordered type, but which we take to be non-negative integer. We assume the *shared memory model* of computation introduced in [4]. In this model, a process P can read its own registers and those of its neighbors, but can write only to its own registers.

The *state* of a process is defined by the values of its registers. A *configuration* of the network is a function from processes to states; if γ is the current configuration, then $\gamma(P)$ is the current state of each process P. An *execution* of $\mathcal{A}$ is a sequence of states $e = \gamma_0 \mapsto \gamma_1 \mapsto \ldots \mapsto \gamma_i \ldots$, where $\gamma_i \mapsto \gamma_{i+1}$ means that it is possible for the network to change from configuration γ_i to configuration γ_{i+1} in one step. We say that an execution is *maximal* if it is infinite, or if it ends at a *sink*, i.e., a configuration from which no execution is possible.

The *program* of each process consists of a finite set of *actions* of the following form: $< label > :: < guard > \longrightarrow < statement >$. The *guard* of an action in the program of a process P is a Boolean expression involving the registers of P and its neighbors. The *statement* of an action of P updates one or more variables of P. An action can be executed only if it is *enabled*, i.e., its guard evaluates to true. A process is said to be enabled if at least one of its actions is enabled. A *step* $\gamma_i \mapsto \gamma_{i+1}$ consists of one or more enabled processes executing an action. The evaluations of all guards and executions of all statements of those actions are presumed to take place in one atomic step; this model is called *composite atomicity* [5].

We assume that each transition from a configuration to another is driven by a *scheduler*, also called a *daemon*. If one or more processes are enabled, the daemon *selects* at least one of these enabled processes to execute an action. We assume that the daemon is also *weakly fair*, meaning that, if a process P is continuously enabled, P must eventually be selected by the daemon.

We say that a process P is *neutralized* in the computation step $\gamma_i \mapsto \gamma_{i+1}$ if P is enabled in γ_i and not enabled in γ_{i+1}, but does not execute any action between these two configurations. The neutralization of a process represents the following situation: at least one neighbor of P changes its state between γ_i and γ_{i+1}, and this change effectively makes the guard of all actions of P false.

We use the notion of *round* [5], which captures the speed of the slowest process in an execution. We say that a finite execution $\varrho = \gamma_i \mapsto \gamma_{i+1} \mapsto \ldots \mapsto \gamma_j$ is a *round* if the following two conditions hold:

1. Every process P that is enabled at γ_i either executes or becomes neutralized during some step of ϱ.
2. The execution $\gamma_i \mapsto \ldots \mapsto \gamma_{j-1}$ does not satisfy condition 1.

We define the *round complexity* of an execution to be the number of disjoint rounds in the execution, possibly plus 1 if there are some steps left over.

2.1 Self-Stabilization and Silence

The concept of *self-stabilization* was introduced by Dijkstra [4]. Informally, we say that distributed algorithm is *self-stabilizing* if, starting from a completely arbitrary configuration, the network will eventually reach a legitimate configuration.

More formally, we assume that we are given a *legitimacy predicate* $\mathcal{L}_\mathcal{A}$ on configurations. Let $\mathbb{L}_\mathcal{A}$ be the set of all *legitimate* configurations, *i.e.*, configurations which satisfy $\mathcal{L}_\mathcal{A}$. Then we define $\mathcal{A}$ to be *self-stabilizing* if the following two conditions hold:

1. (Convergence) Every maximal execution contains some member of $\mathbb{L}_\mathcal{A}$.
2. (Closure) If an execution e begins at a member of $\mathbb{L}_\mathcal{A}$, then all configurations of e are members of $\mathbb{L}_\mathcal{A}$.

We say that $\mathcal{A}$ is *silent* if every execution is finite. In other words, starting from an arbitrary configuration, the network will eventually reach a configuration where no process is enabled.

3 The Leader Election Algorithm SSLE

In this section, we present a silent self-stabilizing algorithm, SSLE, that elects the process of minimum ID in the network to be the leader, within $O(n)$ rounds of arbitrary initialization, using $O(\log n)$ space per process.

3.1 A Simplified Algorithm

We first describe a simplified algorithm for the leader election problem. let *Leader* be the process of smallest ID in the network. Let $P.leader$ be a process P's current estimate of the ID of *Leader* and $P.level$ be P's current estimate of its distance to *Leader*.

For convenience, write $P.key = (P.leader, P.level)$, the *key* of P. Keys are ordered lexically, *i.e.*, $P.key < Q.key$ if $P.leader < Q.leader$, or $P.leader = Q.leader$ and $P.level = Q.level$. For any P, let $P.self = (P.id, 0)$, which we call the *self key* of P. $Succ(i, j) = (i, j + 1)$ for any ordered pair (i, j). Let $Min\_Key\_Nbr(P)$ to be the minimum value of $Q.key$ among all $Q \in \mathcal{N}_P$, where $\mathcal{N}_P$ is the set of neighbors of P.

When the simplified algorithm converges, the following conditions will hold:

C1. $P.key \leq (P.id, 0)$

C2. If $P.key > Min\_Key\_Nbr(P)$,
       then $P.key = Succ(Min\_Key\_Nbr(P))$,
       else $P.key = (P.id, 0)$.

It follows easily that, if these conditions hold, $P.leader = Leader.id$ for all P, and $P.level$ will be the distance from P to $Leader$, and hence each process is connected to the $Leader$ by the shortest possible path.

Our simplified algorithm has only two actions, as follows:

A1. If $(P.key > P.self) \vee (P.key \leq Min\_Key\_Nbr(P))$,
    then $P.key \leftarrow P.self$.
A2. If $Succ(Min\_Key\_Nbr(P)) < P.key \leq P.self$,
    then $P.key \leftarrow Succ(Min\_Key\_Nbr(P))$.

If, initially, $P.leader \geq Leader.id$ for all P, the simplified algorithm converges within $diam + 1$ rounds. In this case, $Leader.self = (Leader.id, 0)$ is the smallest possible key. After one round, $Leader.key = Leader.self$, and after $t + 1$ rounds, all processes within distance t of $Leader$ have their final keys.

3.2   The Problem of Fictitious Leaders

The simplified algorithm in Section 3.1 is not self-stabilizing, since because of arbitrary initialization, $P.leader$ could be initialized to a value of ID type which is not the ID of any process in the network. In this case we say that P has a *fictitious leader*. A fictitious leader that is greater than $Leader.id$ is not a problem, but if a fictitious leader is less than $Leader.id$, the network might never get rid of that fictitious ID. We illustrate this possibility with a simple example.

Consider a 2-process network with processes, P_2 and P_3, where $P_i.id = i$, and where initially $P_2.key = (1,0)$ and $P_3.key = P_3.self = (3,0)$. Suppose each process executes one action during each round. After one round, $P_2.key = (2,0)$ and $P_3.key = (1,1)$. After another round, $P_2.key = (1,2)$ and $P_3.key = (3,0)$. After a total of $2t$ rounds, $P_2.key = (1, 2t)$, and $P_3.key = (3,0)$. Thus, the algorithm never stabilizes.

Using a known upper bound on the diameter. The problem of fictitious leaders can be solved if an upper bound, D, on the diameter of the network is given. Simply replace A1 by A1′:

A1′. If $(P.key > P.self) \vee (P.key \leq Min\_Key\_Nbr(P)) \vee (P.level \geq D)$,
     then $P.key \leftarrow P.self$.

By induction, it can be shown that if t rounds have elapsed since initialization, and if a process P has a fictitious leader, then $P.level \geq t$. Thus, after $D + 1$ rounds have elapsed, there will be no fictitious leader in the network. After at most $diam$ additional rounds, the algorithm converges. This method is similar to the Arora and Gouda's algorithm [2].

3.3   Formal Definition of SSLE

SSLE solves the fictitious leader problem by introducing *color waves*.

In SSLE, each process P has the following variables.

- $P.parent \in \mathcal{N}_P \cup \{P\}$, the *parent* of P.

- $P.key = (P.leader, P.level)$, the *key* of P, where $P.leader$ is of ID type, and $P.level$ is a non-negative integer.

- $P.color \in \{0, 1\}$.

- $P.done$, Boolean.

We also define the following functions on keys:

- $Succ(i, j) = (i, j + 1)$

- $(i, j) < (k, \ell) \equiv (i < k) \lor ((i = k) \land (j < \ell))$, *i.e.*, lexical order on keys.

Each process P has the following functions, which can be evaluated by P.

- $Is\_True\_Root(P) \equiv (P.parent = P) \land (P.key = (P.id, 0))$, P is a *true root*.

- $Is\_True\_Chld(P) \equiv (P.key = Succ(P.parent.key)) \land (P.leader < P.id)$, P is a *true child*.

- $Is\_False\_Root(P) \equiv \neg Is\_True\_Root(P) \land \neg Is\_True\_Chld(P)$, P is a *false root*.

- $Is\_Root(P) \equiv Is\_True\_Root(P) \lor Is\_False\_Root(P)$, P is a *root*.

- $Min\_Key\_Nbr(P) = \min \{Q.id : Q \in \mathcal{N}_P\}$, the minimum key of any neighbor.

- $Can\_Improve(P) \equiv Succ(Min\_Key\_Nbr(P)) < P.key$, there is a neighbor of P that would be a better parent than its current parent.

- $Can\_Attach(P) \equiv \exists Q \in \mathcal{N}_P : (Q.key = Min\_Key\_Nbr(P)) \land (Q.color = 1)$, there is a process that P can attach to that is better than its current parent.

- $Best_Nbr(P) = $ a neighbor $Q \in \mathcal{N}_P$ such that $Q.key = Min\_Key\_Nbr(P)$ and $Q.color = 1$. In case there is more than one choice, pick the one of lowest ID. In case there is none, $Best\_Nbr(P)$ is undefined.

- $Chldrn(P) = \{Q \in \mathcal{N}_P : (Q.parent = P) \land Is\_True\_Chld(Q)\}$, the *true children* of P.

- $False\_Chldrn(P) = \{Q \in \mathcal{N}_P : (Q.parent = P) \land (Is\_False\_Root(Q))\}$, the *false children* of P.

- $Done(P) \equiv (\forall Q \in \mathcal{N}_P : Q.key \le Succ(P.key)) \land$
  $(\forall Q \in Chldrn(P) : Q.done)$

We give the table of actions of SSLE in Table 1. The name of each action is listed in the first column, along with its priority number. The guard of each action is the conjunction of up to four *clauses*, listed in the third column. In order for an action to be enabled, its guard must be true, and no action with a lower priority number may be enabled.

We refer to Actions A2 and A3 as *reset actions*. We refer to Actions A1, A2, and A3 as *structure actions*. We refer to Actions A4 and A5 as *color actions*.

Table 1. Actions of SSLE

A1 priority 1	Attach	$Is\_True\_Root(P)$ $Can\_Attach(P)$ $False\_Chldrn(P) = \emptyset$	$\longrightarrow$	$P.parent$ $\leftarrow Best\_Nbr(P)$ $P.key$ $\leftarrow Succ(Best\_Nbr(P))$ $P.color \leftarrow 0$ $P.done \leftarrow Done(P)$
A2 priority 1	Reset False Root	$Is\_False\_Root(P)$	$\longrightarrow$	$P.key \leftarrow (P.id, 0)$ $P.parent \leftarrow P$ $P.color \leftarrow 0$ $P.done \leftarrow Done(P)$
A3 priority 1	Detach True Child	$Is\_True\_Chld(P)$ $Can\_Improve(P)$	$\longrightarrow$	$P.key \leftarrow (P.id, 0)$ $P.parent \leftarrow P$ $P.color \leftarrow 0$ $P.done \leftarrow Done(P)$
A4 priority 2	Color 1	$P.color = 0$ $P.parent.color = 0$ $\forall Q \in Chldrn(P) : Q.color = 1$ $\neg Is\_True\_Root(P) \vee \neg P.done$	$\longrightarrow$	$P.color \leftarrow 1$ $P.done \leftarrow Done(P)$
A5 priority 2	Color 0	$P.color = 1$ $P.parent.color = 1$ $\forall Q \in Chldrn(P) : Q.color = 0$ $\neg Is\_True\_Root(P) \vee \neg P.done$ $\forall Q \in \mathcal{N}_P : Q.key \leq Succ(P.key)$	$\longrightarrow$	$P.color \leftarrow 0$ $P.done \leftarrow Done(P)$
A6 priority 3	Update Done	$P.done \not\equiv Done(P)$	$\longrightarrow$	$P.done \leftarrow Done(P)$

3.4 Overview of SSLE

The correct value of *P.key*, and the value it will achieve eventually if the algorithm is correct, is $P.final\_key = (Leader.id, Level(P))$, where $Level(P)$ is the distance from P to $Leader$. If $P.key < P.final\_key$, we say that P is *inferior*. We define an *inferior tree* to be a tree whose root is inferior. All inferior processes belong to inferior trees, and all inferior trees are false trees. The relations between the various sets of processes and trees are indicated in Figure 1.

As the algorithm progresses, processes leave trees and join other trees. When SSLE has stabilized, all processes belong to one true tree rooted at *Leader*. A

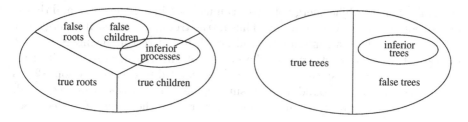

Fig. 1. Relations Among Classes of Processes and Trees

process can easily detect that it is a false root, but a process that is not a root has no way of knowing whether it is a member of a false tree. The problem we face is that an inferior tree can continue to recruit new leaves, even as it deletes itself starting from the root, and might never disappear.

3.5   Color Waves and Energy

Afek and Bremler solve the fictitious leader problem in their message-passing leader election algorithm [1], by using the concept of "power supply," the idea being that a true root continuously supplies "power" to its tree, allowing it to recruit new processes, whereas false trees will eventually run out of "power" and be unable to recruit. In this paper, we introduce a similar concept. Each process P has a *color*, either 0 or 1. Only processes of color 1 are allowed to recruit new members of the tree, and the new recruits always have color 0. In addition, we allow a process P to change color if $P.parent.color = P.color$, and if all its true children have the opposite color. Processes change colors in convergecast waves starting from the leaves of the trees.

A true root "absorbs" the color waves by alternating its own color, but a false root cannot change color. Thus, in a false tree, color waves, which cannot pass each other, eventually cause *color deadlock*, preventing further growth of the tree.

At the same time a false root is enabled to reset (execute Action A2). Thus, a false tree shrinks every round, but is limited in its growth. Deletion of a false root can break the remainder of its tree into multiple smaller false trees, all with the same leader.

In order to prove that, eventually, all inferior trees will be eliminated, we define the *energy* of a tree, and show that the maximum energy of any false tree decreases every round. For any process P, let

$$
\beta(P) = \begin{cases}
1 & \text{if } Is\_Root(P) \wedge (P.color = 0) \\
2 & \text{if } Is\_Root(P) \wedge (P.color = 1) \\
\beta(P.parent) & \text{if } Is\_True\_Chld(P) \wedge (P.color = 0) \wedge \\
 & (P.parent.color = 1) \\
\beta(P.parent) + 2 & \text{otherwise}
\end{cases}
$$

We define the *energy* of a tree to be the maximum value of $\beta(P)$ for any process P in that tree, and we define B to be the maximum value of the energy of any inferior tree. The energy of a tree can increase in only one way, and that is by its root executing a color action. Thus a true tree can increase its energy, but a false tree, such as an inferior tree, although it can recruit members, cannot increase its energy. Furthermore, the energy of any tree decreases if its root leaves the tree. Thus, since every false root is enabled to execute Action A2, its energy decreases every round. Finally, since no new inferior trees can be created, except by fragmentation of an existing inferior tree, the value of B decreases every round.

Since the energy of any tree cannot exceed $2simp + 2$, the time required for all inferior trees to be deleted is $O(simp)$. Once there are no more inferior processes in the network, SSLE will stabilize within $O(simp)$ additional rounds. There will then be just one tree T, rooted at $Leader$, which will be a breadth-first-search spanning tree of the network.

After it has stabilized, SSLE may not yet be silent, since Actions A4, A5, and A6 may continue to execute. In a convergecast wave starting at the leaves of T, $P.done$ will be set to true for all P. When $Leader.done$ holds, it has received acknowledgment from all other processes that it has been elected leader, and it ceases to change color, because of the fourth clause of the guard of each color action. Within $O(diam)$ additional rounds, all other nodes stop changing color as well.

Due to arbitrary initialization, $Leader.done$ could be true even if the algorithm is not finished. In this case, within $O(diam)$ time, $Leader.done$ will be set to false, and SSLE will proceed normally.

3.6   Example Execution

In Figure 2, we show the sequence of configurations for an execution of SSLE in one example, where the network consists of six processes in a chain. The IDs of the processes are shown across the top of the figure. Each row shows one configuration. Each process is represented by a box containing three numbers. The leftmost number in the box representing a process P is $P.leader$, the middle number is $P.level$, and the rightmost number is $P.color$. Arrows represent parent pointers. If no arrow is shown from the box representing P, then $P.parent = P$. In this example, $Leader$ is the fifth node in the chain, and $Leader.id = 2$. We assume that $P.done$ is initially false for all P.

In our example computation, the initial configuration contains one inferior tree consisting of the first four processes. The other two processes form singleton trees. For simplicity, we will assume that all enabled processes are selected at each step; thus, each round consists of one step. When a process executes an action, the name of that action is shown. For example, during the eighth step, the first process, whose ID is 6, executes Action A1 to join the tree whose leader is 4; changing its key from $(6,0)$ to $(4,2)$ and changing its $color$ from 1 to 0. We do not show Action A6 in the figure, nor do we show the values of $P_i.done$.

As the inferior tree grows to the right, it captures the rightmost two nodes, but also shrinks on the left as its processes executes A2. After six steps, the inferior tree is gone. The tree rooted at $Leader$ then grows until it captures all

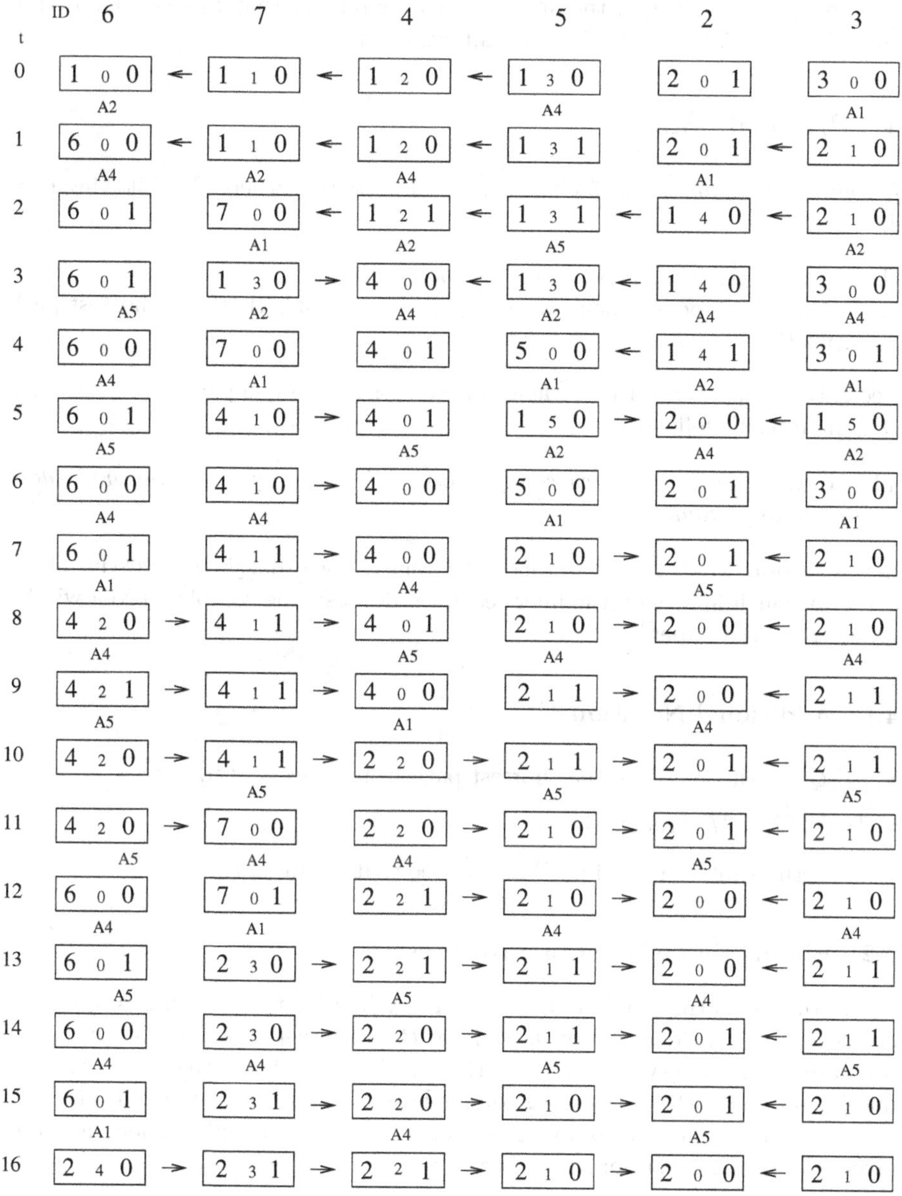

t \ ID	6	7	4	5	2	3
0	1 0 0 (A2)	← 1 1 0	← 1 2 0 (A4)	← 1 3 0	2 0 1 (A4)	3 0 0 (A1)
1	6 0 0 (A4)	← 1 1 0 (A2)	← 1 2 0 (A4)	← 1 3 1	2 0 1 (A1)	← 2 1 0
2	6 0 1	7 0 0 (A1)	← 1 2 1 (A2)	← 1 3 1 (A5)	← 1 4 0	← 2 1 0 (A2)
3	6 0 1 (A5)	1 3 0 (A2) →	4 0 0 (A4) ←	1 3 0 (A2) ←	1 4 0 (A4)	3 0 0 (A4)
4	6 0 0 (A4)	7 0 0 (A1)	4 0 1 (A1)	5 0 0 (A1) ←	1 4 1 (A2)	3 0 1 (A1)
5	6 0 1 (A5)	4 1 0 →	4 0 1 (A5)	1 5 0 (A2) →	2 0 0 (A4) ←	1 5 0 (A2)
6	6 0 0 (A4)	4 1 0 (A4)	4 0 0 →	5 0 0 (A1)	2 0 1	3 0 0 (A1)
7	6 0 1 (A1)	4 1 1	4 0 0 (A4) →	2 1 0 →	2 0 1 (A5) ←	2 1 0
8	4 2 0 (A4) →	4 1 1 →	4 0 1 (A5)	2 1 0 (A4) →	2 0 0 ←	2 1 0 (A4)
9	4 2 1 (A5) →	4 1 1 →	4 0 0 (A1)	2 1 1 →	2 0 0 (A4) ←	2 1 1
10	4 2 0 (A5) →	4 1 1 →	2 2 0 (A4) →	2 1 1 (A5) →	2 0 1 ←	2 1 1 (A5)
11	4 2 0 (A5) →	7 0 0 (A4)	2 2 0 (A4) →	2 1 0 →	2 0 1 (A5) ←	2 1 0
12	6 0 0 (A4)	7 0 1 (A1)	2 2 1 →	2 1 0 (A4) →	2 0 0 ←	2 1 0 (A4)
13	6 0 1 (A5)	2 3 0 →	2 2 1 (A5) →	2 1 1 →	2 0 0 (A4) ←	2 1 1
14	6 0 0 (A4)	2 3 0 (A4) →	2 2 0 →	2 1 1 (A5) →	2 0 1 ←	2 1 1 (A5)
15	6 0 1 (A1)	2 3 1 →	2 2 0 (A4) →	2 1 0 →	2 0 1 (A5) ←	2 1 0
16	2 4 0 →	2 3 1 →	2 2 1 →	2 1 0 →	2 0 0 ←	2 1 0

Fig. 2. Example Computation of SSLE on a Chain of Six Processes

processes after 16 steps. All processes have now chosen 2 as the leader ID, their choices will not change, and SSLE has stabilized.

We encourage the reader to verify that, in this example, $B = 7$ initially, then drops to 5 in the first round, then to 4, then 3, then 2. $B = 1$ after five rounds, and $B = 0$ thenceforth.

Although we only show the first 16 steps, we remark that *Leader.done* is true after 21 steps. All actions will cease after 25 steps.

4   Proof of SSLE

A *legitimate configuration* for SSLE is a configuration where the following conditions hold.

1. All processes belong to a true tree rooted at *Leader*.
2. If P is any process, then $P.level$ is equal to the length of the shortest path from P to *Leader*.

Recall that $simp \leq n - 1$ is the length of the longest simple path in the network. Our main result follows.

Theorem 1. *From arbitrary configuration, SSLE is self-stabilizing and silent within $O(simp)$ rounds.*

In this section, we sketch the proof of Theorem 1. The proof sketches are intuitive, and only touch lightly on the finer technical details. The complete proof will be given in the full paper.

4.1   Additional Notation

- $||P, Q||$ = the length of the shortest path from process P to process Q.
- $Level(P) = ||P, Leader||$.
- T_P = the subtree rooted at P of the tree that contains P.

4.2   Elimination of Inferior Processes

Recall that B is the maximum energy of any inferior tree, if there is any; otherwise $B = 0$. By definition of β, we have $B \leq 2simp + 2$. We will show that B decreases during every round. Thus, there will be no inferior trees and hence no inferior processes after $2simp + 2$ rounds have elapsed from initialization.

In the statements and proofs of Lemmas 1 and 2, we will consider just one given step of the execution, $\gamma_{t-1} \mapsto \gamma_t$.

Lemma 1. *If R is a false root at γ_{t-1} and also at γ_t, then the energy of T_R does not increase during the step.*

Proof. (Sketch.) Since R cannot execute a color action, $\beta(R)$ cannot change. By induction on the length of the parental path from P to R, we can show that, if $P \in T_R$ both before and after the step, $\beta(P)$ cannot increase. In particular, if $P.color$ changes from 1 to 0, $\beta(P)$ decreases by 2, while $\beta(P)$ is unchanged in all other cases.

Suppose, on the other hand, that P joins $\mathcal{T}_R$ during the step, by attaching to a process $Q \in \mathcal{T}_R$. Then $Q.color = 1$ both before and after the step, and $P.color = 0$ after the step. $\beta(P) = \beta(Q)$ after the step, and $\beta(Q)$ does not change.

Lemma 2. *If R is a false root and $S \in \mathcal{T}_R$ at γ_{t-1}, where $S \neq R$, and if S is a false root at γ_t, then the energy of $\mathcal{T}_S$ at γ_t is less than the energy of $\mathcal{T}_R$ at γ_{t-1}.*

Proof. (Sketch.) During the step, $S.parent$ leaves the tree, making S a root. By induction on the length of the parental chain from S to R, we can prove that $\beta(S)$ at γ_t is less then $\beta(R)$ at γ_{t-1}. Each step of the induction requires examining several cases, depending on the colors of the processes both before and after the step.

The rest of the proof is similar to that of Lemma 1.

Lemma 3. *If $B > 0$, then B decreases during the next round.*

Proof. (Sketch.) By Lemmas 1 and 2, B cannot increase at any step. Since any inferior root is a false root, and every false root is enabled to execute Action A2, every inferior root will reset during the round. By Lemma 2, B will decrease.

Lemma 4. *After $2simp + 2$ rounds have elapsed from initialization, there are no inferior processes.*

Proof. (Sketch.) By the definition of β, $B \leq 2simp + 2$. By Lemma 3, $B = 0$ after $2simp + 2$ rounds. Since every inferior process must belong to an inferior tree, we are done.

4.3 Convergence after Elimination of Inferior Processes

After there are no more inferior processes, *Leader* is a true root within at most one more round, after which *Leader* remains a true root. SSLE then stabilizes within $O(simp)$ additional rounds, as we shall explain in this section.

Although it appears to be intuitively obvious that SSLE will stabilize, we have failed to find a simple proof. Our proof, which will appear in the journal version, uses a complex potential argument.

The complexity of our argument is caused by the fact that only processes whose color is 1 can recruit, and thus recruitment of processes by $\mathcal{T}_{Leader}$ can be delayed if processes are forced to wait to change color. This delay has two rather different causes, making it difficult to obtain a proper potential to measure the maximum number of rounds needed to stabilize.

One source of the delay is *color deadlock*, which we have already discussed. If the sequence of colors of a parental chain in $\mathcal{T}_{Leader}$ is of the form $(01)^*$, *i.e.*, maximally impacted color waves, it is color deadlocked except at the root end. The "traffic jam" is slowly cleared out as *Leader* absorbs the waves by alternating its own color.

Much worse is the delay caused if all processes have color 0. In this case, none of the processes in the tree can recruit. A color wave can only start at the leaves of the tree, which can be very far from the root, and no process in the tree can recruit until that color wave reaches it.

We say that a process P is *exact* if $P.key = P.final\_key$. At some step within $O(simp)$ rounds of initialization, every exact process which is a member of $\mathcal{T}_{Leader}$ will have color 1. Neighbors of those processes of color 1 will attach to them by executing structure actions. Within $O(diam)$ rounds after every exact process in $\mathcal{T}_{Leader}$ has had a chance to have color 1, all processes will join $\mathcal{T}_{Leader}$ and become exact.

Potentials. The arguments used to prove convergence make use of a potential Σ, whose definition is quite complex.

Let:

$$\mathcal{T} = \mathcal{T}_{Leader}$$
$$\mathcal{T}^* = \{P \in \mathcal{T} : P.level = Level(P)\}$$
$$\mathcal{T}[1] = \{P \in \mathcal{T} : P.color = 1\}$$

$$\theta(P) = \begin{cases} -\infty & \text{if } P \notin \mathcal{T} \\ 0 & \text{if } P = Leader \\ \theta(P.parent) + 2 & \text{if } P \in \mathcal{T}, P \neq Leader, \\ & \quad \text{and } P.color = P.parent.color \\ \theta(P.parent) - 2 & \text{if } P \in \mathcal{T}, P \neq Leader, \\ & \quad \text{and } P.color \neq P.parent.color \end{cases}$$

$$\epsilon(P, Q) = \begin{cases} \theta(Q) + 1 & \text{if } Q \in \mathcal{N}_P \cap \mathcal{T}[1] \text{ and } Succ(Q.key) < P.key \\ & \quad \text{and } Is\_True\_Root(P) \text{ and } False\_Chldrn(P) = \emptyset \\ -\infty & \text{otherwise} \end{cases}$$

$$\epsilon(P) = \max_Q \{\epsilon(P, Q)\}$$

$$\zeta(P, Q) = \begin{cases} \theta(Q) + 2 & \text{if } \neg Is\_True\_Root(P) \text{ and } Q \in \mathcal{N}_{P.parent} \cap \mathcal{T}[1] \\ & \quad \text{and } Is\_True\_Root(P.parent) \\ & \quad \text{and } Succ(Q.key) < P.parent.key \\ -\infty & \text{otherwise} \end{cases}$$

$$\zeta(P) = \max_Q \{\zeta(P, Q)\}$$

$$\eta(P, Q) = \begin{cases} \theta(Q) + 3 & \text{if } Q \in \mathcal{N}_P \cap \mathcal{T}[1] \text{ and } \neg Is\_True\_Root(P) \\ & \quad \text{and } Succ(Q.key) < P.key \\ -\infty & \text{otherwise} \end{cases}$$

$$\eta(P) = \max_Q \{\eta(P, Q)\}$$

$$\sigma(P) = \max \{\theta(P), \epsilon(P), \zeta(P), \eta(P)\}$$

$$\Sigma = \max \{\sigma(P)\}$$

Note that Σ depends only on the configuration. Chasing definitions, it is fairly easy to verify that $0 \leq \Sigma < 2simp - 1$.

Let γ^* be the first configuration in the execution at which *Leader* is a true root and there are no inferior processes. Let Σ^* be the value of Σ at that configuration.

We omit the proof of the following lemma, which is very technical and several pages long.

Lemma 5. *If Leader is a true root and there are no inferior processes, Then, for any integer $c > 0$, Leader will execute a color action at least c times during the next $\Sigma + 5c - 4$ rounds, provided Leader.done is false during those rounds.*

The color potential. We define a function τ on $\mathcal{T}$, which we call the *color potential*, as follows:

- $\tau(Leader)$ = the number of times *Leader* has executed a color action since γ^*.
- If $P \in \mathcal{T}$ and $P \neq Leader$, then

$$\tau(P) = \begin{cases} \tau(P.parent) & \text{if } P.color = P.parent.color \\ \tau(P.parent) + 1 & \text{if } P.color \neq P.parent.color \end{cases}$$

Lemma 6. *Suppose the configuration is good, $P \in \mathcal{T}$, and P remains in $\mathcal{T}$ after the next step. Then, during that step, $\tau(P)$ increases by 1 if P executes a color action, and is unchanged otherwise.*

Proof. By induction on $P.level$. If $P.level = 0$, then $P = Leader$, and we are done by definition of τ. Otherwise, let $Q = P.parent$. Suppose $P.color$ changes. By the guards of the color actions, $P.color = Q.color$ and hence $\tau(P) = \tau(Q)$ before the step, and Q cannot execute a color action during that step. By the inductive hypothesis, $\tau(Q)$ does not change; thus $\tau(P)$ increases by 1, by the definition of τ.

Suppose $Q.color$ changes. By the guards of the color actions, $P.color \neq Q.color$ and hence $\tau(P) = \tau(Q) + 1$ before the step, and P cannot execute a color action during that step. By the inductive hypothesis, $\tau(Q)$ increases by 1; thus $\tau(P) = \tau(Q)$ after the step, by the definition of τ, and hence is unchanged.

Suppose neither P nor Q executes a color action. By the inductive hypothesis, $Q.color$ remains unchanged, and thus $\tau(P)$ remains unchanged, by the definition of τ.

Lemma 7. *Eventually, $\mathcal{T}^*$ contains every process.*

Proof. By induction on $Level(P)$. $Leader \in \mathcal{T}^*$ within $2simp + 2$ rounds. Within $simp$ additional rounds, $Leader.done$ is false. Suppose $P \neq Leader$. Pick $Q \in \mathcal{N}_P$ such that $Level(Q) = Level(P) - 1$. By the inductive hypothesis, $Q \in \mathcal{T}^*$ eventually. By Lemma 5, P will eventually execute Action A5, which implies that $P \in \mathcal{T}^*$ at that time.

Lemma 8. *Let γ_P be the first good configuration where $P \in \mathcal{T}^*$. Then $\tau(P) \leq 3Level(P)$ at γ_P.*

Proof. By induction on $Level(P)$. If $Level(P) = 0$, then $P = Leader$, $\gamma_P = \gamma^*$, and we are done, by definition of τ. Suppose $Level(P) = L \geq 1$. Assume that $\tau(P) > 3L$ at γ_P. Let $Q = P.parent$. Then, $\tau(Q) \geq 3L$ and $Q \in T^*$. By the inductive hypothesis, $\tau(Q)$ was at most $3L - 3$ at the configuration γ_Q. After Q changes color two more times, P must have joined T^*, and $\tau(Q) \leq 3L - 1$ by Lemma 6. Thus, $\tau(P) \leq 3L$ at γ_P, contradiction.

Let B_0 be the value of B at initialization.

Lemma 9. SSLE *stabilizes within* $B_0 + \Sigma^* + 15(diam)$ *rounds of arbitrary initialization.*

Proof. Let P be any process, and let $L = Level(P)$. By Lemma 3, the configuration γ^* is reached within $B_0 + 1$ of initialization. Let γ_P be the first configuration after γ^* at which $P \in T^*$. By Lemma 8, $\tau(P) \leq 3L$ at γ_P.

Let γ' be the configuration $B_0 + simp + \Sigma^* + 15L$ rounds after initialization. By Lemma 5, $\tau(Leader) \geq 3L + 1$ at γ'.

Suppose that γ_P occurs after γ'. Then $\tau(P) \geq \tau(Leader) \geq 3L + 1$ at γ_P, contradiction. Since $L \leq diam$, our result follows.

Lemma 10. SSLE *is silent within* $B_0 + simp + \Sigma^* + 18(diam) + 2$ *rounds.*

Proof. Let $L = \max\{Level(P)\}$. By Lemma 9, SSLE stabilizes within $B_0 + simp + \Sigma^* + 15(diam)$ rounds. Within L rounds additional rounds, $Leader.done$ holds. Let $\Theta = \max\{\theta(P) : \theta(P) + 2Level(P) > 0\}$, with the default value $\Theta = -L$ if $\theta(P) + 2Level(P) = 0$ for all P. Let $\Delta = \frac{1}{2}\Theta + L$, which is an integer since θ is even. $\Delta \leq 2L$, and as long as $\Delta > 0$, it must decrease by at least 1 every round, since every process P where $\theta(P) + 2Level(P) > 0$ and $\theta(P) = \Theta$ must execute a color action. When $\Delta = 0$, no further actions can be executed.

Our main result, Theorem 1, follows immediately from Lemma 10.

5   Conclusion

We present a silent self-stabilizing asynchronous distributed algorithm, SSLE, for election of a leader of a network, where processes have unique IDs. The algorithm stabilizes in $O(n)$ rounds, using $O(\log n)$ space per process, and becomes silent after an additional $O(diam)$ rounds, under the weakly fair daemon.

SSLE is also silent and self-stabilizing under the *unfair daemon*. The proof will be given in the journal version.

References

1. Afek, Y., Bremler, A.: Self-Stabilizing Unidirectional Network Algorithms by Power-Supply. In: 8th Annual ACM Symposium on Discrete Algorithms, pp. 111–120 (1997)
2. Arora, A., Gouda, M.G.: Distributed Reset. IEEE Transactions on Computers 43, 1026–1038 (1994)

3. Awerbuch, B., Kutten, S., Mansour, Y., Patt-Shamir, B., Varghese, G.: Time Optimal Self-stabilizing Synchronization. In: 25th Annual ACM Symposium on Theory of Computing, pp. 652–661 (1993)
4. Dijkstra, E.W.: Self-stabilizing Systems in Spite of Distributed Control. Communications of the Association for Computing Machinery 17, 643–644 (1974)
5. Dolev, S.: Self-Stabilization. MIT Press, Cambridge (2000)
6. Dolev, S., Herman, T.: Superstabilizing Protocols for Dynamic Distributed Systems. Chicago J. Theor. Comput. Sci. 1997-4, 1–40 (1997)

Tiara: A Self-stabilizing Deterministic Skip List

Thomas Clouser[1], Mikhail Nesterenko[1,*], and Christian Scheideler[2]

[1] Deparment of Computer Science, Kent State University, Kent, OH, USA
[2] Institute of Computer Science, Technical University of Munich, Garching, Germany

Abstract. We present *Tiara* — a self-stabilizing peer-to-peer network maintenance algorithm. Tiara is truly deterministic which allows it to achieve exact performance bounds. Tiara allows logarithmic searches and topology updates. It is based on a novel *sparse 0-1 skip list*. We rigorously prove the algorithm correct in the shared register model. We then describe its extension to a ring and incorporation of crash tolerance.

1 Introduction

Due to the rise in popularity of peer-to-peer systems, dynamic overlay networks have recently received a lot of attention. An overlay network is a logical network formed by its participants across a wired or wireless domain. In open peer-to-peer systems, participants may frequently enter and leave the overlay network either voluntarily or due to failure. As peer-to-peer systems can contain millions of users, faults and inconsistencies should be regarded as the norm rather than an exception. Hence, overlay networks require mechanisms that continuously counter such disturbances. Simplistic ad hoc approaches that handle individual fault conditions do not adequately perform in case of unanticipated, complex or systemic failures. In practice many peer-to-peer systems, such as KaZaA, Bittorrent, Kademlia, use heuristic methods in order to maintain their topology. Moreover, solutions presented in research publications focus on constructing scalable and well-structured overlay networks in an efficient manner [1,2,3,4,5,6,7,8,9] while offering only ad hoc solutions to fault tolerance. For the overlay networks that are based on a sorted list or ring (e.g., [2,3,5,9]), recovery can be achieved as long as this base structure can be maintained. However, jointly maintaining such list and the complete structure is rather tricky.

One can argue that if nodes are randomly distributed, a sorted list or ring with a sufficient number of redundant connections will not disintegrate with high probability. However, it is not clear whether practical systems always satisfy such randomization assumption. In addition, the problem of generating high-quality trusted random numbers in a peer-to-peer systems is far from trivial. Moreover, it is known that an adversary can quickly degrade the randomness of the peer-to-peer system even if perfectly random numbers are reliably generated [10]. Thus, some researchers [11,12] argue that overlay network architects need to consider holistic approaches to fault tolerance and recovery, such as self-stabilization. In

---

* This research is supported in part by NSF Career award CNS-0347485.

S. Kulkarni and A. Schiper (Eds.): SSS 2008, LNCS 5340, pp. 124–140, 2008.
© Springer-Verlag Berlin Heidelberg 2008

this paper we present Tiara. To the best of our knowledge, Tiara is the first self-stabilizing skip-list based overlay network algorithm that supports logarithmic searches and updates.

Related literature. Several algorithms presented in the literature focus on stabilizing parts of overlay networks. Onus et al. [12] present several high-atomicity solutions to linearizing an overlay network. Shaker and Reeves [13] describe a distributed algorithm for forming a directed ring network topology. Hérault et al. [14] describe a spanning tree formation algorithm for overlay networks. Cramer and Fuhrmann [15] show that ISPRP — a ring-based overlay network is, in certain cases, self-stabilizing. Caron et al. [16] describe a snap-stabilizing prefix tree for peer-to-peer systems. Bianchi et al. [17] present a stabilizing search tree for overlay networks optimized for content filters.

Several randomized overlay network algorithms have also been proposed. Dolev and Kat [18] introduce the HyperTree and use it as a basis for their self-stabilizing peer-to-peer system. Dolev et al. [19] describe a self-stabilizing intrusion-tolerant overlay network.

Pugh [20] introduce skip lists as an alternative to balanced tree structures. Munro et al. [21] describe a deterministic algorithm for skip list construction. Awerbuch and Scheideler [3], Aspnes and Shah [2], and Harvey et al. [5] extend the randomized skip list to distributed environments. Harvey and Munro [22] present a deterministic distributed skip list.

Our contribution. In this paper we present Tiara. It stabilizes a novel 0-1 distributed skip list. Specifically, we demonstrate a self-stabilizing algorithm for a sorted list and then show how to extend it to a self-stabilizing algorithm for a skip list. Tiara can construct these structures without any knowledge of global network parameters such as the number of nodes in the system, each node utilizes only the information available to its immediate neighbors. Moreover, Tiara preserves network connectivity so long as the initial network is connected. That is, Tiara reconstructs the connectivity of the base sorted list on the basis of skip list links. We rigorously prove Tiara correct in an asynchronous communication register based model.We describe how Tiara can be extended to a ring structure and how it can incorporate crash resistance.

Organization of the paper. First, we introduce our computational model. Then, we describe a self-stabilizing algorithm for the sorted list and formally prove it correct. We then extend it to a self-stabilizing algorithm for Tiara discuss various extensions and efficiency improvements. We complete the paper with future research directions and open problems.

2   Model

A peer-to-peer system consists of a set N of processes. Each process has a unique integer identifier. A process contains a set of variables and actions. An action has the form $\langle name \rangle : \langle guard \rangle \longrightarrow \langle command \rangle$. *name* is a label, *guard* is a Boolean predicate over the variables of the process and *command* is a sequence assigning new values to the variables of the process. For each pair of processes a and b, we define a Boolean variable (a, b) that is shared among them. Two processes a and b are *neighbors* if this variable is **true**. The *neighborhood* of a process a is defined as the set of all of its neighbors. Sets of neighbors may be maintained on different *levels*. A neighborhood of process a at level i is denoted and denoted $a.i.NB$. The *right neighborhood* of a, denoted $a.i.R$, is the set of neighbors of a with identifiers larger than a. That is, $a.i.R \equiv \{b : b \in a.i.NB : b > a\}$. Similarly, the *left neighborhood* of a, denoted $a.i.L$, are a's neighbors with smaller identifiers. That is, $a.i.L \equiv \{b : b \in b.i.NB : b < a\}$. Naturally, the union of $a.i.R$ and $a.i.L$ is $a.i.NB$.

When describing a link we always state the smaller identifier first. That is, a is less than b in (a, b). Two processes a and b are *consequent* if there is no process c whose identifier is between a and b. That is, $\mathbf{cnsq}(a, b) \equiv (\forall c :: (c < a) \vee (b < c))$. The *length* of a link (a, b) is the number of processes c such that $a < c < b$. By this definition the length of a link that connects consequent processes is zero.

A *system state* is an assignment of a value to the variables of each process. An action is *enabled* in some state if its guard is **true** at this state. A *computation* is a maximal fair sequence of states such that for each state s_i, the next state s_{i+1} is obtained by executing the command of an action that is enabled in s_i. This disallows the overlap of action execution. That is, action execution is *atomic*. The execution of a single action is a *step*. Maximality of a computation means that the computation is infinite or it terminates in a state where none of the actions are enabled. Such state is a *fixpoint*. In a computation the action execution is *weakly fair*. That is, if an action is enabled in all but finitely many states of an infinite computation then this action is executed infinitely often. This defines an *asynchronous* program execution model.

A state *conforms* to a predicate if this predicate is **true** in this state; otherwise the state *violates* the predicate. By this definition every state conforms to predicate **true** and none conforms to **false**. Let T and U be predicates over the state of the program. Predicate T is *closed* with respect to the program actions if every state of the computation that starts in a state conforming to T also conforms to T. Predicate T *converges* to U if T and U are closed and any computation starting from a state conforming to T contains a state conforming to U. The program *stabilizes* to T if **true** converges to T. Since we will focus on self-stabilizing algorithms for overlay networks, and self-stabilization is only possible for overlay networks that are initially connected, we identify with **true** any state where the graph is connected.

While most of our program model is fairly conventional, we would like to draw the reader's attention to our way of modelling overlay network link management. If one process updates its neighborhood, the change affects the neighbors of other processes. For example, if process a adds b to its neighborhood by creating a link (a, b), this also means that a is atomically added to b's neighborhood. On the other hand, if a removes b from its neighborhood, then also a is removed from b's neighborhood.

3   Core Tiara Description, Correctness Proof and Complexity Estimate

In its core, Tiara contains two components: the bottom component (b-Tiara) that maintains the processes at the lowest level in sorted order and the skip-list component (s-Tiara) that constructs the higher levels of Tiara. These components are interdependent. s-Tiara relies on b-Tiara to sort the lowest level, while s-Tiara may append links to the bottom level to preserve the connectivity of the system.

We present the components and prove them correct bottom up starting with b-Tiara. However, the presentation of b-Tiara is divided into two parts: the growing and trimming. We prove the stabilization of the growing part first as the stabilization of s-Tiara depends on its correct operation. We prove the stabilization of the trimming part last as it depends on the stabilization of s-Tiara.

3.1   The Bottom Component of Tiara (b-Tiara) and Stabilization of Grow

Description. The objective of b-Tiara is to transform the system into a linear graph with the processes sorted according to their identifiers. The algorithm for b-Tiara is shown in Fig. 1. The only variables that b-Tiara manipulates are the neighbor sets for each process u — $u.0.NB$. The *right neighborhood* of u, denoted $u.0.R$ is a subset of $u.0.NB$ with the identifiers greater than u. Since $u.0.R$ can be computed from $u.0.NB$ as necessary, $u.0.R$ is not an independent variable but a convenient shortcut. The *left neighborhood* $u.0.L$ is defined similarly.

Each process u has two pairs of actions: *grow* and *trim* that operate to the right and to the left of u. Action *grow right* is enabled if u discovers that its right neighbor s has a left neighbor t that is not a neighbor of u. In this case u adds t to its neighborhood. That is, u adds a link (u, t) to the graph. Even though u is the left neighbor of s, t may be either to the left or to the right of u. That is $t < u$ or $t > u$. Regardless of this relation, u connects to t. Action *grow left* operates similarly in the opposite direction.

process u
variables
    $u.0.NB$ — set of neighbor processes of u.
shortcuts
    $u.0.L \equiv \{z : z \in u.0.NB : z < u\}$, $u.0.R \equiv \{z : z \in u.0.NB : z > u\}$
actions
grow right: $(s \in u.0.R) \wedge (t \in s.0.L) \wedge (t \notin u.0.NB) \longrightarrow$
    $u.0.NB := u.0.NB \cup \{t\}$
trim right: $(s, t \in u.0.R) \wedge (t \in s.0.L) \wedge (\forall z : z \in u.0.R : z \leq s) \wedge (\forall z : z \in s.0.L : z \geq u) \longrightarrow$
    $u.0.NB := u.0.NB/\{s\}$
grow left and *trim left* are similar

Fig. 1. The bottom component of Tiara (b-Tiara)

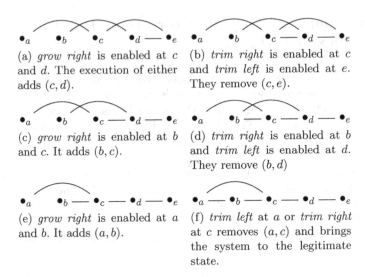

(a) *grow right* is enabled at c and d. The execution of either adds (c, d).

(b) *trim right* is enabled at c and *trim left* is enabled at e. They remove (c, e).

(c) *grow right* is enabled at b and c. It adds (b, c).

(d) *trim right* is enabled at b and *trim left* is enabled at d. They remove (b, d)

(e) *grow right* is enabled at a and b. It adds (a, b).

(f) *trim left* at a or *trim right* at c removes (a, c) and brings the system to the legitimate state.

Fig. 2. Example computation of *b-Tiara*. The processes are listed in increasing order of their identifiers.

Action *trim right* eliminates extraneous links from the graph. This action removes link (u, s) if u has a neighbor s that satisfies the following properties. The guard for *trim right* stipulates that there has to be another process t that is a neighbor of both u and s. Hence, if (u, s) is removed the connectivity of the graph is preserved. Also, all right neighbors of u must be smaller than or equal to s and all left neighbors of s are greater than or equal to u. The latter condition is necessary to break symmetry and prevent continuous growing and trimming of the same link. Action *trim left* operates similarly in the reverse direction. We show an example operation of b-Tiara in Fig. 2.

Correctness proof. Denote $B(N)$ the graph that is induced by the processes of the system and the links of b-Tiara. We define the following predicate: $\mathcal{GI} \equiv (\forall a, b \in N :: \mathbf{cnsq}(a, b) \Rightarrow \exists(a, b))$. That is, $\mathcal{GI}$ states that two consequent processes are also neighbors.

Lemma 1. *If a computation of b-Tiara starts from a state where $B(N)$ is connected, it is connected in every state of this computation.*

Proof: The actions of b-Tiara do not disconnect $B(N)$. Indeed, the actions that remove links are *trim right* and *trim left*. Consider *trim right*. It removes a link (a, b) if there exists a node c such that there are links (a, c) and (c, b). Thus, the removal of (a, b) does not disconnect the graph. The argument for *trim left* is similar. □

Lemma 2. *If a computation of b-Tiara starts from a state where $B(N)$ is connected, b-Tiara stabilizes to $\mathcal{GI}$.*

Proof: To prove the lemma we need to show that (i) $\mathcal{GI}$ is closed under the execution of the actions of b-Tiara and (ii) regardless of the initial state, every computation contains a state satisfying $\mathcal{GI}$. Let us consider closure first. The *grow* actions may not violate $\mathcal{GI}$ as they only add links. The *trim* action may affect $\mathcal{GI}$ by disconnecting two processes a and b. However, *trim right*, which removes link (a, b), is only enabled at process a if there is a process c such that $a < c < b$. Therefore, if a and b are consequent, *trim right* is disabled. The reasoning is similar for *trim left*. Hence the closure.

To show convergence, let us assume that there are two consequent processes a and b that are not neighbors. That is $b \notin a.0.NB$. Since the graph itself is connected, there is a path ρ between a and b. If there are multiple paths, we shall consider the shortest one. Let the length of ρ be the sum of the lengths of its constituent links. The execution of a *trim* action does not change the length of ρ. The execution of any of the *grow* actions does not increase the length of ρ. Path ρ must contain at least one segment d, e, f such that both d and f are either smaller than e or larger than e. In this case *grow right*, or respectively, *grow left*, is enabled in both d and f. The execution of this action decreases the length of the path. Hence, throughout the computation, the length of ρ decreases until it is zero and a and b are neighbors. The lemma follows. $\square$

3.2 The Skip List Component of Tiara (s-Tiara)

Description. The objective of s-Tiara is to establish a skip list on top of the linearized graph created by b-Tiara. The structure maintained by s-Tiara is a *sparse 0-1 skip list*. At each level i, node u maintains a set of neighbors $u.i.NB$. Out of this set, the rightmost and leftmost neighbors are defined as right and left skip links: $u.i.rs$ and $u.i.ls$. A node may not have a right or left skip link at some level if it is on either end of the list.

We denote right and left skip list neighbors of u at level $i - 1$ as v and x respectively. Nodes w and y are respectively right and left neighbors of v and x at the same level. We illustrate this notation in Fig. 3 as we will be using it extensively throughout the correctness proof of the algorithm.

If both nodes u and v exist at level i and $u.i.rs = v$ then this link is *0-skip link*. If u and w exist at level i and $u.i.rs = w$, then this link is a *1-skip link*. A process that exists at level $i - 1$ is *up* if it also exists at level i, it is *down* otherwise. If a process that 1-skip link spans is down it is a *cage*. For example u, v and w form a cage if $u.i.rs$ links to w and v is down. The middle process is *inside* the cage. Refer to Fig. 4 for the illustration of the concept of a cage. The sparse 0-1 skip list has two rules of organization. First, all links are either 0 or 1 skip links. Second, if a node is on level i and it is not on the end of the list on level $i - 1$ then at least one of its links is a 1 skip link.

Fig. 3. Aliases for neighbors of u in *s-Tiara*. $v \equiv u.(i - 1).rs$, $w \equiv v.(i - 1).rs$, $x \equiv u.(i - 1).ls$, and $y \equiv x.(i - 1).ls$, where $u.i.rs$ and $u.i.ls$ are right and left skip-list neighbors of u at level i, respectively.

(a) u is adjacent to the cage on the left.

(b) u is inside the cage.

(c) u is adjacent to the cage on the right.

Fig. 4. Possible cages with respect to node u

process u
parameter $i \geq 0$: **integer** — level of the skip list
variables
    $u.i.NB$ — set of neighbor processes of u at level i
shortcuts
    $v \equiv u.(i-1).rs,\ \ w \equiv v.(i-1).rs,\ \ x \equiv u.(i-1).ls,\ \ y \equiv x.(i-1).ls$
    $u.i.R \equiv \{z : z \in u.i.NB : z > u\},\ \ u.i.L \equiv \{z : z \in u.i.NB : z < u\}$
    $u.i.rs \equiv \begin{cases} (s : s \in u.i.R : (\forall t : t \in u.i.R : t \geq y)), & \text{if } u.i.R \neq \varnothing \\ \bot, & \text{otherwise} \end{cases}$
    $u.i.ls$ is defined similarly
    exists$(z,i) \equiv ((z \neq \bot) \wedge (z.i.NB \neq \varnothing))$
    valid$(u,i) \equiv ((((u.i.ls = y) \vee (u.i.ls = x) \vee (u.i.ls = \bot)) \wedge (u.i.rs = w)) \vee$
        $(((u.i.rs = v) \vee (u.i.rs = w) \vee (u.i.rs = \bot)) \wedge (u.i.ls = y)) \vee$
        $((u.i.ls = \bot) \wedge (u.i.rs = \bot)) \vee$
        $\neg(\textbf{exists}(x,i) \wedge \textbf{exists}(u,i) \wedge \textbf{exists}(v,i)))$
actions for $i > 0$
upgrade right: **valid**$(u,i) \wedge \neg$**exists**$(v,i) \wedge (v \neq \bot) \wedge (w \neq \bot) \wedge (u.i.rs \neq w) \longrightarrow$
        $u.i.NB := u.i.NB \cup \{w\}$
upgrade left is similar
bridge right: **valid**$(u,i) \wedge $**exists**$(u,i) \wedge $**exists**$(v,i) \wedge (u.i.rs \neq v) \longrightarrow$
        $u.i.NB := u.i.NB \cup \{v\}$
bridge left is similar
prune: **valid**$(u,i) \wedge $**exists**$(u,i) \wedge (u.i.NB \neq \{u.i.rs, u.i.ls\}) \longrightarrow$
        $u.0.NB := u.0.NB \cup u.i.NB/\{u.i.rs, u.i.ls\},$
        $u.i.NB := \{u.i.rs, u.i.ls\}$
downgrade right: $\neg$**valid**$(u,i) \wedge \neg((u.i.rs = v) \vee (u.i.rs = w) \vee (u.i.rs = \bot)) \longrightarrow$
        $u.0.NB := u.0.NB \cup u.i.R,$
        $u.i.R := \varnothing$
downgrade left is similar
downgrade center: $\neg$**valid**$(u,i) \wedge $**exists**$(x,i) \wedge $**exists**$(u,i) \wedge $**exists**$(v,i) \longrightarrow$
        $u.0.NB := u.0.NB \cup u.i.NB,$
        $u.i.NB := \varnothing$

Fig. 5. The skip list component of Tiara (s-Tiara)

The the algorithm is shown in Fig. 5. As before, to simplify the presentation we introduce a few shortcuts. Sets $u.i.R$ and $u.i.L$ are the subsets of $u.i.NB$ that contain the identifiers of u's neighbors with respectively higher and lower identifiers than u. We define $u.i.rs$ to be the neighbor with the link of the smallest length among $u.i.R$. To put another way, $u.i.rs$ connects to u's right neighbor

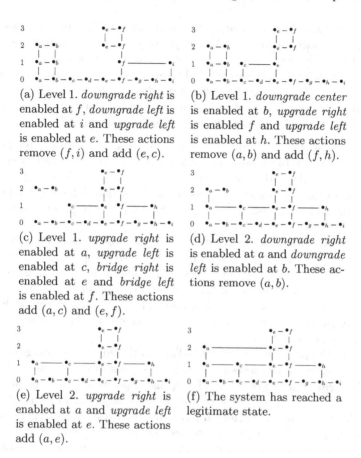

(a) Level 1. *downgrade right* is enabled at f, *downgrade left* is enabled at i and *upgrade left* is enabled at e. These actions remove (f, i) and add (e, c).

(b) Level 1. *downgrade center* is enabled at b, *upgrade right* is enabled f and *upgrade left* is enabled at h. These actions remove (a, b) and add (f, h).

(c) Level 1. *upgrade right* is enabled at a, *upgrade left* is enabled at c, *bridge right* is enabled at e and *bridge left* is enabled at f. These actions add (a, c) and (e, f).

(d) Level 2. *downgrade right* is enabled at a and *downgrade left* is enabled at b. These actions remove (a, b).

(e) Level 2. *upgrade right* is enabled at a and *upgrade left* is enabled at e. These actions add (a, e).

(f) The system has reached a legitimate state.

Fig. 6. *s-Tiara*. We list the processes in the increasing order of their identifiers. *b-Tiara* has stabilized to $\mathcal{GI}$. In each state we only mention the enabled actions that are relevant to the discussion. We do not illustrate the operation of *prune*.

with the smallest identifier. Note that $u.i.rs$ is $\perp$ if $u.i.R$ is empty. Shortcut $u.i.ls$ is defined similarly.

Predicate $\mathbf{exists}(z, i)$ is **true** if node z is present at all and if $z.i.NB$ is not empty. Node u may read only its immediate neighbor states. Thus, u may only invoke **exists** on its neighbors and itself. Observe that **exists** is defined to return **false** if it is invoked on a non-existent node. For example, if u is at the right end of the list at level i and u invokes $\mathbf{exists}(u.i.rs, i)$. In this case $\mathbf{exists}(u.i.rs, i)$ returns **false**. Predicate $\mathbf{valid}(u, i)$ captures the correct state of the system. Specifically, it states that if u exists at level i then the length of the skip links should not be more than 1 and either x or v does not exist at level i. The latter condition guarantees that at least one link of u is a 1 skip link.

The actions of s-Tiara are as follows. Action *upgrade right* establishes a link to w at level i if v is not up. That is, this link is a 1 skip link. If u is not up, *upgrade right* brings u up to level i. Action *upgrade left* operates similarly in the opposite direction. Actions *bridge right* and *left* establish 0 skip links if both nodes being connected are up. Action *prune* eliminates the links other than $u.i.rs$ and $u.i.ls$ from $u.i.NB$. In case the links are not 0 or 1 skip, action *downgrade right* completely removes the right neighborhood of u. Action *downgrade left* operates similarly. And the last action *downgrade center* eliminates three consecutive up nodes. This ensures that there could not be two consecutive 0 skip links. An example computation of s-Tiara is shown in Fig. 6.

Correctness proof. Our proof proceeds as follows. We state five predicates on the level i of s-Tiara. In the sequence of lemmas we show that if the lower levels of s-Tiara have stabilized, then level i of s-Tiara stabilizes to these predicates. The conjunction of these predicates implies the stabilization of level i of s-Tiara. We then use this fact as an inductive step in the convergence proof of stabilization of s-Tiara.

Before proceeding with the proof, we introduce notation and terminology we are going to use. Denote $S(N)$ the graph induced by the processes of the system as well as the links of b-Tiara and s-Tiara. Throughout the discussion we consider process u and its neighbors as defined in the description of s-Tiara. A node u is *middle* at level i if it has both left and right neighbors as well at least one two hop neighbor. That is, $\mathbf{middle}(u,i) \equiv (\mathbf{exists}(v,i-1) \wedge \mathbf{exists}(x,i-1) \wedge (\mathbf{exists}(y,i-1) \vee \mathbf{exists}(w,i-1)))$.

Below are the predicates to which s-Tiara stabilizes. Predicate **good_links**.i states that process u connects to processes at most two hops away. Predicate **one_links**.i enforces the rules of 0-1 skip list. Specifically, it stipulates that u should either be inside the cage or should have adjacent cages to the left or to the right. Predicates **zero_left_links**.i and **zero_left_links**.i ensure that the 0-links are in place. That is, the processes that are consequent at level $i-1$ and are up, are also connected at level i. Predicate **only_good_links**.i states that the neighborhood of u does not have links other than rs and ls.

$\mathbf{good\_links}.i \equiv (\forall u :: \neg\mathbf{exists}(u.i) \vee$
$\qquad ((u.i.rs = v) \vee (u.i.rs = w) \vee (u.i.rs = \bot) \wedge$
$\qquad ((u.i.ls = y) \vee (u.i.rs = x) \vee (u.i.ls = \bot))$

$\mathbf{one\_links}.i \equiv (\forall u : \mathbf{middle}(u,i) :$
$\qquad (\neg\mathbf{exists}(u,i) \wedge (x.i.rs = v) \wedge (v.i.ls = x)) \vee$
$\qquad (\neg\mathbf{exists}(v,i) \wedge (\neg\mathbf{exists}(w,i-1) \vee (u.i.rs = w))) \vee$
$\qquad (\neg\mathbf{exists}(x,i) \wedge (\neg\mathbf{exists}(y,i-1) \vee (u.i.ls = y))))$

$\mathbf{zero\_right\_links}.i \equiv (\forall u :: \neg\mathbf{exists}(u.i) \vee \neg\mathbf{exists}(v.i) \vee (u.i.rs = v))$

$\mathbf{zero\_left\_links}.i \equiv (\forall u :: \neg\mathbf{exists}(u.i) \vee \neg\mathbf{exists}(x.i) \vee (u.i.ls = x))$

$\mathbf{only\_good\_links}.i \equiv (\forall u :: \neg\mathbf{exists}(u.i) \vee (u.i.NB = \{u.i.rs, u.i.ls\}))$

Lemma 3. *Assuming that neighbor relations at level $i-1$ do not change throughout the computation, s-Tiara stabilizes to* **good_links**.i

Proof: In proving this and consequent lemmas we show a stronger property of closure and convergence of the predicate for a particular process u. This implies the stabilization of the predicate for all u at the specified level.

Let us show closure first. The topology at level $i - 1$ does not change. Hence once $u.i.rs$ points to one or two hop neighbors v or w, the neighbor's relative positions do not change. Similar argument applies to $u.i.ls$. Let us consider the actions and how they affect **good_links**.i. Let us start with the actions of u. Actions *upgrade right* and *bridge right* do not violate the predicate since they set $u.i.rs$ to respectively w and v. Similar argument applies to *upgrade left* and *bridge left*. Action *prune* does not affect the predicate since it does not modify either $u.i.rs$ or $u.i.ls$. Neither do *downgrade right* and *downgrade left* since they respectively set $u.i.rs$ and $u.i.ls$ to $\perp$. Action *downgrade center* removes u from level i altogether and hence cannot violate the predicate. The nodes further than two hops away never connect to u. Hence the actions of other nodes cannot violate the predicate either.

Let us now address convergence. The predicate can be violated only if u is up. It is violated if either $u.i.rs$ or $u.i.ls$ points to a node other than u's one or two-hop neighbors. In this case either *downgrade right* or *downgrade left* are enabled that bring the links in compliance with the predicate. $\square$

Lemma 4. *Assuming that neighbor relations at level $i-1$ do not change throughout the computation and* **good_links**.i *is satisfied, s-Tiara stabilizes to* **one_links**.i

Proof: As a first step, we would like to make the following observation: once a cage is formed, it is never destroyed. For example, assume that u, v and w form a cage. The actions of u, and, similarly, w do not affect this link. Also, if v is down, the only actions it can use to come up is *upgrade right* or *upgrade left*. However, both are disabled since u and v are up. This observation guarantees the closure of **one_links**.i.

Let us discuss convergence. Assume that u is down. We consider two cases: u is initially down and u is initially up and never goes down. If u is down, the only way, u can come up is through execution of *upgrade right* or *upgrade left* at u, w or y. In all cases cages adjacent to u are formed and the predicate is satisfied. If u is down, then *upgrade right* is enabled in x and *upgrade left* in v. Thus if u does not come up, then x or v execute these *upgrade* actions. In which case a cage is formed with u inside. This satisfies the predicate as well.

Assume that u is up. If it ever goes down, the foregoing discussion applies. The only remaining case is if u stays up for the remainder of the computation. Throughout a computation of b-Tiara a node can come up only once. Indeed, a node comes up only if it forms a cage. Since a cage is never destroyed, the node never goes down. This means that a node can go down only once. Let us consider the state of the computation where u's neighbors x and v do not change their up and down position. Both x and v cannot be simultaneously up in this state, as it enables *downgrade center* at u. The execution of this action brings u down. However, we assumed that u stays up for the remainder of the computation. Thus, either x or v are down. Assume, without loss of generality, that v is down. If w does not exist at level $i - 1$, **one_links**.i is satisfied. Assume that w exists. If link $u.i.rs = w$ is present, **one_links**.i is also satisfied. However, if it is not present, then *upgrade right* is enabled in u. Its execution establishes the link, forms a cage and satisfies the predicate. $\Box$

Lemma 5. *Assuming that neighbor relations at level $i-1$ do not change throughout the computation and* **good_links**.i *as well as* **one_links**.i *are satisfied, s-Tiara stabilizes to* **zero_left_links**.i *and* **zero_right_links**.i

Proof: We prove the lemma for **zero_right_links**.i only. The proof for the other predicate is similar. Let us argue closure. If **one_links**.i is satisfied processes do not go up or down. Thus, the only actions that can be enabled are *bridge* and *prune*. The execution of either action maintains the validity of **zero_left_links**.i. Hence the closure.

Let us address convergence. The predicate is violated only if the neighbor processes u and v are both up and they do not have a link at level i. If **one_links**.i is satisfied, u forms a cage to its left, while v forms a cage to its right. Recall that the cages are never destroyed. In this case u has *bridge right* while v has *bridge left* enabled. When either action is executed the predicate is satisfied. $\Box$

Lemma 6. *Assuming that neighbor relation at level $i - 1$ does not change throughout the computation and* **good_links**.i, **one_links**.i, **zero_right_links**.i *as well as* **zero_left_links**.i *are satisfied, s-Tiara stabilizes to* **only_good_links**.i

Proof: (outline) The satisfaction of **good_links**.i, **one_links**.i, **zero_right_links**.i and **zero_left_links**.i leaves only one possible action enabled — *prune*. In this case there are links in $u.i.NB$ besides $u.i.rs$ and $u.i.ls$ and they are moved to $u.0.NB$. $\Box$

Lemma 7. *If a computation of Tiara starts from a state where $S(N)$ is connected, this computation contains a state where $B(N)$ is connected.*

Proof: The non-trivial case is where $S(N)$ is connected while $B(N)$ is not. That is, the overall graph connectivity is achieved through the links at the higher levels of Tiara. Let X and Y be two graph components of $B(N)$ such that they are connected in $S(N)$. Let $i > 0$ be the lowest level where X and Y are connected. Assume, without loss of generality that there is a pair of processes $a \in X$ and $b \in Y$, such that $a.i.rs = b$. In this case *downgrade right* is enabled at a. The execution of *downgrade right* connects X And Y in $B(N)$. The lemma follows. $\Box$

Define

$$SI \equiv (\forall i : i > 0 : \textbf{good\_links}.i \wedge \textbf{one\_links}.i \wedge$$
$$\textbf{zero\_right\_links}.i \wedge \textbf{zero\_left\_links}.i \wedge \textbf{only\_good\_links}.i)$$

Lemma 8. *Tiara stabilizes to SI.*

Proof: According to Lemma 7, every computation contains a state where $B(N)$ is connected. Due to Lemma 2, if $B(N)$ is connected, b-Tiara stabilizes to

$\mathcal{GI}$. The remainder of the proof is by induction on the levels of s-Tiara. If $B(N)$ is connected and $\mathcal{GI}$ is satisfied the topology of the level 0 does not change. Hence, the requisite five predicates are vacuously satisfied. Assume that these predicates are satisfied for all levels $i - 1$. Once the predicates are satisfied, none of the actions for processes at level $i - 1$ are enabled. This means that the topology at this level does not change. Applying Lemmas 3, 4 5 and 6 in sequence we establish that the five predicates are satisfied at level i. Hence the lemma.   □

3.3   Stabilization of Trim in b-Tiara

Link (a, b) is *independent* if there exists no link (c, d) different from (a, b) such that $c \leq a$ and $b \leq d$. Consider an arrangement where the nodes are positioned in the increasing order of their identifiers.

Lemma 9. *If a computation of b-Tiara that starts in a state where the graph is connected and contains an independent link of non-zero length, this computation also contains a suffix of states without this link.*

Proof: Let (a, b) be an independent link of non-zero length. None of the *grow* actions create independent links. The only action that makes a link independent is a *trim* of another independent link. Thus, if an independent link is deleted, it is never added. Thus, to prove the lemma it is sufficient to show that (a, b) is eventually deleted.

Link (a, b) is non-zero length. This means that the node c consequent to a is not the same as b. In other words $a < c < b$. b-Tiara stabilizes to $\mathcal{GI}$ which ensures that a and c are connected. If c and b are not connected, both of them have a *grow* action enabled that connects them. Observe that (a, b) is independent. This means that all the right neighbors of a are to the left of b and all the left neighbors of b are to the right of a. Moreover, we just showed that there exists a node c such that $a < c < b$ and there are links $c \in a.R$ and $c \in b.L$. This means that *trim right* is enabled at a and *trim left* is enabled at b. The execution of either action deletes (a, b).   □

We define the following predicate: $\mathcal{TI} \equiv (\forall a, b \in N :: \exists(a, b) \Rightarrow \mathbf{cnsq}(a, b))$

Lemma 10. *If Tiara starts in a state where it satisfies $\mathcal{GI}$ and $\mathcal{SI}$, then it stabilizes to $\mathcal{TI}$*

Proof: (outline) The conjunct of $\mathcal{GI}$ and $\mathcal{TI}$ is closed under the execution of b-Tiara. Note also that if $\mathcal{GI}$ and $\mathcal{SI}$ are satisfied, then the actions s-Tiara are disabled. Hence the closure of $\mathcal{TI}$.

Let us consider convergence. Since the actions of s-Tiara are disabled, they do not add links to $B(N)$. If $\mathcal{TI}$ does not hold, then there is at least one independent link of non-zero length. If the graph is connected the *grow* actions never create an independent link. Consider a computation of b-Tiara that starts in an illegitimate state. Let l be the length of the longest independent link. Since the state is not legitimate, $l > 0$. According to previous discussion, new links of length l do not appear. Let (a, b) be the independent link of length l. According to Lemma 9, (a, b) is eventually removed. Thus, all links of length l are eventually removed. The lemma can be easily proven by induction on l. $\qquad\square$

The discussion in this section culminates in the following theorem.

Theorem 1. *Tiara stabilizes to the conjunction of $\mathcal{GI}$, $\mathcal{SI}$ and $\mathcal{TI}$.*

4   Tiara Usage, Implementation and Extensions

Searches. Tiara maintains a skip list [20,21] which is equivalent to a distributed balanced search tree. Hence the searches in Tiara proceed similar to searches in such trees. Let b be a right neighbor of a at some level i of Tiara. The *right interval* of a, denoted $[a, b)$, is the range of identifiers between a and b. *Left interval* is defined similarly. If a does not have a right neighbor, its interval is not finite. That is, a's interval contains all process identifiers greater than a. Similarly, if a lacks left neighbor it's interval is infinite on the left. Thus in any level, the collection of intervals contains the complete range of identifiers.

Suppose a, c and b are consequent at level $i - 1$ of Tiara and a and b are consequent at level i. That is c is in the cage. Since the identifiers are sorted, c belongs to the interval $[a, b)$. If a node is down, then one if its neighbors is up. Thus a client process that has a pointer to a node in Tiara and wishing to advance up the skip list only needs to examine the node's neighbors.

Assuming that a client process connects to an arbitrary node in Tiara, the search proceeds first upward then downward in the skip list. In the upward phase, the client is moving up the list looking for the node whose interval contains the identity. Since every level contains the complete id-range, this phase terminates. Once the range is found, the client advances downward evaluating the cages it encounters to narrow the search range. This procedure continues until the desired node x is located or it is established that x belongs to the interval of the consequent nodes at the bottom level. The latter case means that x is not present in the system. There are $O(log|N|)$ levels in Tiara. Thus, the upward and the downward phases take $O(log|N|)$ number of steps.

Joins and leaves. We assume that each process has two read-only Boolean variables maintained by the environment: *join* and *leave*. Since the variables are read-only, stabilization of their operation is the responsibility of the environment. Let us consider join operation first. The joining node x connects to an arbitrary node of the network. The variable *join* is set to **true**. We assume that the environment may only set *join* to **false** after the node successfully inserts itself at the bottom level of Tiara. The joining node executes a search to find the bottom level interval $[a, b)$ to which it belongs. Then, x makes a and b its right and left neighbors respectively. After a and b discover the presence of a node whose *join* is set to **true**, they remove link (a, b). Then, the upper levels of Tiara adjust. The insertion of the node at the bottom level entails at most a constant number of steps at each level of Tiara. Since the search takes at most $O(log|N|)$ steps, the total number of steps required for node join is also in $O(log|N|)$.

Let us discuss the leave operation. The environment sets *leave* to **true** to indicate that the node x requests disconnect. We assume that *leave* cannot be set when *join* is set and it cannot be set back to **false** until the node disconnects. When the right and left neighbors of x notice that the *leave* of x is set to **true**, the neighbors add a link bypassing x at the bottom level. Node x can then disconnect. The higher levels of Tiara execute the regular Tiara actions to accommodate the missing node. At most a constant number of adjustment steps is required at each level. Hence the total number of steps required for the node to leave Tiara is in $O(log|N|)$.

Crash resistance. Tiara can be separated into disconnected components by the crash of even a single process. Tiara can be fortified against separation due to crashes in the following manner. At the bottom, each process maintains a crash-redundancy link to its right neighbor's neighbor. That is, the bottom level list becomes doubly connected. Thus, it can tolerate a single crash. The crash tolerance can be further improved by adding similar links to more distant processes. In an asynchronous model there is no reliable way to distinguish a crashed process from a slow one [23]. Thus, to accomplish this, the processes need to be equipped with failure detectors [24,25]. A failure detector alerts the process if its neighbor crashes. Then, Tiara stabilizes to a legitimate state corresponding to the system without the crashed process.

Extension to ring. Tiara can be extended to a ring structure similar to Chord [9]. The idea is as follows. For b-Tiara, as well as for each level of s-Tiara, the lowest id-process needs to add a special wraparound link to the highest-id process. This wraparound link maintenance is carried out by the process without left neighbors. After b-Tiara and s-Tiara stabilize, the lowest-id process at each level is the only such process. The highest-id process at each level is the only process without right neighbors.

Once the process determines that it has no left neighbors it starts positioning the wraparound link. Essentially, the process continues to move the link to a right neighbor of the destination of the link. Note that this movement stops once the wraparound link reaches the highest-id process at that level. If the maintainer of the wraparound link determines that it has left neighbors, it destroys its wraparound link. Refer to a technical report [26] for a detailed description of this extension.

Other improvements. There is a number of modifications to Tiara that make it more efficient and applicable. At each level of Tiara, up to two out of three nodes may be promoted to the next level. Although the number of levels is logarithmic with respect to the system size, it may still be relatively large. The number of levels may be decreased by modifying Tiara to promote fewer nodes. For example, we can allow the nodes at level i to skip up to two or three neighbors at level $i - 1$. This would require for each node to maintain data about its extended neighborhood.

The *grow* operation of b-Tiara may force a process to acquire up to $O(|N|)$ neighbors during stabilization. This may require devoting extensive memory resources of each node to neighborhood maintenance. A simple way to mitigate it is to execute *trim* operations before *grow*. That is, if a process finds that it has both *trim* and *grow* actions enabled. It executes *trim*. Care must be taken to ensure that action execution is still weakly fair.

5   Future Work

We presented Tiara — a first deterministic self-stabilizing peer-to-peer system with a logarithmic diameter. It provides a blueprint for a realistic system. We envision several directions of extending this work: further efficiency improvements, such as keeping the runtime and the degree of the self-stabilization process low, and adding features required by practical systems. One interesting area to explore designing self-stabilizing algorithms for overlay networks that are guaranteed to have both small diameter and high expansion. This task is far from trivial as the known non-stabilizing algorithms that satisfy these properties (e.g., [3,4]) appear to require complicated self-stabilization mechanisms. A desirable scalability property of peer-to-peer networks is low *congestion* — the ability to handle multiple concurrent search requests. Another important property is resistance to *churn* — continuous leaving and joining of nodes. Thus, lowering Tiara's congestion and improving its resistance to churn is a significant avenue of future research.

References

1. Andersen, D., Balakrishnan, H., Kaashoek, F., Morris, R.: Resilient overlay networks. In: SOSP 2001: Proceedings of the eighteenth ACM symposium on Operating systems principles, pp. 131–145. ACM, New York (2001)
2. Aspnes, J., Shah, G.: Skip graphs. In: SODA 2003: Proceedings of the fourteenth annual ACM-SIAM symposium on Discrete algorithms, pp. 384–393. Society for Industrial and Applied Mathematics, Philadelphia (2003)
3. Awerbuch, B., Scheideler, C.: The hyperring: a low-congestion deterministic data structure for distributed environments. In: SODA 2004: Proceedings of the fifteenth annual ACM-SIAM symposium on Discrete algorithms, pp. 318–327. Society for Industrial and Applied Mathematics, Philadelphia (2004)
4. Bhargava, A., Kothapalli, K., Riley, C., Scheideler, C., Thober, M.: Pagoda: a dynamic overlay network for routing, data management, and multicasting. In: SPAA 2004: Proceedings of the sixteenth annual ACM symposium on Parallelism in algorithms and architectures, pp. 170–179. ACM, New York (2004)
5. Harvey, N.J.A., Jones, M.B., Saroiu, S., Theimer, M., Wolman, A.: Skipnet: a scalable overlay network with practical locality properties. In: USITS 2003: Proceedings of the 4th conference on USENIX Symposium on Internet Technologies and Systems, p. 9. USENIX Association, Berkeley (2003)
6. Malkhi, D., Naor, M., Ratajczak, D.: Viceroy: a scalable and dynamic emulation of the butterfly. In: PODC 2002: Proceedings of the twenty-first annual symposium on Principles of distributed computing, pp. 183–192. ACM, New York (2002)

7. Ratnasamy, S., Francis, P., Handley, M., Karp, R., Schenker, S.: A scalable content-addressable network. In: SIGCOMM 2001: Proceedings of the 2001 conference on Applications, technologies, architectures, and protocols for computer communications, pp. 161–172. ACM, New York (2001)

8. Rowstron, A.I.T., Druschel, P.: Pastry: Scalable, decentralized object location, and routing for large-scale peer-to-peer systems. In: Guerraoui, R. (ed.) Middleware 2001. LNCS, vol. 2218, pp. 329–350. Springer, Heidelberg (2001)

9. Stoica, I., Morris, R., Liben-Nowell, D., Karger, D.R., Kaashoek, M.F., Dabek, F., Balakrishnan, H.: Chord: a scalable peer-to-peer lookup protocol for internet applications. IEEE/ACM Trans. Netw. 11(1), 17–32 (2003)

10. Awerbuch, B., Scheideler, C.: Group spreading: A protocol for provably secure distributed name service. In: Díaz, J., Karhumäki, J., Lepistö, A., Sannella, D. (eds.) ICALP 2004. LNCS, vol. 3142. Springer, Heidelberg (2004)

11. Alima, L.O., Haridi, S., Ghodsi, A., El-Ansary, S., Brand, P.: Position paper: Self-.properties in distributed k-ary structured overlay networks. In: Babaoğlu, Ö., Jelasity, M., Montresor, A., Fetzer, C., Leonardi, S., van Moorsel, A., van Steen, M. (eds.) SELF-STAR 2004. LNCS, vol. 3460. Springer, Heidelberg (2005)

12. Onus, M., Richa, A.W., Scheideler, C.: Linearization: Locally self-stabilizing sorting in graphs. In: ALENEX 2007: Proceedings of the Workshop on Algorithm Engineering and Experiments, January 2007. SIAM, Philadelphia (2007)

13. Shaker, A., Reeves, D.S.: Self-stabilizing structured ring topology p2p systems. In: P2P 2005: Proceedings of the Fifth IEEE International Conference on Peer-to-Peer Computing, Washington, DC, USA, pp. 39–46. IEEE Computer Society, Los Alamitos (2005)

14. Hérault, T., Lemarinier, P., Peres, O., Pilard, L., Beauquier, J.: Brief announcement: Self-stabilizing spanning tree algorithm for large scale systems. In: Datta, A.K., Gradinariu, M. (eds.) SSS 2006. LNCS, vol. 4280, pp. 574–575. Springer, Heidelberg (2006)

15. Cramer, C., Fuhrmann, T.: Isprp: a message-efficient protocol for initializing structured p2p networks. In: IPCCC 2005: Proceedings of the 24th IEEE International Performance Computing and Communications Conference, April 2005, pp. 365–370. IEEE, Los Alamitos (2005)

16. Caron, E., Desprez, F., Petit, F., Tedeschi, C.: Snap-stabilizing prefix tree for peer-to-peer systems. In: Masuzawa, T., Tixeuil, S. (eds.) SSS 2007. LNCS, vol. 4838, pp. 82–96. Springer, Heidelberg (2007)

17. Bianchi, S., Datta, A., Felber, P., Gradinariu, M.: Stabilizing peer-to-peer spatial filters. In: ICDCS 2007: Proceedings of the 27th International Conference on Distributed Computing Systems, Washington, DC, USA, p. 27. IEEE Computer Society, Los Alamitos (2007)

18. Dolev, S., Kat, R.I.: Hypertree for self-stabilizing peer-to-peer systems. Distributed Computing 20(5), 375–388 (2008)

19. Dolev, D., Hoch, E., van Renesse, R.: Self-stabilizing and byzantine-tolerant overlay network. In: Tovar, E., Tsigas, P., Fouchal, H. (eds.) OPODIS 2007. LNCS, vol. 4878, pp. 343–357. Springer, Heidelberg (2007)

20. Pugh, W.: Skip lists: a probabilistic alternative to balanced trees. Commun. ACM 33(6), 668–676 (1990)

21. Munro, J.I., Papadakis, T., Sedgewick, R.: Deterministic skip lists. In: SODA 1992: Proceedings of the third annual ACM-SIAM symposium on Discrete algorithms, pp. 367–375. Society for Industrial and Applied Mathematics, Philadelphia (1992)

22. Harvey, N.J.A., Munro, J.I.: Deterministic skipnet. Inf. Process. Lett. 90(4), 205–208 (2004)
23. Fischer, M., Lynch, N., Patterson, M.: Impossibility of distributed consensus with one faulty process. Journal of the ACM 32(2), 374–382 (1985)
24. Chandra, T., Hadzilacos, V., Toueg, S.: The weakest failure detector for solving consensus. Journal of the ACM 43(4), 685–722 (1996)
25. Chandra, T., Toueg, S.: Unreliable failure detectors for reliable distributed systems. Communications of the ACM 43(2), 225–267 (1996)
26. Clouser, T., Nesterenko, M., Scheideler, C.: Tiara: A self-stabilizing deterministic skip list. Technical Report TR-KSU-CS-2008-04, Department of Computer Science, Kent State University (June 2008)

Local Synchronization on Oriented Rings

Doina Bein[1], Ajoy K. Datta[2], Chitwan K. Gupta[2], and Lawrence L. Larmore[2]

[1] University of Texas at Dallas, USA
siona@utdallas.edu
[2] University of Nevada, Las Vegas, USA
{datta,guptac,larmore}@cs.unlv.edu

Abstract. We consider the local mutual exclusion (LME) problem on a ring network. We present two self-stabilizing distributed algorithms, with local mutual exclusion, for the dining philosophers problem on a bidirectional oriented ring with two distinguished processes. The first algorithm, which uses the composite atomicity model, works under an unfair distributed daemon. The second algorithm, which uses the read-write atomicity model, works under a weakly fair daemon. Both algorithms use at most two extra bits per process to enforce local mutual exclusion. Both algorithms are derived from a simpler algorithm using transformations which can be applied to other algorithms on the ring. The technique can be generalized to more complex topologies.

Keywords: Local mutual exclusion, transformer, oriented ring, self-stabilization, synchronization.

1 Introduction

Local mutual exclusion (LME) has many applications in distributed systems. LME is the property that adjacent processes, which might use the same resource, are not allowed to enter their critical sections at the same time.

An LME *transformer* starts with an algorithm $\mathcal{A}$ on a network that may not satisfy the LME condition, and produces a distributed algorithm $\mathcal{B}$ which satisfies LME. It is desirable for the transformer to preserve certain properties of $\mathcal{A}$. For example, if $\mathcal{A}$ is *self-stabilizing*, then $\mathcal{B}$ should also be self-stabilizing.

Previous Work

Hoover and Poole [10] and Gouda [6] proposed self-stabilizing solutions for the Dining Philosophers' (DP) problem that use a central daemon and a distinguished process. Gouda and Haddix [7,8] proposed a transformer, called an *alternator*, that transforms a system that executes actions serially into a system that executes actions concurrently. Their transformer uses $\log d$ bits per process, where d is the length of the longest cycle ($d = 2$ if the graph has no cycles).

S. Kulkarni and A. Schiper (Eds.): SSS 2008, LNCS 5340, pp. 141–155, 2008.

Huang [9] gives a transformer on a network with an arbitrary topology, but subject to a coloring and an orientation condition on the edges. Starting from an algorithm that works under the *weakly fair* central daemon, the transformed algorithm satisfies LME and works under the weakly fair distributed daemon, but does not work under the unfair daemon. Nestorenko and Arora [1] give an LME transformation which refines from composite atomicity to read-write atomicity.

Our Contributions

We present two self-stabilizing LME distributed algorithms for the dining philosophers problem on a ring with two distinguished processes; Algorithm B in Section 5, using the composite atomicity model and Algorithm C in Section 6, using the read-write atomicity model. These algorithms are obtained by using transformers, starting with Algorithm A, a naive algorithm given in Section 4. Both transformers require at most two extra bits per process to enforce local mutual exclusion, and Algorithm B uses one more bit in each of the two distinguished processes, to ensure that it works under the unfair daemon. In Section 7, we give a transformer that changes an serial algorithm on the ring to a distributed algorithm with the LME condition and which works under the unfair daemon, while preserving self-stabilization.

Outline of the Paper

In Section 2, we describe the models. In Section 3, we define the dining philosophers problem. In Section 4, we give a naive algorithm for the dining philosophers problem. In Section 5, we give a transformed algorithm, Algorithm B, for the dining philosophers problem which satisfies LME, in the composite atomicity model under the unfair daemon. Algorithm B is also silent. In Section 6, we give a transformed algorithm, Algorithm C, for the dining philosophers problem which satisfies LME, in the read-write atomicity model under the weakly fair daemon. In Section 7, we define a general transformer for the ring. In Section 8, we discuss future work.

2   Preliminaries

We are given a ring network, consisting of processes $P_1, \ldots P_n$, $n \geq 3$. We assume the *shared memory model* of computation introduced in [3]. In this model, a process P can read its own registers and those of its neighbors, but can write only to its own registers. The evaluations of all guards and executions of all statements of actions are presumed to take place in one atomic step; this model is called *composite atomicity* [5]. In the *read-write atomicity* model [4], a process can either read one neighbor or write to its own shared variables in a step, but not both. We assume that each transition from a configuration to another is driven by a *scheduler*, also called a *daemon*. If one or more processes are enabled, the daemon *selects* at least one of these enabled processes to execute an action. The daemon is *weakly fair* if every continuously enabled process must eventually be selected; if the daemon has no such restriction, it is *unfair*.

2.1 Local Mutual Exclusion

We say that a distributed algorithm satisfies the *local mutual exclusion* (LME) property if no two neighboring processes may be in their critical section at the same time. This does not necessarily mean that they cannot be *selected* during the same step. For example, in Algorithms B and C given in this paper, not every action causes a process to enter its critical section, and it is possible for two neighboring processes to act at the same time, as long as at most one of them is in its critical section.

2.2 Self-stabilization and Silence

The concept of *self-stabilization* was introduced by Dijkstra [3]. Informally, we say that distributed algorithm is *self-stabilizing* if, starting from a completely arbitrary configuration, the network will eventually reach a legitimate configuration. We refer the reader to [3] for a detailed discussion of the property.

We say that $\mathcal{A}$ is *silent* if every execution is finite. In other words, starting from an arbitrary configuration, the network will eventually reach a configuration where no process is enabled.

3 The Dining Philosophers Problem

In this section, we describe the *dining philosophers* problem, introduced by Dijkstra [2]. We use terminology taken from Lynch [11].

Each philosopher P_i is represented by two processes, the *user* U_i, and the *agent*, which we also call P_i. U_i, which we think of as controlled by an application, can request that P_i enter its critical section. Once P_i enters its critical section, U_i will eventually signal that it is *satisfied*, after which P_i can leave its critical section. U_i can then repeat its at arbitrary times, infinitely often.

In Dijkstra's original formulation, each P_i must use two resources ("forks") to enter its critical section, and each resource can only be used by one agent at a time. That is, two neighboring agents can be in their critical sections simultaneously. A solution to the dining philosophers problem must avoid conflict *i.e.*, satisfy the LME property, and must also avoid deadlock and starvation.

4 Algorithm A

We now give a distributed algorithm, Algorithm A, for the dining philosophers problem on ring. All agent processes are anonymous, *i.e.* they all have the same program and do not use any ID information.

Algorithm A enforces local mutual exclusion, provided that the scheduler selects only one process during each step. If two neighboring processes should

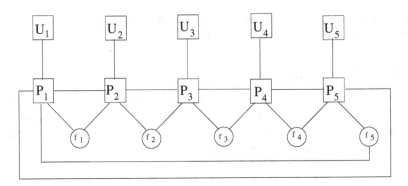

Fig. 1. Network of Processes and Resources for the Dining Philosophers Problem, for $n = 5$ (Taken from Figure 11.2 of [11])

be selected simultaneously, conflict will occur as both try to enter their critical sections at the same time.

Starvation is also a problem with Algorithm A, unless the scheduler is careful to select every process that is waiting to enter its critical section eventually.

In Section 5, we transform Algorithm A into Algorithm B, which avoids both conflict and starvation, even with the unfair daemon, and which uses the composite atomicity model.

In Section 6, we transform Algorithm A into Algorithm C, which uses the read-write atomicity model, and which avoids conflict. However, to avoid starvation, Algorithm C requires the daemon to be weakly fair.

4.1   Formal Definition of Algorithm A

We write:

$$Left(P_i) = \begin{cases} P_n & \text{if } i = 1 \\ P_{i-1} & \text{otherwise} \end{cases}$$

$$Right(P_i) = \begin{cases} P_1 & \text{if } i = n \\ P_{i+1} & \text{otherwise} \end{cases}$$

Variables of Algorithm A

Any agent process P has the following shared variable.

$P.state \in \{waiting, executing, idle\}$.

Any user process U has the following shared variable.

$U.state \in \{request, sat\}$. The value of this variable is not controlled by the algorithm; rather, by an outside application.

Predicates of Algorithm A

$Free(P) \equiv (Left(P).state \neq executing) \wedge (Right(P).state \neq executing)$
$Conflict(P) \equiv ((P.state = executing) \wedge \neg Free(P))$

$CS\_Error(P) \equiv$ Either $P.state = executing$ and P is not in its critical section, or P is in its critical section and $P.state \neq executing$.

$Error(P) \equiv Conflict(P) \vee CS\_Error(P)$

Macros of Algorithm A

$Enter\_CS(P)$: P enters its critical section.

$Leave\_CS(P)$: P leaves its critical section.

Algorithm A gives a solution to the dining philosophers problem if the scheduler has the following two properties:

1. No two adjacent processes are simultaneously selected to execute Action A3.
2. If $P.state = waiting$, then P will eventually be selected.

The first condition is *local mutual exclusion*, while the second condition is *fairness*. It is desirable to have an algorithm for the dining philosophers problem that does not depend on the benevolence of the scheduler. In the next section, we overcome that limitation.

In all the action tables in this paper, each action is given a priority. In order for an action to be enabled, its guard must be true, and no action with a lower priority number may be enabled.

Table 1. Actions of Algorithm A

A1 priority 1	Correct Error	$Error(P)$	$\longrightarrow$	$P.state \leftarrow idle$ $Leave\_CS(P)$
A2 priority 2	Start Wait	$P.state = idle$ $User(P).state = request$	$\longrightarrow$	$P.state \leftarrow waiting$
A3 priority 2	Enter CS	$P.state = waiting$ $Free(P)$	$\longrightarrow$	$P.state \leftarrow executing$ $Enter\_CS(P)$
A4 priority 2	Leave CS	$P.state = executing$ $User(P).state = sat$	$\longrightarrow$	$P.state \leftarrow idle$ $Leave\_CS(P)$

5 Algorithm B

We now give a distributed algorithm, Algorithm B, for the dining philosophers problem on a almost anonymous ring with two distinguished processes; the other processes we call *normal*. We use the same topology as in the previous section, but we allow the distinguished processes to have separate programs.

Each distinguished process has all the same shared variables as the normal processes, plus two additional "special" shared variables. A normal neighbor of a distinguished process does not know that its neighbor is distinguished. The distinguished neighbor of a distinguished process P, which we call $Partner(P)$, can read P's special shared variables, but its normal neighbor cannot.

Overview of Algorithm B. Each process has a *control bit* $P.S \in \{0,1\}$, which plays the same role as the control bit defined by Huang [9]. P_1 and P_n each have a *lock bit*, $P.lock \in \{0,1\}$, which also plays the same rule as Huang's control bit; it also has a Boolean flag. Both $P.lock$ and $P.flag$ are special shared variables.

Local mutual exclusion is enforced by the control bits and the lock bits. The easiest way to visualize this is to think of each edge as having a "token" which is always held by one of the two processes. A process P is *Ready* if it holds the tokens of both of its incident edges. That way, two neighboring processes can never be *Ready* simultaneously. Call the edge between the two distinguished processes the *special* edge, and the others *normal edges*. The location of the token for each normal edge is determined by the control bits at each end, while the location of the token for the special edge is determined by the lock bits. In each case, the token is at the left end of the edge if the bits agree, and at the right end if the bits disagree.

When a normal process P is *Ready*, i.e. holds both of its edge tokens, it can enter the critical section, provided it has has a pending request from its user process, indicated by the fact that $P.state = waiting$. When P enters its critical section, it releases both tokens by reversing its control bit. In order to prevent deadlock, a normal process also releases its tokens if it is *Ready* and it has not received a request.

The need for the special edge should now be clear. If all processes were normal, the LME mechanism could deadlock. For example, and if all their control bits are the same, all tokens are on the left ends of their edges, and no process could ever become *Ready*. We break the deadlock by allowing the token on the special edge to move independently.

Token Priority. To avoid deadlock, edge tokens are prioritized. A distinguished process that holds its normal edge token and has a pending request holds onto that token until it gets the special edge token, but if it has the special edge token only, it releases it. This technique is used by Huang [9].

Fairness. Huang's synchronizer works under the weakly fair daemon, but not the unfair daemon. In order to make Algorithm B work under the unfair daemon, we make use of the flag bits. A distinguished process yields the special edge token to its partner only if it sees that its partner has raised its flag. If we did not use this feature, the unfair daemon could cause that token to shuttle endlessly back and forth between the two distinguished processes if neither has a pending request, while refusing to select any other process.

5.1   Formal Definition of Algorithm B

Algorithm B uses all the same variables, predicates, and macros as Algorithm A, together with some additional ones.

Additional Shared Variables of Algorithm B

$P.S \in \{0, 1\}$, the control bit, a normal shared variable.

$P.lock \in \{0, 1\}$, if $P \in \{P_1, P_n\}$, the lock bit, a special shared variable.

$P.flag$ Boolean, if $P \in \{P_1, P_n\}$, a special shared variable.

Additional Predicates of Algorithm B

$$S\_Ready(P) \equiv \begin{cases} P.S = Right(P).S & \text{if } P = P_1 \\ P.S \neq Left(P).S & \text{if } P = P_n \\ (P.S = Right(P).S) \, \wedge \\ \quad (P.S \neq Left(P).S) & \text{otherwise} \end{cases}$$

$Lock\_Ready(P_1) \equiv P_1.lock \neq P_n.lock$

$Lock\_Ready(P_n) \equiv P_n.lock = P_1.lock$

$$Ready(P) \equiv \begin{cases} S\_Ready(P) \wedge Lock\_Ready(P) & \text{if } P \in \{P_1, P_n\} \\ S\_Ready(P) & \text{otherwise} \end{cases}$$

Additional Macros of Algorithm B

$Reverse(P.S)$: Change $P.S$ from 0 to 1 or vice versa.

$Reverse(P.lock)$: Change $P.lock$ from 0 to 1 or vice versa, if $P \in \{P_1, P_n\}$.

5.2   Proofs for Algorithm B

Lemma 1
(a) *From an arbitrary configuration, the network will reach a legitimate config- uration within one round.*
(b) *From a legitimate configuration, the network will never reach an illegitimate configuration.*

Proof. If $Error(P)$, then P is enabled to execute Action B1, and will do so within one round. No action can cause $Error(P)$ to become true.

Henceforth, we will assume that the network is always in a legitimate configuration.

Let $Num(P) =$ the number of times $Reverse(P.S)$ has executed
since the network was initialized

Table 2. Actions of Algorithm B

B1 priority 1	Correct Error	$Error(P)$	$\longrightarrow$	$P.state \leftarrow idle$ $Leave\_CS(P)$
B1 priority 2	Start Wait	$P.state = idle$ $User(P).state = request$	$\longrightarrow$	$P.state \leftarrow waiting$
B2 priority 2	Raise Flag	$P \in \{P_1, P_n\}$ $P.state = waiting$ $S\_Ready(P)$ $\neg P.flag$	$\longrightarrow$	$P.flag \leftarrow$ TRUE
B3 priority 2	Lower Flag	$P \in \{P_1, P_n\}$ $(P.state \neq waiting \ \vee$ $\neg S\_Ready(P))$ $P.flag$	$\longrightarrow$	$P.flag \leftarrow$ FALSE
B4 priority 2	Yield Control Token	$P \in \{P_1, P_n\}$ $Lock\_Ready(P)$ $Partner(P).flag$ $\neg P.flag$	$\longrightarrow$	$Reverse(P.lock)$
B5 priority 2	Yield Lock Token	$P.state \neq waiting$ $S\_Ready(P)$	$\longrightarrow$	$Reverse(P.S)$

B6 priority 2	Enter CS	$P.state = waiting$
		 $Ready(P)$
		 $Free(P)$
			$\longrightarrow$	$P.state \leftarrow executing$
				 $Enter\_CS(P)$
				 $Reverse(P.S)$
				 if $P \in \{P_1, P_n\}$ **then**
				 $Reverse(P.lock)$
				 $P.flag =$ FALSE
				 endif

B7 priority 2	Leave CS	$P.state = executing$ $User(P).state = sat$	$\longrightarrow$	$P.state \leftarrow idle$ $Leave\_CS(P)$

$$\tau(P_i) = \begin{cases} 0 & \text{if } i = 1 \\ \tau(P_{i-1}) + 1 & \text{if } i > 1 \text{ and } P_{i-1}.S = P_i.S \\ \tau(P_{i-1}) - 1 & \text{otherwise} \end{cases}$$

$$\Delta(P) = Num(P) - Num(P_1) - \tfrac{1}{2}\tau(P)$$

Lemma 2. *For any process P, $\Delta(P)$ never changes.*

Proof. (Sketch.) No action of any process can change the value of $\Delta(P)$.

$$\text{Let } T = \frac{n(n-1)}{4} + nNum(P_1) + \tfrac{1}{2}\sum_{i=2}^{n}\tau(P_i) \tag{1}$$

Remark 1. T is an integer, and $nNum(P_1) \leq T \leq nNum(P_1) + \frac{n(n-1)}{2}$.

Lemma 3. *During any given step, T increases by the number of processes that execute Reverse(P.S) during that step.*

Proof. Execution of $Reverse(P_i.S)$ causes $\tau(P_i)$ to increase by 2 if $i > 1$, and hence causes T to increase by 1. Execution of $Reverse(P_1.S)$ causes $Num(P_1)$ to increase by 1 and causes $\tau(P_i)$ to decrease by 2 for all $i > 1$, and hence causes T to increase by 1.

Lemma 4. *Eventually some process will execute Reverse(P.S), i.e., Action B5 or B6.*

Proof. By Lemma 1, we can assume there is no error.

There must be at least one process which is S-enabled, namely the process with the minimum value of τ.

Case I: Some $P \neq \{P_1, P_2\}$ is S-enabled. If $P.state \neq waiting$, P can execute Action B5. If $P.state = waiting$, neither neighbor may enter its critical section since it is not S-enabled. If a neighbor is already in its critical section, it must eventually execute Action B7. P simply waits until $Free(P)$, and can then execute Action B6.

Case II: Both P_1 and P_n are S-enabled. If one of those is not waiting, it can execute Action B5. If both are waiting, then one of them is lock-enabled, and is thus enabled to execute Action B6.

Case III: $S\_Ready(P_1)$ and $\neg S\_Ready(P_n)$. If $P_1.state \neq waiting$, then P_1 can execute Action B5. Otherwise, eventually either P_n will become $S\_enabled$, reducing to Case II, or $Free(P_1)$ and $P_1.flag$ will become true, after which P_1 can execute B6.

Lemma 5. *If $P.state = waiting$ for any process P, P will eventually enter its critical section.*

Proof. By Lemmas 3 and 4, T grows without bound. Since the other two terms of (1) are bounded, $Num(P_1)$ must increase without bound. By Lemma 2, $Num(P)$ must also increase without bound, and hence P must eventually execute Action B6.

Combining the results of the above lemmas, we conclude:

Theorem 1. *Algorithm B solves the dining philosophers problem in the composite atomicity model under a distributed unfair daemon, avoiding conflict after the first round, and avoiding starvation.*

6   Algorithm C

In this section we present Algorithm C, a modification of Algorithm B which uses read-write atomicity instead of composite atomicity. Algorithm C runs under the weakly fair daemon.

6.1   Formal Definition of Algorithm C

Algorithm C uses almost exactly the same shared variables, functions, and macros as Algorithm B. One exception is that the variable $P.flag$ for a distinguished process is not used.

When a process P evaluates a guard of an action of Algorithm C, it uses the stored copies of the shared variables of its neighbors instead of the current variables. When P executes a read action, it reads the values of the shared variables of one of its neighbors. To guarantee that the algorithm makes progress, P uses a local round robin queue to rotate between its alternatives, so that it will eventually read any given neighbor, and will eventually execute every non-read action that is enabled.

Table 3. Actions of Algorithm C

C1 priority 1	Correct Error	$Error(P)$	$\longrightarrow$	$P.state \leftarrow idle$ $Leave\_CS(P)$
C2 priority 2	Read Neighbor	Round-robin	$\longrightarrow$	$Read\_Nbr(P)$
C3 priority 3	Start Wait	$P.state = idle$ $User(P).state = request$	$\longrightarrow$	$P.state \leftarrow waiting$
C4 priority 3	Yield Lock Token	$P \in \{P_1, P_n\}$ $Lock\_Ready(P)$	$\longrightarrow$	$Reverse(P.lock)$
C5 priority 3	Yield Control Token	$P.state \neq waiting$ $S\_Ready(P)$	$\longrightarrow$	$Reverse(P.S)$
C6 priority 3	Enter CS	$P.state = waiting$ $Ready(P)$ $Free(P)$	$\longrightarrow$	$P.state \leftarrow executing$ $Enter\_CS(P)$ $Reverse(P.S)$ **if** $P \in \{P_1, P_n\}$ **then** $Reverse(P.lock)$ **endif**
C7 priority 3	Leave CS	$P.state = executing$ $User(P).state = sat$	$\longrightarrow$	$P.state \leftarrow idle$ $Leave\_CS(P)$

Theorem 2. *Algorithm C solves the dining philosophers problem in the read-write atomicity model, under the weakly fair daemon.*

We will give the detailed proof of Theorem 2 in the full paper. The proof is essentially the same as that of Algorithm B, with appropriate modifications because of the change of model.

One problem with the read-write atomicity model is that a process might execute an action which has been neutralized by a change in a neighbor's state, if the process does not yet know that the neighbor has changed state. Algorithm C avoids this problem by using a *gentlemen's rule*; a process never "seizes" an edge token, but rather waits until it is freely given. This way, if a process is mistaken about the state of its neighbor, that mistake is always on the "safe side." If P has given the edge token to Q, but Q does not know it yet, neither process will make use of the resource. represented by the token.

Starvation cannot be avoided without making use of the weak fairness of the daemon. Suppose P is enabled to enter its critical section, and Q is another process which is not enabled to execute any action except a read action, and Q already has correct copies of its neighbors shared variables. If the daemon selects just Q at every step, Q will read the same values from its neighbors endlessly, and Q will starve. On the other hand, a weakly fair daemon is required to select Q eventually. If Q is a process enabled to enter its critical section.

7   A General Transformer on the Ring

We assume the same topology as in the earlier sections. The processes of the network are P_i for all $1 \leq i \leq n$, P_i and P_{i+1} are neighbors, and P_n and P_1 are neighbors. As in Section 5, we refer to P_1 and P_n as *distinguished* and the other processes as *normal*; similarly, we refer to the edge between P_1 and P_n as *special* and the other edges as normal.

Suppose we are given an algorithm $\mathcal{A}$ consisting of a program, $\mathcal{A}_P$, for each process P. These programs could all be identical, or not. We assume that $\mathcal{A}$ is self-stabilizing under the weakly fair central daemon. We construct a transformed algorithm $T(\mathcal{A})$, which satisfies the LME property, and is self-stabilizing under the unfair daemon.

Overview of the Transformer. The construction is essentially the same as the construction of Algorithm B from Algorithm A in Section 5. For simplicity, we assume that in $\mathcal{A}$, a process is in its critical section for only an instant.

We use the same control and lock bits that we used for Algorithms B and C.

7.1   Formal Definition of the Transformer

Variables of Transform($\mathcal{A}$). Any process P has the following shared variables.

Table 4. Actions of Transform($\mathcal{A}$)

D1 priority 1	Raise Flag	$P \in \{P_1, P_n\}$ $A\_Ready(P)$ $S\_Ready(P)$ $\neg P.flag$	$\longrightarrow$	$P.flag \leftarrow$ TRUE
D2 priority 1	Lower Flag	$P \in \{P_1, P_n\}$ $(A\_Ready(P) \vee \neg S\_Ready(P))$ $P.flag$	$\longrightarrow$	$P.flag \leftarrow$ FALSE
D3 priority 1	Yield Lock	$P \in \{P_1, P_n\}$ $Lock\_Ready(P)$ $Partner(P).flag$ $\neg P.flag$	$\longrightarrow$	$Reverse(P.lock)$
D4 priority 1	Yield Control	$\neg A\_Ready(P))$ $S\_Ready(P)$ $\neg P.done \vee (P \neq P_1)$	$\longrightarrow$	$Reverse(P.S)$ $P.done \leftarrow Done(P)$
D5 priority 1	Critical Section	$A\_Ready(P)$ $Ready(P)$	$\longrightarrow$	$P.state \leftarrow idle$ $Execute\_CS(P)$ $Reverse(P.S)$ **if** $P \in \{P_1, P_n\}$ **then** $\quad Reverse(P.lock)$ $\quad P.flag =$ FALSE **endif** $P.done \leftarrow Done(P)$
D6 priority 2	Update Done	$P.done \neq Done(P)$	$\longrightarrow$	$P.done \leftarrow Done(P)$

All the shared variables of P defined for the algorithm $\mathcal{A}$.

$P.S \in \{0, 1\}$.

$P.lock \in \{0, 1\}$, if $P \in \{P_1, P_n\}$.

$P.flag$ Boolean, if $P \in \{P_1, P_n\}$.

$P.done$ Boolean.

$P_1.lock$ and $P_1.flag$ can only be read by P_n, not by P_2. Similarly, $P_n.lock$ and $P_n.flag$ can only be read by P_1, not by P_{n-1}.

Predicates of Transform($\mathcal{A}$)

$A\_Ready(P) \equiv P$ is enabled to execute some action of $\mathcal{A}_P$.

$$S\_Ready(P) \equiv \begin{cases} P.S = Right(P).S & \text{if } P = P_1 \\ P.S \neq Left(P).S & \text{if } P = P_n \\ (P.S = Right(P).S) \land \\ \quad (P.S \neq Left(P).S) & \text{otherwise} \end{cases}$$

$Lock\_Ready(P_1) \equiv P_1.lock \neq P_n.lock$

$Lock\_Ready(P_n) \equiv P_n.lock = P_1.lock$

$$Ready(P) \equiv \begin{cases} S\_Ready(P) \land Lock\_Ready(P) & \text{if } P \in \{P_1, P_n\} \\ S\_Ready(P) & \text{otherwise} \end{cases}$$

$$Done(P) \equiv \begin{cases} \neg A\_Ready(P) & \text{if } P = P_n \\ \neg A\_Ready(P) \land Right(P).done & \text{otherwise} \end{cases}$$

Partners

The two distinguished processes recognize each other as *partners*. Write $Partner(P_1) = P_n$, and $Partner(P_n) = P_1$.

Macros of Transform($\mathcal{A}$)

Reverse($P.S$): Change $P.S$ from 0 to 1 or vice versa.

Reverse($P.lock$): Change $P.lock$ from 0 to 1 or vice versa, if $P \in \{P_1, P_n\}$.

Execute_CS(P): P executes an enabled action of $\mathcal{A}$.

Theorem 3. *If $\mathcal{A}$ is self-stabilizing under the weakly fair central daemon, then $T(\mathcal{A})$ is self-stabilizing under the unfair daemon, and satisfies the LME condition. If $\mathcal{A}$ is silent, then $T(\mathcal{A})$ is silent.*

Proof. (Sketch.) We first note that $T(\mathcal{A})$ satisfies the LME condition, since no two neighboring processes can execute an action of $\mathcal{A}$. Given a computation of $T(\mathcal{A})$, we can derive a computation of $\mathcal{A}$ by ignoring all actions except D5 and replacing each step which has more than one instance of Action D5 into multiple steps of $\mathcal{A}$. Since no two simultaneous instances of D5 can occur on adjacent processes, the corresponding actions of $\mathcal{A}$ cannot influence each other. As in Algorithm B in Section 5, the flags of the distinguished processes work to ensure that that execution of $\mathcal{A}$ is weakly fair, since it is impossible for even an unfair daemon to ignore any one process forever while selecting other processes. Thus, if every weakly fair execution of $\mathcal{A}$ is eventually in a legitimate state, so is every execution of $T(\mathcal{A})$.

If $\mathcal{A}$ is silent, then, as $T(\mathcal{A})$ executes, eventually $\neg A\_Ready(P)$ for all P. In a wave starting at P_n, $P.done$ will become true for all P. When $P_1.done$ holds, P_1

will be unable to execute Action D4. Eventually, $\neg S\_Ready(P)$ for all $P \neq P_1$, and the network will be unable to execute any action.

8 Conclusion and Future Work

In this paper, we give two distributed algorithms for the classic dining philosophers problem [3] in an almost anonymous ring. One of those uses the composite model of atomicity and works under an unfair distributed daemon, while the other uses the read-write model of atomicity and works under a weakly fair distributed daemon.

Using the technique used in Section 5, we show how to transform any composite atomicity model self-stabilizing algorithm on the ring which works under the weakly fair central daemon to a composite atomicity model self-stabilizing algorithm which works under the unfair distributed daemon. If the original algorithm is silent, the transformed algorithm will also be silent.

Using the technique used in Section 6, we can transform any composite atomicity model self-stabilizing algorithm on the ring which works under the weakly fair central daemon to a read-write atomicity model self-stabilizing algorithm which works under the weakly fair distributed daemon. The new algorithm will not be silent; in fact it appears to be impossible to construct a silent algorithm with read-write atomicity as it is usually defined, since a process has no way of knowing that it already has the correct values of its neighbors' variables. We will give this transformer in the full paper.

Other Topologies. Our techniques work for any tree topology; in fact, the needed transformations are much simpler in that case. We hope to extend our results to topologies other than the ring or tree.

References

1. Nesterenko, M., Arora, A.: Stabilization-Preserving Atomicity Refinement. Journal of Parallel and Distributed Computing 62, 766–791 (2002)
2. Dijkstra, E.W.: Hierarchical Ordering of Sequential Processes. Acta Informatica 1, 115–138 (1971)
3. Dijkstra, E.W.: Self Stabilizing Systems in Spite of Distributed Control. Communications of ACM 17, 643–644 (1974)
4. Dolev, S., Israeli, A., Moran, S.: Self-stabilization of Dynamic Dystems Dssuming Dnly Dead/write Dtomicity. Distributed Computing 7, 3–16 (1993)
5. Dolev, S.: Self-Stabilization. MIT Press, Cambridge (2000)
6. Gouda, M.G.: The Stabilizing Philospher: Asymmetry by Memory and by Action. Tech. Report TR-87-12. University of Texas at Austin (1987)
7. Gouda, M.G., Haddix, F.F.: The Linear Alternator. In: Proceedings of the 3rd Workshop on Self-stabilizing Systems, pp. 31–47. Carleton University Press (1997)

8. Gouda, M.G., Haddix, F.F.: The Alternator. Distributed Computing 20, 21–28 (2007)
9. Huang, S.T.: The fuzzy philosophers. In: Rolim, J.D.P. (ed.) IPDPS-WS 2000. LNCS, vol. 1800, pp. 130–136. Springer, Heidelberg (2000)
10. Hoover, D., Poole, J.: A Distributed Self-stabilizing Solution For the Dining Philosophers Problem. IPL 41, 209–213 (1989)
11. Lynch, N.A.: Distributed Algorithms. Morgan Kaufmann, San Francisco (1996)

Stabilization of Max-Min Fair Networks without Per-flow State

Jorge A. Cobb[1] and Mohamed G. Gouda[2]

[1] Department of Computer Science
The University of Texas at Dallas
cobb@utdallas.edu
[2] Department of Computer Science
The University of Texas at Austin
gouda@cs.utexas.edu

Abstract. Let a *flow* be a sequence of packets sent from a source computer to a destination computer. Routers at the core of the Internet do not maintain any information about the flows that traverse them. This has allowed for great speeds at the routers, at the expense of providing only best-effort service. In this paper, we consider the problem of fairly allocating bandwidth to each flow. We assume some flows request a constant amount of bandwidth from the network. The bandwidth that remains is distributed fairly among the rest of the flows. The fairness sought after is max-min fairness, which assigns to each flow the largest possible bandwidth that avoids affecting other flows. The distinguishing factor to other approaches is that routers only maintain a constant amount of state, which is consistent with trends in the Internet (such as the proposed Differentiated Services Internet architecture). In addition, due to the need for high fault-tolerance in the Internet, we ensure our protocol is self-stabilizing, that is, it tolerates a wide variety of transient faults.

Keywords: Stabilization, max-min fairness, quality of service, computer networks.

1 Introduction

As the Internet grows, scalability at the core of the Internet has become a significant concern. To provide simple best-effort service, core routers do not need to maintain any state information about the flows of packets that traverse them. To provide more advance forms of quality of service, such as guaranteeing bandwidth or delay, the Differentiated Services Architecture [1,2], which maintains only a constant amount of state per router, is favored over the Integrated Services Architecture [3,4], where each core router maintains state for each individual flow.

In this paper, we focus on providing fair bandwidth allocation among different flows in a core network. There are many different notions of fairness, and each of these leads to a different optimization objective. We adopt the notion of *max-min fairness*. A bandwidth allocation is max-min fair [5], if no flow can

S. Kulkarni and A. Schiper (Eds.): SSS 2008, LNCS 5340, pp. 156–172, 2008.

be allocated a higher bandwidth without hurting another flow having equal or lower bandwidth.

Max-min fairness satisfies many intuitive fairness properties, and it has been studied extensively [6,7,8,9]. However, all of these proposed algorithms need-per flow state.

In this paper, we present a fault-tolerant distributed algorithm for the computation of max-min bandwidth allocations. Our algorithm only requires a constant amount of state information at each router.

Although constant-state algorithms have been presented earlier, [10,11], they have disregarded fault tolerance altogether. Our algorithm is presented formally and is shown to be stabilizing, i.e., resilient against a wide-variety of transient faults.

The organization of this paper is as follows. Section 2 presents our notation and defines stabilization. We assume two types of flows in our system: rigid flows, whose bandwidth is constant, and adaptive flows, whose bandwidth is determined by the max-min algorithm. Section 4 presents our signaling protocol and how it is used to support rigid flows. Section 5 defines max-min fairness formally and introduces adaptive flows. The stabilization of our algorithm is discussed in Section 6. Finally, concluding remarks are given in Section 7.

2   Notation and Stabilization

A *system* consists of a set of processes, and a set of communication channels between these processes. The *topology* of the system consists of a connected undirected graph, where each node represents one process in the system, and each edge between two nodes p and q indicates that processes p and q are neighbors in the system. Neighboring processes are joined by a pair of communication channels allowing them to exchange messages.

Each process is assumed to have access to a real-time clock. Clock values need not be synchronized between processes. The only requirement is that clocks of different processes advance at (approximately) the same rate.

Each *process* in a system is specified by finite sets of constants, variables, and actions. The values of each variable are taken from some bounded domain of values. Each action of a process p is of the form

$$\langle \text{guard} \rangle \rightarrow \langle \text{assignment} \rangle$$

where $\langle \text{guard} \rangle$ can be in one of three forms: a) local, b) receiving, or c) timeout, as follows.

A local guard is a boolean expression over the constants and variables of process p. A receiving guard of the form **rcv** m evaluates to true if there is a message of type m in one of the incoming channels of p. Finally, a timeout action is executed when the clock of p has reached a certain value.

In the above action, $\langle \text{assignment} \rangle$ is a sequence of assignment statements, each of which is of the form

$$x := \text{E}(y, \dots) \textbf{ if } P$$

where x is a variable in process p, E is an expression of the same type as variable x, and y is a either a constant or a variable in process p. Executing this assignment statement assigns the value of expression E to variable x provided predicate P is true. Otherwise, the value of x is left unchanged.

A *state* of a system S is specified by one value for each variable, taken from the domain of values of that variable, in each process in S, and the contents of each communication channel in S.

A *transition* of a system S is a triple of the form

$$(s, ac, s')$$

where s and s' are two states of system S and ac is an action in some process in S such that the following two conditions hold.

  i. *Enablement:* The guard of action ac is true at state s.
 ii. *Execution:* Executing the assignment of action ac, when system S is in state s, yields system S in state s'.

A *computation* of a system S is a sequence of the form

$$(s_0, ac_0, s_1), (s_1, ac_1, s_2), \ldots$$

where each element $(s_i, ac_i, s_{(i+1)})$ is a transition of S such that the following two conditions hold.

  i. *Maximality:* Either the sequence is infinite or it is finite and its last element $(s_{(z-1)}, ac_{(z-1)}, s_z)$ is such that the guard of every action in system S is false at state s_z, and timeout actions cannot evaluate to true by increasing the value of the clocks in the system.
 ii. *Fairness:* If the sequence has an element $(s_i, ac_i, s_{(i+1)})$ and the guard of some action ac is true at state $s_{(i+1)}$, then the sequence has a later element $(s_k, ac_k, s_{(k+1)})$ where ac_k is ac or the guard of ac is false at state $s_{(k+1)}$.

A *predicate* P of a system S is a boolean expression over the variables in all processes in system S and the contents of the channels in S.

A system S is called P-*stabilizing* iff every computation of S has a suffix where P is true at every state of the suffix [12,13,14].

Stabilization is a strong form of fault-tolerance. Normal behavior of the system is defined by predicate P. If a fault causes the system to a reach an abnormal state, i.e., a state where P is false, then the system will converge to a normal state where P is true, and remain in the set of normal states as long as the execution remains fault-free.

3   Network Model

Consider a computer network as depicted in Fig. 1. It consists of a set of core routers surrounded by access networks. Access routers serve as intermediate points between the core network and the access networks.

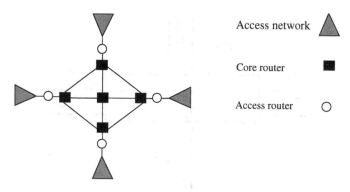

Fig. 1. Core network

Consider a computer in an access network that generates data packets that must cross the core network to reach their destination at a different access network. We denote this sequence of packets as a *flow*.

As it is commonly assumed [15,16,17,18], access routers maintain information about each individual flow, while core routers, for scalability purposes, do not. In our case, core routers will maintain only a constant amount of information regarding the flows that traverse them.

We model this by having three types of processes in our system: source processes, router processes, and destination processes. Each source process corresponds to the actions that an access router must perform for an individual flow. Thus, there are multiple source processes per access router, and each source process is associated with a single destination process at a different access router.

Routers have multiple processes, one per output channel, as shown in Fig. 2(a). Therefore, the path traverse by a flow is abstracted as shown in Fig. 2(b). That is, data begins at a source process, it traverses multiple router processes, and ends at a destination process.

The path across the core network between a source and destination is assumed to be constant, which may be implemented with mechanisms such as MPLS [19]. Route changes across a core network are rare, and thus, they are viewed as faults in our system.

There are two types of sources: rigid and adaptive. A source is *rigid* if the bandwidth it reserves from the network is non-changing. A source is *adaptive* if it must probe the network to determine how much bandwidth it is allowed to use. Routers only keep aggregate (and hence constant) amount of information regarding the flows that traverse them. Through signaling messages, the sources are able to modify this aggregate information in order to maintain its accuracy.

To ensure correct synchronization of values between sources and routers, we require some bounds on the delay of signaling messages. Routers must give signaling messages high priority, ensuring that the end-to-end delay does not exceed ε seconds. Messages exceeding this bound are discarded. This can be accomplished in a variety of ways, including timestamping each message with its inception time, or with the accumulated queuing delay that the packet has encountered

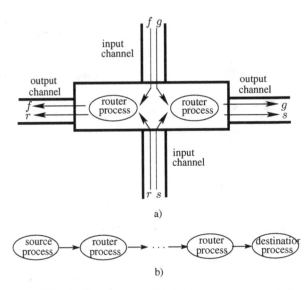

Fig. 2. Processes and flows in a core router

along its path. We thus incorporate this assumption on end-to-end delays into our system model.

We conclude by defining the fairness we expect to achieve for adaptive sources. We will consider max-min fairness [5], which is intuitively is defined as follows: bandwidth is allocated to each flow so that an increase of the bandwidth allocated to any flow f must be done at the expense of decreasing the bandwidth of a flow g where the bandwidth allocated to g is smaller than that of f.

The bandwidth allocation to each flow can be defined iteratively as follows. For each pair of neighboring processes p and q, we define the following variables:

- Let $B(p, q)$ initially have the bandwidth of channel $ch(p, q)$ *minus* the bandwidth of the rigid flows traversing channel $ch(p, q)$. B will contain the unallocated bandwidth of the channel.
- Let $F(p, q)$ be the set of adaptive flows traversing channel $ch(p, q)$. F will contain the set of flows whose bandwidth has not yet been determined.

The following steps are repeated until all flows have been assigned a bandwidth, i.e., until F is empty for all edges.

- Let (p, q) be an edge such that

$$\frac{B(p, q)}{|F(p, q)|} = \min_{x,y}\left\{\frac{B(x, y)}{|F(x, y)|}\right\}$$

- For every flow $f \in F(p, q)$, assign to f a bandwidth of

$$\frac{B(p, q)}{|F(p, q)|}$$

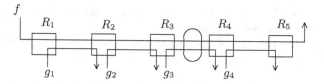

Fig. 3. Max-Min Fairness example

- For every edge (x, y) other than (p, q),
  - Reduce $B(x, y)$ by the sum of the bandwidths of the flows in $F(p, q)$ that also traverse (x, y).
  - Remove from $F(x, y)$ any flow that is also in $F(p, q)$.
- $F(p, q)$ is assigned the empty set and $B(p, p)$ is assigned zero.

As a simple example, consider Fig. 3, where we have five routers and five flows. Flow f traverses the entire network, while the remaining flows traverse only a single hop. Assume all links have equal capacity C, except for the link (R_3, R_4), which has capacity $C/2$.

To maximize the throughput of the system, each of flows g_1, g_2 and g_4 must be assigned a bandwidth of C, g_3 must be assigned a bandwidth of $C/2$, while flow f must be assigned a bandwidth of zero, which of course is unfair to f.

Under max-min fairness, at each link, we divide the bandwidth by its number of flows, and find the minimum of these values. This occurs at link (R_3, R_4), with a value of $((C/2)/2) = C/4$, while all other links have a value of $C/2$. Thus, f and g_3 are assigned a bandwidth of $C/4$ each. Also, since f traverses the other three links, their bandwidth is reduced by $C/4$.

We thus have a bandwidth of $3 \cdot C/4$ left at each of the remaining three links. Since each of these has only one flow, then g_1, g_2, and g_4 are assigned a bandwidth of $3 \cdot C/4$.

Finally, throughout the paper, we use the terms bandwidth and data rate interchangeably.

4   Rigid-Source Signaling

In this section, we present our signaling protocol, and show how it may be used by the rigid sources to reserve bandwidth from the network. It is a variation of a signaling protocol we presented in [20,21] for a different network model. The protocol presented here however is strengthened to become stabilizing.

We make the following assumptions about the rigid sources:

- First, the set of rigid sources is assumed to be fixed. The reason for this requirement is that converging to a stable assignment of bandwidth to sources is not possible if the set of sources changes over time. We make this assumption also for the adaptive sources.
- Since the set of rigid sources are fixed, we do not address the steps required to setup/tear-down a source, and focus only on refreshing/correcting information at the routers. This is a practical assumption in some core networks,

where flows would correspond to "data pipes" across the core, and the set of these pipes changes infrequently.
- We assume that the sum of the bandwidth requirements of all the rigid flows sharing a link is less than the bandwidth of the link.

As mentioned earlier, routers only maintain a constant amount of state information. Hence, each router maintains, for each of its output channels, the sum of the bandwidths of the rigid flows that traverse that channel. The remaining bandwidth of the channel will be distributed among the adaptive flows.

The objective of the signaling protocol is to maintain the above information current at each router, even though faults occur. For example, source processes may die, or the path between a source and its destination may change.

To maintain updated the state at each router along its path, each rigid source sends a *Reserve* message periodically. This message contains the desired bandwidth of its flow, and, as mentioned earlier, it is sent across the path with high priority and bounded round-trip time.

The router process maintains two variables, R and its "shadow copy" $\widehat{R}$. Variable R contains the sum of the bandwidth of the rigid flows. The router also maintains a boolean bit s, known as the "shadow bit". Every T seconds, where T is a predefined constant, the router updates its state in the following way:

$$s, R, \widehat{R} := \neg s, \widehat{R}, 0$$

That is, the s bit is flipped, the shadow copy $\widehat{R}$ is assigned to R, and the shadow copy $\widehat{R}$ is cleared to zero.

The objective of the *Reserve* message is to add the bandwidth of the flow to $\widehat{R}$ exactly once before the above assignments are done. In this way, the bandwidth of the flow will always be included in R. This is accomplished as follows.

The *Reserve* message contains a bit vector s, with one bit for each router along the path of the flow. These bits are the last-known values of the s bit of each router along the path. The bandwidth of the flow is added to the shadow variable only if the state has been updated (and thus s has changed) from the time of the previous *Reserve* message of the flow. That is, the following two steps are performed at the ith router whenever it receives a *Reserve*(r, s) message, where r is the bandwidth of the flow.

- If $s_i \neq s$, then, assign $\widehat{R} + r$ to $\widehat{R}$, and assign s to s_i.
- Forward the *Reserve*(r, s) message along the next hop to the destination of the flow.

When the destination receives this message, it returns a *ReserveAck* message back to the source, containing the updated vector s. A new *Reserve* message is not sent until an acknowledgment is received for the previous *Reserve* message.

We next address how often the source of a flow should send a *Reserve* message. As mentioned earlier, we assume a bound, ε, on the time for a signaling message to traverse the network. A signaling message created at time t is discarded by a router if it is received at a time greater than $t + \varepsilon$. State updates of different

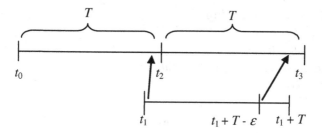

Fig. 4. Timing of *Reserve* messages

routers are not required to be synchronized. The only assumption is that each scheduler performs updates at least T seconds apart.

Consider Fig. 4, and consider a router along the path of flow f. A state update occurs in the router at time t_0, and another at time t_2. At time t_1, the source of f transmits a *Reserve* message, which arrives at the router in the interval (t_0, t_2). Thus, at least one *Reserve* message from f must arrive at the router in the interval (t_2, t_3). In the worst case, t_1 is almost equal to t_2, which implies that the next *Reserve* message must arrive at the router no later than $t_1 + T$, i.e., it must be sent no later than $t_1 + T - \varepsilon$. Furthermore, the next *Reserve* cannot be sent until a *ReserveAck* is received for the first *Reserve*, which at the latest will occur at time $t_1 + 2 \cdot \varepsilon$. Thus, we require

$$t_1 + 2 \cdot \varepsilon < t_1 + T - \varepsilon.$$

That is, $3 \cdot \epsilon < T$, and the interval between successive transmissions of *Reserve* messages should be at most $T - \varepsilon$.

The above signaling protocol is robust to a variety of faults. E.g., if a source dies, then all the bandwidth reservation from the source will be removed within $2 \cdot T$ seconds, as follows. Within the first T seconds, $\widehat{R}$ is set to zero. Since the source has died, its bandwidth is never added to $\widehat{R}$, and within the next T seconds, $\widehat{R}$ is assigned to R. Similarly, if the path of a source changes, routers along the previous path will remove information about the source in $2 \cdot T$ seconds, while routers along the new path will add information about the source. If the information at the routers is incorrect, it will also correct itself within $2 \cdot T$ seconds.

We are now ready to present the specification of the source, router, and destination processes. The source process is specified as follows.

process *src*[i]
const

r	:	**integer**	{data rate}
d	:	**process id**	{destination}
ε	:	**integer**	{max. e2e delay}

var

s	:	**bit vector**	{shadow-bit vector}
t	:	**integer**	{time msg is sent}

begin

rcv $ack\_f(i, d, s)$ $\rightarrow$ **skip**

☐

   timeout $clock \in [t + 2 \cdot \varepsilon,\ t + T - \varepsilon]$ $\rightarrow$
       send $Reserve(i, d, r, s)$ **to** $dst[d]$
       $t := clock;$

☐

   $t + T - \varepsilon < clock < t$ $\rightarrow$ $t := clock;$
end

The source process contains two actions. In the first action, it receives a *ReserveAck* message, which has traversed the network from the destination back to the source. The only purpose of the message is to update the bit vector s, which is done as a side effect of receiving the message. Thus, the right-hand side of the action is empty.

The second action is a timeout action, in which a *Reserve* message is sent to the destination. Variable t stores the time at which the last *Reserve* message was sent. To ensure old *Reserve* and *ReserveAck* messages have left the network before sending a new one, *Reserve* messages are sent with at least $2 \cdot \varepsilon$ seconds in between. Furthermore, to ensure the message arrives in time at the routers, the message should be sent no later than time $t + T - \varepsilon$. We assume that execution of actions is done such that the timeout will be executed within the right time interval. Failure to do so is considered a fault.

The last action is a sanity action in which t is restored to a sensible value in case of a fault.

The specification of the router is as follows.

process $router[i]$
const
   C :   **integer**   {channel bandwidth}
   T :   **integer**   {shadow interval}
var
   s :   **boolean** {shadow bit}
   $R, \widehat{R}$:   **integer**   {fixed bandwidth}
   t :   **integer**   {time of last timeout}
begin
   rcv $Reserve(x, y, r, s)$ $\rightarrow$
          $\widehat{R} := \widehat{R} + r$ **if** $s_i \neq s$
          $s_i := s;$
          send $Reserve(x, y, r, s)$ **to** $dst[y];$

☐

   rcv $ReserveAck(x, y, r, s)$ $\rightarrow$
          send $ReserveAck(x, y, r, s)$ **to** $src[x];$

☐

   timeout $clock > t + T$ $\rightarrow$
       $s, R, \widehat{R} := \neg s, \widehat{R}, 0;$

$t := clock;$

⟦

$clock < t \quad \rightarrow \quad t := clock;$
end

In the first action, a *Reserve* message is received, and is forwarded along the next hop to the destination. Before forwarding the message, the rate of the flow is added to the shadow variable $\widehat{F}$, provided a state change has occurred from the last time a *Reserve* message from this flow was received, i.e., $s_i \neq s$. Also, s_i is updated to the value of s before forwarding the message. This ensures that the flow is counted only once in $\widehat{F}$.

In the second action, a *ReserveAck* is received. The router simply forwards the message in the direction of the source.

In the third action, the router changes its state after T seconds from its last state change. Thus, $\widehat{R}$ is assigned to R, $\widehat{R}$ is set to zero, and bit s is flipped. The time of the state change is recorded in t.

The last action is a sanity action to restore t to a sensible value in case of a fault.

The specification of the destination process is given next.

process $dst[i]$
begin
   rcv $Reserve(x, i, r, s) \quad \rightarrow$
        send $ReserveAck(x, i, r, s)$ **to** $src[x];$
end

It simply consists of a single action that receives a *Reserve* message and returns a *ReserveAck* in the direction of the source of the message.

5   Adaptive-Source Signaling

We next address how to modify the system to support adaptive sources. The system should converge to a state where all adaptive sources have been given their max-min fair share of the network bandwidth.

Consider the algorithm to compute max-min fairness given in Sec. 3. In order to implement it, at each iteration we need to know, for each link, the number of flows whose bandwidth has not been allocated, and the total bandwidth that remains unallocated on the link.

This suggests that the information we maintain at the router is as follows:

- The sum of the bandwidths of adaptive flows that are not bottlenecked at this router, that is, flows who cannot increase their bandwidth because another router is preventing them from doing so. We will denote this sum as A.
- The total number of adaptive flows that are bottlenecked at this router, denoted by n. The bandwidth allocated to these flows will be the total bandwidth C of the channel minus A above divided by the number of flows n. We denote this bottleneck bandwidth by B, i.e., $B = (C - A)/n$.

In order for this information to be updated at the routers, the source needs to know which router is its bottleneck router, what is the bottleneck bandwidth of that router, and inform all other routers of this limit on the flow's bandwidth. Furthermore, this information may change over time, as the system converges to a steady state.

We thus require sources to send a *Probe* message along the path to their destination. The message contains the rate r currently being used by the source, and whether the source is considered bottlenecked or not at each router. With this information, the router can determine which of the following four cases apply to the flow:

1. If the flow is bottlenecked at the router and its rate r is greater than the bottleneck bandwidth B of the router ($r > B$), then the flow remains bottlenecked at the router, but its new rate should be decreased to B.
2. If the flow is bottlenecked at the router and $r < B$, then the flow should be no longer considered bottlenecked at this router. Thus, its bandwidth r is added to A, and the number of bottlenecked flows n at the router is decreased by one.
3. If the flow is not bottlenecked at this router and $r > B$, then the flow must become bottlenecked at this router. Hence, n increases by 1, and A decreases by r.
4. If the flow is not bottlenecked at this router, and $r < B$, then the state of the flow and the router remain the same.

In order to refresh the information in a fault-tolerant manner, we also introduce shadow copies of n and A, i.e., $\widehat{n}$ and $\widehat{A}$. Furthermore, in order for the source to be aware of which routers consider it to be bottlenecked, each *Probe* message carries an additional bitmap b, where b_i is true if the flow is bottlenecked at router i along its path.

We now present the specification of the source, router, and destination processes.

process $src[i]$
const
d	:	**process id**	{destination}
ε	:	**integer**	{min. interpacket time}

var
s	:	**bit vector**	{shadow-bit vector}
b	:	**bit vector**	{bottleneck-bit vector}
r, r', r''	:	**integer**	{allocated rate}
t	:	**integer**	{time msg is sent}

begin
  rcv $ProbeAck(i, d, r'', s, b)$ $\rightarrow$
        $r := r'$;
        $r' := r''$;

☐

  timeout $clock \in [t + 2 \cdot \varepsilon, \, t + T - \varepsilon]$ $\rightarrow$
      send $Probe(i, d, r, r', \infty, s, b)$ **to** $dst[d]$;

$$t := clock;$$

▯

$$t + T - \varepsilon < clock < t \quad \rightarrow \quad t := clock;$$
end

An adaptive source has several more variables than a rigid source. It contains a bitmap b (discussed above) and three bandwidth variables, r, r', r'', that are included in each *Probe* message.

Variable r contains the current bandwidth of the source, i.e., this value has been added to the bandwidth sum A at each router. On the other hand, r' contains the updated bandwidth, that is, the new value that should be stored at the routers. Finally, r'' is initialized to infinity, and, as the *Probe* message traverses to the destination, r'' stores the minimum of the bottleneck bandwidths of the routers along the path.

In the first action, the source receives a *ProbeAck* message. The values of r and r' are updated. The values of s and b are updated as a side effect of receiving the message.

The timeout action is similar to the timeout action of a rigid source, except that a *Probe* message is sent instead of a *Reserve* message. The last action is again, a corrective action for the value of t.

process $router[i]$
const

C	: **integer**	{channel bandwidth}
T	: **integer**	{shadow interval}

var

s	: **boolean**	{shadow bit}
$n, \widehat{n}$	: **integer**	{bottlenecked users}
$A, \widehat{A}$	: **integer**	{adaptive bandwidth}
$R, \widehat{R}$	: **integer**	{fixed bandwidth}
t	: **integer**	{time of last timeout}

begin
  rcv $Reserve(x, y, r, s) \quad \rightarrow$
      $\widehat{R} := \widehat{R} + r \quad$ **if** $s_i \neq s$
      $s_i := s;$
      send $Reserve(x, y, r, s)$ **to** $dst[y];$

▯

  rcv $ReserveAck(x, y, r, s) \quad \rightarrow$
      send $ReserveAck(x, y, r, s)$ **to** $src[x];$

▯

  rcv $Probe(x, y, r, r', r'', s, b) \quad \rightarrow$
      {add flow to shadow variables}
      $\widehat{n} := \widehat{n} + 1 \quad\quad$ **if** $s_i \neq s \wedge b_i;$
      $\widehat{A} := \widehat{A} + r \quad\quad$ **if** $s_i \neq s \wedge \neg b_i;$
      {change flow from category if necessary}

$$n, \widehat{n}, := n - 1, \widehat{n} - 1 \quad \text{if } r' < B \wedge \boldsymbol{b}_i;$$
$$A, \widehat{A} := A + r', \widehat{A} + r' \quad \text{if } r' < B \wedge \boldsymbol{b}_i;$$
$$n, \widehat{n} := n + 1, \widehat{n} + 1 \quad \text{if } r' \geq B' \wedge \neg \boldsymbol{b}_i;$$
$$A, \widehat{A} := A - r, \widehat{A} - r \quad \text{if } r' \geq B' \wedge \neg \boldsymbol{b}_i;$$

{update values before forwarding}
$$\boldsymbol{s}_i, \boldsymbol{b}_i := s, (r' \geq B);$$
$$r'' := \min(r'', B)$$
send $Probe(x, y, r, r', r'', \boldsymbol{s}, \boldsymbol{b})$ **to** $dst[d]$

[]

rcv $ProbeAck(x, y, r'', \boldsymbol{s}, \boldsymbol{b}) \quad \rightarrow$
    send $ProbeAck(x, y, r'', \boldsymbol{s}, \boldsymbol{b})$ **to** $src[x]$

[]

timeout $clock > t + T \quad \rightarrow$
    $s, n, A, R, \widehat{n}, \widehat{A}, \widehat{R} := \neg s, \widehat{n}, \widehat{A}, \widehat{R}, 0, 0, 0;$
    $t := clock;$

[]

$clock < t \quad \rightarrow \quad t := clock;$
end

The router contains seven actions. The first two are the same as before: they receive messages originating from rigid sources.

The last two actions are also similar to before. The last action restores the value of t to a sensible value, and the timeout action performs a state change of the router by assigning the shadow variables to their corresponding regular variables, and flipping the shadow bit.

In the third action, a *Probe* message is received. The first step consists of adding the bandwidth information of the flow to the shadow variables, provided the shadow bit indicates this is necessary. The second step consists of evaluating the four conditions mentioned above to ensure the flow is correctly placed in the bottlenecked or not bottlenecked category. In this action, B and B' are defined as follows.

$$B = \frac{C - A - R}{n} \qquad B' = \frac{C - A - R - r}{n + 1}$$

The destination is similar to before; it receives a *Probe* message and returns a *ProbeAck* message.

process $dst[i]$
begin
  rcv $Probe(x, i, r, r', r'', \boldsymbol{s}, \boldsymbol{b}) \quad \rightarrow$
      send $ProbeAck(i, d, r'', \boldsymbol{s}, \boldsymbol{b})$ **to** $src[x];$
end

6   Stabilization of Max-Min Fairness

We next present an overview of the stabilization properties of our system. Detailed proofs will be available in [22]. Below, we refer only to *Probe* and *ProbeAck* messages of adaptive sources. Similar lemmas and theorems can be derived for messages from rigid sources. As discussed earlier, routing between access networks is outside the scope of the paper. We simply assume that routing is stabilizing[1], and thus the routing tables converge to a sound and stable set of values. This, combined with the timing restrictions on sending messages, gives the following.

Lemma 1. *The system stabilizes to the following predicate: every $Probe(x, y, \ldots)$ message is located only along the path from x to y, and every $ProbeAck(x, y, \ldots)$ message is located only along the path from y to x.*

Similarly, due to the time restrictions on the sending of messages by the source and the fast processing of messages at the routers, we have the following.

Lemma 2. *The system stabilizes to the following predicate: for every x and y, the number of $Probe(x, y, \ldots)$ messages plus the number of $ProbeAck(x, y, \ldots)$ messages is at most one.*

We next consider the relationship between the rates of the sources and the information stored at the routers. Before this, the following two lemmas are necessary. First, due to the timing of the state changes of the routers and the timing on the generation of signaling messages by the source we have the following.

Lemma 3. *Every computation of the system has a suffix such that the following holds. In every state u_i of the suffix, if the shadow bit of a router at state u_i differs from its value at a later state u_j, then the router has received a Probe message between u_i and u_j for every adaptive source that traverses the router.*

Due to the above, we obtain the following relationship of the shadow bits of messages, routers, and sources.

Lemma 4. *The system stabilizes to the conjunction of the following predicates:*

- *if there exists a $Probe(x, y, \ldots, s, \ldots)$ message along the ith hop of the path from source x and destination y, then,*
  - $\langle \forall j, (src[x].s_j = router[j].s) \Rightarrow (Probe.s_j = router[j].s) \rangle$,
  - $\langle \forall j, (src[x].s_j \neq router[j].s \land i \leq j) \Rightarrow (Probe.s_j = src[x].s_j) \rangle$,
  - $\langle \forall j, (Probe.s_j \neq src[x].s_j) \Rightarrow (i > j \land Probe.s_j = router[j].s) \rangle$,

  where $router[j]$ is the jth router along the path from source x to destination y.
- *if there exists a $ProbeAck(x, y, \ldots, s, \ldots)$ message along the path from destination y back to source x, then*

$$\langle \forall j, (ProbeAck.s_j \neq src[x].s_j) \Rightarrow (ProbeAck.s_j = router[j].s) \rangle$$

---

[1] Most routing protocols such as link-state routing and distance-vector routing are in essence stabilizing.

From the above, we can derive the relationship between the aggregate bandwidth information at the routers and the bandwidth information of each individual source, as follows.

Theorem 1. *Let $S(i)$ be the set of adaptive sources whose flows traverse router i. Let $b(x), s(x), r(x), r'(x)$ be the fields in the Probe and ProbeAck messages of source x, and if neither of the two messages are in transit, then these values correspond to the variables of the source.*

Then, the system stabilizes to the following predicate. For all i,

- $router[i].A = (\sum x,\ x \in S(i),\ \alpha(x) \cdot r(x) + \alpha'(x) \cdot r'(x))$, *and*
- $router[i].n = |\{x,\ x \in S(i) \wedge b(x)_i\}|$, *and*
- $router[i].\widehat{A} = \left(\sum x,\ x \in S(i),\ \widehat{\alpha}(x) \cdot r(x) + \widehat{\alpha'}(x) \cdot r'(x)\right)$, *and*
- $router[i].\widehat{n} = |\{x,\ x \in S(i) \wedge b(x)_i \wedge s(x)_i = router[i].s\}|$

where

- $\alpha(x) = 1$ *if $\neg b(x)_i$ and either there is a Probe message along the path from $src[x]$ to $router[i]$ or there is no message from $src[x]$ in the network. It is zero otherwise.*
- $\alpha'(x) = 1$ *if $\neg b(x)_i$ and either there is a Probe message along the path from $router[i]$ to the destination of $src[x]$, or there is a ProbeAck message along the path from the destination back to $src[x]$. It is zero otherwise.*
- $\widehat{\alpha}(x) = 1$ *if $\alpha(x) = 1 \wedge (router[i].s = s(x)_i)$. It is zero otherwise.*
- $\widehat{\alpha'}(x) = 1$ *if $\alpha'(x) = 1 \wedge (router[i].s = s(x)_i)$. It is zero otherwise.*

Finally, the bandwidth values must converge to the max-min allocation for each flow. The first lemma serves as a stepping stone for an induction proof leading to the main theorem.

Lemma 5. *Let B_0 be the bandwidth assigned to the first set of flows in the max-min algorithm. Then, every computation has a suffix where all of the following hold.*

- *For any i, $router[i].B \geq B_0$.*
- *For any i, each of $src[i].r$, $src[i].r'$, $src[i].r''$ are at least B_0.*
- *For each Probe message, each of $Probe.r$, $Probe.r'$, $Probe.r''$ are at least B_0.*
- *For each ProbeAck message, $ProbeAck.r'' \geq B_0$.*

Theorem 2. *Let $S^A(i)$ and $S^R(i)$ be the set of adaptive and rigid sources, respectively, whose flows traverse $router[i]$. Then, the system stabilizes to the following predicate. For all i and j,*

- *if $src[j]$ is an adaptive source, then $src[j].r$ equals the max-min fair bandwidth corresponding to the source, and*
- $router[i].R = \left(\sum x,\ x \in S^R(i),\ src[x].r\right)$, *and*
- $router[i].A = \left(\sum x,\ x \in S^A(i) \wedge \neg src[x].b_i,\ src[x].r\right)$, *and*
- $router[i].n = |\{x,\ x \in S^A(i) \wedge src[x].b_i\}|$

7   Concluding Remarks

Above, we did not discuss the stabilization time of our system. The stabilization predicate of Theorem 1 can be shown to stabilize in $O(T)$ time, where T is the interval between state changes at a router.

The stabilization time of Theorem 2, on the other hand, still remains an open problem. It can be shown that if bandwidth values are discrete, then the convergence time is in the order of $O(N \cdot \Delta)$, where N is the number of discrete bandwidth values, and Δ is the time interval between signaling messages from a source. We have shown in Sec. 4 that $\Delta \leq T - \varepsilon$, so in the worst case the convergence time is $O(N \cdot T)$, unless a tighter bound is imposed on Δ.

References

1. Heinanen, J., Baker, F., Weiss, W., Wroclawski, J.: Assured forwarding phb group. Internet RFC 2597
2. Jacobson, V., Nichols, K., Poduri, K.: An expedited forwarding phb. Internet RFC 2598
3. Braden, R., Clark, D., Shenker, S.: Integrated services in the internet architecture. Internet RFC 1633
4. Wroclawski, J.: Specification of controlled-load network element service, Internet RFC 2211 (1997)
5. Boudec, J.-Y.L.: Rate adaptation, congestion control and fairness (2008), http://icalwww.epfl.ch/PS_files/LEB3132.pdf
6. Abraham, S., Kumar, A.: A stochastic approximation approach for max-min fair adaptive rate control of abr sessions with mcrs. In: Proceedings of IEEE INFO-COM, New York, NY (March 1999)
7. Charny, A.: An algorithm for rate allocation in a packet switching network with feedback, M.S. thesis, Massachusetts Institute of Technology (May 1994)
8. Hou, Y.T., Tzeng, H.H.Y., Panwar, S.S.: A generalized max-min rate allocation policy and its distributed implementation using the abr flow control mechanism. In: Proceedings of IEEE Infocom, San Francisco, CA (March 1998)
9. Ros, J., Tsai, W.K.: A general theory of constrained max-min rate allocation for multicast networks. In: IEEE International Conference on Networks, Singapore (2000)
10. Sarkar, S., Ren, T., Tassiulas, L.: Achieving fairness in multicasting with almost stateless rate control. In: Proceedings of the conference on Scalability and Traffic Control in IP Networks, SPIE, ITcom (2002)
11. Kim, Y., Tsai, W.K., Iyer, M., Ros, J.: Minimum rate guarantee without per-flow information. In: ICNP 1999: Proceedings of the Seventh Annual International Conference on Network Protocols, Washington, DC, USA, p. 155. IEEE Computer Society, Los Alamitos (1999)
12. Arora, A., Gouda, M.: Closure and convergence: A foundation of fault-tolerant computing. IEEE Transactions on Software Engineering 19(11), 1015–1027 (1993)
13. Dolev, S., Herman, T.: Superstabilizing protocols for dynamic distributed systems. Chicago Journal of Theoretical Computer Science 1997(4) (1997)
14. Dijkstra, E.W.: Self-stabilizing systems in spite of distributed control. Commun. ACM 17(11), 643–644 (1974)

15. Stoica, I., Zhang, H.: Providing guaranteed services without per-flow management. In: Proc. of the ACM SIGCOMM Conference (1999)
16. Zhang, Z., Duan, Z., Gao, L., Hou, Y.T.: Decoupling QoS control from core routers: A novel bandwidth architecture for scalable support for guaranteed services. In: Proc. ACM SIGCOMM Conference (2000)
17. Kaur, J., Vin, H.M.: Core-stateless guaranteed rate scheduling algorithms. In: Proc. of the IEEE INFOCOM Conf. (2001)
18. Kaur, J., Vin, H.M.: Core stateless guaranteed throughput networks. In: Proc. of the IEEE INFOCOM Conf. (2003)
19. Callon, R., Doolan, P., Feldman, N., Fredette, A., Swallow, G., Viswanathan, A.: A framework for multiprotocol label switching, Internet draft draft-ietf-mpls-framework-02.txt (1997)
20. Cobb, J.: Preserving quality of service without per-flow state. In: Proc. IEEE International Conference on Network Protocols (ICNP) (November 2001)
21. Cobb, J.: Scalable quality of service across multiple domains. Computer Communications 28(18), 1997–2008 (2005)
22. Cobb, J.A., Gouda, M.G.: Stabilization of max-min fair networks without per-flow state, Department of Computer Science Technical Report, The University of Texas at Dallas (September 2008)

Convergence Time Analysis of Self-stabilizing Algorithms in Wireless Sensor Networks with Unreliable Links

Hirotsugu Kakugawa* and Toshimitsu Masuzawa**

Osaka University
1-3 Machikaneyama, Toyonaka, Osaka 560-8531, Japan
{kakugawa,masuzawa}@ist.osaka-u.ac.jp

Abstract. Wireless sensor network is a set of many tiny sensor nodes each of which consists of a microprocessor with sensors and wireless communication device. Because centralized control is hard to achieve in a large scale sensor network, self-* is a key concept to design such a network. In this paper, as one of self-* properties, we investigate self-stabilization algorithms which is a promising theoretical background for wireless sensor network protocols. T. Herman [Procs. International Workshop of Distributed Computing, 2003] proposed a transformation scheme of self-stabilizing algorithm in abstract computational model to sensor network model. However, it is not known that whether expected convergence time of transformed algorithms is finite or not. We show upper bound of expected convergence time of some self-stabilizing algorithms in explicit formulas.

Keywords: Wireless sensor network, self-stabilization, self-organization, probabilistic self-stabilization, convergence time.

1 Introduction

1.1 Background

Wireless sensor network is a set of large number of sensor nodes, each of which is equipped with wireless communication device and sensors to monitor environment. Software design for wireless sensor networks is challenging because resource on each node is limited and wireless communication is unreliable. In addition, a set of sensor nodes in operation changes because new sensor nodes are deployed in ad-hoc manner and a sensor node stop working when its battery is exhausted. Therefore, in design of dynamic distributed system such as

---

* This work is supported in part by Grant-in-Aid for Scientific Research ((B)20300012 and (B)17300020) of JSPS, "Special Coordination Funds for Promoting Science and Technology: Yuragi Project" of MEXT, and Kayamori Foundation of Informational Science Advancement.

** This work is supported in part by Grant-in-Aid for Scientific Research ((B)19300017) of JSPS, and Global COE (Centers of Excellence) Program of MEXT.

S. Kulkarni and A. Schiper (Eds.): SSS 2008, LNCS 5340, pp. 173–187, 2008.

wireless sensor network, self-∗ (self-organizing, self-configuring, self-managing, self-optimizing, self-repairing, etc) is a key concept for system design.

Different from ad-hoc approaches, we take a formal approach to design distributed algorithms for wireless sensor networks because formal approach gives us theoretical foundation for design, verification and performance analysis. Specifically, we adopt self-stabilization as a theoretical background for self-organizing and self-repairing distributed systems. Self-stabilization is a theoretical framework for non-masking fault-tolerant distributed systems [1,2,3]. Specifically, self-stabilizing distributed systems have the following important advantages for large and complex modern distributed systems, and hence different from ad-hoc design approaches, self-stabilization is one of formal backgrounds for system design with self-∗ property of wireless sensor network.

1.2   Related Works

Although self-stabilization is undoubtedly important in distributed systems, design and verification of a self-stabilizing distributed algorithm is a hard task because such a system must recover from arbitrary soft errors. That is, we must assume that, at the beginning of computation, local variables of nodes and contents of messages may be corrupted arbitrarily. By this reason, many self-stabilizing distributed algorithms are designed under abstract computational model (coarse-grained atomic action with distributed shared memory) for simplicity of design and verification. However, big semantic gap lies between such an abstract computational model and real distributed systems (fine-grained atomic action in parallel with message passing). Several model transformation methods that fill the gap have been proposed so far to execute such self-stabilizing distributed algorithms in real distributed systems.

- *Transformation with exact model equivalence.* Transformation in this category guarantees that execution of a transformed algorithm is exactly the same as executing under the abstract computational model. A transformation proposed in [4] is based on optimistic concurrency control from database theory, and update of a local state of a node is considered as a transaction. We call transformation of this category *heavyweight* because runtime overhead is large to guarantee model equivalence.
- *Transformation with inexact model equivalence.* Transformation in this category does not guarantee model equivalence, and a transformed algorithm may produce execution that never occurs in the abstract computational model. Transformations proposed in [5,6,7] are based on caching of neighbor states without any cache coherency protocols to simulate distributed shared memory. We call transformation of this category *lightweight* because runtime overhead is small.

We review lightweight transformation proposed in [5,6,7]. In each method, each node maintains a cache of neighbor node, and each node v_i sends its local state to each neighbor node v_j to update cache of local state of v_i at v_j

immediately [5] or periodically [6,7]. In [5], Huang, Wuu and Tsai propose a lightweight transformation for general networks with reliable FIFO communication links, and this is the first paper that proposes lightweight transformation. In [6], Herman presents a lightweight transformation for wireless sensor networks. He assumes that each node has correct cache of each neighbor node in initial configuration, and he also assumes communication is reliable. By these assumptions, correctness of each cache is maintain by sending new local state when a node updates its local state. However, these two assumption is unrealistic in sensor networks.

In [7], under assumption that each node receives a packet from neighbor with probability $0 < p < 1$, Turau and Weyer show that lightweight transformation by [6] yields a probabilistically self-stabilizing algorithm that converges to legitimate configuration with probability 1 from initial configuration in which caches are incorrect. Unfortunately, the authors do not show whether expected convergence time is finite or not.

1.3   Contribution of This Paper

In this paper, we show upper bound of expected convergence time of some self-stabilizing algorithms in sensor networks obtained by lightweight transformation. To the best knowledge of the authors, expected convergence time analysis for lightweight transformation is unknown. Main contribution of this paper is two-fold.

- We propose a general methodology to derive upper bound on expected convergence time of self-stabilizing algorithms by lightweight transformation (Theorem 1). In particular, we assume that each node fails to receive a packet with some probability even if a system in converging, which makes convergence time analysis non-trivial.
- As a case study, we show expected convergence time analysis of some self-stabilizing algorithms and give (finite) upper bounds in explicit formulas.

Organization of this paper is as follows. In section 2, we descrive computational models and self-stabilization. In section 3, lightweight transformation scheme for our implementation is presented. In section 4, we show some upper bounds on expected convergence time of self-stabilizing algorithms. In section 5, we give concluding remarks of this paper.

2   Preliminary

2.1   Abstract Computational Model

Let $V = (v_1, v_2, ..., v_n)$ be a set of nodes and $E \subseteq V \times V$ be a set of bidirectional communication links in a distributed system. Then, the topology of the distributed system is represented as an undirected graph $G = (V, E)$. The number of nodes is denoted by n. We assume that G is a connected and simple graph. By N_i, we denote a set of neighbor nodes of v_i. By $v_i.x$, we denote local variable x at node v_i. A set of local variables defines local state of a node. Let $v_i.q$ be the local state (tuple of all local variables) of node $v_i \in V$. A tuple of local states of nodes $(v_1.q, v_2.q, ..., v_n.q)$ forms a *configuration* (global state) of a distributed system, and let Γ be a set of all configurations.

An algorithm of each node v_i is given as a set of guarded commands:

$$*[\ Grd_1 \rightarrow Act_1 \ \Box \ Grd_2 \rightarrow Act_2 \ \Box \ Grd_3 \rightarrow Act_3 \ \Box \ \cdots \ ]$$

As a communication model, we assume that each node can read local states of neighbor nodes, which is called the *state reading model*. Although a node can read local state of neighbor nodes, it can update its local state only.

Each Grd_j $(j = 1, 2, ...)$ is called a *guard* and it is a predicate on v_i's local state and local states of its neighbor nodes. Each Act_j is called an *action* which updates local state of v_i, and the next local state is computed from current local state of v_i and those of its neighbor nodes. We say that v_i is *enabled* in configuration γ if and only if at least one guard of v_i is true in γ.

An atomic step of each node v_i consists of the following three internal substeps: (1) read local states of neighbor nodes and evaluate guards, (2) execute a command that is associated to a true guard, if any, and (3) update its local state. Following two types of schedulers are often assumed in the literature of self-stabilizing distributed algorithms. (1) *The central daemon*: At each step, only one enabled node is selected arbitrarily, and a selected node executes an atomic step. (2) *The distributed daemon*: At each step, arbitrary non-empty set of enabled nodes are selected, and selected nodes execute their atomic steps in parallel.

For any configuration γ, let γ' be any configuration that follows γ. Then, we denote this transition relation by $\gamma \rightarrow \gamma'$. For any configuration γ_0, a *computation* e starting from γ_0 is a maximal (possibly infinite) sequence of configurations $e = \gamma_0, \gamma_1, \gamma_2, ...$ such that $\gamma_t \rightarrow \gamma_{t+1}$ for each $t \geq 0$.

2.2   Computational Model for Sensor Networks

In this paper, we adopt the following computational model for sensor networks.

Each node communicates via wireless communication device, however, it is assumed that packet loss or collisions cannot be detected by any node. We assume that message delay is zero because two nodes directly communicate with each other via wireless communication. A set of nodes that are in the communication range of v_i forms a set of neighbor N_i of v_i, and it is assumed that a variable N_i is available at v_i for each node v_i. It is assumed that communication is bidirectional, i.e., $v_k \in N_i$ if and only if $v_i \in N_k$. Each packet transmitted by node v_i is locally broadcast to nodes N_i. Each packet by v_i is received by each neighbor node $v_k \in N_i$ independently with probability p, conversely, each node $v_k \in N_i$ drops a packet from v_i independently with probability $1 - p$. Note that, when v_i transmits a packet, $v_j \in N_i$ may receive and $v_k \in N_i$ may not receive it probabilistically. Each node is equipped with a local clock and speed of local clocks of nodes are the same, however, we do not assume that clock values are not synchronized.

Each node takes an action on receive event or timer event. We assume that timer events of nodes do not occur simultaneously.

- Receive event: On event that a node successfully receives a packet, a message handler of a node is invoked atomically.
- Timer event: On event that an interval timer of a node ticks, a timer handler of a node is invoked atomically.

2.3   Self-stabilization

Self-stabilization property is defined as an ability to converge to a correct system operation in finite time from arbitrary initial configuration. Let S be a 3-tuple $S = (\Gamma, \Lambda, \rightarrow)$, where Γ is a finite set, Λ is a subset of Γ, and $\rightarrow$ is a mapping from Γ to Γ. A 3-tuple $S = (\Gamma, \Lambda, \rightarrow)$ can be viewed as a transition system defined by given network topology and algorithm. The concept of self-stabilization is formally defined as follows [1].

Definition 1. *A system $S = (\Gamma, \Lambda, \rightarrow)$ is* self-stabilizing *with respect to $\Lambda \subseteq \Gamma$ if and only if the following two conditions hold: (1) Convergence: Starting from arbitrary configuration, configuration eventually becomes one in Λ, and (2) Closure: For any configuration $\lambda \in \Lambda$, any configuration γ such that $\lambda \rightarrow \gamma$ is also in Λ. Each $\lambda \in \Lambda$ is called a* legitimate configuration. *and Λ is called a set of legitimate configurations.*   □

A configuration just after some soft errors occur or just after node removal and/or deployment (i.e., change of N_i values) occur is considered as a new initial configuration, and self-stabilization guarantees convergence from such a configuration.

3   Lightweight Transformation Scheme

3.1   Transformation Algorithm

Outline of our lightweight transformation scheme is shown in Figure 1, which is essentially the same as the ones proposed in [5,6,7], and it converts a self-stabilizing algorithm in the abstract computational model (defined in section 2.1) into a program in the sensor network model (defined in section 2.2).

Let $v_i.q$ be a (set of) local variable(s) of node v_i in the original algorithm. Then, in a transformed algorithm, each v_i maintains a cache $v_i.C[v_k, q]$ of $v_k.q$ for each neighbor node $v_k \in N_i$. Algorithm logic in a transformed algorithm is kept unchanged except each access to $v_k.q$ in the original algorithm is replaced by an access to its cache $v_i.C[v_k, q]$. Periodically, by interval timer event, each node v_i locally broadcasts a packet that contains its local variable(s) $v_i.q$. We call such a message packet as *state packet*. Each node neighbor node receives

---

Local variables of node v_i
 $v_i.q$ — the (set of) local variable(s) of original algorithm;
 $v_i.C[v_k, q]$ — cache of $v_k.q$ for each neighbor $v_k \in N_i$;
Code of node v_i
 on timer :
  transmit $\langle v_i.q \rangle$;
 on message $\langle q \rangle$ **from** $v_k \in N_i$ **:**
  $v_i.C[v_k, q] := q$;
  Update $v_i.q$ by running guarded commands of original algorithm
   except access to each $v_k.q \in N_i$ is replaced by $v_i.C[v_k, q]$;

Fig. 1. Lightweight transformation scheme

a state packet independently with probability p. When node v_i receives a state packet that contains $v_j.q$ from its neighbor v_j, it updates $v_i.C[v_j, q]$ to cache the latest value of $v_j.q$.

It is important to remember that the lightweight transformation scheme does not preserve the abstract computational model because update of $v_i.q$ by v_i is not immediately observable by its neighbor nodes. That is, an execution which never occurs in the abstract computational model may occur in a transformed algorithm executed in real wireless sensor networks. However, in this paper, we show that transformed algorithm probabilistically converges to legitimate configuration by showing explicit upper bound on the expected number rounds to converge.

3.2 Legitimate Configurations

We describe definition of legitimate configurations of a transformed algorithm. Let $S_A = (\Gamma_A, \Lambda_A, \rightarrow_A)$ be a self-stabilizing system in the abstract computational model which is non-reactive, and let $S_S = (\Gamma_S, \Lambda_S, \rightarrow_S)$ be a transformed system in the sensor network model. A set of configurations Γ_S is obtained by augmenting each configuration $\gamma_A \in \Gamma_A$ in such a way that a state of a node v_i in $\gamma_S \in \Gamma_S$ is a tuple of (1) the values of local variables of node v_i in γ_A and (2) the value of local cache $v_i.C[v_k, x]$ for each neighbor $v_k \in N_i$ and local variable x.

For any configuration $\gamma_S \in \Gamma_S$, we say γ_S is *cache coherent for node* v_i if and only if $\forall v_j \in N_i : v_j.C[q, v_i] = v_i.q$ for each local variable q, i.e., each neighbor v_j of v_i caches the current local state of node v_i. We say a configuration γ_S is *cache coherent* if and only if γ_S is cache coherent for each node v_i [6]. We say node v_i is *cached-state consistent in configuration* γ_S if and only if v_i is not enabled (i.e., no true guard) in γ_S. Intuitively, in a cached-state consistent configuration, each node need not update its local variable according to its cache of neighbor states, and note that cached-state consistency does not imply cache coherency.

A set of legitimate configurations Λ_S in sensor network model is defined from $S_A = (\Gamma_A, \Lambda_A, \rightarrow_A)$ as follows. A configuration $\gamma_S \in \Gamma_S$ is in Λ_S if and only if γ_S is cache coherent and each node $v_i \in V$ is cached-state consistent in γ_S. Note that, in sensor network model, a legitimate configuration λ_S is stable under packet loss because configuration never change on such events. In other words, packet loss does not break legitimacy of configuration.

4   Convergence Time Analysis in Sensor Networks

First we derive a useful formula that will be used in our analysis. Let k be any integer such that $k \geq 1$. For each $i = 1, 2, ..., k$, let $Z_i(p)$ be a random variable distributed according to the geometric distribution with parameter p. We define a random variable $Z(k, p)$ by

$$Z(k, p) = \max_{1 \leq i \leq k} \{Z_i(p)\}, \tag{1}$$

and expectation of $Z(k, p)$ is

$$\mathbf{E}[Z(k, p)] = \sum_{t=1}^{\infty} t \cdot \mathbf{Pr}[Z(k, p) = t]. \tag{2}$$

In [8], Szpankowski and Rego derive non-recurrent expression for $\mathbf{E}[Z(k, p)]$, and Figure 2 shows graph of $\mathbf{E}[Z(k, p)]$ for some p.

$$\mathbf{E}[Z(k, p)] = - \sum_{k'=1}^{k} (-1)^{k'} \frac{{}_kC_{k'}}{(1 - (1 - p)^{k'})} \tag{3}$$

Informally, the random variable $Z(k, p)$ is defined as follows.

We have k coins, and head (tail) of each coin appears with probability p (resp., $1 - p$). At the first iteration, we flip all of the k coins at the same time. In the second iteration, we flip only tail coins by the first iteration. In the third iteration, we flip only tail coins by the second iteration. We repeat such coin flips until no coin is tail. Let $Z(k, p)$ be a random variable for the total number of iterations.

In our problem setting, the definition of the random variable $Z(k, p)$ and its expectation $\mathbf{E}[Z(k, p)]$ can be interpreted as follows.

- If node v_i transmits its state packet $\mathbf{E}[Z(\delta_i, p)]$ times, each neighbor of v_i is expected to receive the state packet at least once.
- In our transformation setting, each node transmits its state packet in every round. Thus, in $\mathbf{E}[Z(\delta_i, p)]$ expected rounds, each neighbor of v_i is expected to receive the state packet of v_i at least once.
- Conversely, in $\mathbf{E}[Z(\delta_i, p)]$ expected rounds, for each neighbor $v_j \in N_i$, v_i is expected to receive a state packet of v_j at least once.
- In $\mathbf{E}[Z(2|E|, p)]$ rounds, all the node are expected to receive state packets at least once from all neighbors.

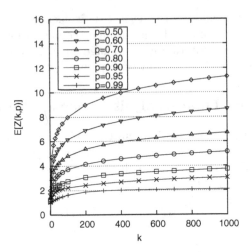

Fig. 2. Graph of $\mathbf{E}[Z(k,p)]$

4.1 On Upper Bound of Convergence Time

We show general framework for deriving convergence time analysis of self-stabilizing systems for the sensor network model.

Let $S = (\Gamma, \Lambda, \rightarrow)$ be a self-stabilizing algorithm (in either abstract and sensor network models). Let F be a predicate on configurations Γ such that $F(\gamma) \Leftrightarrow \gamma \in \Lambda$, that is, $F(\gamma)$ is true if and only if γ is a legitimate configuration.

For given $S = (\Gamma, \Lambda, \rightarrow)$, let K be some integer and let F_i be a predicate on configuration for each $i = 1, 2, ..., K$ such that

- For each $i = 1, 2, ..., K$, starting from any configuration in which F_{i-1} is true[1], S eventually reaches a configuration in which F_i is true,
- F_i is closed, that is, for any configuration $\gamma \in \Gamma$ such that $F_i(\gamma)$, $F_i(\gamma')$ holds for any configuration γ' such that $\gamma \rightarrow \gamma'$, and
- $F = F_1 \wedge F_2 \wedge \cdots \wedge F_K$.

Such a set of predicates $\{F_i : i = 1, 2, ..., K\}$ is called a *convergence stair* of S [9]. Intuitively, starting from any configuration, the system gradually increases satisfied predicates, and finally, all predicates are satisfied which implies configuration is legitimate.

Let $\{F_i : i = 1, 2, ..., K\}$ be a convergence stair of S, and let $T(\gamma, F_i)$ be a random variable for the number of execution steps (rounds[2]) from configuration γ to some configuration in which F_i is true. Then, we define

$$\tau(F_i, F_j) = \max_{\substack{\gamma \in \Gamma \text{ s.t.} \\ F_i(\gamma) \text{ is true}}} \left\{ \mathbf{E}[T(\gamma, F_j)] \right\}. \qquad (4)$$

---

[1] We assume that $F_0(\gamma)$ is true for any $\gamma \in \Gamma$.

[2] For the sake of simplicity, we assume that configuration transitions within a single round in the sensor network model are collapsed into a single transition.

Note that $\tau(F_i, F_j)$ is the upper bound of the expected number of executions from a configuration γ_i such that $F_i(\gamma_i)$ is true to any configuration γ_j such that $F_i(\gamma_j)$ is true.

Theorem 1 below states that upper bound on expected convergence time of a self-stabilizing system is the sum of expected convergence time for each convergence step of predicate of a convergence stair.

Theorem 1. *For any self-stabilizing system* $S = (\Gamma, \Lambda, \rightarrow)$ *and let* $\{F_i : i = 1, 2, ..., K\}$ *be a convergence stair of* S. *Then, we have*

$$\tau(true, F_K) \leq \sum_{i=1}^{K} \tau(F_{i-1}, F_i). \tag{5}$$

In the following subsections, we implicitly use Theorem 1 and convergence stairs to derive upper bound of expected convergence time of transformed self-stabilizing algorithm.

4.2   Spanning Tree Algorithm BFS

Self-stabilizing algorithm for breadth-first search (BFS) spanning tree with a distinguished node under central daemon is shown in Figure 3 [10] [3]. We call this algorithm BFS in this paper. In BFS, the distinguished node v_R plays as the root of BFS tree. Each node v_i maintains a local variable for the distance $v_i.d$ from the root node and parent node $v_i.f$ in a BFS tree from its neighbor nodes.

Convergence of BFS proceeds from the root node. The root node v_R eventually fixes its local variables ($v_R.d = 0$ and $v_R.f = v_R$), Local variables of other nodes are maintained so that its parent node has the smallest distance from the root. Basically, convergence proceeds from the root node to other nodes in the order of the hop distance from the root node. However, this convergence scenario is interfered by some nodes that incorrectly hold small hop distanced from the root node. Thus, our upper bound is based on this observation.

Theorem 2. *For any network* G *with packet transmission probability* p, *expected convergence time of Algorithm BFS is bounded by*

$$T(BFS, G, p) = (2D + 1) \cdot \mathbf{E}[Z(2|E|, p)] \tag{6}$$

rounds.

Proof. The upper bound is derived in two steps. First we derive upper bound on the expected number of rounds to reach a configuration in which no node v_i holds smaller value than its hop distance from the root node v_R, i,e, $v_i.d <$

---

[3] Algorithm presented in Figure 3 is modification of the algorithm presented in [10] in such a way that Figure 3 does not use the number of nodes in the algorithm and two guarded-commands are merged into one.

Local variable of node v_i
  $v_i.d$: integer — the distance of v_i from the root node
  $v_i.f \in N_i$ — parent node of v_i in a BFS tree
Guarded commands of the root node v_R
$*[$ // GC0: Set root values
    $(v_R.d \neq 0) \vee (v_R.f \neq v_R)$
      $\rightarrow$ $v_R.d := 0;\ v_R.f := v_R$
$]$
Guarded commands of non-root node v_i
$*[$ // GC1: Select a parent
    $(v_i.d \neq \min\{v_j.d : v_j \in N_i\} + 1) \vee (v_i.f \neq v_k$ s.t. $v_k.d = \min\{v_j.d : v_j \in N_i\})$
      $\rightarrow$ $v_i.d := \min\{v_j.d : v_j \in N_i\} + 1;$
        $v_i.f := v_k$ s.t. $v_k.d = \min\{v_j.d : v_j \in N_i\};$
$]$

Fig. 3. Algorithm BFS [10]

$\mathrm{dist}(v_R, v_i)$. We will show that expected number of rounds for this is bounded by $D \cdot \mathbf{E}[Z(2|E|, p)]$ rounds. Then, convergence proceeds from the root node to other nodes in the order of hop distance from the root node. We show that expected number of rounds for this is bounded by $(D+1) \cdot \mathbf{E}[Z(2|E|, p)]$ rounds. In total, we have the upper bound $(2D+1) \cdot \mathbf{E}[Z(2|E|, p)]$.

First, we assume that any initial configuration γ_0 in which there is a node v_i such that $v_i.d < \mathrm{dist}(v_R, v_i)$. For any configuration γ, we denote, by $d(\gamma)$, the smallest value of $v_i.d$ among such nodes (if any) in configuration γ. Let γ_1 be a configuration such that state packet of each node v_i is successfully received by each neighbor node of v_i after γ_0.

Suppose that, in configuration γ_1, there exists a node, say v_j, such that $v_j.d < \mathrm{dist}(v_R, v_j)$. Then, we claim that $d(\gamma_0) < d(\gamma_1)$ holds. Let v_k be any node in γ_1 such that $v_k.d = d(\gamma_1)$. Then, v_k receives state packet at least once from each neighbor node from γ_0 to γ_1. Because we have $v_k.d < \mathrm{dist}(v_R, v_k)$ in γ_1 by assumption, each received value from any neighbor is larger than or equal to $d(\gamma_0)$. Hence, by algorithm definition, the value of $v_k.d$ in γ_1 is larger than $d(\gamma_0)$, i.e., $d(\gamma_0) < d(\gamma_1)$ holds.

Repeating the same observation D times, we have configuration γ_D in which $d(\gamma_D) \geq D$ holds (or $d(\gamma_D)$ is undefined) within at most $D \cdot \mathbf{E}[Z(2|E|, p)]$ expected rounds.

Next, we estimate upper bound on the expected number of rounds for convergence process from the root node to other nodes. Let

$$W_\ell = \{v_j \in V : \mathrm{dist}(v_R, v_j) = \ell\}, \text{ and}$$

$$M_\ell = \sum_{v_j \in W_\ell} |N_j|.$$

By definition, $W_0 = N_R$, $|W_0| = |N_R| = M_0$, and $M_\ell \leq 2|E|$ for any ℓ.

The state packet of the root node v_R is received at least once by each node $v_j \in W_0$ within expected $\mathbf{E}[Z(M_0, p)]$ rounds, and hence its local variables $v_j.d$ and

$v_j.f$ are fixed and remain unchanged in the following execution. Then, the state packet of each node $v_j \in W_1$ is received at least once by each node $v_j \in M_1$ within expected $\mathbf{E}[Z(M_1,p)]$ rounds, and hence its variables $v_j.d$ and $v_j.f$ are fixed and remain unchanged in the following execution. Repeating this observation, variables $v_j.d$ and $v_j.f$ for each process $v_j \in V$ are fixed within

$$\sum_{\ell=0}^{D} \mathbf{E}[Z(M_\ell,p)] \leq (D+1) \cdot \mathbf{E}[Z(2|E|,p)]$$

expected rounds, and convergence is done.

In total, we have the bound $(2D+1) \cdot \mathbf{E}[Z(2|E|,p)]$.

4.3 Maximal Independent Set Algorithm MIS

Self-stabilizing algorithm for maximal independent set (MIS) with no node identifier under central daemon is shown in Figure 4 [11]. We call this algorithm MIS in this paper.

Definition 2. *For any γ configuration of MIS, γ is cached-state consistent if and only if, for each node v_i,*

- *$v_i.x = 0$ implies $v_i.C[v_j,x] = 1$ for some $v_j \in N_i$, and*
- *$v_i.x = 1$ implies $v_i.C[v_j,x] = 0$ for any $v_j \in N_i$.*

Note that no node is enabled in a cached-state consistent configuration γ.

Lemma 1. *Let γ be any cached-state consistent configuration in which there exists at least one node v_i such that $v_i.x = 1$. Then, in any configuration γ' that follows γ, there is at least one node, say v_j, such that $v_j.x = 1$.*

Lemma 2. *Let γ_0 be any cached-state consistent configuration in which $v_i.x = 0$ for any node v_i. Then, expectation of the round number in which a node, say v_j, such that $v_j.x = 1$ appears for the first time is bounded by $\mathbf{E}[Z(\delta,p)]$.*

```
Local variable of node v_i
    v_i.x ∈ {0,1} — v_i.x = 1 iff v_i is a member of MIS
Guarded commands of node v_i
*[    // GC1: Join MIS.
        (v_i.x = 0) ∧ (∀v_k ∈ N_i[v_k.x ≠ 1])
        → v_i.x := 1;
        // GC2: Leave MIS.
    □ (v_i.x = 1) ∧ (∃v_k ∈ N_i[v_k.x = 1])
        → v_i.x := 0;
]
```

Fig. 4. Algorithm MIS [11]

Theorem 3. *For any network G with packet transmission probability p, expected convergence time of Algorithm MIS is bounded by*

$$T(MIS, G, p) = \mathbf{E}[Z(\delta, p)] + \beta(G)/p^{\Delta} + \mathbf{E}[Z(2|E|, p)] \qquad (7)$$

rounds, where $\beta(G)$ is the independence number of graph G.

Proof. Starting from any initial configuration, a node, say v_i, such that $v_i.x = 1$ appears within $\mathbf{E}[Z(\delta, p)]$ expected rounds by Lemma 2. Then, by Lemma 1, there is at least one node, say v_j, such that $v_j.x = 1$ in any configuration. We will show later that expected rounds so that each node computes MIS is at most $\beta(G)/p^{\Delta}$. Then, within $\mathbf{E}[Z(2|E|, p)]$ expected rounds, cache at each node becomes consistent. Thus, we have upper bound $\mathbf{E}[Z(\delta, p)] + \beta(G)/p^{\Delta} + \mathbf{E}[Z(2|E|, p)]$.

Now we show the bound of expectation $\beta(G)/p^{\Delta}$. Because there is at least one node v_i such that $v_i.x = 1$ at each round by Lemma 1, we observe such a node at each round. With probability $p^{|N_i|} \geq p^{\Delta}$, a packet sent by v_i is successfully received by all the neighbors N_i simultaneously. When this event occur, each $v_j \in N_i$ sets $v_j.C[v_i, x] = 1$ and, as a result, we have $v_j.x = 0$. Then, the values $v_i.x = 1$ and $v_j.x = 0$ for each $v_j \in N_i$ are fixed in any configuration thereafter because $v_i.C[v_j, x] = 0 \wedge v_j.C[v_i.x] = 1 \wedge v_j.x = 0$ for any $v_j \in N_i$.

By expectation of geometric distribution, some node v_i such that $v_i.x = 1$ and its neighbors fix their values of x at every expected $1/p^{|N_i|} \leq 1/p^{\Delta}$ rounds. Because the number of MIS nodes is at most $\beta(G)$, the expected number of rounds to compute MIS is bounded by $\beta(G)/p^{\Delta}$.

We have better analysis in case the network is complete.

Theorem 4. *For any complete network K with packet transmission probability p, expected convergence time of Algorithm MIS is bounded by*

$$T(MIS, K, p) = \mathbf{E}[Z(\delta, p)] + 2\mathbf{E}[Z(n-1, p)] \qquad (8)$$

rounds.

Proof. By the same reason discussed in the proof of Theorem 3, $\mathbf{E}[Z(\delta, p)] + \mathbf{E}[Z(n-1, p)]$ rounds are necessary to bound the number of rounds at the beginning and the end of converging computation. Below we show a bound $\mathbf{E}[Z(n-1, p)]$.

To show a bound $\mathbf{E}[Z(n-1, p)]$, we assume a configuration in which there is at least one node v_i such that $v_i.x = 1$. Because there is at least one node v_i such that $v_i.x = 1$ in any configuration by Lemma 1, we observe such a node at each round.

Let $n_0(\leq n)$ be the number of nodes v_i such that $v_i.x = 1$. At each round, a node, say v_i such that $v_i.x = 1$, sends a state packet. Other nodes receive it with probability p, and fail to receive it with probability $1 - p$. Our goal is to derive the number of rounds such that only one node with $x = 1$ remains.

To evaluate the upper bound of the expected number rounds, without loss of generally, we can assume that, for some node v_i, only v_i sends state packet at every round. Then, for other node v_j, the value of $v_j.x$ becomes 0 by successfully receiving a state packet of v_i which occurs with probability p, and the value of $v_j.x$ remains 0 thereafter. Thus, the upper bound of the expected number of rounds such that all the nodes except v_i to have $x = 0$ is given by $\mathbf{E}[Z(n-1,p)]$. That is, after $\mathbf{E}[Z(n-1,p)]$ expected rounds, only v_i is a node such that $x = 1$.

The analysis above applies for the self-stabilizing algorithm for maximal independent set (MIS) proposed in [12].

4.4 Maximal Independent Set Algorithm CDS

Self-stabilizing algorithm for connected dominating set (CDS) for node clustering with unique node identifier under central daemon is shown in Figure 5 [13]. We call this algorithm CDS in this paper. It is assumed that a spanning tree over a network is given by constants $v_i.d$ (distance from the root) and $v_i.f$ (parent node in the tree) for each node v_i, and a node v_i is the root node of a given spanning tree if and only if $v_i.d = 0$ and $v_i.f = v_i$. Each node v_i maintains two local variables $v_i.x$ and $v_i.y$. Node v_i is a member of CDS if and only if $v_i.x = 1$, and local variable $v_i.y$ is for internal use.

Constant
  $v_i.f$: parent node v_i in a spanning tree;
  $v_i.d$: distance of v_i from the root of a spanning tree;
Local variable of node v_i
  $v_i.x \in \{0,1\}$ — $v_i.x = 1$ iff v_i is a member of CDS;
  $v_i.y \in \{0,1\}$ — (internal) $v_i.y = 1$ iff v_i is a member of MIS;
Guarded commands of node v_i
*[// GC1: The root joins MIS and CDS.
    $(d_i = 0) \wedge ((v_i.x = 0) \vee (v_i.y = 0))$
        $\rightarrow\ v_i.x := 1;\ v_i.y := 1;$
    // GC2: Non root joins MIS.
  □ $(v_i.d > 0) \wedge (v_i.y = 0) \wedge (\forall v_j \in N_i : v_j.d > v_i.d \vee v_j.y = 0)$
        $\rightarrow\ v_i.y := 1;$
    // GC3: Non root leaves MIS.
  □ $(v_i.d > 0) \wedge (v_i.y = 0) \wedge (\exists v_j \in N_i : v_j.d \leq v_i.d \wedge v_j.y = 1)$
        $\rightarrow\ v_i.y := 1;$
    // GC4: Non root joins CDS.
  □ $(v_i.d > 0) \wedge \neg Grd_2 \wedge \neg Grd_3 \wedge (v_i.x = 0) \wedge (\exists v_j \in N_i : v_j.f = v_i \wedge v_j.y = 1)$
        $\rightarrow\ v_i.x := 1;$
    // GC5: Non root leaves CDS.
  □ $(v_i.d > 0) \wedge \neg Grd_2 \wedge \neg Grd_3 \wedge (v_i.x = 1) \wedge (\forall v_j \in N_i : v_j.f \neq v_i \vee v.j.y = 0)$
        $\rightarrow\ v_i.x := 0;$
]

Fig. 5. Algorithm CDS [13]

We denote, by v_R, the root node of a given spanning tree. Convergence proceeds as follows. First, the value of $v_R.x$ and $v_R.y$ is fixed by the root node v_R. Then, for each $\ell = 1, 2, ..$ in increasing order, nodes whose distance from the root is ℓ decide their values of local variable y. Finally, each node decides the values of their local variable x.

Theorem 5. *For any network G with packet transmission probability p, expected convergence time of Algorithm CDS is bounded by*

$$T(\mathsf{CDS}, G, p) = \mathbf{E}[Z(\Delta, p)] + D \cdot T(\mathsf{MIS}, G, p) + \mathbf{E}[Z(2|E|, p)] \tag{9}$$

rounds, provided a given spanning tree is a depth-first search tree, where D is the height of the tree.

Proof. First, state packet of the root node v_R is received by every neighbor nodes of v_R. The expected number of rounds for this is $\mathbf{E}[Z(|N_R|, p)]$ rounds, which is bounded by $\mathbf{E}[Z(\Delta, p)]$.

Next, for each $\ell = 1, 2, ..., D$, in this order, a set of nodes whose distance from the root node is ℓ in a spanning tree computes MIS to decide the value of $v_i.y$, and the value of $v_i.y$ is transmitted to all of their neighbors via state packet. Expected number of rounds for this step is trivially bounded by $T(\mathsf{MIS}, G, p)$ by Theorem 3. Because MIS computation is done for each $\ell = 1, 2, ..., D$, at most $D \cdot T(\mathsf{MIS}, G, p)$ expected rounds are required to fix the value of $v_i.y$ for each node v_i.

Finally, each node v_i fixes the value of $v_i.x$ according to the value of $v_i.y$. The value of $v_i.x$ is transmitted to its neighbor nodes in $\mathbf{E}[Z(2|E|, p)]$ expected rounds, and the system converges.

In total, we have at most $\mathbf{E}[Z(\Delta, p)] + D \cdot T(\mathsf{MIS}, G, p) + \mathbf{E}[Z(2|E|, p)]$ expected rounds to converge.

5   Conclusion

In this paper we present convergence time analysis of self-stabilizing distributed algorithms for sensor network obtained by lightweight transformation. Although previous works show only that a transformed algorithm converges with probability one for enough long time and do not show any explicit convergence time, this paper presents non-trivial and explicit upper bound on convergence time. Because our upper bound may not be tight, derivation of better upper bound is the next challenge. Our next project is to compare with our upper bound, simulation results and measurement with real sensor network.

References

1. Dijkstra, E.: Self-stabilizing systems in spite of distributed control. Communications of the ACM 17(11), 643–644 (1974)
2. Schneider, M.: Self-stabilization. ACM Computing Surveys 25(1), 45–67 (1993)
3. Dolev, S.: Self-stabilization. MIT Press, Cambridge (2000)

 4. Mizuno, M., Kakugawa, H.: A transformation of self-stabilizing programs for distributed computing environments. In: Babaoğlu, Ö., Marzullo, K. (eds.) WDAG 1996. LNCS, vol. 1151, pp. 304–321. Springer, Heidelberg (1996)
 5. Huang, S.T., Wuu, L.C., Tsai, M.S.: Distributed execution model for self-stabilizing systems. In: Proceedings of the 14th International Conference on Distributed Computing Systems (ICDCS), pp. 432–439 (1994)
 6. Herman, T.: Models of self-stabilization and sensor networks. In: IWDC 2003. LNCS, vol. 2918, pp. 205–214. Springer, Heidelberg (2003)
 7. Turau, V., Weyer, C.: Randomized self-stabilizing algorithms for wireless sensor networks. In: de Meer, H., Sterbenz, J.P.G. (eds.) IWSOS 2006. LNCS, vol. 4124, pp. 74–89. Springer, Heidelberg (2006)
 8. Szpankowski, W., Rego, V.: Yet another application of a binomial recurrence, order statistics. Computing 43, 401–410 (1990)
 9. Gouda, M.: The triumph and tribulation of system stabilization. In: Helary, J.-M., Raynal, M. (eds.) WDAG 1995. LNCS, vol. 972. Springer, Heidelberg (1995)
10. Huang, S.T., Chen, N.S.: A self-stabilizing algorithm for constructing breadth-first trees. Information Processing Letters 41, 109–117 (1992)
11. Shukla, S., Rosenkrantz, D., Ravi, S.: Observation on self-stabilizing graph algorithms for anonymous networks. In: Proceedings of the Second Workshop on Self-Stabilizing Systems, WSS (1995)
12. Ikeda, M., Kamei, S., Kakugawa, H.: A space-optimal self-stabilizing algorithm for the maximal independent set problem. In: Proceedings of the 3rd International Conference on Parallel and Distributed Computing, Applications and Technologies (PDCAT), pp. 70–74 (2002)
13. Kamei, S., Kakugawa, H.: A self-stabilizing distributed approximation algorithm for the minimum connected dominating set. In: Proceedings of the 9th IPDPS Workshop on Advances in Parallel and Distributed Computational Models, APDCM (2007)
14. Turau, V.: Linear self-stabilizing algorithms for the independent and dominating set problems using an unfair distributed scheduler. Information Processing Letters 103(3), 88–93 (2007)
15. Chen, N.S., Yu, H.P., Huang, S.T.: A self-stabilizing algorithm for constructing spanning trees. Information Processing Letters 39, 147–151 (1991)

Self-stabilizing Mobile Robot Formations with Virtual Nodes

Seth Gilbert[1], Nancy Lynch[2], Sayan Mitra[3,*], and Tina Nolte[2]

[1] Ecole Polytechnique Fédérale, Lausanne
[2] Massachusetts Institute of Technology
[3] University of Illinois at Urbana-Champaign

Abstract. In this paper, we describe how virtual infrastructure can be used to coordinate the motion of mobile robots in a 2-dimensional plane in the presence of dynamic changes in the underlying mobile ad hoc network, i.e., nodes joining, leaving, or failing. The mobile robots cooperate to implement a VSA Layer, in which a virtual stationary automaton (VSA) is associated with each region of the plane. The VSAs coordinate among themselves to distribute the robots as needed throughout the plane. The resulting motion coordination protocol is self-stabilizing, in that each robot can begin the execution in any arbitrary state and at any arbitrary location in the plane. In addition, self-stabilization ensures that the robots can adapt to changes in the desired formation.

1 Introduction

We study the problem of coordinating autonomous mobile devices. Consider, for example, firefighting robots deployed in forests and other fire-prone wilderness areas. Significant levels of coordination are required in order to combat the fire: the fire should be surrounded, "firebreaks" should be created, and it should be doused with water; in additiona, the firefighters may need to direct the actions of (potentially autonomous) helicopters carrying water. Similar scenarios arise in a variety of contexts, including search and rescue, emergency disaster response, remote surveillance, and military engagement, among many others. In fact, autonomous coordination has long been a central problem in mobile robotics.

We focus on a generic coordination problem that captures many of the complexities associated with these real-world scenarios. We assume that the mobile robots are deployed in a large two-dimensional plane, and that they can coordinate via local communication using wireless radios. The robots must arrange themselves to form a particular pattern, specifically, they must spread themselves evenly along a continuous curve drawn in the plane. In the firefighting example described above, this curve might form the perimeter of the fire.

These types of coordination problems can be quite challenging due to the dynamic and unpredictable environment that is inherent to wireless ad hoc networks. Robots may be continuously joining and leaving the system, and they

---

* Supported by NSF CSR program (Embedded & Hybrid systems area) under grant NSF CNS-0614993.

may fail. In addition, wireless communication is notoriously unreliable due to collisions, contention, and various wireless interference.

Virtual infrastructure has been proposed as a new tool for building reliable and robust applications in unreliable wireless ad hoc networks (e.g., [1,2,3,4]). The basic principle motivating virtual infrastructure is that many of the challenges in a dynamic networks could be avoided if there were real network infrastructure available. Unfortunately, in many contexts, such infrastructure is unavailable. Thus, the virtual infrastructure abstraction emulates real infrastructure in ad hoc networks. It has already been observed that virtual infrastructure simplifies several important problems, including distributed shared memory [2], tracking mobile devices [5], and geographic routing [1].

In this paper, we rely on a virtual infrastructure known as the Virtual Stationary Automata Layer (VSA Layer) [6,7]. Each robot is modelled as a *client* which interacts with *virtual stationary automata* (VSAs) via a (virtual) communication service. VSAs are distributed throughout the world, each assigned permanently to its own region. An advantage of VSAs is that they are less likely to fail than an individual mobile robot. Notice that the VSAs do not actually exist in the real world; they are emulated by the underlying mobile robots.

The VSA Layer is modeled in the Timed Input/Output Automata (TIOA) [8] framework. In TIOA parlance, an *emulation* is an implementation relationship between two sets of TIOAs: those that specify the VSA Layer and those that implement it. The emulation transforms an algorithm designed for the VSA Layer into an algorithm that runs directly on the mobile robots. An execution resulting from this transformation looks as if the original program is running on the VSA Layer; formally, the traces of the transformed system, restricted to non-broadcast actions at the client nodes, are traces of the VSA Layer. In [6,7], we show how to emulate the VSA Layer in a wireless network of mobile robots.

Here, we show how to use the VSA Layer to implement a reliable and robust protocol for coordinating mobile robots. The protocol relies on the VSAs to peform the coordination. Each VSA decides based on its local information which robots to keep in its own region and which to assign to neighboring regions. For each robot that remains, the VSA determines where the robot should go. In order that the robot coordination be robust, our coordination protocol is *self-stabilizing*, meaning that each robot can begin in an arbitrary state, in an arbitrary location in the network, and yet the distribution of the robots will converge to the specified curve. When combined with a self-stabilizing implementation of the VSA Layer, as is presented in [6,7], we end up with an entirely self-stabilizing solution for the problem of autonomous robot coordination.

Self-stabilization provides many advantages. Given the unreliable nature of wireless networks, occasionally (due to aberrant interference) messages may be lost, disrupting the protocol; a self-stabilizing algorithm can readily recover from this. In addition, a self-stabilizing algorithm can cope with more dynamic coordination problems when the desired formation of robots may change. In the firefighting example above the formation of firefighting robots must adapt as the fire evolves. A self-stabilizing algorithm can easily adapt to these changes.

The remainder of this paper is organized as follows. First, in Section 2, we discuss some of the related work. Next, in Section 3, we discuss the VSA Layer model. In Section 4 we describe the motion coordination problem, and describe our algorithm that solves it. In Section 5, we show that the algorithm is correct, and in Section 6, we show that the algorithm is self-stabilizing.

2   Related Work

The problem of motion coordination has been studied in a variety of contexts, including: flocking [9]; rendezvous [10,11,12]; aggregation [13]; deployment and regional coverage [14]; and pattern formation [15]. Control theory literature contains several algorithms for achieving spatial patterns [16,17,18,19]. These assume that agents process information and communicate reliably and synchronously.

Asynchronous vision-based model have also been investigated in [15,20,21,22] and [23]. In this model, agents are asynchronous, oblivious, and anonymous. Each agent repeatedly performs *look, compute*, and *move* actions to compute its next target position based on the current position of other visible agents. The class of patterns that can be formed depends on the common knowledge of the agents, such as common compass and common coordinates [15,23].

We have previously presented a protocol for coordinating mobile devices using virtual infrastructure in [24]. This earlier protocol relies on a more powerful class of virtual infrastructure (see [6,7]), and hence, our new protocol is somewhat simpler (and more elegant). Moreover, the new protocol is self-stabilizing, which allows both for better fault-tolerance, and also the ability to tolerate dynamic changes in the desired pattern of motion. Virtual infrastructure has also been considered in [25] in the context of coordinating airplane flight.

3   Virtual Stationary Automata

The Virtual Stationary Automata (VSA) infrastructure has been presented earlier in [6,7]. The architecture of this abstraction layer is shown in Figure 1. In this section, we informally describe these components.

Network tiling. We fix R to be a closed, bounded and connected subset of $\mathbb{R}^2$, and U, P to be two totally ordered index sets. R models the physical space in which the robots reside; we call it the *deployment space*. U and P serve as the index sets for regions in R and for the participating robots, respectively. A network tiling divides R into a set of *regions* $\{R_u\}_{u \in U}$, such that: (i) for each $u \in U$, R_u is a closed, connected subset of R, and (ii) for any $u, v \in U$, R_u and R_v may overlap only at their boundaries. For any $u, v \in U$, the corresponding regions are said to be *neighbors* if $R_u \cap R_v \neq \emptyset$. This neighborhood relation, *nbrs*, induces a graph on the set of regions. We assume that the resulting graph is connected. Throughout this paper, we assume that each region has at most four neighbors; generalizing to an arbitrary number of neighbors is straightforward. We define

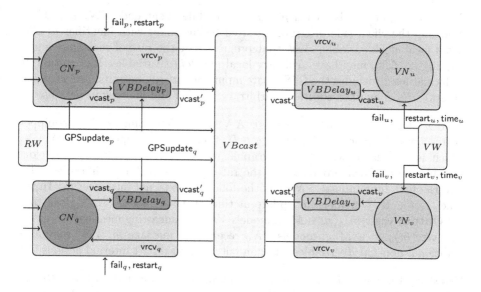

Fig. 1. Virtual Stationary Automata layer

the distance between regions u and v, denoted $regDist(u,v)$, as the minimum number of hops between u and v in the graph. The diameter of the graph, i.e., the distance between the farthest regions, is denoted by D, and the largest Euclidean distance between any two points in any region is denoted by r.

Real World (RW) Automaton. RW is an external source of occasional but reliable time and location information for participating robots. The RW automaton is parameterized by: (a) $v_{max} > 0$, a maximum speed, and (b) $\epsilon_{sample} > 0$, a maximum time gap between successive updates for each robot. The RW automaton maintains three key variables: (a) a continuous variable now representing true system time; now increases monotonically at the same rate as real-time starting from 0. (b) An array $vel[P \rightarrow R \cup \{\bot\}]$; for $p \in P$, $vel(p)$ represents the current velocity of robot p. Initially $vel(p)$ is set to $\bot$, and it is updated by the robots when their velocity changes. (c) an array $loc[P \rightarrow R]$; for $p \in P$, $loc(p)$ represents the current location of robot p. Over any interval of time, robot p may move arbitrarily in R provided its path is continuous and its maximum speed is bounded by v_{max}. Automaton RW performs the GPSupdate$(l,t)_p$ action, $l \in R, t \in \mathbb{R}_{\geq 0}, p \in P$, to inform robot p about its current location and time. For each p, some GPSupdate$(,)_p$ action must occur every ϵ_{sample} time.

Virtual World (VW) Automaton. VW is an external source of occasional but reliable time information for VSAs. Similar to RW's GPSupdate action for clients, VW performs time$(t)_u$ output actions notifying VSAs of the current time. One such action occurs at time 0, and they are repeated at least every ϵ_{sample} time thereafter. Also, VW nondeterministically issues fail$_u$ and restart$_u$ outputs for each $u \in U$, modelling the fact that VSAs may fail and restart.

Mobile client nodes. For each $p \in P$, the mobile client node CN_p is a TIOA modeling the client-side program executed by the robot with identifier p. CN_p has a local clock variable, *clock* that progresses at the rate of real-time, and is initially $\bot$. CN_p may have arbitrary local non-*failed* variables. Its external interface at least includes the GPSupdate inputs, vcast$(m)_p$ outputs, and vrcv$(m)_p$ inputs. CN_p may have additional arbitrary non-fail and non-restart actions.

Virtual Stationary Automata (VSAs). A VSA is a deterministic clock-equipped abstract virtual machine. For each $u \in U$, there is a corresponding VSA VN_u which is associated with the geographic region R_u. VN_u has a local clock variable *clock* which progresses at the rate of real-time. (It is initially $\bot$ before the first time input.) VN_u has the following external interface: (a) **Input** time$(t)_u, t \in \mathbb{R}^{\geq 0}$, models an update at time t; it sets node VN_u's *clock* to t. (b) **Output** vcast$(m)_u, m \in Msg$, models VN_u broadcasting message m. (c) **Input** vrcv$(m)_u, m \in Msg$, models VN_u receiving a message m. VN_u may have additional non-*failed* variables and non-fail and non-restart internal actions.

VBDelay *Automata.* Each client and VSA node is associated with a *VBDelay* buffer that delays messages when they are broadcast for up to e time. This buffer takes as input a vcast(m) from the node and relays the message to the *VBcast* service after some delay of at most e. In the case of VSA nodes, there is no delay.

VBcast *Automaton.* Each client and virtual node has access to the virtual broadcast communication service *VBcast*. The service is parameterized by a constant $d > 0$ which bounds message delays. *VBcast* takes each vcast$'(m, f)_i$ input (from the delay buffers) and delivers the message m via vrcv(m) at each client or virtual node that is in the same region as the initial sender, when the message was first sent, along with those in neighboring regions. The *VBcast* service guarantees that in each execution of *VBcast* there is a correspondence between vrcv(m) actions and vcast$'(m, f)_i$ actions such that: (i) each vrcv occurs *after and within* d *time* of the corresponding vcast$'$, (ii) at most one vrcv at a process is mapped to each vcast$'$. (iii) a message originating from some region u must be received by all robots that are in R_u or its neighbors throughout the transmission period.

A VSA layer *algorithm* is an assignment of a TIOA program to each client and VSA. We denote the set of all V-algorithms is as *VAlgs*. We now define a *VLayer*, i.e., a VSA layer with failure-prone clients and VSAs.

Definition 1. *Let alg be an element of Valgs. VLNodes[alg], the fail-transformed nodes of the VSA layer parameterized by alg, is the composition of each alg(i), modified so as to fail by crashing, with a* VBDelay *buffer, for all* $i \in P \cup U$. *VLayer[alg], the VSA layer parameterized by alg, is the composition of VLNodes[alg] with RW∥VW∥VBcast.*

4   Motion Coordination Using Virtual Nodes

In this paper we fix $\Gamma : A \rightarrow R$ to be a simple, differentiable curve on R that is parameterized by arc length. The domain set A of parameter values is an interval in the real line. We also fix a particular network tiling given by the collection of regions $\{R_u\}_{u \in U}$ such that each point in Γ is also in some region R_u. Let $A_u \triangleq \{p \in A : region(\Gamma(p)) = u\}$ be the domain of Γ in region u. We assume that A_u is convex for every region u; it may be empty for some u. The local part of the curve Γ in region u is the restriction $\Gamma_u : A_u \to R_u$. We write $|A_u|$ for the length of the curve Γ_u. We define the *quantization* of a real number x with quantization constant $\sigma > 0$ as $q_\sigma(x) = \lceil \frac{x}{\sigma} \rceil \sigma$. We fix σ, and write q_u as an abbreviation for $q_\sigma(|A_u|)$, q_{min} for the minimum nonzero q_u, and q_{max} for the maximum q_u.

Our goal is to design an algorithm for mobile robots such that, once the failures and recoveries cease, within finite time all the robots are located on Γ and as time progresses they eventually become equally spaced on Γ. Formally, if no fail and **restart** actions occur after time t_0, then:

(1) there exists a constant T, such that for each $u \in U$, within time $t_o + T$ the set of robots located in R_u becomes fixed and its cardinality is roughly proportional to q_u; moreover, if $q_u \neq 0$ then the robots in R_u are located on[1] Γ_u, and

(2) as time goes to infinity, all robots in R_u are evenly spaced[2] on Γ_u.

4.1   Solution Using Virtual Node Layer

The VSA Layer is used as a means to coordinate the movement of client nodes, i.e., robots. A VSA controls the motion of the clients in its region by setting and broadcasting target waypoints for the clients: VSA VN_u, $u \in U$, periodically receives information from clients in its region, exchanges information with its neighbors, and sends out a message containing a calculated target point for each client node "assigned" to region u. VN_u performs two tasks when setting the target points: (1) it re-assigns some of the clients that are assigned to itself to neighboring VSAs, and (2) it sends a target position on Γ to each client that is assigned to itself. The objective of (1) is to prevent neighboring VSAs from getting depleted of robots and to achieve a distribution of robots over the regions that is proportional to the length of Γ in each region. The objective of (2) is to space the nodes evenly on Γ within each region. The client algorithm, in turn, receives its current position information from RW and computes a velocity vector for reaching its latest received target point from a VSA.

Each virtual node VN_u uses only information about the portions of the target curve Γ in region u and neighboring regions. We assume that all client nodes know the complete curve Γ; however, we could model the client nodes in u as receiving external information about the nature of the curve in region u and neighboring regions only.

---

[1] For a given point $\mathbf{x} \in R$, if there exists $p \in A$ such that $\Gamma(p) = \mathbf{x}$, then we say that the point $\mathbf{x}$ is on the curve Γ; abusing the notation, we write this as $\mathbf{x} \in \Gamma$.

[2] A sequence $\mathbf{x}_1, \ldots, \mathbf{x}_n$ of points in R is said to be *evenly spaced* on a curve Γ if there exists a sequence of parameter values $p_1 < p_2 \ldots < p_n$, such that for each i, $1 \leq i \leq n$, $\Gamma(p_i) = \mathbf{x}_i$, and for each i, $1 < i < n$, $p_i - p_{i-1} = p_{i+1} - p_i$.

```
 1   Signature:
 2     Input time(t)ᵤ, t ∈ ℝ≥⁰
 3     Input vrcv(m)ᵤ, m ∈ ({cn-update} ×P ×R) ∪ ({vn-update} ×U ×ℕ)
 4     Output vcast(m)ᵤ, m ∈ ({vn-update} ×{u} ×ℕ) ∪ ({target-update} ×(P → R))
 5
 6   State:
 7     analog clock: ℝ≥⁰∪ {⊥}, initially ⊥.
 8     M:P→R, initially ∅.
 9     V : U → ℕ, initially ∅.
10
11   Trajectories:
12     evolve if clock ≠ t then d(clock) = 1 else d(clock) = 0
13     stop when Any precondition is satisfied.
14
15   Transitions:
16     Input: time(t)ᵤ
17     Effect: if clock ≠ t ∨ t mod δ ∉ (0, e + 2d + 2ε] then M, V ← ∅; clock ← t
18
19     Input: vrcv(⟨cn-update, id, loc⟩)ᵤ
20     Effect: if u = region(loc) and clock mod δ ∈ (0, d] then M(id) ← loc; V ← ∅
21
22     Output: vcast(⟨vn-update, u, n⟩)ᵤ
23     Precondition: (clock mod δ) = d+ε and n= |M|≠ 0 and V≠ {⟨u, n⟩}
24     Effect: V ← {⟨u, n⟩}
25
26     Input vrcv(⟨vn-update, id, n⟩)ᵤ
27     Effect: if id ∈ nbrs(u) then V(id) ← n
28
29     Output vcast(⟨target-update, target⟩)ᵤ
30     Precondition: (clock mod δ) = e + 2d + 2ε and M ≠ ∅
31                   target = calctarget(assign(id(M), V), M)
32     Effect: M, V ← ∅
```

Fig. 2. TIOA $VN(k, \rho_1, \rho_2)_u$ with parameters: safety k; damping ρ_1, ρ_2

4.2   Client Node Algorithm (CN)

The algorithm for the client node $CN(\delta)_p, p \in P$ follows a round structure, where rounds begin at times that are multiples of δ. At the beginning of each round, a CN stops moving and sends a cn-update message to its local VSA (that is, the VSA in whose region the CN currently resides). The cn-update message tells the local VSA the CN's id and its current location in R. The local VN then sends a response to the client, i.e., a target-update message. Each such message describes the new target location $\mathbf{x}_p^*$ for CN_p, and possibly an assignment to a different region. CN_p computes its velocity vector $\mathbf{v}_p$, based on its current position $\mathbf{x}_p$ and its target position $\mathbf{x}_p^*$, as $\mathbf{v}_p = (\mathbf{x}_p - \mathbf{x}_p^*)/\|\mathbf{x}_p - \mathbf{x}_p^*\|$ and communicates $v_{max}\mathbf{v}_p$ to RW, moving it with maximum velocity towards the target.

4.3   Virtual Stationary Node Algorithm (VN)

The algorithm for virtual node $VN(k, \rho_1, \rho_2)_u, u \in U$, appears in Figure 2, where $k \in \mathbb{Z}^+$ and $\rho_1, \rho_2 \in (0, 1)$ are parameters of the TIOA. VN_u collects cn-update messages sent at the beginning of the round from CN's located in region R_u, and aggregates the location and round information in a table, M. When $d + \epsilon$ time

```
1    function assign(assignedM: 2^P, y: nbrs^+(u) → ℕ) =
2       assign: P → U, initially {⟨i, u⟩} for each i ∈ assignedM
3       n: ℕ, initially y(u); ra: ℕ, initially 0
4       if y(u) > k then
5          if q_u ≠ 0 then
6             let lower = {g ∈ nbrs(u): (q_g/q_u)y(u) > y(g)}
7             for each g ∈ lower
8                ra ← min(⌊ρ_2 · ⌈(q_g/q_u)y(u) − y(g)⌉/2(|lower|+1)⌋, n − k)
9                update assign by reassigning ra nodes from u to g
10               n ← n − ra
11          else if {v ∈ nbrs(u): q_v ≠ 0} = ∅ then
12             let lower = {g ∈ nbrs(u) : y(u) > y(g)}
13             for each g ∈ lower
14                ra ← min(⌊ρ_2 · ⌈y(u) − y(g)⌉/2(|lower|+1)⌋, n − k)
15                update assign by reassigning ra nodes from u to g
16                n ← n − ra
17          else ra ← ⌊ (y(u) -k)/ |{v ∈ nbrs(u): q_v ≠ 0}| ⌋
18             for each g ∈ {v ∈ nbrs(u): q_v ≠ 0}
19                update assign by reassigning ra nodes from u to g
20       return assign
21
22   function calctarget(assign: P → U, locM: P → R) =
23       seq: indexed list of pairs in A × P, sorted by the index A and then , P, initially the list:
24          ⟨p, i⟩, ∀i ∈ P : (assign(i)= u) and (locM(i) ∈ Γ_u) and p= Γ_u^{-1}(locM(i))
25       for each i ∈ P : assign(i) ≠ null
26          if assign(i) = g ≠ u then locM(i) ← o_g
27          else if locM(i) ∉ Γ_u then locM(i) ← choose {min_{x∈Γ_u}{dist(x, locM(i))}}
28          else let p = Γ_u^{-1}(locM(i)), seq(k) = ⟨p, i⟩
29             if k = first(seq) then locM(i) ← Γ_u(inf(A_u))
30             else if k = last(seq) then locM(i) ← Γ_u(sup(A_u))
31             else let seq(k − 1) = ⟨p_{k−1}, i_{k−1}⟩
32                seq(k + 1) = ⟨p_{k+1}, i_{k+1}⟩
33                locM(i) ← Γ_u(p + ρ_1 · ((p_{k−1}+p_{k+1})/2 − p))
34       return locM
```

Fig. 3. Functions assign and calctarget for the case where $VN(k, \rho_1, \rho_2)_u$ has at most 4 neighbors

passes from the beginning of the round, VN_u computes from M the number of client nodes assigned to it that it has heard from in the round, and sends this information in a vn-update message to all of its neighbors.

When VN_u receives a vn-update message from a neighboring VN, it stores the CN population information in a table, V. When $e + d + \epsilon$ time from the sending of its own vn-update passes, VN_u uses the information in its tables M and V about the number of CNs in its and its neighbors' regions to calculate how many CNs assigned to itself should be reassigned and to which neighbor. This is done through the assign function, and these assignments are then used to calculate new target points for local CNs through the calctarget function (see Figure 3).

If the number of CNs assigned to VN_u exceeds the minimum *safe number* k, then assign reassigns some CNs to neighbors. Let In_u denote the set of neighboring VNs of VN_u that are on the curve Γ and $y_u(g)$, denote the number $num(V_u(g))$ of CNs assigned to VN_g, where g is either u or a neighbor of u. If $q_u \neq 0$, meaning VN_u is on the curve then we let $lower_u$ denote the subset of $nbrs(u)$ that are on the curve and have fewer assigned CNs than VN_u has after normalizing with $\frac{q_g}{q_u}$. For each $g \in lower_u$, VN_u reassigns the smaller of the following two quantities of CNs to VN_g: (1) $ra = \rho_2 \cdot [\frac{q_g}{q_u} y_u(u) - y_u(g)]/2(|lower_u| + 1)$, where $\rho_2 < 1$ is a *damping factor*, and (2) the remaining number of CNs over k still assigned to VN_u.

If $q_u = 0$, meaning VN_u is not on the curve, and VN_u has no neighbors on the curve (lines 11–15), then we let $lower_u$ denote the subset of $nbrs(u)$ with fewer assigned CNs than VN_u. For each $g \in lower_u$, VN_u reassigns the smaller of the following two quantities of CNs: (1) $ra = \rho_2 \cdot [y_u(u) - y_u(g)]/2(|lower_u| + 1)$ and (2) the remaining number of CNs over k still assigned to VN_u. VN_u is on a *boundary* if $q_u = 0$, but there is a $g \in nbrs(u)$ with $q_g \neq 0$. In this case, $y_u(u) - k$ of VN_u's CNs are assigned equally to neighbors in In_u (lines 17–19).

The calctarget function assigns to every CN_p in the region of VN_u a target point $locM_u(p)$, either in region u or one of u's neighbors. The target point $locM_u(p)$ is computed as follows: If CN_p is assigned to VN_g, $g \neq u$, then its target is set to the center $\mathbf{o}_g$ of region g (lines 26–26); if CN_p is assigned to VN_u but is not located on the curve Γ_u then its target is set to the nearest point on the curve, nondeterministically choosing one (lines 27–27); if CN_p is either the first or last client node on Γ_u then its target is set to the corresponding endpoint of Γ_u (lines 29–30); if CN_p is on the curve but is not the first or last client node then its target is moved to the mid-point of the locations of the preceding and succeeding CNs on the curve (line 33). For the last two computations a sequence seq of nodes on the curve sorted by curve location is used (line 24). Lastly, VN_u broadcasts new waypoints via a target-update message to its clients.

Round length. Let r be the maximum Euclidean distance between points in neighboring regions. It can take $\frac{r}{v_{max}}$ time for a client to reach its target. After the client arrives, the VN may have failed. Let d_r be the time it takes a VN to restart. During each round: a client sends a cn-update, the VNs exchange information, clients receive target-updates, clients move to their new target and restart any VNs. This requires that δ satisfy $\delta > 2e + 3d + 2\epsilon + r/v_{max} + d_r$.

5   Correctness of Algorithm

In this section we describe the steps in proving Theorem 1; the complete proofs will appear in the full version of the paper. We define round t as the interval of time $[\delta(t - 1), \delta \cdot t)$. That is, round t begins at time $\delta(t - 1)$ and is completed by time $\delta \cdot t$. We say $CN_p, p \in P$, is *active* in round t if node p is not failed throughout round t. A VN_u, $u \in U$, is *active* in round t if there is some active CN_p such that $region(\mathbf{x}_p) = u$ for the duration of rounds $t - 1$ and t. Thus, by definition, none of the VN s is active in the first round.

Let $In(t) \subseteq VN$ denote the identifiers $u \in U$ such that VN_u is active in round t and $q_u \neq 0$. The set $Out(t) \subseteq VN$ denote the identifiers $u \in U$ such that VN_u is active in round t and $q_u = 0$. The set $C(t)$ is the subset of active CNs at round t, and $C_{in}(t)$ and $C_{out}(t)$ are the sets of active CNs located in regions with ids in $In(t)$ and $Out(t)$, respectively, at the beginning of round t.

For every pair of regions u, w and for every round t, we define $y(w, t)_u$ to be the value of $V(w)_u$ (i.e., the number of clients u believes are available in region w) immediately prior to VN_u performing a vcast$_u$ in round t. If there are no new client failures or recoveries in round t, then for every pair of regions $u, w \in nbrs^+(v)$, we can conclude that $y(v, t)_u = y(v, t)_w$, which we denote simply as $y(v, t)$. We define $\rho_3 \triangleq \frac{q_{max}^2}{(1-\rho_2)\sigma}$.

For the rest of this section we fix a particular round number t_0 and assume that $\forall p \in P$, no fail$_p$ or recover$_p$ events occur at or after round t_0. First we establish that in every round $t \geq t_0$: (1) If $y(u, t) \geq k$ for some $u \in U$, then $y(u, t + 1) \geq k$; (2) $In(t) \subseteq In(t + 1)$; (3) $Out(t) \subseteq Out(t + 1)$. Next, we identify a round $t_1 \geq t_0$ after which the set of regions $In(t)$ and $Out(t)$ remain fixed. That is, we show that there exists a round $t_1 \geq t_0$ such that for every round $t \in [t_1, t_1 + (1 + \rho_3)m^2n^2]$: (1) $In(t) = In(t_1)$; (2) $Out(t) = Out(t_1)$; (3) $C_{in}(t) \subseteq C_{in}(t + 1)$; and (4) $C_{out}(t + 1) \subseteq C_{out}(t)$. We fix t_1 such that it satisfies the above conditions. The next lemma states that eventually, regions bordering on the curve stop assigning clients to regions that are on the curve.

Lemma 1. *There exists some round $t_2 \in [t_1, t_1 + (1 + \rho_3)m^2n^2]$ such that for every round $t \in [t_2, t_2 + (1 + \rho_3)m^2n]$: if $u \in Out(t)$ and $v \in In(t)$ and if u and v are neighboring regions, then u does not assign any clients to v in round t.*

Fix t_2 for the rest of this section such that it satisfies Lemma 1. From the above discussion, it follows that in every round $t \geq t_1$, $In(t) = In(t_1)$ and $Out(t) = Out(t_1)$; we denote these simply as In and Out. The next lemma states a key property of the assign function after round t_1. For a round $t \geq t_1$, consider some VN_u, $u \in Out(t)$, and assume that VN_w is the neighbor of VN_u assigned the most clients in round t. Then we can conclude that VN_u is assigned no more clients in round $t + 1$ than VN_w is assigned in round t. A similar claim holds for regions in $In(t)$, but in this case with respect to the *density* of clients with respect to the quantized length of the curve. The next lemma states that there exists a round T_{out} such that in every round $t \geq T_{out}$, the set of CNs assigned to region $u \in Out(t)$ does not change.

Lemma 2. *There exists a round $T_{out} \in [t_2, t_2 + m^2n$ such that in any round $t \geq T_{out}$, the set of CNs assigned to VN_u, $u \in Out(t)$, is unchanged.*

For the rest of the section we fix T_{out} to be the first round after t_0, at which the property stated by Lemma 2 holds. This implies that in every round $t \geq T_{out}$, $C_{In}(t) = C_{In}(t_1)$ and $C_{Out}(t) = C_{Out}(t_1)$; we denote these simply as C_{In} and C_{Out}. The next lemma states a property similar to that of Lemma 2 for VN_u, $u \in In$, and the argument is similar to the proof of Lemma 2.

Lemma 3. *There exists a round $T_{stab} \in [T_{out}, T_{out} + \rho_3m^2n]$ such that in every round $t \geq T_{stab}$, the set of CNs assigned to VN_u, $u \in In$, is unchanged.*

We prove that the number of clients located in regions with ids in Out is upper-bounded by $O(m^3)$. Next, fixing T_{stab} to be the first round after T_{out} at which the property stated by Lemma 3 holds, we are able to prove that the number of clients assigned to each VN_u, $u \in In$, in the stable assignment after T_{stab} is proportional to q_u within a constant additive term. From line 27 of Figure 3, it follows that by the beginning of round $T_{stab} + 2$, all CNs in C_{in} are located on the curve Γ, satisfying our first goal. The next lemma states that the locations of the CNs in each region $u \in In$, are evenly spaced on Γ_u in the limit; it is proved by analyzing the behavior of calctarget as a discrete time dynamical system.

Lemma 4. *Consider a sequence of rounds $t_1 = T_{stab}, \dots, t_n$. As $n \to \infty$, the locations of CNs in u, $u \in In$, are evenly spaced on Γ_u.*

Thus we conclude by summarizing the results in this section:

Theorem 1. *If there are no* fail *or* restart *actions for robots at or after some round t_0, then within a finite number of rounds after t_0:*

1. *The set of CNs assigned to each VN_u, $u \in U$, becomes fixed, and the size of the set is proportional to the quantized length q_u, within an a constant additive term $\frac{10(2m-1)}{q_{min}\rho_2}$.*
2. *All client nodes in a region $u \in U$ for which $q_u \neq 0$ are located on Γ_u and evenly spaced on Γ_u in the limit.*

6   Self-stabilization

In this section we show that the VSA-based motion coordination scheme is self-stabilizing. Specifically, we show that when the VSA and client components in the VSA layer start out in some arbitrary state (owing to failures and restarts), they eventually return to a reachable state. Thus, the visible behavior, or *traces*, of $VLayer[MC]$ running with some reachable state of $Vbcast\|RW\|VW$, eventually, becomes indistinguishable from a reachable trace of $VLayer[MC]$.

We first show that our motion coordination algorithm $VNodes[MC]$ is self-stabilizing to some set of legal states L_{MC}. Then, we show that these legal states correspond to reachable states of $VLayer[MC]$; hence, the traces of our motion coordination algorithm, where clients and VSAs start in an arbitrary state, eventually look like reachable traces of the correct motion coordination algorithm. Here MC is the motion coordination algorithm of Section 4.

6.1   Definitions and General Results

We begin with some basic claims. Through out this section A, A_1, A_2, etc., are sets of actions and V is a set of variables. An (A, V)-sequence is a (possibly infinite) alternating sequence of actions in A and trajectories of V. Given (A, V)-sequences α, α' and $t \geq 0$, α' is a *t-suffix of α* if there exists a closed (A, V)-sequence α'' of duration t such that $\alpha = \alpha''\alpha'$. α' is a *state-matched t-suffix of α* if it is a t-suffix of α, and the first state of α' equals the last state of α''.

Given a set of (A_1, V)-sequences S_1, a set of (A_2, V)-sequences S_2, and $t \geq 0$, S_1 is said to *stabilizes in time t* to S_2 if each state-matched t-suffix α of each sequence in S_1 is in S_2. This *stabilizes to* relation is transitive as per the following:

Lemma 5. *Let S_i be a set of (A_i, V)-sequences, for $i \in \{1, 2, 3\}$. If S_1 stabilizes to S_2 in time t_1, and S_2 stabilizes to S_3 in time t_2, then S_1 stabilizes to S_3 in time $t_1 + t_2$.*

Let $\mathcal{A}$ be any TIOA with set of states $Q_{\mathcal{A}}$, and L be a nonempty subset of $Q_{\mathcal{A}}$. L is said to be a *legal set* for $\mathcal{A}$ if it is closed under the transitions and closed trajectories of $\mathcal{A}$. For any $L \subseteq Q_{\mathcal{A}}$, $Start(\mathcal{A}, L)$ is defined to be the TIOA that is identical to $\mathcal{A}$ except with starting states L. We define $U(\mathcal{A}) \triangleq Start(\mathcal{A}, Q_{\mathcal{A}})$ and $R(\mathcal{A}) \triangleq Start(\mathcal{A}, \mathsf{Reach}_{\mathcal{A}})$, where $\mathsf{Reach}_{\mathcal{A}}$ is the set of reachable states of $\mathcal{A}$.

Definition 2. *Let $\mathcal{B}$ and $\mathcal{A}$ be compatible TIOAs, and L be a legal set for the composed TIOA $\mathcal{A} \| \mathcal{B}$. $\mathcal{A}$ self-stabilizes in time t to L relative to $\mathcal{B}$ if the set of executions of $U(\mathcal{A}) \| \mathcal{B}$ stabilizes in time t to executions of $Start(\mathcal{A} \| \mathcal{B}, L)$.*

As per the theory of stabilizing emulations, assume we have a stabilizing VSA layer emulation such that each algorithm $alg \in VAlgs$ stabilizes in some t_{Vstab} time to traces of $U(VLNodes[alg]) \| R(RW \| VW \| Vbcast)$ that satisfy the additional property that for any $u \in U$, if there exists a client that has been in region u and alive for d_r time and no alive clients in the region failed or left in that time, then VSA V_u is not failed. In the context of this work, this means that if VSA layer algorithm MC is such that $VLNodes[MC]$ self-stabilizes in some time t to L_{MC} relative to $R(RW \| VW \| Vbcast)$, then we can conclude that physical node traces of the emulation algorithm on MC stabilize in time $t_{Vstab} + t$ to client traces of executions of the VSA layer started in legal set L_{MC} and that satisfy the above failure-related properties.

6.2 Self-stabilization of Our Algorithm

We now describe two legal sets for $VLayer[MC]$, the second a subset of the first. The first is a set of states that results after the first GPSupdate at each client and the first time at each virtual node. It is easy to verify that this is a legal set.

Definition 3. *We define L_{MC}^1 to be the set of states $x \in X_{VLayer[MC]}$ such that the following hold:*

1. $x \lceil X_{Vbcast \| RW \| VW} \in Reach_{Vbcast \| RW \| VW}$.
2. $\forall u \in U : \neg failed_u : clock_u \in \{RW.now, \perp\} \wedge (M_u \neq \emptyset \Rightarrow clock_u \mod \delta \in (0, e + 2d + 2\epsilon])$.
3. $\forall p \in P : \neg failed_p \Rightarrow \mathbf{v}_p \in \{RW.vel(p)/v_{max}, \perp\}$.
4. $\forall p \in P : \neg failed_p \wedge \mathbf{x}_p \neq \perp:$
   (a) $\mathbf{x}_p = RW.loc(p) \wedge clock_p = RW.now$.
   (b) $\mathbf{x}_p^* \in \{\mathbf{x}_p, \perp\} \vee \|\mathbf{x}_p^* - \mathbf{x}_p\| < v_{max}(\delta \lceil clock_p/\delta \rceil - clock_p - d_r)$.
   (c) $Vbcast.reg(p) = region(\mathbf{x}_p) \vee clock \mod \delta \in (e+2d+2\epsilon, \delta-d_r+\epsilon_{sample})$.

Part 1 means that x restricted to the state of $Vbcast \| RW \| VW$ is a reachable state of $Vbcast \| RW \| VW$. Part 2 means that the nonfailed VSAs have *clocks* that are either equal to real-time or $\perp$, and have nonempty M only after the beginning of a round and up to $e + 2d + 2\epsilon$ time into a round. Part 3 requires that nonfailed clients have velocity vectors that are equal either to $\perp$ or equal to the client's velocity vector in RW, scaled down by v_{max}. Part 4 has three sub-parts and they assert that nonfailed clients with non-$\perp$ positions have (a) positions equal to their actual location and local *clocks* equal to the real-time, (b) targets equal to $\perp$ or the current location or a point reachable from the current location before a certain time (d_r), and (c) *Vbcast* last region updates that match the current region or the time is within a certain time window in a round. The following stabilization result is also easy to verify.

Lemma 6. *VLNodes[MC] is self-stabilizing to L^1_{MC} in time $t > \epsilon_{sample}$ relative to the automaton $R(Vbcast\|RW\|VW)$.*

The main legal set L_{MC} for our algorithm is described as the set of reachable states from a set of *reset* states.

Definition 4. *Define $Reset_{MC}$ to be the set of states $x \in X_{VLayer[MC]}$ such that the following properties hold:*

1. $x \in L^1_{MC}$.
2. $\forall p \in P : \neg failed_p \Rightarrow [tosnd^-_p = tosnd^+_p = \lambda \wedge (\mathbf{x}_p = \perp \vee [\mathbf{x}^*_p \neq \perp \wedge \mathbf{v}_p = 0])]$.
3. $\forall u \in U : \neg failed_u \Rightarrow to\_send_u = \lambda$.
4. $\forall \langle m, u, t, P' \rangle \in vbcastq : P' = \emptyset$.
5. $RW.now \mod \delta = 0 \wedge \forall p \in P : \forall \langle l, t \rangle \in RW.updates(p) : t < RW.now$.

L_{MC} *is the set of reachable states of $Start(VLayer[MC], Reset_{MC})$.*

Part 2 states that each nonfailed client has empty queues in its *VBDelay* and either has a position variable equal to $\perp$ or else has both a non-$\perp$ target and 0 velocity. Part 3 requires that each nonfailed VSA has an empty queue in its *VBDelay*. By Part 4 there are no pending messages in *Vbcast*, and Part 5 means that the time is the starting time for a round and that no GPSupdates have yet occurred at this time. It is easy to see that that L_{MC} is a legal set for *VLayer[MC]*. We show that starting from a state in L^1_{MC}, we reach a reset state which implies that eventually we arrive at a state in L_{MC}.

Lemma 7. *Executions of VLayer[MC] started in states in L^1_{MC} stabilize in time $\delta + d + e$ to executions started in states in L_{MC}.*

Now we can combine our stabilization results to conclude that *VLNodes[MC]* started in an arbitrary state and run with $R(Vbcast\|RW\|VW)$ stabilizes to L_{MC} in time $\delta + d + e + \epsilon_{sample}$. From transitivity of stabilization and 7, the next result follows.

Theorem 2. *VLNodes[MC] is self-stabilizing to L_{MC} in time $\delta + d + e + \epsilon_{sample}$ relative to $R(Vbcast\|RW\|VW)$.*

6.3   Relationship between L_{MC} and Reachable States

We just showed that $VLNodes[MC]$ is self-stabilizing to L_{MC} relative to the automaton $R(Vbcast\|RW\|VW)$. However, in order to conclude anything about the traces of $VLayer[MC]$ after stabilization, we need to show that traces of $VLayer[MC]$ starting in a state in L_{MC} are reachable traces of $VLayer[MC]$. We do this by first defining a simulation relation between states of $VLayer[MC]$ and then showing that for each state x in L_{MC} there is a reachable state y of $VLayer[MC]$ such that x is related to y under the simulation relation. This implies that the trace of any execution fragment starting with x is the trace of an execution fragment starting with y, which is a reachable trace of $VLayer[MC]$.

In order to show that each state in L_{MC} is related to some reachable state of $VLayer[MC]$, it is enough to show that each state in $Reset_{MC}$ is related to a reachable state of $VLayer[MC]$. The proof proceeds by providing a construction of an execution of $VLayer[MC]$ for each state in L_{MC}.

Lemma 8. *For each state $x \in Reset_{MC}$, there exists a reachable state y of $VLayer[MC]$ such that $x\mathcal{R}_{MC}y$.*

From these results it follows that the set of trace fragments of $VLayer[MC]$ starting from $Reset_{MC}$ is contained in the set of traces of $R(VLayer[MC])$. Bringing our results together we arrive at the main theorem:

Theorem 3. *The traces of $VLNodes[MC]$, starting in an arbitrary state and executed with automaton $R(Vbcast\|RW\|VW)$, stabilize in time $\delta + d + e + \epsilon_{sample}$ to reachable traces of $R(VLayer[MC])$.*

Thus, despite starting from an arbitrary configuration of the VSA and client components in the VSA layer, if there are no failures or restart of client nodes at or after some round t_0, then within a finite number of rounds after t_0, the clients are located on the curve and equally spaced in the limiting sense.

References

1. Dolev, S., Gilbert, S., Lahiani, L., Lynch, N.A., Nolte, T.A.: Virtual stationary automata for mobile networks. Technical Report MIT-LCS-TR-979 (2005)
2. Dolev, S., Gilbert, S., Lynch, N., Shvartsman, A., Welch, J.: Geoquorums: Implementing atomic memory in ad hoc networks. In: Fich, F.E. (ed.) DISC 2003. LNCS, vol. 2848, pp. 306–320. Springer, Heidelberg (2003)
3. Dolev, S., Gilbert, S., Lynch, N.A., Shvartsman, A.A., Welch, J.: Geoquorums: Implementing atomic memory in mobile ad hoc networks. Distributed Computing (2005)
4. Chockler, G., Gilbert, S., Lynch, N.: Virtual infrastructure for collision-prone wireless networks. In: Proceedings of PODC (to appear, 2008)
5. Nolte, T., Lynch, N.A.: A virtual node-based tracking algorithm for mobile networks. In: ICDCS (2007)
6. Dolev, S., Gilbert, S., Lahiani, L., Lynch, N., Nolte, T.: Virtual stationary automata for mobile networks. In: OPODIS (2005)

7. Nolte, T., Lynch, N.A.: Self-stabilization and virtual node layer emulations. In: Masuzawa, T., Tixeuil, S. (eds.) SSS 2007. LNCS, vol. 4838, pp. 394–408. Springer, Heidelberg (2007)

8. Kaynar, D.K., Lynch, N., Segala, R., Vaandrager, F.: The Theory of Timed I/O Automata. Synthesis Lectures on Computer Science. Morgan Claypool, San Francisco (2005)

9. Jadbabaie, A., Lin, J., Morse, A.S.: Coordination of groups of mobile autonomous agents using nearest neighbor rules. IEEE Trans. on Automatic Control 48(6), 988–1001 (2003)

10. Ando, H., Oasa, Y., Suzuki, I., Yamashita, M.: Distributed memoryless point convergence algorithm for mobile robots with limited visibility. IEEE Trans. on Robotics and Automation 15(5), 818–828 (1999)

11. Lin, J., Morse, A., Anderson, B.: Multi-agent rendezvous problem. In: IEEE CDC 2003 (2003)

12. Martinez, S., Cortes, J., Bullo, F.: On robust rendezvous for mobile autonomous agents. In: IFAC World Congress (2005)

13. Gazi, V., Passino, K.M.: Stability analysis of swarms. IEEE Trans. on Automatic Control 48(4), 692–697 (2003)

14. Cortes, J., Martinez, S., Karatas, T., Bullo, F.: Coverage control for mobile sensing networks. IEEE Trans. on Robotics & Automation 20(2), 243–255 (2004)

15. Suzuki, I., Yamashita, M.: Distributed autonomous mobile robots: Formation of geometric patterns. SIAM Journal of computing 28(4), 1347–1363 (1999)

16. Fax, J., Murray, R.: Information flow and cooperative control of vehicle formations. IEEE Trans. on Automatic Control 49, 1465–1476 (2004)

17. Clavaski, S., Chaves, M., Day, R., Nag, P., Williams, A., Zhang, W.: Vehicle networks: achieving regular formation. In: ACC (2003)

18. Blondel, V., Hendrickx, J., Olshevsky, A., Tsitsiklis, J.: Convergence in multiagent coordination consensus and flocking. In: IEEE CDC-ECC 2005, pp. 2996–3000 (2005)

19. Olfati-Saber, R., Fax, J., Murray, R.: Consensus and cooperation in networked multi-agent systems. Proceedings of the IEEE 95(1), 215–233 (2007)

20. Prencipe, G.: Corda: Distributed coordination of a set of autonomous mobile robots. In: ERSADS, pp. 185–190 (May 2001)

21. Flocchini, P., Prencipe, G., Santoro, N., Widmayer, P.: Pattern formation by autonomous robots without chirality. In: SIROCCO, 147–162 (June 2001)

22. Efrima, A., Peleg, D.: Distributed models and algorithms for mobile robot systems. In: van Leeuwen, J., Italiano, G.F., van der Hoek, W., Meinel, C., Sack, H., Plášil, F. (eds.) SOFSEM 2007. LNCS, vol. 4362, pp. 70–87. Springer, Heidelberg (2007)

23. Prencipe, G.: Achievable patterns by an even number of autonomous mobile robots. Technical Report TR-00-11 (2000)

24. Lynch, N., Mitra, S., Nolte, T.: Motion coordination using virtual nodes. In: IEEE CDC 2005 (December 2005)

25. Brown, M.D.: Air traffic control using virtual stationary automata. Master's thesis, MIT (September 2007)

An Application of
Specification-Based Design of Self-stabilization
to Tracking in Wireless Sensor Networks

Murat Demirbas[1] and Anish Arora[2]

[1] Computer Science & Engineering Dept.
University at Buffalo, SUNY, Buffalo, NY, 14260
demirbas@cse.buffalo.edu
[2] Computer Science & Engineering Dept.
The Ohio State University, Columbus, OH, 43210
anish@cse.ohio-state.edu

Abstract. In previous work, we have designed a tracking protocol, Stalk, for wireless sensor networks and proved it to be self-stabilizing at the pseudo-code (I/O automata) level. However, it is very challenging to achieve and verify self-stabilization of the same protocol at the implementation (TinyOS) level due to the size of the corresponding program at the implementation level. In this paper, we present a lightweight and practical method for specification-based design of stabilization and illustrate this method on the Stalk protocol as our case study.

1 Introduction

In previous work [1] we presented a self-stabilizing tracking service, Stalk, for sensor networks. There, we used I/O automata specification language for describing Stalk, and gave formal proofs of correctness and self-stabilization for this I/O language program. The implementation languages for sensor network platforms are, however, more finer-grained than the abstract I/O language. For the mote [2] platform, the implementation language is a dialect of C, called NesC [3], and the runtime environment TinyOS [4] consists of a collection of system components for network protocols and sensor drivers. With a conservative estimate, the 20 lines of I/O code we wrote for Stalk will correspond to 2000 lines of code (including the libraries for networking and sensing) at the implementation level. Even though we formally verified Stalk at the I/O language level, proving correctness and self-stabilization of the corresponding implementation at the TinyOS level by studying 2000 lines of code is a very challenging task.

There have been several work on fault-tolerance preserving refinements [5,6,7, 8]. One can consider using these refinements for implementing Stalk in TinyOS, however, these refinements do not have compiler/code-transformer tool support and, hence, their adoption in practice is limited. In this case, it would be hard to prove manually that our implementation at the TinyOS level is in fact a stabilization-preserving refinement of Stalk at the I/O automata level.

S. Kulkarni and A. Schiper (Eds.): SSS 2008, LNCS 5340, pp. 203–217, 2008.
© Springer-Verlag Berlin Heidelberg 2008

Contributions of this paper: In this paper we present a lightweight and practical method for specification-based design of stabilization. More specifically, we show that we can use ordinary refinements (for which a lot of compiler/tool support exists) and still achieve a specification-based design of stabilization under suitable conditions. We illustrate our lightweight and practical specification-based design method on the Stalk protocol as our case study.

An outline of our lightweight method for specification-based design of stabilization. Given a high-level system specification A, the specification-based approach [5, 6] is to design a tolerance wrapper W such that adding W to A yields a fault-tolerant system. The goal is to ensure that for any low-level implementation C of A adding a low-level implementation W' of W would also yield a fault-tolerant system. Since the refinements from A to C and W to W' can be done independently, specification-based design enables a posteriori or dynamic addition of fault-tolerance. That is, given a concrete implementation C, it is possible to add fault-tolerance to C by first designing an abstract tolerance wrapper W using solely an abstract specification A of C, and then adding a concrete refinement W' of W to C.

We next present a brief outline of our method for adopting ordinary refinements for specification-based design of stabilization in terms of a series of challenges and fixes.

Challenge: Refinements do not preserve fault-tolerance. Ordinary refinements do not preserve fault-tolerance and do not support fault-tolerance composition: Even though the abstract system composed of the fault-intolerant tracking program A and the self-stabilization wrapper W is self-stabilizing, when A and W are refined into C and W' at the implementation level, the concrete system might not be stabilizing since starting from faulty states C may interfere with and invalidate the recovery strategy of W'. Even when one proves that starting from faulty states A does not interfere with W, since ordinary refinements are concerned only with computations starting from good states, computations of C that start from faulty states are unconstrained and may be interfering with W'.

Fix: Use atomic wrappers to avoid interference. In order to prevent the interferences between the wrapper and the application code outside the good states, we use atomic wrappers at both the abstract and the concrete systems. When an atomic wrapper is executed it corrects the application to a good state in a single step, and the application code does not have the opportunity to interfere with the execution and the recovery strategy of the wrapper. Similarly, we also require that the wrapper self-stabilizes atomically in order to prevent the application to interfere with the self-stabilization of the wrapper when starting from a faulty state for the wrapper.

Challenge: Atomic wrappers are infeasible for distributed systems. In a distributed system, global system state is not available for instantaneous access. So, it is unrealistic to assume a wrapper that can in one step correct the entire application state, which is distributed across the system/network.

Fix: Use local atomic wrappers per each process. For effective specification-based design of stabilization of distributed systems, we restrict our attention to wrappers local to each process of the distributed system. At the abstract level, $A = ([] \, i :: \, A_i)$ [1], we design the wrappers to be decomposable as local wrappers, one for every process i; i.e., $W = ([] \, i :: \, W_i)$. While refining to a distributed implementation $C = ([] \, i :: \, C_i)$ we refine these local and atomic wrappers to be composed with the application code C_i at each process i; i.e., $W' = ([] \, i :: \, W'_i)$

Challenge: Composed system as a whole may still fail to be stabilizing. By using local and atomic wrappers we achieve stabilization for each process both at the abstract and concrete system levels. However, even though all the processes are individually stabilizing, the system may fail to stabilize as a whole due to the continuous introduction of corruptions to the system by the processes that are in a faulty state at the time. Consider a scenario where process j is not yet stabilized but i is. If they interact, i may receive bad input from j, and its state may become bad. Next, when j is corrected to a good state, since i is not yet stabilized, i can in turn infect j. This cycle may repeat infinitely, and even though i and j are individually stabilizing, the system may fail to stabilize as a whole.

Fix: Use a compositional framework. In order to ensure that stabilization of individual processes leads to stabilization of the system as a whole, we borrow ideas from literature on compositional approaches to stabilization. One simple idea is stabilization through composition of layers [10]. In the traditional stabilization by layers approach lower-level processes are oblivious to the existence of higher-level processes, and higher-level processes can read (but not write) the state of a lower-level process. Processes can corrupt each other, but only in a predetermined controlled way since lower-level processes cannot be affected by the state of higher-level ones. Also, the order in which correction must take place is the same direction; the correction of higher-levels depend on that of lower-levels. In order to ensure that stabilization compose at the system level, we adopt a layered composition technique at the abstract system level and assert that the concrete system preserve the layered composition structure of the abstract system.

Application to Stalk. To recap, we make the following assumptions in our method:

---

[1] A formula $(op \, i : R.i : X.i)$ denotes the value obtained by performing the (commutative and associative) op on the $X.i$ values for all i that satisfy $R.i$. As special cases, where op is conjunction, we write $(\forall i : R.i : X.i)$, and where op is disjunction, we write $(\exists i : R.i : X.i)$. Thus, $(\forall i : R.i : X.i)$ may be read as "if $R.i$ is true then so is $X.i$", and $(\exists i : R.i : X.i)$ may be read as "there exists an i such that both $R.i$ and $X.i$ are true". Where $R.i$ is true, we omit $R.i$. This notation is adopted from [9]. In the above formula, the operator $[]$ denotes the union of automata/processes.

1. Wrappers are local to each process and are atomic.
2. Identical layered composition structure is used by the abstract and concrete systems.

These two assumptions are satisfied by a rich class of implementations. In our case, Stalk satisfies both assumptions. The correctors (wrappers) in Stalk are local to each process and atomic: the process is atomically put into a locally consistent state with respect to the processes it interacts. Also Stalk algorithm imposes a static structure on the information flow. There is no communication from a higher level process to a lower level process in Stalk. The direction of communication in the protocol is always from lower level processes to higher level processes. Due to this structural constraint, the same layered composition structure is applicable at both the abstract and concrete systems.

We show, using these two assumptions, that an ordinary refinement suffices for the fault-intolerant tracking algorithm, and a self-stabilization preserving refinement suffices for the wrappers. The reason we use a stabilization-preserving refinement for the wrapper is to ensure that the concrete wrapper is able to stabilize from the corruption of its variables. Since there are a lot of tool support for ordinary refinements, refinement of the tracking algorithm can be done automatically via a compiler. Since the wrappers are small and simple their proof of self-stabilization can be achieved easily even at the implementation level.

Outline of the rest of the paper. We present the system model in Section 2. We then prove in Section 3 that the refinement method we described above is amenable for the specification-based design approach. We discuss the refinement of Stalk to a self-stabilizing implementation in Section 4. After presenting the related work in Section 5, we conclude the paper in Section 6.

2   Model

Let Σ be a state space.

Definition. A *system* S is a finite-state automaton (Σ, T, I) where T, the set of transitions, is a subset of $\{(s_0, s_1) : s_0, s_1 \in \Sigma\}$ and I, the set of initial states, is a subset of Σ.

A computation of S is a maximal sequence of states such that every state is related to the subsequent one with a transition in T, i.e., if a computation is finite there are no transitions in T that start at the final state.

We refer to an abstract system as a *specification*, and to a concrete system as an *implementation*. For convenience in this paper we assume that the specification and the implementation use the same state space. In general, the state space of the implementation can be different than that of the specification since the implementations often introduce some components of states that are not used by the specifications. We handle this by relating the states of the concrete implementation with the abstract specification via an abstraction function. The abstraction function is a *total* mapping from Σ_C, the state space of the implementation C, *onto* Σ_A, the state space of the specification A. That is, every state in C is mapped to a state in A, and correspondingly, every state in A is an image of some state in C. All definitions and theorems in this chapter are readily extended with respect to the definition of the abstraction function. The soundness and completeness of these abstraction functions are discussed in detail in [11].

Henceforth, let C be an implementation and A a specification.

Definition. C is a *refinement* of A, denoted $[C \subseteq A]_{init}$, iff every computation of C that starts from an initial state is a computation of A.

Definition. C is an *everywhere refinement* [5] of A, denoted $[C \subseteq A]$, iff every computation of C is a computation of A.

A fault is a perturbation of the system state. Here, we focus on transient faults that may arbitrarily corrupt the process states. The following definition captures a standard tolerance to transient faults.

Definition. C *is stabilizing to* A iff every computation of C has a suffix that is a suffix of some computation of A that starts at an initial state of A.

This definition of stabilization allows the possibility that A is stabilizing to A, that is, A is self-stabilizing.

We define a wrapper to be a system over Σ and formulate the "addition" of one system to another in terms of the operator $[]$ (pronounced "box") which denotes the union of automata.

Let A and C be distributed systems composed of processes A_i and C_i respectively; i.e., $A = ([] i :: A_i)$ and $C = ([] i :: C_i)$. We say that a wrapper W_i for each process A_i is local and atomic iff W_i when executed self-stabilizes (if its state is corrupted) and corrects A_i to a good state (locally consistent state) in a single step.

3   Adopting Ordinary Refinements for Specification-Based Design

In this section we prove that we can adopt ordinary refinements for the specification-based design of stabilization under suitable conditions. One of these conditions is the use of a layered composition structure of the processes in the system. Stabilization through composition of layers asserts that the correction and the corruption relations are to the same direction and form a directed acyclic graph. *Corruption relation* denotes for each process in a bad state which other processes it can corrupt. That is the corruption relation constrains the processes an uncorrected process can potentially corrupt. *Correction relation* denotes for each process the prior correction of which other processes its correction depends on. That is, the correction relation constrains the order in which correction must occur. In cases where the correction and corruption relations are in reverse directions, persistent corruption cycles may be formed: even though all the processes are individually stabilizing, the system may fail to stabilize due to the continuous introduction of corruptions to the system via these corruption cycles. However,

in the case of layered composition since both correction and corruption relations
are in the same direction, corruption cycles do not exist. Therefore, in this case,
if all processes are individually stabilizing, then the system as a whole is also
stabilizing [10].

Theorem 1 formally states the conditions under which ordinary refinements
are usable for the specification-based design of stabilization: Given local and
atomic wrappers (premise 3) that achieve stabilization of the abstract system
(premise 1), ordinary refinement of the application code at each process (premise
2) when composed with everywhere refinement of the abstract wrapper (premise
4) —provided that the layered composition structure of the abstract is preserved
(premise 5)— results into a concrete system that is self-stabilizing to the abstract
system specifications.

Theorem 1. If

1. $([]i :: [A_i [] W_i])$ is stabilizing to A_i,
2. $(\forall i :: [C_i \subseteq A_i]_{init})$,
3. $(\forall i :: [W_i' \subseteq W_i])$,
4. $(\forall i :: W_i$ is local and atomic), and
5. the correction & corruption relations of the abstract system are to the same
   direction, and the concrete system preserves the correction & corruption
   relations of the abstract

then $([]i :: [C_i [] W_i])$ is stabilizing to $([]i :: A_i)$.

Proof. From premises 3 and 4 it follows that $(\forall i :: W_i'$ is local and atomic), and
hence C_i cannot interfere with the recovery strategy of W_i'. Thus, from premises
2, 3, and 4, it follows that $(\forall i :: [C_i [] W_i]$ is stabilizing to $[A_i [] W_i])$. Even
though, at this point we have stabilization at the process level, the system as a
whole may fail to be stabilizing due to corruption cycles. Premise 5 takes care of
this concern as we discussed above. The conclusion follows from this result and
premise 1.   □

Theorem 1 shows that an ordinary refinement suffices for the fault-intolerant
application, and a self-stabilization preserving refinement suffices for the wrappers. The reason we use a stabilization-preserving refinement (e.g., everywhere
refinements) for the wrapper is to ensure that the concrete wrapper is able to
stabilize from the corruption of its variables. Since there are a lot of tool support
for ordinary refinements, refinement of the tracking algorithm can be done automatically via a compiler. Since the wrappers are small and simple their proof
of self-stabilization can be achieved easily even at the implementation level.

4   Refinement of Stalk to the Implementation Level

In this section, we present a refinement of the abstract Stalk program to the
TinyOS implementation level by showing that Theorem 1 is applicable for this
refinement. We start by recalling some of the properties of Stalk and pointing
out which concepts of Theorem 1 they correspond to. We then continue with a
discussion of the refinement to the implementation level.

Input: **object**$_i$
eff: if $c \neq i \ \wedge \ lvl(i) = 0$ then
$\quad\quad c := i$
$\quad\quad gtime := now + g$

Output: **send (gquery)**$_{i,j}$
pre: $j \in gnbrquery$
eff: $gnbrquery := gnbrquery - \{j\}$
$\quad\quad$ if $gnbrquery = \emptyset$ then
$\quad\quad\quad gtime := now + g * r^{lvl(i)}$

Input: **receive (gquery)**$_{j,i}$
eff: if $p = h(i)$ then
$\quad\quad gqack := j$

Output: **send (ack_gquery)**$_{i,j}$
pre: $gqack = j$
eff: $gqack := \bot$

Input: **receive (ack_gquery)**$_{j,i}$
eff: if $c \neq \bot \ \wedge \ p = \bot$ then
$\quad\quad p := j$

Output: **send (grow)**$_{i,j}$
pre: $now = gtime \ \wedge \ c \neq \bot \ \wedge$
$\quad\quad ((j = p \ \wedge \ p \in nbr(i)) \ \vee \ (j = h(i) \ \wedge \ p = \bot))$
eff: if $p = \bot$ then
$\quad\quad\quad p := h(i)$
$\quad\quad gtime := \infty$

Input: **receive (grow)**$_{j,i}$
eff: $c := j$
$\quad\quad$ if $lvl(i) = MAX$ then
$\quad\quad\quad p := i$
$\quad\quad$ if $p = \bot$ then
$\quad\quad\quad gnbrquery := nbr(i)$

Fig. 1. Stalk protocol: grow actions at process i

4.1   Brief Summary of Stalk

For achieving scalability, STALK employs a hierarchical structure by using a hierarchical partitioning of the sensor network into clusters based on radius. The tracking structure is a path rooted at the highest level of the hierarchy. Each process in the *tracking path* has at most one child, either at its level or one below it in the hierarchy, and the mobile object resides at the leaf of the tracking path, at the lowest level. Each process in the path points to a process that is generally closer to the object and has more recent information about its location.

Input: **no_object**$_i$
eff: if $lvl(i) = 0 \ \wedge \ c \neq \perp$ then
$$c := \perp$$
$$stime := now + s$$

Output: **send (shrink)**$_{i,j}$
pre: $now = stime \ \wedge \ c = \perp \ \wedge \ j = p$
eff: $p := \perp$
$$stime := \infty$$

Input: **receive (shrink)**$_{j,i}$
eff: if $c = j$ then
$$c := \perp$$
$$stime := now + s * r^{lvl(i)}$$

Fig. 2. Stalk protocol: shrink actions at process i

We implement move-triggered updates to the tracking path by means of two operations, *grow* and *shrink*. The grow operation enables a path to grow from the new location of the object to increasingly higher levels of the hierarchy and connect to the original path at some level. The shrink operation cleans branches deserted by the object. Shrinking also starts at the lowest level and climbs to increasingly higher levels.

A hierarchical partitioning of a network inevitably results in multi-level cluster boundaries: even though two processes are neighbors they might be contained in different clusters at all levels (except the top) of the hierarchy. If a process were to always propagate grows and shrinks to its clusterhead, a small movement of the object back and forth across a multi-level cluster boundary could result in work proportional to the size of the network rather than the distance of the move. To resolve this "dithering" problem, Stalk allows one *lateral link* per level in our tracking path. A process occasionally connects to the original path with a lateral link to a neighboring process rather than by propagating a link to its parent in the hierarchy. Stalk limits the lateral link count per level in order not to upset the locality properties of the find operation.

To implement **Tracker**, each process i maintains a child pointer c, a parent pointer p, a set *gnbrquery* to keep track of which neighbors it has send a query in the last invocation of grow, a variable *gqack* to keep track of which neighbor to reply to, a grow timer *gtime*, and a shrink timer *stime*. In the initial states, $i.c = i.p = \perp$ and $i.gtime = i.stime = \infty$ for all i. The grow actions are presented in Figure 1 and the shrink actions are presented in Figure 2.

In order to correct for the case where a process i may have a valid child but no parent or a valid parent but no child, Stalk uses two simple actions as in Figure 3. In order to detect and dissociate a child at process i, Stalk employs a heartbeat mechanism as in Figure 4. The actions in Figure 3 are stateless (they do not introduce any new state), and the actions in Figure 4 introduces only one variable (a soft-state variable) to keep track of a timeout.

Internal: **start-shrink**$_i$
pre: $(c = \bot \land p \neq \bot$
            $\land \ stime \notin [now, now + s * r^{lvl(i)}])$
      $\lor \ [p \in nbr(i) \ \land \ c \in nbr(i)]$
eff: $c := \bot$
      $stime := now + s * r^{lvl(i)}$

Internal: **start-grow**$_i$
pre: $c \neq \bot$
            $\land \ p = \bot \ \land \ gtime \notin [now, now + g * r^{lvl(i)}]$
eff: if $lvl(i) = MAX$ then
                $p = i$
      if $p = \bot$ then
                $gnbrquery := nbr(i)$

Fig. 3. Stalk protocol: correction actions at process i

4.2 Application of Theorem 1 to Stalk

Stalk provides local specifications for the fault-intolerant tracking program: The Tracker$_i$ automata presented in Figures 1 and 2 corresponds to A_i in Theorem 1. Stalk also provides local and atomic wrappers for each Tracker$_i$: The parallel composition of the correction actions in Figures 3 and 4 corresponds to W_i in Theorem 1. Since, in [1], we proved that Tracker$_i$ composed with the correction actions are self-stabilizing, premise 1 is satisfied. Since the correction actions for the Tracker$_i$ automata are all local and atomic (they put Tracker$_i$ in a locally-consistent state in one step), premise 4 is satisfied.

Stalk imposes a static layered structure on the processes: There is no communication from a higher level process to a lower level process; the direction of communication is from lower level processes to higher level processes. Due to this structural constraint, the same layered composition structure is applicable at both the abstract and concrete systems; hence, premise 5 is satisfied.

Next, we consider the refinement of Stalk to the implementation level. In order for Theorem 1 to be applicable, we need to show that premises 2 and 3 are satisfied by our refinement of Stalk.

Premise 2 asserts that the implementation of the Tracker$_i$ automata should be a refinement from the initial states. Since there are a lot of tool support for ordinary refinements, refinement of the tracking algorithm can be done automatically via a compiler. For example, the IOA toolkit [12] supports the design, analysis, verification, and refinement of programs written in I/O automata notation. The toolkit includes analysis tools such as the IOA simulator [13] and interfaces to theorem-proving tools [14] as well as compilers for generation of distributed code in commercial programming languages [15]. Even if the implementation of Tracker$_i$ automata is performed manually, the verification process for ordinary refinements are, in general, easier than that of fault-tolerance preserving and compositional refinements. Since an ordinary refinement from initial states of

---

Output: **send (heartbeat)**$_{i,j}$
pre: $now = next \ \wedge \ j = p$
eff: $next := now + b * r^{lvl(i)}$

Input: **receive (heartbeat)**$_{j,i}$
eff: if $c = \perp$ then $c := j$
       if $c = j$ then
              $timeout := now + (b + 2\delta m/r) * r^{lvl(i)}$

Internal: **timeout_expire**$_i$
pre: $now = timeout \ \wedge \ c \neq \perp \ \wedge \ c \neq i$
eff: $c := \perp$

Internal: **heartbeat_set**$_i$
pre: $p \neq \perp \ \wedge \ next \notin [now, now + b * r^{lvl(i)}]$
eff: $next := now + b * r^{lvl(i)}$

Internal: **timeout_set**$_i$
pre: $c \neq \perp \ \wedge \ c \neq i$
       $\wedge \ timeout \notin [now, now + (b + 2\delta m/r) * r^{lvl(i)}]$
eff: $timeout := now + (b + 2\delta m) * r^{lvl(i)}$

Fig. 4. Stalk protocol: heartbeat actions at process i

the Tracker$_i$ automata is sufficient, one does not have to consider refinements from every state for the purposes of this implementation.

Premise 3 asserts that the abstract wrappers should be everywhere refined. Since sensor nodes [16] have a single thread of control, the concrete level wrappers are made atomic easily by making them to run till completion upon invocation. Hence, if we prove self-stabilization of the concrete wrappers, then this implies that the concrete wrappers are everywhere refinements of the abstract ones. Since the wrappers are small and simple, their proof of self-stabilization can be achieved easily even manually, without any tool support. Model-checking based approaches may also be used for this purpose: For example, [17] can accept a wrapper written in C language as input, and check the self-stabilization properties of the wrapper.

(Remark:) An interesting research question is the feasibility of automating the translation process from the abstract wrappers to the concrete wrappers. To implement the abstract wrapper at the concrete level, the code translator may use the abstraction function from C to A in the reverse direction. Note that the wrapper synthesized for the abstract model A is readily available for mapping back to C because the abstraction function is defined as onto. (In fact in [18] a similar method is presented for mapping the counterexamples in the abstract model to counterexamples in the concrete model.) Since abstract wrappers are often stateless (as in Figure 3), in these cases the translator would only be responsible for cleaning out the extra implementation state it introduces at the

concrete. Soft-state approaches and watch-stop timer based reset approaches might be useful for automating this cleaning task. *(End of remark.)*

Since all the premises are satisfied, we can conclude, by a simple application of Theorem 1, that the resultant implementation of Stalk at the TinyOS level is self-stabilizing to the abstract specifications.

5   Related Work

In this section, we review the previous work on fault-tolerance preserving refinements and compositional frameworks for self-stabilization.

5.1   Fault-Tolerance Preserving Refinements

Our previous work on stabilization preserving refinements. We have shown in [5] that refinements in general are not fault-tolerance preserving, that is, even though A is fault-tolerant, a refinement C of A may not be fault-tolerant. We are therefore led to considering special classes of refinements. In our previous research, we have identified two fault-tolerance preserving refinements: everywhere refinements [5] and convergence refinements [6].

Intuitively speaking, everywhere refinements demand that the implementations always satisfy the specifications from every state. Further, for effective design of fault-tolerance in distributed systems, we identify the subclass of *local everywhere refinements*: these refinements are decomposable into parts each of which must always be satisfied by some system process from *all* of its states without relying on its environment (including other processes).

Intuitively speaking, convergence refinement implies that even in the unreachable states the computations of the concrete system C track the computations of the abstract system A, although some states that appear in the computations of A may disappear in the computations of C, and hence, C preserves convergence properties (e.g., stabilization) of A.

In contrast to previous work on fault-tolerance preserving refinements, we have shown that the refinements we have identified have nice compositionality properties making them suitable for specification-based design of fault-tolerance. For example, convergence refinement enables a non-stabilizing implementation C to be made stabilizing without knowing the implementation details of C but knowing only an abstract specification A that C satisfies. More specifically, given C that is a convergence refinement of A, first stabilization of A is designed by devising an abstract wrapper W for A. Stabilization of C is then achieved by adding to C any convergence refinement of W; the refined wrapper is oblivious to the implementation details of C.

The lightweight method we present in this paper enables the use of ordinary refinements (for which a lot of compiler/tool support exists) in the specification-based design of stabilization in lie of an everywhere or convergence refinement.

Method by Z. Liu and M. Joseph. Liu and Joseph [7] have considered designing fault-tolerance via transformations. In their work, an abstract program

A is refined to a more concrete implementation C and then based on the refined program C and the fault actions F that are introduced in the refinement process, further precautions (such as using a checkpointing & recovery protocol) are taken to render C fault-tolerant. Liu and Joseph design the tolerance based on the concrete program, while we design our wrappers based on the abstract program.

Method by L. Lamport and S. Merz. In [8], Lamport and Merz claim that there is no need for a special technique for formal specification and verification of fault-tolerance systems, and that refinement of fault-tolerance programs could be achieved using temporal logic of actions (TLA) and a hierarchical proof method.

Towards this end, they show how a message-passing Byzantine agreement program (of [19]) can be derived from its high-level specification. (The authors, however, do not discuss how their example can be generalized into a method for designing arbitrary fault-tolerant programs.) They first present three specifications for the Byzantine agreement program: a high-level problem specification, a mid-level specification of the algorithm, and a low-level specification for message-passing model. Then they prove that each specification implements the next-higher one.

The authors claim that little ingenuity is required for proofs of refinements since a hierarchical proof strategy is adopted. However, it should be noted that a considerable amount of ingenuity is still required for coming up with the refinement programs in the first place. The authors also admit in the discussion section of the paper that their method is "not yet feasible for reasoning at the level of executable code, except in special applications or for small parts of a system."

Fault-tolerance preserving atomicity refinements. Fault-tolerance preserving refinements have been studied in the context of atomicity refinement in [20, 21], whereas in our work we study them in the more general context of computation-model refinement.

McGuire and Gouda [22] have developed an execution model that can be used in translating abstract network protocol specifications written in a guarded-command language into C programs using Unix sockets. Their framework cannot handle arbitrary state corruptions we considered here, and only allows the following faults: message loss, message ordering, and message duplication.

Semantics of fault-tolerance preserving refinements. Leal [23] has also observed that refinement tools are inadequate for preserving fault-tolerance. The focus of his work is on defining the semantics of tolerance preserving refinements of components.

5.2   Compositional Frameworks for Self-stabilization

Scalable design of stabilization through composition idea has been around for a long time [10]. In the traditional stabilization by layers approach lower-level components are oblivious to the existence of higher-level components, and higher-level components can read (but not write) the state of a lower-level component.

Components can corrupt each other, but only in a predetermined controlled way since lower-level components cannot be affected by the state of higher-level ones. Also, the order in which correction must take place is the same direction, the correction of higher-levels depend on that of lower-levels. Adaptive programming [24] is similar to stabilization by layers, except that the components depend on an environment that may change. If the environment achieves a fixed point for a sufficiently long time, the components stabilize with respect to it.

In [25], a compositional framework for constructing self-stabilizing systems is proposed. The framework explicitly identifies for each component which other components it can corrupt (corruption relation). Additionally, the correction of one component often depends on the prior correction of one or more other components, constraining the order in which correction can take place (correction relation). A global reset [26] is potentially avoided and fault-containment is enabled when possible by using the correction and corruption relations to check and block certain components to prevent formation of fault-contamination cycles.

Depending on what is actually known about the corruption and correction relations, the framework offers several ways to coordinate system correction. In cases where the correction and corruption relations are in reverse directions, persistent corruption cycles may be formed: even though all the components are individually stabilizing, the system may fail to stabilize due to the continuous introduction of corruptions to the system via these corruption cycles. By employing blocking coordinators, the framework breaks these malicious cycles. In cases where both correction and corruption relations are in the same direction, no cycle forms and there is no need for blocking. By including both correction and corruption relations, the framework in [25] subsumes and extends other compositional approaches, such as layered composition, where correction and corruption relations are to the same direction.

In our paper, while developing lightweight and local refinements for designing specification-based self-stabilization to tracking, we restricted our work to the systems where both the correction and corruption relations are to the same direction in both the abstract and the concrete levels. This way we did not have to deal with addition of extra coordinators and blocking at the concrete system level. By adopting the framework in [25] for our refinement method, we can relax our layered composition assumption and allow arbitrary compositions of processes. Using the knowledge of correction-corruption relations between the processes, we can instantiate a corresponding coordinator to ensure that stabilization of processes compose at the abstract level. In fact, then these coordinators become part of the wrappers at the abstract, and by refinement of these wrappers we can achieve stabilization at the concrete level.

6   Concluding Remarks

In this paper we showed that we can use ordinary refinements (for which a lot of compiler/tool support exists) and still achieve a specification-based design of stabilization under suitable conditions. To this end, we assumed that (1) wrappers are local to each process and are atomic, and (2) the concrete system preserves the layered composition structure of the abstract system. Using these two conditions, we showed that an ordinary refinement suffices for the fault-intolerant application, and a self-stabilization preserving refinement suffices for the wrappers. Another advantage of our specification-based design is that it enables a posteriori addition of stabilization. That is, starting with a concrete implementation C, it is possible to add fault-tolerance to C by first designing an abstract tolerance wrapper W using solely an abstract specification A of C, and then adding a concrete refinement W' of W to C.

We have illustrated this lightweight method for specification-based design on the Stalk protocol for wireless sensor networks. We believe that for a rich class of wireless sensor network applications the two conditions we have identified for the applicability of our method holds naturally. In future work, we will provide an actual demonstration of Stalk on the motes as part of our NSF-funded on-going project on pursuer-evader tracking in wireless sensor networks. Also, we will investigate other wireless sensor network applications where our method is applicable for achieving stabilization at the implementation level.

References

1. Demirbas, M., Arora, A., Nolte, T., Lynch, N.: A hierarchy-based fault-local stabilizing algorithm for tracking in sensor networks. In: 8th International Conference on Principles of Distributed Systems (OPODIS), pp. 299–315 (2004)
2. Crossbow technology, Mica2 platform,
   `www.xbow.com/Products/Wireless_Sensor_Networks.htm`
3. Gay, D., Levis, P., von Behren, R., Welsh, M., Brewer, E., Culler, D.: The nesc language: A holistic approach to networked embedded systems. In: PLDI 2003: Proceedings of the ACM SIGPLAN 2003 conference on Programming language design and implementation, pp. 1–11 (2003)
4. Hill, J., Szewczyk, R., Woo, A., Hollar, S., Culler, D., Pister, K.: System architecture directions for network sensors. In: ASPLOS, pp. 93–104 (2000)
5. Arora, A., Demirbas, M., Kulkarni, S.S.: Graybox stabilization. In: Proceedings of the International Conference on Dependable Systems and Networks (ICDSN), pp. 389–398 (July 2001)
6. Demirbas, M., Arora, A.: Convergence refinement. In: Proceedings of the International Conference on Distributed Computing Systems (ICDCS), July 2002, pp. 589–597 (2002); Best paper(1st/335)
7. Liu, Z., Joseph, M.: Transformations of programs for fault-tolerance. Formal Aspects of Computing 4(5), 442–469 (1992)
8. Lamport, L., Merz, S.: Specifying and verifying fault-tolerant systems. In: Langmaack, H., de Roever, W.-P., Vytopil, J. (eds.) FTRTFT 1994 and ProCoS 1994, vol. 863, pp. 41–76. Springer, Heidelberg (1994)
9. Dijkstra, E.W., Scholten, C.S.: Predicate Calculus and Program Semantics. Springer, Heidelberg (1990)
10. Dolev, S.: Self-Stabilization. MIT Press, Cambridge (2000)
11. Demirbas, M.: Scalable design of fault-tolerance for wireless sensor networks. PhD thesis, The Ohio State University (2004)

12. Garland, S.J., Lynch, N.A.: Using i/o automata for developing distributed systems. Foundations of Component-Based Systems, 285–312 (2000)
13. Kaynar, D.K., Chefter, A., Dean, L., Garland, S., Lynch, N., Win, T.N., Ramirez, A.: The ioa simulator. Technical Report 843, MIT Laboratory for Computer Science (2002)
14. Garland, S., Guttag, J.V., Horning, J.: An overview of larch. Functional Programming, Concurrency, Simulation and Automated Reasoning (1993)
15. Tauber, J.A.: Verifiable Code Generation from Abstract I/O Automata. PhD thesis, MIT (2003)
16. Hill, J., Szewczyk, R., Woo, A., Hollar, S., Culler, D., Pister, K.: System architecture directions for network sensors. In: ASPLOS, pp. 93–104 (2000)
17. Hatcliff, J., Dwyer, M.B., Pasareanu, C.S., Robby: Foundations of the bandera abstraction tools, pp. 172–203 (2002)
18. Clarke, E.M., Grumberg, O., Jha, S., Lu, Y., Veith, H.: Counterexample-guided abstraction refinement. In: Computer Aided Verification, pp. 154–169 (2000)
19. Lamport, L., Shostak, R., Pease, M.: The Byzantine generals problem. ACM Transactions on Programming Languages and Systems (1982)
20. Nesterenko, M., Arora, A.: Stabilization-preserving atomicity refinement. In: Jayanti, P. (ed.) DISC 1999. LNCS, vol. 1693, pp. 254–268. Springer, Heidelberg (1999)
21. Beauquier, J., Datta, A.K., Gradinariu, M., Magniette, F.: Self-stabilizing local mutual exclusion and daemon refinement. In: International Symposium on Distributed Computing, pp. 223–237 (2000)
22. McGuire, T.M.: Correct implementation of network protocols. PhD thesis, University at Texas at Austin (2004)
23. Leal, W.: A Foundation for Fault Tolerant Components. PhD thesis, The Ohio State University (2001)
24. Gouda, M.G., Herman, T.: Adaptive programming. IEEE Transactions on Software Engineering 17, 911–921 (1991)
25. Leal, W., Arora, A.: Scalable self-stabilization via composition and refinement. In: Proceedings of the 24th International Conference on Distributed Computing Systems (ICDCS). IEEE, Los Alamitos (2004)
26. Arora, A., Gouda, M.G.: Distributed reset. IEEE Transactions on Computers 43(9), 1026–1038 (1994)

Our Brothers' Keepers: Secure Routing with High Performance*

Alex Brodsky and Scott Lindenberg

University of Winnipeg
515 Portage Ave, Winnipeg, MB, Canada, R3B 2E9
{abrodsky,slindenb}@acs.uwinnipeg.ca

Abstract. The Trinity [1] spam classification system is based on a distributed hash table that is implemented using a structured peer-to-peer overlay. Such an overlay must be capable of processing hundreds of messages per second, and must be able to route messages to their destination even in the presence of failures and malicious peers that misroute packets or inject fraudulent routing information into the system. Typically there is tension between the requirements to route messages securely and efficiently in the overlay.

We describe a secure and efficient routing extension that we developed within the I3 [2] implementation of the Chord [3] overlay. Secure routing is accomplished through several complementary approaches: First, peers in close proximity form overlapping groups that police themselves to identify and mitigate fraudulent routing information. Second, a form of random routing solves the problem of entire packet flows passing through a malicious peer. Third, a message authentication mechanism links each message to it sender, preventing spoofing. Fourth, each peer's identifier links the peer to its network address, and at the same time uniformly distributes the peers in the key-space.

Lastly, we present our initial evaluation of the system, comprising a 255 peer overlay running on a local cluster. We describe our methodology and show that the overhead of our secure implementation is quite reasonable.

Keywords: Secure routing, peer authentication, distributed hash tables.

1 Introduction

Systems such as Trinity [1], LOCKSS [4], and others are based on distributed hash tables that are implemented on top of peer-to-peer structured overlays. These overlays differ from better known peer-to-peer systems such as BitTorrent in three fundamental ways. First, these overlays are closed, meaning that only authorized hosts may join the overlay. Second, these overlays must be secure and function even in the presence of failures, denial of service attacks, and malicious peers. Third, performance is paramount, meaning that each peer in the these overlays must be able to forward hundreds of messages per second.

Although securing closed overlays seems more manageable than the task of securing open overlays, the task presents several challenges. First, identifying, authenticating and

---

* This research was supported by an NSERC Discovery grant.

S. Kulkarni and A. Schiper (Eds.): SSS 2008, LNCS 5340, pp. 218–232, 2008.

authorizing peers and authenticating the messages that they send is not easy because the mechanisms must be fault tolerant, allow revocation, and must not significantly impact performance. Second, securely routing messages, dealing with host and network failures, and most importantly, dealing with malicious peers and the fraudulent routing information that they inject into the overlay is challenging in itself, let alone without significantly impacting performance.

As part of the Trinity project [1], we have designed, implemented, and tested a secure closed overlay based on the I3 [2] Chord [3] implementation. Our design comprises a distributed and fault tolerant identification, authentication, and authorization mechanism; a key assignment scheme that encodes a peer's network location yet ensures that the keys are uniformly distributed in the key space; a self-policing scheme based on groups of local peers; and a form of random routing that ensures that no (malicious) peer is a choke-point between any two other peers.

In addition to describing our approaches, we present a performance evaluation, which was performed on a local cluster that hosted overlays consisting of 255 peers. We compare the performance of our system in "secure" and "insecure" modes, and show that the performance penalty for secure operation is acceptable.

The rest of the paper is organized as follows: Section 2 describes our assumptions and the Chord protocol. Section 3 describes the three parts of our approach and Section 4 describes our evaluation of the system. Lastly, Section 5 and 6 describe related work, and discuss future work.

2 Preliminaries

We selected the Chord [3] structured overlay to provide lookup services for the Trinity [1] system because Chord has good performance characteristics and provides control over the location of peers within the overlay, making it easier to secure [5,6].

The Chord [3] overlay structure assigns each peer a unique key, k, from a 160-bit key-space[1] and organizes the peers into a single ring in the numerical order of their keys. The predecessor and successor of key k are the keys k_p and k_s, respectively, belonging to peers in the ring, such that $k - k_p$ and $k_s - k$, respectively, are minimal (see Figure 1). Intuitively, the peer to whom key k is assigned is located between its predecessor and successor, the peers to whom the keys k_p and k_s are assigned. If a key k is not assigned to a peer in the ring, then the peer whose key is the successor to k is responsible for the key. Consequently, each peer is responsible for all the possible key values between it and its predecessor.

When a peer joins the ring, it locates its position within the ring by sending a "find successor" request with its own key, k, to a "well known" peer that is already in the ring. The request is routed to the current predecessor of k, whose successor is therefore also the successor of k. The predecessor replies to the new peer, informing it of both the successor and itself. The new peer then informs the successor and predecessor of its existence and assumes its location in ring. Lastly, the peer builds its routing table, called a finger table.

---

[1] All operations on the keys are performed mod 2^{160}.

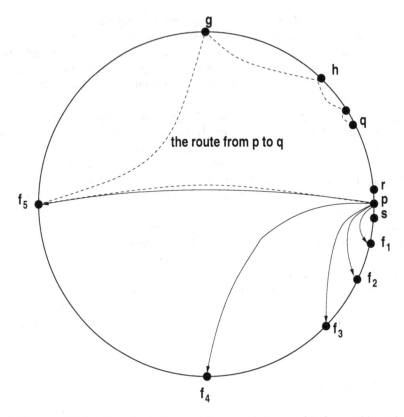

Fig. 1. The peers labeled f_i are in p's finger table, peer g is in peer f_5's finger table, and peer h is in peer g's finger table. Peers r and s are the predecessor and successor of peer p

The finger table is used by the peer to forward a message toward its eventual destination. The finger table comprises keys of select peers in the ring. Typically, the table contains $O(\log N)$ keys of peers that are $\frac{1}{2^i}$ of a ring away, $i = 1 \ldots \log(N)$, where N is the number of peers in the ring (see Figure 1). To forward a message to the peer responsible for key k, the peer with the closest preceding key to k is selected from the finger table, and the message is forwarded directly to that peer. Thus, the distance to the destination peer is decreased by at least half, and after at most $O(\log N)$ such hops, the message arrives at the destination. If the closest preceding peer is the current peer, then the message is forwarded directly to the peer's successor, its destination.

The finger table is populated by performing additional "find successor" queries with key values of the form $k + 2^i$, for $0 < i < 160$. Additional ongoing "find successor" queries, at regular intervals, are used to update the finger table as well as the peer's successor and predecessor. Also, a simple heart-beat mechanism tracks when peers leave the ring.

Unfortunately, the system as described, is susceptible to many attacks. First, the overlay uses an unreliable message-based transport protocol, User Datagram Protocol (UDP), that is susceptible to spoofing because the source address of a message can easily be forged. Thus, the source of the message cannot be (reliably) determined. Second, the system, as described, allows any host to become a peer, which is problematic for a closed overlay and can lead to the admittance of malicious peers. Third, as a result of the first two weaknesses, the overlay is susceptible to denial of service attacks because large numbers of messages and requests can be injected into the overlay by external hosts.

Fourth, the overlay relies on the correct behaviour of all of its constituents. For example, all peers must correctly forward and reply to "find successor" requests. Malicious peers can inject fraudulent routing information into the overlay by replying with incorrect "find successor" replies, dropping requests, or misdirecting the requests. Consequently, a few collaborating malicious peers could cause segments of the ring to "drop out". This is a problem even if peers are initially identified and authenticated prior to joining because peers may be compromised and an initially nonmalicious peer may become malicious.

We assume that all malicious hosts are computationally bounded and cannot forge or decrypt messages that are signed or encrypted using the standard 2048-bit RSA public key system. We make no assumptions about the number of malicious hosts—machines that have not joined the ring—or the security of the channel, meaning that malicious hosts may be able to view the messages as they transit the Internet. This corresponds to the resources available to spammers today in the form of large bot-nets. Correspondingly, we do assume that such malicious hosts do not have control over the IP address that they are assigned.

We assume that a small fraction (5%) of peers—hosts that are authorized to join the ring—are malicious; either from the start or because they were compromised at some point after joining. We can make this assumption because the peers will be set up and monitored by qualified system administrators, and because the peers will be checked by the ring's administrators before they are authorized to join the ring. The challenge then, is to limit the ability of the malicious peers to collaborate and disrupt the overlay, to detect malicious peers, and evict them from the overlay.

3 Design and Implementation

Our implementation is an extension of the I3 [2] code-base. Our implementation comprises five parts: (i) a key assignment scheme that links each peer's key with its network address[2] while at the same time uniformly distributing the peers' keys in the ring; (ii) a distributed identification, authentication, and (revocable) authorization mechanism that allows the overlay to control what peers are admitted into the ring; (iii) a message authentication mechanism that links each message to its sender; (iv) a self-policing mechanism based on overlapping groups composed of proximate peers; and (v) a simple form of random routing that avoids the possibility of any peer becoming a choke point between two other peers.

3.1 Key Assignment

As was observed in [5] and [6], it is harder for malicious peers to collaborate when they are uniformly distributed in the ring than when they are clustered. Consequently, peers

---

[2] Both IP address and port number.

should be assigned keys from a uniform distribution. Thus, prior to joining, each peer is expected to choose a key from the uniform distribution on the key space. However, there is nothing that prevents malicious peers from choosing keys that facilitate collaboration. Furthermore, a randomly selected key, only encodes the peers position within the ring, not the network, which another peer would need to contact it directly. Lastly, the choice of the peer's network address is typically limited and in most cases beyond the control of the peer, malicious or otherwise.

We leverage this restriction to assign keys to peers so that the peers have no choice in their key, the key is unique, the key encodes a peer's network address, and the key appears to be chosen from the uniform distribution on the key space. To determine its key a peer concatenates its IP address and port number, both in network byte order, to create a 6 byte string. This string is passed through the SHA-1 function, generating a 20 byte hash. The hash is the same length as a key, 20 bytes, and appears as if it was chosen from the uniform distribution on the key space.[3] Lastly, the IP address and the port number replace the 6 least significant bytes of the hash, as suggested in [6].

The resulting 20 byte key, can easily be validated by extracting the 6 least significant bytes, passing them from the SHA-1 function, and comparing the 14 most significant bytes of the resulting hash and the key—they should match. The 14 most significant bytes of the key look as if they were drawn from a uniform distribution, ensuring that the peers are uniformly distributed throughout the ring. Lastly, the key uniquely identifies each peer because the IP address of each peer is necessarily unique. Thus, each peer can be uniquely identified.

3.2   Distributed Identification, Authentication and Authorization

A peer must be identified, authenticated, and authorized before it can join the overlay. The peer's key uniquely identifies the peer, but it does not authenticate the peer, which is a prerequisite for authorization. Since the maliciousness of a peer may be discovered only after it joins the ring, authorization must be revocable, in order to facilitate the excommunication of such peers.

Authentication is accomplished by using a public key signature system—each new peer generates a public-private key-pair. A peer authenticates a message by first embedding its 20-byte key into the message and then signing it. However, two problems remain: distribution of the public key, and the authorization of the peer. Both problems are solved simultaneously by leveraging the Domain Name System (DNS) [7,8].

Each ring is identified by a domain name in the DNS database and each authorized peer in the ring has corresponding a TXT entry within the domain, identified by the peer's key and storing a certificate that contains the peer's public key. The authority responsible for authorizing peers is also responsible for signing the certificates and for adding or removing the TXT entries.

When a peer receives a message from another peer, it checks its cache for the sender's public key, if present then the sender is authorized to participate in the ring. Otherwise, the receiver performs a DNS lookup for the sender's key in the ring's domain. If found,

---

[3] In reality the hash is uniformly chosen from key subspace of cardinality 2^{48}, the size of the input string.

the sender's public key is added to the cache and the sender is deemed to be authorized. If not, a negative entry is added to the cache, causing the peer to ignore all future messages from the sender until the negative entry expires. Authorizations are revoked by removing the corresponding TXT entry from the DNS database and informing all peers of the revocation via a broadcast.

We leverage the DNS system because it has proven to be relatively robust and fault tolerant. In fact, robustness can be increased by simply adding more name servers. Furthermore, a DNS query is only needed when a new peer joins. In theory, peers could broadcast the certificates they receive from their DNS queries, informing the ring of the joining peer. Thus, an attack on the DNS system would only prevent new peers from joining the ring. One problem with our approach is that authenticating each message using a public key signature is prohibitively expensive.

3.3 Message Authentication

A message is linked to its sender because it contains the sender's key and then signed by the sender. Since the keys are unique and contain the sender's network address, each message can be traced to its origin. Consequently, if fraudulent messages are detected, the sender can be identified with certainty and excommunicated.

Unfortunately, signing and verifying all messages using a public key signature system is expensive. For example, to determine the overhead of using a public key signature system, we ran a two peer ring on a single 1.60GHz Intel Xeon E5310 (4-core) server with 2 gigabytes of RAM, and had one peer ping the other. This nullified the any potential network related slowdown, and allocated one CPU to each peer, thus avoiding any issues associated with sharing a CPU. Without message authentication, the system performed about 4000 pings per second—approximately 8000 messages per second. With message authentication, using public key signatures, the number of pings per second dropped to 15—a slowdown by a factor of 300!

We solve this problem by using message authentication codes (MAC) as the default authentication mechanism. The Chord overlay structure exhibits good temporal locality with respect to communication, meaning that if a peer communicates directly with another peer, it will do so repeatedly in the future. The first time two peers communicate directly, they exchange shared secret keys (using public key encryption), and use shared keys to authenticate all messages to each other. Using HMAC based authentication, the performance of our system went back up to about 3500 pings per second.

3.4 Our Brothers' Keepers

Chord overlay structure relies on peers behaving properly: forwarding requests that they cannot satisfy and replying truthfully to requests that they can satisfy. However, if a malicious peer does not forward requests, or even worse, misdirects the requests or sends fraudulent replies, the overlay structure can be subverted. In particular, maligning the "find successor" requests, which are used by peers to find their position within the ring and construct finger tables, can create loops and partitions within the ring, rendering the overlay dysfunctional. That is, a few collaborating malicious peers could cause segments of the ring to "drop out".

Realistically, we can neither ensure that no malicious peer will ever join, nor can we ensure that no peer will ever be compromised. Malicious peers are distinguished by their behaviour that, when detected, can be quashed by excommunicating the peer. Thus, by increasing the system's ability to detect malicious behaviour, the amount of damage caused by a malicious peer can be limited. Since our key assignment scheme ensures that with high probability two malicious peers will not be near each other in the ring, we use a peer group approach to improve detection of malicious behaviour, i.e., the peer's proximate peers keep it honest.

Each peer in the ring, is associated with a peer group of size g, where g is a small odd number, such as 5, 7, 9, 11, etc. The group comprises the peer itself—the group leader— and $g - 1$ of its closest peers: $\frac{g-1}{2}$ closest preceding peers and $\frac{g-1}{2}$ closest succeeding peers. Thus, each peer belongs to g overlapping groups of size g. Furthermore, given our assumption about the uniform distribution of malicious peers, the chance of a group having multiple malicious peers is small.

When a new peer joins the ring, it queries its predecessor and successor for their group memberships, constructs its own group membership list from the responses, and then queries the other peers in its group to confirm their membership. On an ongoing basis, the peers in a group query each other's membership lists, updating them as peers join or leave. In closed overlays, particularly in the case of Trinity, we assume that the rate at which peers join and leave the ring is relatively low. Hence, a peer's group membership list will not change often.

In fact, a peer is only added to a group only after it has been verified by the group's leader, ensuring that group lists only contain valid peers. These group lists also provide a fast mechanism for finding a new successor or predecessors if the current one leaves (or fails) the ring.

A peer's group membership list, should be consistent with those of the group's members, e.g., if the group of peer p is (n, o, p, q, r), then peer q's group should be (o, p, q, r, s). Thus, if a peer sends a group list that is inconsistent with the lists of other group members, it is considered malicious, or at least untrustworthy. Consequently, malicious peers cannot easily send fraudulent "find successor" responses about their group members, because similar queries to their neighbours would unmask them. The result is that peers cannot send out false "find successor" replies to any of its neighbouring peers without being excommunicated.

However, it is also necessary to ensure that remote peers are also honest, i.e., those peers that are not within a peer's group. This is accomplished by leveraging the group structure. Specifically, a peer's "find successor" response is be verified by querying a member of its peer group, and is based on the fact that peers in the same group will have similar finger tables.

Recall, that a peer's ith finger table entry contains the successor to key $k + 2^i$, where k is the peer's key. Assuming that peers are uniformly distributed in the ring, if peers with keys k and k' are adjacent, then the successors to $k + 2^i$ and $k' + 2^i$ will likely be close to each other in the ring, if not the same peer. Thus, there will be considerable overlap between the groups associated with the ith finger table entries of the two peers. Consequently, a "find successor" response can be verified by resending the query to a member of the responder's group.

To facilitate this approach, and to verify the consistency of the groups associated with the finger table entries, our implementation uses an expanded finger table that stores the keys of the peer's entire group rather than just the peer's key—the finger table stores g keys per entry. Furthermore, a peer's "find successor" response includes the keys of the peer's entire group. Since "find successor" queries are sent on an ongoing basis, the finger table entries are updated and checked on a regular basis. Lastly, storing entire groups in the finger table, instead of single peers, facilitates the implementation of a simple randomized routing scheme, mitigating the problem of packet dropping by malicious peers.

3.5 Randomized Routing

Even if a malicious peer does not send fraudulent routing responses, it can still cause problem by simply dropping all messages. If a malicious peer is a choke-point between two other peers—all messages from one peer to the other are routed through it—then none of the messages may get through. Detecting this behaviour is problematic because the I3 Chord implementation and many other overlay systems use lightweight connectionless unreliable transport protocols, such as UDP. Consequently, it is impossible to distinguish between poor network connectivity and a misbehaving peer. Fortunately, our scheme can mitigate both problems. We note that we cannot ensure that no messages will be lost; only that with high probability, not all the messages will pass through the same peer, while in transit.

We use a variant of randomized routing [9]. Traditional randomized routing forwards the message to a randomly chosen peer in the system, and then from that peer to the destination. This can dramatically increase the latency, particularly if the destination peer is close to the sender but the randomly chosen peer is far away. Instead, in our scheme, multiple messages between two peers take different but comparable length paths, ensuring that a choke-point can not form.

When a message arrives at a peer, the peer classifies the message's destination as either local, near, or far. If the destination is local, then the message has arrived at its destination. If the destination is near, then the message is destined to a neighbour of the peer and is forwarded directly to its destination. Otherwise, a peer is selected and the message is forwarded to it.

According to the traditional deterministic forwarding protocol, the peer whose key most closely precedes the message destination is chosen from the finger table, and the message is forwarded to this peer. In our implementation, a group is chosen from the finger table such that the group leader's most closely precedes the message destination. Then, a peer is randomly chosen from this group and the message is forwarded to it.[4] Since the finger tables of the peers in a group are similar, the route taken between two peers will differ in the peers that the messages transit. However, as discussed in the preceding section, these peers are near each other within the ring, implying that the total number of hops will not vary greatly.

The correctness of the protocol does not change as long as the key of the peer selected from the finger table precedes the message destination, and since all peers in a group

----

[4] The selection process also ensures that the peer precedes the message destination.

are, by definition, near each other, the size of each hop is will differ by an additive constant, resulting in a small variance in the number of hops that a message takes.

Lastly, the malicious peer detection and the random routing scheme depend on the fact that the routing tables of proximate peers are similar. Consequently, the group size, g, cannot be too large because the farther a peer is from the group leader, the less similar is its routing table. Furthermore, using a larger group size requires larger messages and a larger finger table. At the same time, a group size should be large enough to tolerate peer failures and ensure that messages have a sufficient number of routes that they can take. Consequently, a group size of 5 to 15 should suffice.

4 Evaluation

To evaluate the performance of our implementation we used a 255 peer ring running on a 26 machine cluster running OpenBSD 4.3 and 4.2. One of these machines was an Intel Xeon X3210 2.13GHz Quad-core based server with 4GB of RAM, which ran 5 peers on it and served as the name server for the cluster. Each of the remaining 25 machines was an Intel Pentium 4 2.80 GHz based desktop with 1 GB of RAM. Each of these desktops ran 10 peers each and all the machines were interconnected via a Cisco WS-C2924–XL-EN and a Cisco WS-C3548-XL-EN managed switches that were locked at 10 Mb/s half-duplex—the mean latency between any two machines in the cluster was 0.5 milliseconds, with a negligible variance. We performed several different tests to measure the latency, throughput, and capacity of our implementation in both secure and insecure modes, in order to compare the overhead associated with secure mode.

4.1 Latency and throughput

We first compared the latency and throughput overhead of secure versus insecure operation. Since peers regenerate and exchange their shared keys at regular intervals, different parts of ring had different loads at different times. To compensate for this, a series of test runs were performed, spanning a sufficiently large time interval, and the minimums over these test runs were used.

Each test comprises two communicating peers: the initiator, which conducts and times the test, and the responder, which serves as the other end-point of the communication. The latency test measures the round trip time of a ping and its echo. The initiator pings the responder, which echos the ping—both the ping and the echo are routed through the overlay. The test is repeated sequentially a set number of times and the count is divided by the total time, yielding the round trip time per ping. The throughput test measures how fast packets (or messages) can be sent through the overlay. The initiator sends a throughput request to the responder, indicating the number of packets the responder should send back. The responder sends the requested number of packets (through the overlay) as quickly as possible, and the initiator measures the time difference between the arrival of the first and last packets—the number of packets divided by the difference is the throughput.

Our evaluation fixed one of the five peers on the 4-core server to be the initiator, and used the 250 peers running on the 25 desktops as responders. For both latency and

Table 1. Summary statistics of round trip times to peers and packets per second from peers

	Latency			Throughput		
	Insecure Op. RTT (sec)	Secure Op. RTT (sec)	Relative Difference	Insecure Op. Pkts / sec	Secure Op. Pkts / sec	Relative Difference
Mean	0.002874	0.003457	20.2%	6148	4946	19.4%
Median	0.002897	0.003483	20.2%	6389	5087	20.4%
Maximum	0.003542	0.004282	20.9%	7794	6566	15.8%
Minimum	0.000759	0.000880	15.9%	3107	2643	14.9%
Std. Dev.	0.000335	0.000411	N/A	1164	930	N/A

throughput measurements, the initiator performed 12 test series consisting of 10 test runs that consisted of 250 tests, once for each peer. Each latency test performed 10 pings at a time and each throughput test had the responder send back 1000 packets. Each series takes the minimum measurement for each peer over the 10 runs. The minimums for each peer from the 12 series are averaged to yield the latency or throughput measurement.

Table 1 displays the mean, median, maximum, minimum, and standard deviation round trip times and throughput measured for all 250 peers. The table shows the measurements for both insecure mode operation and secure mode operation, and the overhead of the secure mode.

The measured latency in secure mode is 20% greater than in insecure mode. Although, this seems high, it is important to remember that there were 10 peers running on each host, making the system CPU bound and that the time difference, 0.6 milliseconds, is negligible compared to the typical latency between two hosts in the Internet.

The throughput in secure mode is also on average 20% lower. This is due to the cost of authenticating messages: the sender has to sign each message and the receiver has to verify the message. Since message authentication is a CPU bounded task, its effect will be less when only one peer is running on each server.

It is more instructive to view the round trip times for each peer and throughput from each peer in a sorted order. The graph in Figure 2 shows the round trip times to all the peers for both insecure and secure operation modes, in ascending order of times measured in insecure mode. The graph in Figure 3 shows the throughput from all the peers for both insecure and secure operation modes, in descending order of times measured in insecure mode.

Several artifacts are immediately visible in Figure 2: First, four peers have much lower round trip times. These peers are the successors and predecessors of the peer performing the ping, and hence both the ping and the response only take one hop. Second, there is large jump in round trip times for both insecure and secures modes; approximately, 0.0025 and 0.003 seconds respectively. Since the minimum latency between two peers in the cluster is 0.0005 seconds, this means that pings to and from all the other peers take between 6 and 9 hops, which makes sense for a ring of 255 peers. Lastly, and most importantly, the relative difference in latency between insecure and secure operation remains fixed, at 0.06 milliseconds per hop.

Figure 3 also exhibits a couple important features. First, the graph has a step feature, corresponding to the distances between the initiator and the responders. The closer a responder is to the initiator, the higher the measured throughput. Second, the relative

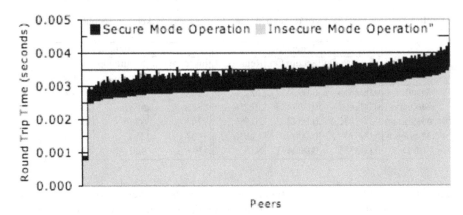

Fig. 2. Round trip times to peers

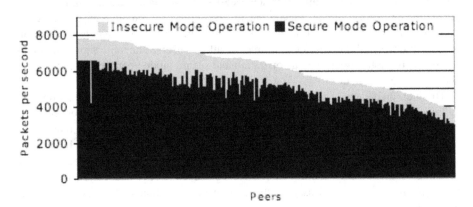

Fig. 3. Throughput from peers

decrease in throughput between insecure and secure operation remains relatively constant. As before the primary reason for the reduction is the cost of message authentication and is noticeable because 10 peers were running on each singe-core machine.

4.2 Capacity

The capacity of an overlay is the measure of the number of messages that the system can deliver per unit time. To measure the system's capacity we implemented a game of hot-potato over the overlay: A set number of messages (potatoes) are injected into the system. The potatoes are randomly passed from peer to peer, and counter in each potato tracks the number of times the potato is passed. By varying the number of concurrent potatoes in the system, we control the system's load.

When a peer receives a potato, it increments the potato's counter, generates a random key, and sends the potato to the peer responsible for the random key. To ensure that no potato is dropped, the receiving peer acknowledges the potato, and the sender acknowledges the acknowledgment. Only after receiving the second acknowledgment does the

Table 2. Number of passes per second that a message takes

# of msgs	10	20	30	40	50	60	70	80	160
Insecure Mode Operation									
Mean	163	134	107	86	72	60	51	45	23
Median	163	134	106	86	72	60	51	45	22
Std. Dev.	3.3	2.8	2.1	2.3	2.0	1.6	1.4	1.8	2.4
Maximum	172	141	113	92	77	65	54	50	33
Minimum	156	127	103	81	67	56	48	42	19
Secure Mode Operation									
Mean	138	115	93	76	62	53	45	40	20
Median	137	115	94	76	62	53	45	39	19
Std. Dev.	3.4	2.0	2.1	1.6	1.4	1.3	1.6	1.8	2.6
Maximum	147	120	98	79	68	55	49	46	29
Minimum	131	109	89	71	58	47	42	36	15

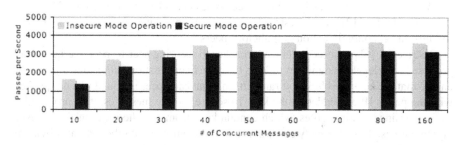

Fig. 4. Capacity of overlay.

receiver commence the next potato pass. If potato's originator receives it, and the potato has been in the system for a minimum amount of time, e.g., 60 seconds, the number of passes per second for the potato is computed, by dividing the value of the potato's pass counter by the number of seconds that the potato was in the system. The potato's time to live counter is then decremented, and if nonzero, the potato's pass counter is reset and the potato is injected into the system again. This ensures a period of consistent load.

In each of the runs, the first measurement from the first 75 ejected potatoes was used. Table 2 exhibits the mean, median, standard deviation, maximum, and minimum number of passes per second that a potato achieved under different system loads: 10, 20, 30, 40, 50, 60, 70, 80, and 160 potatoes in the system. Note: a pass consists of a 3-message exchange between two peers in the system and message delivery may take multiple hops within the overlay.

As the load increases, the number of passes per second of a potato decreases because the likelihood that a peer may need to process multiple potatoes at once increases. However, passes per second of a potato does not yield a measure of the capacity of the system as a whole. The capacity of the system is the number of passes per second that the system performs over all. This is equal to the average number of passes per second multiplied by the number potatoes in the system.

Figure 4 exhibits the capacity of the system for both insecure and secure operation modes. The capacity of the system is 3600 and 3150 passes per second in insecure and secure operation modes, respectively. In both cases the system becomes saturated at 50 potatoes, but capacity does not degrade as the number of potatoes increases. The relative difference in capacity is 12.5%, and is predominately affected by the CPU bounded task of message authentication.

As the size of the ring increases, the number of hops per pass will increase logarithmically. Consequently, the number of passes per second will increase because the number of hops per pass grows at a much slower rate than the number of peers in the ring. Thus, the capacity of the system should increase as the size of the ring grows.

5   Related Work

The challenge of securing peer-to-peer systems has been around since their advent. Sit and Morris [5] first identified a set of design principles for securing peer-to-peer systems and described a taxonomy of various attacks against them. This work was extended by Wallach [10] who investigated the security aspects of systems such as CAN [11], Chord [3], Pastry [12], and Tapestry [13], and discussed issues such as key assignment, routing, and excommunication of malicious peers.

Castro et al. [6] proposed several approaches to securing peer-to-peer overlays. They proposed to delegate assignment of keys to trusted certification authorities, that would ensure that the keys are chosen at random, and that each peer is bound to a unique key, with the peer's IP embedded in the key. To securely route messages, they proposed to use constrained routing tables, which contain keys from specific locations in the overlay. In our case Chord already constrains a key's location within the overlay, obviating the need for constrained routing tables. In fact, our self-policing and random routing mechanisms leverage this constraint.

Castro et al. [6] also proposed a routing failure test that tries to determine what nodes are malicious. Their approach also sends multiple copies of the message through diverse routes to ensure message delivery. Our approach is similar but less resource intensive. Our system uses the peer groups to detect faulty routing information, and to ensure that no peer is a choke-point between two other peers. Our system does not attempt to ensure the delivery of all messages, but instead attempts to ensure that some messages will be delivered.

There are many different ways to secure peer-to-peer systems. For example systems such as LOCKSS [4], use majority voting replicas and computationally rate-limiting cryptographic puzzles [14]. Unfortunately, these approaches severely impact system performance and are not practical in the context where good performance is a necessity.

Lastly, some of the mechanisms used in our extension are also used in the design of accountable systems [15]. The goal of accountable systems is to detect and provide unforgable proof of a peer's misbehaviour. Such proof is a necessary component of any system that allows for the excommunication of malicious peers. PeerReview [15] uses witness peers to validate a peer's behaviour and to construct a proof of a peer's misbehaviour. However, unlike in our system, the witnesses are not proximate and compare the log of a peer's actions to a simulation of the peer. In our system the veracity of a peer's response can be checked by comparing it to that of its neighbours and does not require a simulation of the peer.

6   Conclusion and Future Work

We have designed and implemented a secure and efficient extension to the I3 [2] implementation of the Chord structured overlay [3]. Our extension is aimed at closed overlays in which membership is tightly controlled. This context requires mechanisms for peer identification, authentication, and authorization, mechanisms for message authentication, and mechanisms to mitigate the behaviour of malicious peers in the overlay, which are unavoidable.

Our implementation uses a simple hashing scheme to generate keys that are linked to peer's network address, and are uniformly distributed in the key space. The keys are embedded into messages, linking each message to its sender via an efficient two-part authentication mechanism, combining public key and HMAC message authentication. Secure routing is implemented via self-policing peer groups that force malicious peers to either behave properly or face detection. Lastly, these groups are leveraged for a simple random routing scheme that prevents choke-points within the overlay.

Our evaluation, which was performed on a local cluster, has demonstrated that our implementation's overhead, of about 20%, is primarily due to CPU bounded operations. We believe that this effect will significantly decrease under normal conditions in the larger Internet context where latency will dominate, and where multiple peers are not running on the same host.

To validate this hypothesis, we intend to perform a more realistic evaluation using the Planet-Lab platform, which spans the world and will allow us to test much larger overlays. We are in the process of implementing the Trinity [1] e-mail classification system on top of our secure overlay. This will provide additional opportunities to identify and solve performance bottlenecks in our implementation.

References

1. Brodsky, A., Brodsky, D.: A distributed content independent method for spam detection. In: Proc. of the 1st USENIX Workshop on Hot Topics in Understanding Botnet (2007)
2. Stoica, I., Adkins, D., Zhuang, S., Shenker, S., Surana, S.: Internet indirection infrastructure. IEEE/ACM Transactions on Networks 12(2), 205–218 (2004)
3. Stoica, I., Morris, R., Karger, D., Kaashoek, M.F., Balakrishnan, H.: Chord: A scalable peer-to-peer lookup service for internet applications. In: Proc. of the ACM SIGCOMM 2001 Conference (2001)
4. Maniatis, P., Rosenthal, D., Roussopoulos, M., Baker, M., Giuli, T., Muliadi, Y.: Preserving peer replicas by rate-limited sampled voting. In: Proc. of the 19th ACM Symposium on Operating Systems Principles (2003)
5. Sit, E., Morris, R.: Security considerations for peer-to-peer distributed hash tables. In: Druschel, P., Kaashoek, M.F., Rowstron, A. (eds.) IPTPS 2002. LNCS, vol. 2429. Springer, Heidelberg (2002)
6. Castro, M., Druschel, P., Ganesh, A., Rowstron, A., Wallach, D.: Secure routing for structured peer-to-peer overlay networks. In: Proc. of the 5th ACM Symposium on Operating System Design and Implementation (2002)
7. Mockapetris, P.: RFC 1034 – Domain Names - Concepts and Facilities. Internet Engineering Task Force (1987)

8. Mockapetris, P.: RFC 1035 – Domain Names - Implementation and Specification. Internet Engineering Task Force (1987)
9. Leighton, T., Maggs, B., Ranade, A., Rao, S.: Randomized routing and sorting on fixed-connection networks. J. Algorithms 17(1), 157–205 (1994)
10. Wallach, D.: A survey of peer-to-peer security issues. In: Okada, M., Pierce, B.C., Scedrov, A., Tokuda, H., Yonezawa, A. (eds.) ISSS 2002. LNCS, vol. 2609, pp. 42–57. Springer, Heidelberg (2003)
11. Ratnasamy, S., Francis, P., Handley, M., Karp, R., Shenker, S.: A scalable content-addressable network. In: Proc. of the ACM SIGCOMM 2001 Conference, pp. 161–172 (2001)
12. Rowstron, A., Druschel, P.: Pastry: Scalable, decentralized object location, and routing for large-scale peer-to-peer systems. In: Guerraoui, R. (ed.) Middleware 2001. LNCS, vol. 2218, p. 329. Springer, Heidelberg (2001)
13. Zhao, B., Kubiatowicz, J., Joseph, A.: Tapestry: An infrastructure for fault-tolerant wide-area location androuting. Technical report (April 04, 2001)
14. Dwork, C., Naor, M.: Pricing via processing or combatting junk mail. In: Brickell, E.F. (ed.) CRYPTO 1992. LNCS, vol. 740, pp. 139–147. Springer, Heidelberg (1993)
15. Haeberlen, A., Kouznetsov, P., Druschel, P.: Peerreview: practical accountability for distributed systems. In: Proceedings of the 21st ACM Symposium on Operating Systems Principles, pp. 175–188 (2007)

Pharewell to Phishing

Taehwan Choi[1], Sooel Son[1], Mohamed G. Gouda[1], and Jorge A. Cobb[2]

[1] The University of Texas at Austin
{ctlight,samuel,gouda}@cs.utexas.edu
[2] The University of Texas at Dallas
cobb@utdallas.edu

Abstract. The conventional wisdom has always been that users should refrain from entering their sensitive data (such as usernames, passwords, and credit card numbers) into http(or white) pages, but they can enter these data into https (or yellow) pages. Unfortunately, this assumption is not valid as it became clear recently that, through human mistakes or Phishing or Pharming attacks, a displayed yellow page may not be the same one that the user has intended to request in the first place. In this paper, we propose to add a third class of secure web pages called brown pages. We show that brown pages are more secure than yellow pages especially in face of human mistakes and Phishing and Pharming attacks. Thus users can enter their sensitive data into brown pages without worry. We present a login protocol, called the Transport Login Protocol or TLP for short. An https web page that is displayed on the browser is classified brown by the browser if and only if this web page has been called into the browser either through TLP or from within another brown page that had been called earlier into the browser through TLP.

1 Introduction

When a user needs to display a web page on his browser, the user follows any one of four direction rules, described below, to request that his browser calls the page and displays it on the screen. If the requested page is an (insecure) http page, then the browser calls the page and displays it without any firm guarantee that the displayed page is the one that the user has requested. On the other hand, if the requested page is a (secure) https page, then the browser displays the page only after it has authenticated that the page is the one that the user has requested. Unfortunately, as described below, the authentication procedure is vulnerable to human mistakes, by the user, and to Phishing and Pharming attacks [1], by adversarial web sites. And so it is possible that the displayed page may not be the one requested by the user after all.

The user may not mind that the displayed page is different from the page that he has requested for two reasons. First, both the displayed page and the page that the user has requested have similar graphics and colors and the user may not notice that the displayed page is actually not the one that he has requested even in the presence of security indicators [2]. Second, the user may notice that the displayed page is not the one that he has requested, but he may believe that

S. Kulkarni and A. Schiper (Eds.): SSS 2008, LNCS 5340, pp. 233–245, 2008.
© Springer-Verlag Berlin Heidelberg 2008

the displayed page is a legitimate redirection that was requested by the page that he has requested. In any case, the user may proceed to enter some sensitive data, such as his credit card number, into the displayed page which may happen to be an adversarial page.

This paper is dedicated to prevent these scenarios from occurring. Towards this end, we propose to introduce a new class of https web pages, which we refer to as brown pages. As discussed below, brown pages are secure against human mistakes and Phishing and Pharming attacks. Thus, when a user requests that his browser calls and displays an https page and then the browser displays the page and classifies it brown, the user knows that the displayed page is indeed the one that he has requested and so he can proceed to enter his sensitive data into it.

In order for the browser to be able to classify a called https page brown, the browser needs to call this page through a login protocol that is completely secure against human mistakes and Phishing and Pharming attacks. In this paper, we present and discuss the design and implementation of such a login protocol.

2   Attack Scenarios

In this section, we describe three attack scenarios, caused by human mistakes or Phishing or Pharming attacks[3,4]. In each one of these scenarios, a user intends to call into his browser a particular https page, but he ends up calling a wrong https page into his browser.

1. **Human Mistakes**
   A user intends to enter the URL `https://www.amazon.com` into the URL box of his browser. But he enters the wrong URL `https://www.anazon.com` by mistake.

2. **Phishing Attacks**
   A user receives an email that urges the user to click on a link described as leading to the web site `https://www.amazon.com`. By clicking on this link, the user ends up in the wrong web site `https://www.anazon.com`.

3. **Pharming Attacks**
   For the convenience of its users, the web site `https://www.amazon.com` allows its users to call the web site using the alternative insecure URL `http://www.amazon.com`. Now, the DNS of a user can be manipulated so that when the user uses this insecure URL to request the web site, the user's DNS directs the request to an adversarial web site that redirects the user's browser to the wrong web site `https://www.anazon.com`.

In each one of these three scenarios, the user intended to call into his browser the web site `https://www.amazon.com`, but he ends up calling the wrong web site `https://www.anazon.com`. The user does not notice the switch, from `https://www.amazon.com` to `https://www.anazon.com`, because the two web sites have similar logos, graphics, and colors, and maybe similar URLs. Thus the user proceeds to enter his sensitive information (such as username, password, or credit card numbers) into the wrong web site. The objective of this paper is to outline a proposal to counter these three attack scenarios.

One method to counter these scenarios is to advise the user to be careful and check the URL box of the displayed https web page on his browser before he enters his sensitive data into the displayed web page. However, it is very difficult for a user to remember and follow this advice every time he requests an https web page.

A second method to counter these scenarios is to make the browser check, before it displays an https web page, that this page is indeed the one that the user wants. Unfortunately, the browser can not tell whether or not the user wants the web page whose URL is in the URL box.

The method that we adopt in this paper to counter these scenarios is as follows. Browser B of user U displays an https page from a web site S when and only when the following three conditions hold.

1. User U has requested the page.
2. Site S has verified that sometime in the past user U has registered and stored his login data in site S.
3. Browser B has verified that sometime in the past user U has registered and stored his login data in site S.

If any one of these three conditions does not hold, then the browser of user U refuses to display the requested page. The correctness of this method is based on the reasonable assumption that each web site in which user U registers is a legitimate, rather than an adversarial, site. Next, we argue that this method can counter the above three scenarios.

Consider the first scenario. If user U intends to request the web site `https://www.amazon.com`, but by mistake requests the web site `https://www.amazon.com`, then only one of two outcomes is possible. The most likely outcome is that user U has not registered in the web site `https://www.amazon.com` and so the browser of user U will not display the web page. The second outcome is that user U has registered in the web site `https://www.amazon.com` and so the browser will display the legitimate web page of this site and user U will notice that the displayed page is not the one that he wants.

Now consider the second and third scenarios. In these scenarios, the web site `https://www.amazon.com` is an adversarial site and so user U has not registered in it. Thus, browser of user U will not display the web page.

3   Countering the Attack Scenarios

In this section, we outline our proposal to modify the browser and some web sites in order to counter the attack scenarios, caused by human mistakes and Phishing and Pharming attacks, discussed in the previous section. Our proposal consists of three parts.

1. **White, Yellow, and Brown Pages**
   We propose to modify the browser so that the browser classifies each displayed http web page as white, and classifies each displayed https web page as either yellow or brown. As described below, a user should regard each white page as insecure, each yellow page as mildly secure (which means that the page is vulnerable to human mistakes and Phishing and Pharming attacks), and each brown page as highly secure (which means that the page is secure against human mistakes and Phishing and Pharming attacks).

2. **A New Login Protocol**
   We also propose to add a new login protocol to the browser and to some web sites that need to be (extra) secure against human mistakes and Phishing and Pharming attacks. We call this new login protocol the Transport Login Protocol or TLP for short. When a user invokes TLP on his browser and requests the browser to call a web page on a specified web site, the following three steps are executed. First, the browser and the specified web site use TLP to establish mutual authentication between each other. Second, if the mutual authentication between the browser and the web site succeeds, then the web site redirects the browser to an https web page. Third, the browser calls the secure web page and, upon receiving it, the browser assigns it a brown classification and displays it to the user.

3. **Classification of Web Pages**
   The modified browser assigns a classification, white, yellow, or brown, to each displayed web page, depending on how this page has been called into the browser in the first place. Thus the same displayed https page can be assigned a yellow classification if it is called into the browser one way, and assigned a brown classification if it is called into the browser another way. We adopt the following classification rules.
   (a) Any http page, that is called into the browser, is classified white by the browser.
   (b) Any https page, that is called into the browser using our login protocol TLP, is classified brown by the browser.
   (c) Any https page, that is called into the browser using the TLS protocol[5], is either classified yellow if this page is called from within a displayed white or yellow page, or classified brown if this page is called from within a displayed brown page.

When the browser displays a web page, the browser makes its classification of the displayed page clear to the user by choosing an appropriate background color for the URL box. If the displayed page is white (or yellow or brown respectively), then the background color for the URL box is white (or yellow or brown respectively). Note that the current browser already supports white and yellow classifications of web pages. So the main contributions of this project are merely the addition of brown classifications and the introduction of the new login protocol TLP which can be used in calling brown web pages into the browser.

(Recently, a green classification of https web pages has been introduced to distinguish those https pages that have extended validation certificates[6]. Clearly some green pages, like yellow pages, can still be adversarial, and can still be used in launching Phishing and Pharming attacks as described above. Henceforth, when we refer to yellow pages, we do mean yellow or green pages.)

The policy for entering sensitive data (such as usernames, passwords, and credit card numbers) into a displayed web page depends on the classification of the displayed page. This policy consists of the following three rules.

1. **The White Page Rule**
   A user should never enter sensitive data into a white page.

2. **The Brown Page Rule**
   A user can enter sensitive data into a brown page.

3. **The Yellow Page Rule**
   Before a user can enter sensitive data into a yellow page, the user should have prior knowledge that this data can be entered into this particular page, and the user should check that the URL box of the displayed page has indeed the URL of this particular page.

4 The Current Login Protocol

Our login protocol TLP, described in the next section, enjoys a number of nice features that are not all present in any of the current login protocols. These nice features are as follows.

1. **Immunity to Attacks**
   When a user U uses TLP to log in a site S, then the login succeeds if and only if both browser B of user U and site S can verify that user U has registered (and stored some login data) in site S sometime in the past.

2. **No External Servers**
   All the login data, that are needed by user U to use TLP and successfully log in site S, are stored on site S. Thus TLP does not need any external servers to store some of the login data.

3. **One-Time Login Data**
   In TLP, the login data, that are needed by user U to log in site S, are updated after each successful login of U into S. Therefore, if an adversary somehow steals the login data of user U in site S, then the stolen data becomes useless after the next login of U into S.

4. **Universal Passwords**
   Each user U needs only to memorize one password P, called the TLP universal password of U. User U employs his universal password in the TLP

protocol to log in every web site. No web site S can deduce the TLP universal password of user U from the login data that user U stores in S or from the messages exchanged between the browser of U and site S during the execution of TLP.

5. **Standard Cryptography**
   TLP uses only standard symmetric cryptography and standard secure hash functions. Thus, every time the standards of symmetric cryptography or of hash functions are updated, the standards of TLP are updated accordingly.

Next we argue that none of the login protocols, that have been proposed recently, enjoys all these five features.

The current login protocol over the web consists of two protocols: the standard TLS protocol [5] (which is used to authenticate a secure web site by the browser), and a non-standard password protocol (which is sometimes used to authenticate the secure web site by the user and to authenticate the user by the secure web site). As described in Section 2, this login protocol is vulnerable to human mistakes and Phishing and Pharming attacks, and so it does not enjoy feature 1.

This login protocol can be strengthened using Site Keys which allow a user to authenticate the identity of the web site being logged in [7,8]. Unfortunately, Site Keys can be stolen using Man-In-The-Middle Attacks. Thus the strengthened protocol still does not enjoy feature 1.

The login protocol SRP[9,10] doest not enjoy any of features 3, 4, and 5 above.

The hash-based protocols, such as [11,12,13,14], enjoy the features 2, 4, and 5. They also allow the web site to verify that the user has registered in the site sometimes in the past. Unfortunately, they do no allow the user's browser to verify that the user has registered in the site sometime in the past. Thus these protocols do not enjoy feature 1. Also, some of these protocols, for example [13], do not enjoy feature 2.

The Passpet system[15] does not enjoy features 2 and 3.

5   The New Login Protocol

Our login protocol TLP is to be executed between browser B of user U and web site S. Prior to executing TLP, user U needs to have registered with site S by making its browser B store in S the following tuple of four data items:

$$(H(U), \quad n, \quad H(0, n, P, S), \quad H^2(1, n, P, S))$$

where

> U is the username of the user,
> B is the browser of user U,
> n is a nonce selected at random by browser B,
> H is a standard secure hash function,
>   0 is the character zero,

1 is the character one,

P is the TLP universal password of user U, and

S is the domain name of the web site.

Note that $H(0, n, P, S)$ denotes the application of the secure hash function H to the concatenation of the four data items 0, n, P, and S. Also, $H^2(1, n, P, S)$ denotes two consecutive applications of function H to the concatenation of the four data items 1, n, P, and S. After B stores this tuple in S, B forgets the tuple completely.

Executing TLP between browser B and site S is intended to achieve five objectives.

1. B checks that S is one of the sites where user U had previously registered (and stored the above tuple of four data items).
2. S checks that user U has entered his universal password P to browser B.
3. Both B and S agree on a symmetric session key that they can use to encrypt and decrypt their exchanged messages.
4. B selects a new random nonce n' and stores the following tuple of four data items in S in place of the above tuple:

$$(H(U), \quad n', \quad H(0, n', P, S), \quad H^2(1, n', P, S))$$

   (Therefore, each successful login of browser B into site S causes the tuple of four data items that B had previously stored in S to be replaced by a new tuple of four data items also provided by B.)
5. S sends to B the URL of the next https page that B needs to call, using TLS, along with a cookie identifying user U and testifying that the login procedure between U's browser and S, has been successful. When the next https page is called into B, B assigns this page a brown classification. Moreover browser B assigns any other https page, that is called using TLS from within this brown page, a brown classification .

We adopt the following notation in describing a field in a message that is sent during the execution of TLP.

$$[expression1] < expression2 >$$

This notation means that the value of *expression1* is used as a symmetric key to encrypt the value of *expression2* before the message is sent.

To start executing TLP between B and S, user U enters three data items, namely U, P, and S, to a local web page named `httpl` stored in browser B. Then the execution of TLP proceeds with the following four message exchanges between B and S.

$B \rightarrow S$: {Hello Message}
$\quad U$

$B \leftarrow S$: {Hello-Reply Message}
$\quad n, \quad [H(0, n, P, S)] < SN >$

$B \rightarrow S$: {Login Message}
$\quad U,$
$\quad [H(H^2(1, n, P, S), SN)] < H(1, n, P, S), BN, H^2(1, n', P, S) >,$
$\quad [H(BN, SN)] < n', H(0, n', P, S) >$

$B \leftarrow S$: {Login-Reply Message}
$\quad [H(BN, SN)] < $ URL of next https web page $>,$
$\quad [H(BN, SN)] < $ cookie $>$

The hello message, from B to S, consists of the username of user U who wants to log in site S. On receiving this message, S fetches the tuple

$$(H(U), n, H(0, n, P, S), H^2(1, n, P, S))$$

that B had stored previously in S. Then S uses the data item $H(0, n, P, S)$ as a symmetric key to encrypt a new nonce SN that S selects at random. The result of the encryption is denoted $[H(0, n, P, S)] < SN >$ and is included in the hello-reply message that is sent from S to B.

After B receives the hello-reply message, it computes $H(0, n, P, S)$ and uses it to obtain the nonce SN from the received message. Then, B selects at random two nonces BN and n', and uses the received SN and the computed BN and n' to construct the login message before sending it to site S.

After S receives the login message, it performs four tasks. First, it checks that user U has indeed entered its TLP universal password P into browser B. Second, S extracts the nonce BN from the received message, and now both B and S know BN and SN. Third, S stores the tuple:
$(H(U), \quad n', \quad H(0, n', P, S), \quad H^2(1, n', P, S))$ in place of the earlier tuple. Fourth, S constructs the login-reply message and sends it to browser B.

After B receives the login-reply message, it concludes that S is one of the web sites where user U has previously registered. Moreover, B gets the URL of the https page that B needs to call next using TLS, along with a cookie that identifies user U and testifies to the fact that the login procedure between U's browser and S has been successful.

Figure 1 illustrates the five steps that are needed for a user to use TLP to log in a web site in a domain say xyz.com.

1. The user calls a local web page, for convenience named the httpl page, on his browser and enters his username, his TLP universal password, and the site address www.xyz.com into this page.
2. The browser uses DNS to get the IP address of site www.xyz.com.
3. The browser and site www.xyz.com execute TLP. At the end, the browser receives the URL of a web page on site online.xyz.com and a cookie.

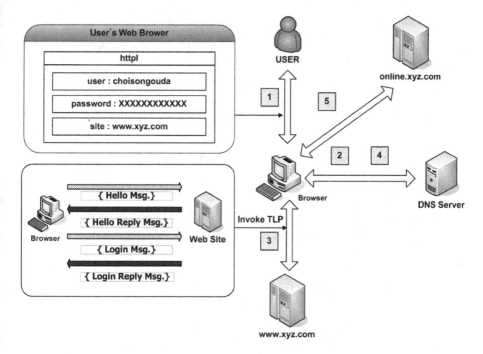

Fig. 1. Using TLP

4. The browser uses DNS to get the IP address of site `online.xyz.com`.
5. The browser and site `online.xyz.com` execute TLS, and the browser gets the required https page at the end. The browser classifies this page brown. It also classifies any other https page, that is called using TLS from within this page, brown.

An argument for the correctness of TLP is presented in [16].

6   User Interface of TLP

As a proof of concept, we have developed a prototype of our Transport Login Protocol TLP. The browser side of our prototype is developed on the Firefox browser using the two technologies of Javascript and HTML. The web site side of our prototype is developed on the Tomcat web server using four technologies: Java, HTML, the JSP (Java Server Page) technology, and the MySQL database technology. Note that the MySQL database technology is used to manage the login tuples, of all users, that are stored in the web site.

We employed standard cryptography in our prototype. In particular, we employed the Secure Hash Algorithm SHA-1 for secure hash, and employed the Advanced Encryption Standard AES for symmetric key cryptography.

The guiding principle in our prototype is to ensure that the user never enters his TLP universal password into a web page that is supplied by a web site, but

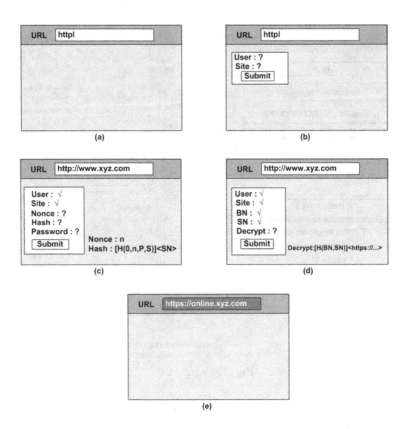

Fig. 2. User Interface of TLP

he can enter his password into a local web page that is supplied by his own browser. It turns out that this principle is hard to fulfill in our prototype in the light of the "Same Origin Policy" that is adopted by the Javascript technology. At the end, however, we were able to fulfill this principle by designing a novel user interface for our prototype. We discuss this user interface next.

Figure 2 details the four steps that need to be taken by a user to log in a web site www.xyz.com.

1. The user first enters httpl into the URL box of his browser and pushes $< return >$; see Figure 4a. This causes a display of the local page httpl to appear as a small window on the left site of the screen; see Figure 4b.
2. The user enters his username and the name of the site www.xyz.com into page httpl then clicks on the $< submit >$ button in this page. This causes page httpl to execute, update its own display, and send a Hello message (the first message in TLP) to site www.xyz.com which replies by sending back the web page http://www.xyz.com. This page contains the two fields, named nonce and hash, of the Hello-Reply message (the second message in TLP); see Figure 4c.

3. The user copies the values of the two fields nonce and hash from the displayed page http://www.xyz.com and enters them into page httpl. The user then enters his password into page httpl and clicks on the $<$ *submit* $>$ button of this page. This causes page httpl to execute, update its own display, and send a Login message (the third message in TLP) to site www.xyz.com which replies by sending back a new web page http://www.xyz.com. This new page contains one field, named decrypt, of the Login-Reply message (the last message in TLP); see Figure 4d.

4. The user copies the value of field decrypt from the displayed page http://www.xyz.com and enters it into page httpl. The user then clicks on the $<$ *submit* $>$ button of page httpl. This causes page httpl to execute, compute the next https page, say page https://online.xyz.com, that needs to be called into the browser, and redirects the browser to call this page using TLS and display it on the screen. Note that in this case the browser assigns the displayed https page a brown classification, and so the background color of the URL box of the displayed page becomes brown as shown in Figure 2e.

Because the browser has classified the displayed page https://online.xyz.com brown, then if the user clicks on any link (of an https page) in page https://online.xyz.com, then the browser will classify the newly called page brown as well.

7   Concluding Remarks

In this paper, we present a comprehensive proposal to counter human mistakes and Phishing and Pharming attacks that may occur when a user attempts to log in a secure web site. Our proposal is based on two ideas. First, we introduce a new classification, brown, of secure https web pages. When the browser of a user U classifies a displayed page brown, user U should conclude that the displayed page is secure and can enter his sensitive data into it. Second, we design a new login protocol, named TLP, that is secure against human mistakes and Phishing and Pharming attacks. The browser of a user U uses TLP to classify a displayed page brown according to two rules:

1. The displayed page is called into the browser using TLP.
2. The displayed page is called into the browser, using TLS, from within another brown page that was displayed earlier on the browser.

Note that TLP is not intended to replace TLS. On the contrary, our vision assigns complementary roles to be played by TLP and TLS: TLP can be used first to securely log in a web domain, then TLS can be used later to securely go from one web site to another within the logged in domain.

Note also that some mildly secure web domains may feel that they are in no danger of facing Phishing or Pharming attacks because adversaries have little incentive to launch such attacks against these domains. (Examples of such domains are those that host electronic reviewing and handling of submitted papers

244 T. Choi et al.

to conferences and journals.) These web domains can keep on employing TLS, as they do presently, both for logging in a domain and for going from one web site to another within this domain.

A nice feature of TLP is that a user can use the same username and same (TLP universal) password to securely log in any web site in the Internet. This means that the user needs only to memorize one username and one password for all web sites. Therefore it is reasonable to demand that each user chooses a long string, say of sixteen characters, to be his TLP universal password. And so TLP becomes naturally secure against online and offline dictionary attacks.

Acknowledgement

The work of Mohamed G. Gouda was supported in part by the US National Science Foundation under grant CNS-0520250.

References

1. Ollmann, G.: The Pharming Guide,
   http://www.ngssoftware.com/papers/ThePharmingGuide.pdf
2. Dhamija, R., Tygar, J., Hearst, M.: Why Phishing Works. In: The Proceedings of the Conference on Human Factors in Computing Systems (CHI 2006) (2006)
3. Group, A.P.W.: Phising activity trends report, (September 2007),
   http://www.antiphishing.org/reports/apwg_report_sept_2007.pdf
4. McMillan, R.: Gartner: Consumers to lose $2.8 billion to phishers in 2006 (2006),
   http://www.networkworld.com/news/2006/
   110906-gartner-consumers-to-lose-28b.html
5. Blake-Wilson, S., Nystrom, M., Hopwood, D., Mikkelsen, J., Wright, T.: Transport Layer Security (TLS) Extensions. RFC 4366 (Proposed Standard) (April 2006)
6. Franco, R.: Website identification and extended validation certificates in IE7 and other browsers. IEBlog (November 2005)
7. PassMark Security, http://www.passmarksecurity.com
8. Bank of America, http://www.bankofamerica.com/privacy/sitekey/
9. Wu, T.: The Secure Remote Password Protocol. In: Proceedings of the 1998 Internet Society Network and Distributed System Security Symposium, pp. 97–111 (1998)
10. Wu, T.: SRP-6: Improvements and Refinements to the Secure Remote Password Protocol. Submission to the IEEE P1363 Working Group
11. Gabber, E., Gibbons, P.B., Matias, Y., Mayer, A.: A Convenient Method for Securely Managing Passwords. In: Financial Cryptography (Feburuary 1997)
12. Kelsey, J., Schneier, B., Hall, C., Wagner, D.: Secure Applications of Low-Entropy Keys. In: Okamoto, E. (ed.) ISW 1997. LNCS, vol. 1396, pp. 121–134. Springer, Heidelberg (1998)
13. Halderman, J.A., Waters, B., Felten, E.W.: A Convenient Method for Securely Managing Passwords. In: 14th International World Wide Web Conference (May 2005)

14. Gouda, M.G., Liu, A.X., Leung, L.M., Alam, M.A.: SPP: An anti-phishing single password protocol. Comput. Netw. 51(13), 3715–3726 (2007)
15. Yee, K.P., Sitaker, K.: Passpet: convenient password management and phishing protection. In: SOUPS 2006: Proceedings of the second symposium on Usable privacy and security, pp. 32–43. ACM, New York (2006)
16. Choi, T., Son, S., Gouda, M.G.: Pharwell to Phishing: Secure Direction and Redirection over the Web. Technical Report TR-08-19, Austin, TX, USA (April 2008)

The Asynchronous Bounded-Cycle Model

Peter Robinson* and Ulrich Schmid

Technische Universität Wien
Embedded Computing Systems Group (E182/2)
Treitlstrasse 1-3, A-1040 Vienna (Austria)
{robinson,s}@ecs.tuwien.ac.at

Abstract. This paper shows how synchrony conditions can be added to the purely asynchronous model in a way that avoids any reference to message delays and computing step times, as well as any global constraints on communication patterns and network topology. Our Asynchronous Bounded-Cycle (ABC) model just bounds the ratio of the number of forward- and backward-oriented messages in certain ("relevant") cycles in the space-time diagram of an asynchronous execution. We show that clock synchronization and lock-step rounds can easily be implemented and proved correct in the ABC model, even in the presence of Byzantine failures. We also prove that any algorithm working correctly in the partially synchronous Θ-Model also works correctly in the ABC model. Finally, we relate our model to the classic partially synchronous model, and discuss aspects of its applicability in real systems.

Key words: Fault-tolerant distributed algorithms, partially synchronous models, clock synchronization.

1   Introduction

Adding synchrony conditions, relating the occurrence times of certain events in a distributed system to each other, is the "classic" approach for circumventing impossibility results like [9] in fault-tolerant distributed computing. The following models in between synchrony and asynchrony, which are all sufficiently strong for solving the pivotal consensus problem, have been proposed in literature: (1) The Archimedean model [20] bounds the ratio between maximum end-to-end delays and minimal computing step times. (2) The classic partially synchronous models [7,5] and the semi-synchronous models [18,3] bound message delays as well as the ratio of minimal and maximal computing step times. (3) The Θ-Model [21,4,22] bounds the ratio between the maximal and minimal end-to-end delay of messages simultaneously in transit. (4) The FAR-Model [8] assumes lower bounded computing step times and message delays with finite average. (5) The Weak Timely Link (WTL) models of [1,13,11] assume that only messages sent via certain links have bounded end-to-end delay. All these models refer to

---

* This research is supported by the Austrian Science Foundation (FWF) projects P17757 and P20529. A brief announcement appeared in the proceedings of PODC'08.

S. Kulkarni and A. Schiper (Eds.): SSS 2008, LNCS 5340, pp. 246–262, 2008.

individual message delays and/or computing step times, and most of them involve explicit time bounds and system-wide (global) constraints. Somewhat an exception is (6) the MMR model [17] suggested for implementing failure detectors in systems with process crashes, which assumes certain order properties for round-trip responses.

This paper shows how to add synchrony assumptions—sufficiently strong for implementing lock-step rounds, and hence for solving any important distributed computing problem—to the asynchronous model in a way that entirely avoids (1) any reference to message delays and computing step times, and (2) any global constraint on communication patterns and network topology. More specifically, our *Asynchronous Bounded-Cycle* (ABC) model bounds the ratio of the *number* of forward- and backward-oriented messages in certain cycles ("relevant cycles") in the space-time diagram of an asynchronous execution. In fact, there is only one scenario that is admissible in the purely asynchronous model but not in the ABC model: A chain C_1 of k_1 consecutive messages, starting at process q and ending at p, that properly "spans" (i.e., covers w.r.t. real-time, see Fig. 2) another causal chain C_2 from q to p involving $k_2 \geqslant k_1 \varXi$ messages, for some model parameter $\varXi > 1$.

Consequently, individual message delays can be arbitrary, ranging from 0 to any finite value; they may even continuously increase. There is no relation at all between computing step times and/or message delays at processes that do not exchange messages; this also includes purely one-way communication ("isolated chains"). For processes that do exchange messages, message delays and step times in non-relevant cycles and isolated chains can also be arbitrary. Only *cumulative* delays of chains C_1 and C_2 in *relevant* cycles must yield the event order as shown in Fig. 2. That is, the *sum* of the message delays along C_2 must not become so small that C_1 could span $k_1 \varXi$ or more messages in C_2. ABC algorithms can exploit the fact that this property allows to "time out" relevant message chains, and hence failure detection.

2   The ABC Model

We consider a system of n distributed processes, connected by a (not necessarily fully-connected) point-to-point network with finite but unbounded message delays. We neither assume FIFO communication channels nor an authentication service, but we do assume that processes know the sender of a received message.

Every process executes an instance of a distributed algorithm and is modeled as a state machine. Its local execution consists of a sequence of atomic, zero-time computing steps, each involving the reception of exactly one[1] message, a state transition, and the sending of zero or more messages to a subset of the processes in the system. Since the ABC model is entirely time-free, i.e., does not introduce any time-related bounds, we restrict our attention to message-driven algorithms [4, 14]: Computing steps at process p are exclusively triggered by a

---

[1] An algorithm cannot learn anything from receiving multiple asynchronous messages at the same time, cp. [6].

single incoming message at p, with an external "wake-up message" initiating p's very first computing step; we assume that this very first step occurs before any message from another process is received.

Among the n processes, at most f may be Byzantine faulty. A faulty process may deviate arbitrarily from the behavior of correct processes as described above; it may of course just crash as well, in which case it possibly fails to complete some computing step and does not take further steps. In order to properly capture the interaction of correct and faulty processes, we conceptually distinguish the receive event that triggers a computing step and the computing step itself. If the process is correct, both occur at the same time. In case of a faulty receiver process, however, we separate the reception of a message, which is not under the receiver's control but initiated by the network, from the processing of this message, which is under the receiver's control and hence arbitrary in case of a faulty receiver. Consequently, even crashed processes eventually receive messages sent by correct processes, and since processes can only receive one message per step, there is a total order on the receive events at every process.

We can now specify admissible executions for our asynchronous message-driven system, cp. [4]: (1) If an infinite number of messages are sent to a correct process, it must execute infinitely many computing steps, and (2) every message sent by a correct process must be received by every [correct or faulty] recipient within finite time. Note that we do not say anything about messages sent by faulty processes here, which are usually unconstrained anyway.

The ABC model just puts one additional constraint on admissible executions. It is based on the space-time diagram [12], which captures the causal flow of information in an admissible execution α. In order to properly include faulty processes, we just drop every message sent by a faulty process (along with both its send and receive step) in the space-time diagram. Note that a similar message dropping can be used for exempting certain messages, say, of some specific type or sent/received by some specific processes, from the ABC synchrony condition. After all, it is the particular algorithm that determines whether the order of certain receive events matters, i.e., whether the involved cycle is relevant or not.

Definition 1 (Execution Graph). *The execution graph G_α is the digraph corresponding to the space-time diagram of an admissible execution α, with nodes $V(G_\alpha) = \Phi$ corresponding to the receive events in α, and edges reflecting the happens-before relation [12] without its transitive closure: (ϕ_i, ϕ_j) is in the edge relation $\rightarrow_\alpha : \Phi \times \Phi$ if and only if one of the following two conditions holds:*

1. *The receive event ϕ_i triggers a computing step where a message m is sent from a correct process p to a process q; event ϕ_j is the receive event of m at q. We call the edge $\phi_i \rightarrow_\alpha \phi_j$ non-local edge or simply message in G_α.*
2. *The events ϕ_i and ϕ_j both take place at the same processor p and there exists no event ϕ_k in α occurring at p with $i < k < j$. The edge $\phi_i \rightarrow_\alpha \phi_j$ is said to be a local edge.*

We will simply write G and $\rightarrow$ instead of G_α and $\rightarrow_\alpha$ when α is clear from the context. Note that we will also consider execution graphs of finite prefixes of executions.

A *causal chain* $\phi_1 \rightarrow \cdots \rightarrow \phi_l$ is a directed path in the execution graph, which consists of messages and local edges. The *length of a causal chain D* is the number of non-local edges (i.e., messages) in D, denoted by $|D|$. A *cycle Z* in G is a subgraph of G that corresponds to a cycle in the undirected shadow graph $\bar{G}$ of G.[2] Since messages cannot be sent backwards in time, every cycle can be decomposed into at least 2 causal chains having opposite directions. We now take a closer look at such cycles, which capture all causal information relevant for ABC algorithms.

Definition 2 (Relevant Cycles). *Let Z be a cycle in the execution graph, and partition the edges of Z into the* backward *edges $\hat{Z}^-$ and the* forward *edges $\hat{Z}^+$ as follows: Identically directed edges are in the same class, and*

$$|Z^+| \leqslant |Z^-|, \tag{1}$$

where $Z^- \subseteq \hat{Z}^-$ and $Z^+ \subseteq \hat{Z}^+$ are the restrictions of $\hat{Z}^-$ resp. $\hat{Z}^+$ to non-local edges (messages). The orientation *of the cycle Z is the direction of the forward edges Z^+, and Z is said to be* relevant *if all local edges are backward edges, i.e., if $\hat{Z}^+ = Z^+$; otherwise it is called* non-relevant.

Fig. 2 shows an example of a relevant cycle: Its orientation is opposite to the direction of all local edges, and the backward messages are traversed oppositely w.r.t. their direction when traversing the cycle according to its orientation. Bear in mind, however, that labelling the edges in a cycle as forward and backward is only of local significance. For example, in Fig. 1, the forward message e in cycle X is actually a backward one in cycle Y (i.e., $e \in X^+$ and $e \in Y^-$).

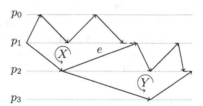

Fig. 1. An execution graph containing relevant cycles X, Y, and the combined cycle $X \oplus Y$, consisting of all edges except the oppositely oriented edge e

Definition 3 (ABC Synchrony Condition). *Let Ξ be a given rational number $\Xi > 1$, and let G be the execution graph of an execution α. Then, α is* admissible *in the ABC model if, for every relevant cycle Z in G, we have*

$$\frac{|Z^-|}{|Z^+|} < \Xi. \tag{2}$$

---

[2] The shadow graph $\bar{G}$ has the same set of vertices as G and, for every edge in G, there is a corresponding undirectional edge in $\bar{G}$.

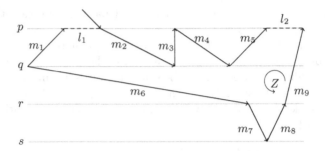

Fig. 2. A relevant cycle Z, where a causal chain $C_2 = m_1 l_1 m_2 \ldots m_5 l_2$ is spanned by the "slow" message chain $C_1 = m_6 m_7 m_8 m_9$. Message m_3 has zero delay.

Note carefully that, compared to the purely asynchronous model, there is no other constraint in the ABC model: Only the ratio of the *number* of backward vs. forward messages in relevant cycles is constrained. There is no reference to end-to-end delays, no delay constraints whatsoever are put on individual messages, and none on messages in non-relevant cycles and isolated chains. Nevertheless, in Section 3, we will prove that the ABC synchrony condition is sufficient for simulating lock-step rounds, and hence for solving e.g. consensus by means of any synchronous consensus algorithm.[3]

3   Clock Sychronization in the ABC Model

In this section, we show that the simple fault-tolerant tick generation algorithm introduced in [22] can be used for clock synchronization in the ABC model. It tolerates up to f Byzantine process failures in a system of $n \geqslant 3f + 1$ processes adhering to the ABC model. In Algorithm 1, every process p maintains a local variable k that constitutes p's local clock as follows: Every process initially sets $k \leftarrow 0$ and broadcasts the message $(tick\ 0)$; for simplicity, we assume that a process sends messages also to itself. If a correct process p receives $f + 1$ $(tick\ \ell)$ messages (catch-up rule, line 3), it can be sure that at least one of them was sent by a correct process that has already reached clock value l. Therefore, p can safely catch-up to l and broadcast $(tick\ k + 1), \ldots, (tick\ l)$. If some process p receives $n - f \geqslant 2f + 1$ $(tick\ k)$ messages (advance rule, line 6) and thus advances its clock to $k + 1$, it follows that at least $f + 1$ of those messages will also be received by every other correct process, which then executes line 3. Hence, all correct processes will eventually receive $n - f$ $(tick\ k)$ messages and advance their clocks to $k + 1$.

We will now prove that the algorithm guarantees progress of clocks and a certain synchrony condition, which can be stated in terms of consistent cuts in the execution graph. Note that using causality as a reference—rather than a common point in time, as in traditional clock synchronization—is natural in the time-free ABC model. Since the classic definition of consistent cuts does not take

---

[3] Weaker ("eventual") variants of the ABC model are introduced in [19].

Algorithm 1. Byzantine Clock Synchronization

1: **VAR** k: integer $\leftarrow$ 0;
2: send (tick 0) to all [once];

/* catch-up rule */
3: **if** received (tick l) from $f + 1$ distinct processes and $l > k$ **then**
4:     send (tick $k + 1$),...,(tick l) to all [once];
5:     $k \leftarrow l$;
    /* advance rule */
6: **if** received (tick k) from $n - f$ distinct processes **then**
7:     send (tick $k + 1$) to all [once];
8:     $k \leftarrow k + 1$;

---

faulty processes into account, we will use the following correct-restricted version tailored to our execution graphs:

Definition 4. *Let G be an execution graph and denote by $\overset{*}{\to}$ the reflexive and transitive closure of the edge relation $\to$. A subset S of events in G is called consistent cut, if (1) for every correct process p, there is an event $\phi \in S$ taking place at p, and (2) the set S is left-closed for $\overset{*}{\to}$; i.e., S contains the whole causal past of all events in S.*

Given an event ϕ_p at process p, we denote by $C_p(\phi_p)$ the clock value *after* executing the computing step corresponding to ϕ_p. Recall that the latter need not be correctly executed if p is faulty. The clock value of a [correct] process p in the frontier of a consistent cut S is denoted by $C_p(S)$; it is the last clock value of p w.r.t. $\overset{*}{\to}$ in S. Since it follows immediately from the code of Algorithm 1 that local clock values of correct processes are monotonically increasing, $C_p(S)$ is the maximum clock value at p over all events $\phi_p \in S$.

We first show that correct clocks make progress perpetually.

Lemma 1 (One Step Progress). *Let S be a consistent cut such that all correct processes p satisfy $C_p(S) \geqslant k$, for a fixed $k \geqslant 0$. Then there is a consistent cut S' where every correct process has set its clock to at least $k + 1$.*

Proof. If all correct processes p_i have a (possibly distinct) clock value $k_i \geqslant k$ in the frontier of S, the code of Algorithm 1 ensures that they have already sent (*tick k*). Since all messages in transit are eventually delivered, there must be a (not necessarily consistent) cut S'', in the frontier of which every correct process has received $n - f$ tick k messages and thus set its clock to $k + 1$. The left-closure of S'' yields the sought consistent cut S'. □

Theorem 1 (Progress). *In every admissible execution of Algorithm 1 in a system with $n \geqslant 3f + 1$ processes, the clock of every correct process progresses without bound.*

Proof. The theorem follows from a trivial induction argument using Lemma 1, in conjunction with the fact that the cut $\mathcal{S}^0$ comprising the initial event ϕ_p^0 of every process p is trivially consistent and satisfies $C_p(\mathcal{S}^0) \geqslant 0$.   □

Lemma 2 (First Advance). *If a correct process q sets its clock to $k \geqslant 1$ in event ψ_q, then there is a correct process p that sets its clock to k using the advance rule in some event ψ_p with $\psi_p \xrightarrow{*} \psi_q$.*

Proof. If q uses the advance rule for setting its clock to k in ψ_q, the lemma is trivially true. If q uses the catch-up rule instead, it must have received $f+1$ (*tick* k) messages, at least one of which was sent by a correct process q' in an event $\psi_{q'} \xrightarrow{*} \psi_q$. If q' also sent its (*tick* k) via the catch-up rule (line 3), we apply the same reasoning to q'. Since every process sends (*tick* k) only once and there are only finitely many processes, we must eventually reach a correct process p that sends (*tick* k) in event $\psi_p \xrightarrow{*} \psi_q$ via the advance rule.   □

Lemma 3 (Causal Chain Length). *Assume that a correct process sets its clock to $k + m$, for some $k \geqslant 0$, $m \geqslant 0$, at some event ϕ', or has already done so. Then, there is a causal chain D of length $|D| \geqslant m$ involving correct processes only, which ends at ϕ' and starts at some event ϕ where a correct process sets its clock to k using the advance rule ($k \geqslant 1$) or the initialization rule ($k = 0$).*

Proof. Let p be the process where ϕ' occurs. If p has set its clock in some earlier computing step $\phi''' \xrightarrow{*} \phi'$, we just replace ϕ' by ϕ''' and continue with the case where p sets its clock to $k + m$ in ϕ'. If p sets its clock in ϕ' using the catch-up rule, applying Lemma 2 yields a correct process that sets its clock to $k + m$ in an event $\psi \xrightarrow{*} \phi'$ using the advance rule. To prove Lemma 3, it hence suffices to assume that p sets its clock to $k + m$ in ϕ' via the advance rule ($k + m \geqslant 1$) or the initialization rule ($k + m = 0$), as we can append the chains cut before to finally get the sought causal chain D.

The proof is by induction on m. For $m = 0$, the lemma is trivially true. For $m > 0$, at least $n - 2f \geqslant f + 1$ correct processes must have sent (*tick* $k + m - 1$). Let q be any such process, and ϕ'' be the event in which (*tick* $k + m - 1$) is sent. Since q also sets its clock to $k + m - 1$ at ϕ'', we can invoke Lemma 2 in case $k + m - 1 \geqslant 1$ to assure that the advance rule is used in ϕ''; for $k + m - 1 = 0$, the initialization rule is used in ϕ''. We can hence apply the induction hypothesis and conclude that there is a causal chain D' of length at least $m - 1$ leading to ϕ''. Hence, appending q's (*tick* $k + m - 1$) message [and the initially cut off chains] to D' provides D with $|D| \geqslant m$.   □

The following Lemma 4 will be instrumental in our proof that Algorithm 1 maintains synchronized clocks. It reveals that when a correct process p updates its clock value in some event ϕ', then all messages of correct processes of a certain lower tick value must have already been received by p, i.e., must originate from the causal cone of ϕ'.

Lemma 4 (Causal Cone). *For some $k \geqslant 0$, suppose that $C_p(\phi') = k + 2\Xi$ at the event ϕ' of a correct process p. Then, for every $0 \leqslant \ell \leqslant k$, process p has already received (tick ℓ) from every correct process.*

Proof. The general proof idea is to show that the arrival of (*tick* ℓ) in some event ϕ'' after ϕ' would close a relevant cycle in which the synchrony assumption (2) is violated. See Fig. 3 for a graphical representation of the scenario described below.

Let $C_p(\phi') = k + 2\Xi$ and assume, for the sake of contradiction, that (*tick* ℓ) from some correct process q was not yet received by p before or at ϕ', for some $\ell \leqslant k$. Consider the last message that p received from q before (or at) ϕ'. If such a message exists, we denote its send event at q as ψ'; otherwise, we simply define ψ' to be the (externally triggered) initial computing step at q.

From Lemma 3, we know that there is a causal chain $D = \phi'_1 \to \cdots \to \phi'$ of length $|D| \geqslant k + 2\Xi - (\ell+1)$, where a (*tick* $\ell+1$) message is sent in ϕ'_1 by some correct process p_1 via the advance rule and, by assumption, $C_p(\phi') = k + 2\Xi$. Since ϕ'_1 executes the advance rule, p_1 must have received $n - f$ (*tick* ℓ) messages to do so. Denoting by $0 \leqslant f' \leqslant f$ the actual number of faulty processes among the $n \geqslant 3f + 1$ ones, it follows that $n - f - f' \geqslant f + 1$ of these messages were sent by correct processes; we denote this set by P_1.

Since Theorem 1 ensures progress of all correct processes, there must be an event ψ_1, coinciding with or occuring after ψ', in which q broadcasts (*tick* ℓ). Eventually, this message is received by p in some event ϕ'', which must be after ϕ' since by assumption (*tick* ℓ) was not received before (or at) ϕ'. Furthermore, we claim that q receives at least $n - f' - f$ (*tick* ℓ) messages from correct processes after (or at) event ψ_1; let P_2 be that set. Otherwise, q would have received at least $n - f' - (n - f' - f) + 1 = f + 1$ (*tick* ℓ) from correct processes by some event $\psi'_1 \overset{*}{\to} \psi_1$, and therefore would have broadcast (*tick* ℓ) already in ψ'_1 according to the catch-up rule.

Since $P_1 \cup P_2$ is of size at most $2n - 2f' - 2f$ and we have only $n - f'$ correct processes, it follows by the pigeonhole principle that $2n - 2f' - 2f - (n - f') = n - 2f - f' \geqslant n - 3f > 0$ correct processes are in $P_1 \cap P_2$. Choose any process $p_0 \in P_1 \cap P_2$, which broadcasts its (*tick* ℓ) in some event ϕ_0. This message is received at q in some event ψ_2, and at p_1 in event ϕ_1.

It is immediately apparent from Fig. 3 that the causal chains $\phi_0 \to \phi_1 \overset{*}{\to} D \overset{*}{\to} \phi''$, $\phi_0 \to \psi_2$, $\psi_1 \overset{*}{\to} \psi_2$, and $\psi_1 \to \phi''$ form a relevant cycle Z: The number of backward messages is $|Z^-| = |D| + 1 \geqslant k - \ell + 2\Xi \geqslant 2\Xi$, since $\ell \leqslant k$; the number of forward messages $|Z^+|$ is 2. But this yields $\frac{|Z^-|}{|Z^+|} \geqslant \frac{2\Xi}{2} = \Xi$, contradicting the ABC synchrony assumption (2). $\qquad\square$

We can now easily prove that Algorithm 1 maintains the following synchrony condition:

Theorem 2 (Synchrony). *For any consistent cut $\mathcal{S}$ in an admissible execution of Algorithm 1 in a system with $n \geqslant 3f+1$ processes, we have $|C_p(\mathcal{S}) - C_q(\mathcal{S})| \leqslant 2\Xi$ for all correct processes p, q.*

Proof. Assume that the maximum clock value in the frontier of $\mathcal{S}$ is $k + 2\Xi$, and let p be a correct process with $C_p(\mathcal{S}) = k + 2\Xi$. From Lemma 4, we know that p must have seen (*tick* ℓ) from every correct process q for any $\ell \leqslant k$. Since $\mathcal{S}$ is

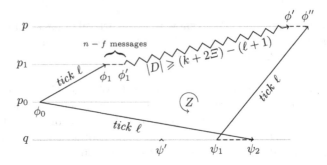

Fig. 3. Proof of Lemma 4

consistent, all the corresponding send events at q must be within S, such that $C_q(S) \geq k$. □

Even though the ABC model is entirely time-free, we can immediately transfer the above synchrony property to real-time cuts according to [15], to derive the following theorem:

Theorem 3 (Clock Precision). *Let $C_p(t)$ denote the clock value of process p at real-time t. For any time t of an admissible execution of Algorithm 1 in a system with $n \geq 3f+1$ processes, we have $|C_p(t) - C_q(t)| \leq 2\Xi$ for all correct processes p, q.* □

Finally, we will show how to build a lock-step round simulation in the ABC model atop of Algorithm 1. A lock-step round execution proceeds in a sequence of rounds $r = 1, 2, \ldots$, where all correct processes take their round r computing steps (consisting of receiving the round $r-1$ messages[4], executing a state transition, and broadcasting the round r messages for the next round) exactly at the same time.

We use the same simulation as in [22], which just considers clocks as phase counters and introduces rounds consisting of 2Ξ phases. Algorithm 2 shows the code that must be merged with Algorithm 1; the round r messages are piggybacked on (*tick k*) messages every 2Ξ phases, namely, when $k/(2\Xi) = r$. The round r computing step is encapsulated in the function start(r) in line 7; start(0) just sends the round 0 messages that will be processed in the round 1 computing step.

To prove that this algorithm achieves lock-step rounds, we need to show that all round r messages from correct processes have arrived at every correct process p before p enters round $r+1$, i.e., executes start($r+1$).

Theorem 4 (Lock-Step Rounds). *In a system with $n \geq 3f+1$ processes, Algorithm 2 merged with Algorithm 1 correctly simulates lock-step rounds in the ABC model.*

---

[4] For notational convenience, we enumerate the messages with the index of the previous round.

Algorithm 2. Lock-Step Round Simulation

1: **VAR** r: integer $\leftarrow 0$;
2: call start(0);

3: Whenever k is updated do
4: **if** $k/(2\varXi) = r + 1$ **then**
5:     $r \leftarrow r + 1$
6:     call start(r)

7: **procedure** start$(r{:}\text{integer})$
8:     **if** $r > 0$ **then**
9:         read round $r - 1$ messages
10:        execute round r computation
11:        send round r messages

Proof. Suppose that a correct process p starts round $r+1$ in event ϕ. By the code, $C_p(\phi) = k$ with $k/(2\varXi) = r + 1$, i.e., $k = 2\varXi r + 2\varXi$. By way of contradiction, assume that the round r message, sent by some correct process q in the event ψ, arrives at p only after ϕ. By the code, $C_q(\psi) = k'$ with $k'/(2\varXi) = r$, i.e., $k' = 2\varXi r$. However, Lemma 4 reveals that p should have already seen $(tick\ 2\varXi r)$ from q before event ϕ, a contradiction. $\square$

Remark: We note that the above proof(s) actually establish *uniform* [10] lock-step rounds, i.e., lock-step rounds that are also obeyed by faulty processes until they fail for the first time: If the messages sent by faulty processes also obey the ABC synchrony condition (2), then the proof of the key Lemma 4 actually establishes a uniform causal cone property: Assuming that (i) process q performs correctly up to and including at least one more step after event ψ', and (ii) p works correctly up to and including event ϕ', then p would receive (though not necessarily process) the message from q in ϕ'', thereby closing a relevant cycle that violates $\varXi$. Hence, p must have received all messages from its causal cone by ϕ' already, which carries over to a uniform version of Theorem 4.

4   Model Indistinguishability

In this section, we will develop a non-trivial "model indistinguishability" argument in order to show that any algorithm designed for the Θ-Model [21, 4, 22] also works correctly in the ABC model. It is non-trivial, since there are (many) admissible ABC executions which are *not* admissible in the Θ-Model. Nevertheless, no simulation will be involved in our argument; the original algorithms can just be used "as is" in the ABC model. This "timing invariance" of algorithms and their properties confirms again that timing constraints are not really essential for solving certain distributed computing problems.

More specifically, provided that $\varXi < \Theta$, we will show that every algorithm designed and proved correct for the Θ-Model preserves all its timing-independent properties when executed in the ABC model. Note that the algorithms analyzed in Section 3 belong to this class.[5]

Like the ABC model, the Θ-Model [21, 4, 22] is a message-driven model, without real-time clocks, and hence also relies on end-to-end delays. If $\tau^+(t)$ resp. $\tau^-(t)$ denotes the (unknown) maximum resp. minimum delay of all messages in transit system-wide between correct processes at time t, it just assumes that there is some $\Theta > 1$ such that

$$\frac{\tau^+(t)}{\tau^-(t)} \leqslant \Theta \tag{3}$$

at all times t in all admissible executions. In the simple static Θ-Model (which is sufficient for our model indistinguishability argument, since it has been shown in [22] to be equivalent to the general Θ-Model from the point of view of algorithms), it is assumed that there are (unknown) upper resp. lower bounds $\infty > \tau^+ \geqslant \tau^+(t)$ resp. $0 < \tau^- \leqslant \tau^-(t)$ on the end-to-end delays of all correct messages in all executions, the ratio of which matches the (known) $\Theta = \frac{\tau^+}{\tau^-}$.

Formally, fix some algorithm A and let $ASYNC$ be the set of executions of A running in a purely asynchronous message-driven system; note that we consider *timed executions* here, i.e., executions along with the occurence times of their events. A *property* P is a subset of the admissible executions in $ASYNC$, i.e., a property is defined via the executions of A that satisfy it. Let $\mathcal{M}$ be the set of admissible executions of A in some model M that augments the asynchronous model, by adding additional constraints like the ABC synchrony condition. Clearly, $\mathcal{M}$ is the intersection of some model-specific safety and liveness properties in $ASYNC$. We say that an execution α is in model M if $\alpha \in \mathcal{M}$, i.e., if α is admissible in M. If $\mathcal{M} \subseteq P$, we say that A *satisfies* property P in the model $\mathcal{M}$. A property P is called *timing-independent*, if $\alpha \in P \Rightarrow \alpha' \in P$ for every pair of causally equivalent executions α, α', i.e., executions where $G_\alpha = G_{\alpha'}$.

First, using a trivial model-indistinguishability argument, it is easy to show that properties of an algorithm proved to hold in the ABC model M_{ABC} also hold in the Θ-Model M_Θ, for any $\Theta < \Xi$: The following Theorem 5 exploits the fact that the relevant cycles in the execution graph G_α, corresponding to an admissible execution α in the Θ-Model, also satisfy the ABC synchrony condition (2), i.e., that α is an admissible execution in the ABC model as well.

Theorem 5. *For any* $\Theta < \Xi$, *it holds that* $M_\Theta \subseteq M_{ABC}$. *Hence, if an algorithm satisfies a property P in the ABC model, it also satisfies P in the Θ-Model.*

Proof. If Z is any relevant cycle in G_α, then no more than $|Z^+|/\Theta$ backward messages can be in Z; otherwise, at least one forward-backward message pair would violate (3). It follows that $|Z^-|/|Z^+| \leqslant \Theta < \Xi$ as required. Hence, $M_\Theta \subseteq M_{ABC} \subseteq P$, since the algorithm satisfies P in the ABC model.   □

---

[5] It is not possible to derive our results from the Θ-based analysis in [22], however, since this would require carrying over timing-dependent properties. And indeed, the Θ-variant [22] of our synchronizer (Algorithm 2) requires rounds consisting of 3Θ phases, rather than 2Ξ phases as in the ABC model.

The converse of Theorem 5 is not true, however: The time-free synchrony assumption (2) of the ABC model allows arbitrary small end-to-end delays for individual messages, violating (3) for every Θ. From a timing perspective, the ABC model is indeed strictly weaker than the Θ-Model, hence $\mathcal{M}_{ABC} \not\subseteq \mathcal{M}_\Theta$. Nevertheless, Theorem 6 below shows that, given an arbitrary finite execution graph G in $\mathcal{M}_{ABC}$, it is always possible to assign end-to-end delays $\in (1, \Xi)$ to the individual messages *without changing the event order* at any process. Let τ be such a delay assignment function, and G^τ be the weighted execution graph obtained from G by adding the assigned delays to the messages. Since Θ-algorithms are message-driven, without real-time clocks, G and G^τ are indistinguishable for every process. Consequently, an algorithm that provides certain timing-independent properties when being run in the Θ-Model also maintains these properties in the ABC model, see Theorem 8.

Theorem 6. *For every finite ABC execution graph G, there is an end-to-end delay assignment function τ, such that the weighted execution graph G^τ is causally equivalent to G and all messages in G^τ satisfy* (3).

Proof. The (quite involved) proof, which utilizes a non-standard cycle-space of a graph and an algebraic treatment of a system of linear inequalities using a variant of Farkas' lemma, can be found in [19]. □

In order to formally prove the claimed "model indistinguishability" of the ABC model and the Θ-Model, we proceed with the following Lemma 5. It says that processes cannot notice any difference in finite prefixes in the ABC model and in the Θ-Model, and therefore make the same state transitions.

Lemma 5 (Safety Equivalence). *If an algorithm satisfies a timing-independent safety property S in the Θ-Model, then S also holds in the ABC model, for any $\Xi < \Theta$.*

Proof. Suppose, by way of contradiction, that there is a finite prefix β of an ABC model execution $\alpha \in \mathcal{M}_{ABC}$, where S does not hold. Furthermore, let β' be a finite extension of β such that all messages sent by correct processes in β arrive in β', and denote the execution graph of β' by $G_{\beta'}$. From Theorem 6, we know that there is a delay assignment τ such that the synchrony assumption (3) of the Θ-Model is satisfied for all messages in the timed execution graph $G^\tau_{\beta'}$, while the causality relation in $G_{\beta'}$ and $G^\tau_{\beta'}$ (and since $G^\tau_{\beta'} \supseteq G^\tau_\beta$ also in G_β and G^τ_β) is the same.

We will now construct an admissible execution γ in the Θ-Model, which has the same prefix $G^\tau_{\beta'}$: If t is the greatest occurrence time of all events in $G^\tau_{\beta'}$, we simply assign an end-to-end delay of τ^+ to all messages still in transit at time t and to all messages sent at a later point in time. Note that γ may be totally different from the ABC-execution α w.r.t. the event ordering *after* the common prefix β'. Anyway, γ is admissible in the Θ-Model since (3) holds for all messages, but violates S, which provides the required contradiction. □

Unfortunately, we cannot use the same reasoning for "transfering" liveness properties, since finite prefixes of an execution are not sufficient to show that "something good" eventually happens. Nevertheless, Theorem 7 below reveals that all properties satisfiable by an algorithm in the Θ-Model are actually safety properties, in the following sense: For every property P (which could be a liveness property like termination) satisfied by A in M_Θ, there is a (typically stronger) safety property $P' \subseteq P$ (like termination within time X) that is also satisfied by A in M_Θ. Hence, there is no need to deal with liveness properties here at all.

For our proof, we utilize the convenient topological framework introduced in [2], where safety properties correspond to the closed sets of executions in $ASYNC$, and liveness properties correspond to dense sets. If a model M is determined solely by safety properties $S_1, \ldots, S_k$, then the set $\mathcal{M} = \bigcap_{i=1}^{k} S_i$—and therefore the model M—is *closed*.

Theorem 7 (Safety-Only in Closed Models). *Let M be a closed model augmenting the asynchronous model, and let $\mathcal{M} \subseteq ASYNC$ be the set of all admissible executions of an algorithm A in M. To show that A satisfies some arbitrary property P in M, it suffices to show that A satisfies the property $P' = P \cap \mathcal{M}$, which is a safety propery.*

Proof. Suppose that A satisfies some property $P \subseteq ASYNC$ in M, i.e., $\mathcal{M} \subseteq P$. Then, $\mathcal{M} = \mathcal{M} \cap P$ and since $\mathcal{M}$ is closed, it follows that $P' = \mathcal{M} \cap P$ is closed (in $ASYNC$) as well. But this is exactly the definition of a safety property $P' \subseteq ASYNC$ and, since $\mathcal{M} \subseteq P' \subseteq P$, it indeed suffices to show that A satisfies P' in M. $\square$

Lemma 6. *The ABC model and the Θ-Model are both closed.*

Proof. We just need to show that the set $\mathcal{M}_\Theta$ resp. $\mathcal{M}_{ABC}$ of executions in the Θ-Model resp. in the ABC model is closed. If some execution violated the end-to-end timing assumption (3) of the Θ-Model resp. the ABC synchrony condition (2), there would be a finite prefix within which this violation has happened. This characterizes a safety property and hence a closed set in $ASYNC$. $\square$

Theorem 7 in conjunction with Lemma 6 reveals that every property satisfiable in the Θ-Model is a safety property. Hence, Lemma 5 finally implies Theorem 8, which complements Theorem 5.

Theorem 8. *All timing-independent properties satisfied by an algorithm in the Θ-Model also hold in the ABC model, for any $\Xi < \Theta$.* $\square$

5   Relation to the Classic Partially Synchronous Model

In this section, we relate the ABC model to the perpetual partially synchronous model (ParSync) introduced in [7]. ParSync stipulates a bound Φ on relative computing speeds and a bound Δ on message delays, relative to an (external) discrete global clock, which ticks whenever a process takes a step: During Φ ticks of the global clock, every process takes at least one step, and if a message m was sent at time k to a process p that subsequently performs a receive step at or after time $k + \Delta$, p is guaranteed to receive m.

First of all, we note that the ABC model and ParSync are equivalent in terms of solvability of timing-independent problems in fully-connected networks: In [22], it was shown that the Θ-Model and ParSync are equivalent is this regard: Since the synchrony parameters Φ, Δ of the ParSync model imply bounded (and non-zero) end-to-end delays, any Θ-algorithm can be run in a ParSync system if $\Theta = \Theta(\Phi, \Delta)$ is chosen sufficiently large. Conversely, using the lock-step round simulation for the Θ-Model provides a "perfect" ParSync system ($\Phi = 1$ and $\Delta = 0$), which obviously allows to execute any ParSync algorithm atop of it. The claimed equivalence thus follows from the model indistinguishability of the ABC model and the Θ-Model established in Section 4.

This problem equivalence does not imply that the models are indeed equivalent, however. First, as shown below, there are problems that can be solved in ABC model but not in ParSync in case of not fully-connected networks. Moreover, whereas we can choose Ξ such that every execution of a message-driven algorithm in ParSync with Φ, Δ is also admissible in the ABC model for some $\Xi > \Theta(\Phi, \Delta)$, we can even conclude from $\mathcal{M}_{\text{ABC}} \supset \mathcal{M}_\Theta$ that some ABC executions cannot be modeled in ParSync. To investigate this issue in more detail, we use the taxonomy of partially synchronous models introduced in [6], which delimits the exact border between consensus solvability and impossibility: It distinguishes whether (c) communication is synchronous (Δ holds) or asynchronous, whether (p) processes are synchronous (Φ holds) or asynchronous, whether (s) steps are atomic (send+receive in a single step) or non-atomic (separate send and receive steps), whether (b) send steps can broadcast or only unicast, and whether (m) message delivery is (globally) FIFO ordered or out-of-order.

We will argue below that the ABC model model must be mapped to the case of asynchronous communication, asynchronous processes, atomic steps, broadcast send and out-of-oder delivery. Using the corresponding "binary encoding" ($c = 0, p = 0, s = 1, b = 1, m = 0$) in [6, Table 1], it turns out that consensus is not solvable in the resulting model. Of course, the apparent contradiction to the solvability of consensus in the ABC model is due to the ABC synchrony condition, which cannot be properly expressed in the framework of [6].

Asynchronous Communication and Asynchronous Processes: Consider a 2-player game where the Prover first chooses Ξ and the Adversary, knowing Ξ, chooses a pair (Φ, Δ). Finally, the Prover has to choose an execution satisfying (2) for Ξ; the Prover wins iff this execution violates the adversary-chosen parameters (Φ, Δ). The Prover has a winning strategy: It suffices to choose any execution containing a relevant cycle as shown in Fig. 2, which respects (2) but lets $|Z^-|$ be greater than both Φ and Δ: While the (slow) message m_6 from q to r is in transit, process q executes more than Δ steps. Moreover, neither process r nor s execute a step during the more than Φ steps of q. As a consequence, both communication and processes must be considered asynchronous ($c = 0, p = 0$).

Atomic Steps and Broadcast: Whereas it is clear that out-of-order delivery ($m = 0$) makes it more difficult to solve problems, one may be wondering whether the "favorable" choices $s = 1$ and $b = 1$, rather than the ABC synchrony condition, make consensus solvable in the ABC model. [6, Table 1] reveals that this is not the case: All entries corresponding to $p = 0, c = 0, m = 0$ are the same (consensus impossible), irrespectively of the choice of b and s. And indeed, the assumption of atomic receive+broadcast steps in the ABC model's definition in Section 2 is just a simplifying abstraction: Every non-atomic broadcast execution (= multiple unicast steps) can be mapped to a causally equivalent atomic receive+broadcast step execution with appropriately adjusted end-to-end delays.[6]

Another major difference between ParSync and the ABC model results from the cumulative and non-global character of the ABC synchrony condition. Since (2) needs to hold only in relevant cycles, which are in fact defined by the specific algorithm employed, the ABC model is particularly suitable for modeling systems with not fully-connected communication graphs: For choosing Ξ, only the cumulative end-to-end delay ratio over certain paths counts.

Consider the execution shown in Fig. 5, for example, which corresponds to a system where process q exchanges messages directly with p (over a 1-hop path P_{qpq}), and indirectly with s (over a 2-hop path P_{qrsrq} via r). As long as the sum of the delays along P_{qrsrq} is less than the cumulative delay of Ξ instances of P_{qpq}, the individual delays along the links between q, r and r, s are totally irrelevant. In the VLSI context, for instance, this gives more flexibility for place-and-route, as well as some robustness against dynamic delay variations. By contrast, in ParSync, very conservative values of Φ, Δ would be needed to achieve a comparable flexibility; obviously, this would considerably degrade the achievable performance system-wide.

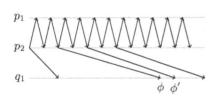

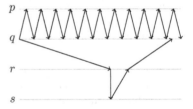

Fig. 4. An execution of a system implementing bounded-size FIFO channels. If the order of ϕ and ϕ' changed, there would be a relevant cycle violating (2) for $\Xi = 4$.

Fig. 5. The long delay on the link between q and r is compensated by the fast delay on the link between r and s

In case of not fully-connected networks, there are even situations which cannot be modeled in ParSync at all. Consider the message-pattern given in Fig. 4 in a system with $\Xi = 4$, for example: The ABC synchrony condition ensures FIFO order of the messages sent from p_2 to q_1, even when their delay is unbounded (and may even continuously grow, as e.g. in a formation of fixed-constellation clusters of spacecraft that move away from each other): If there was a reordering

---

[6] The ABC model can hence also be used for making classic distributed algorithms results applicable to non-atomic models like the Real-Time Model introduced in [16].

of ϕ and ϕ', a relevant cycle with $\Xi = 5$ would be formed, which is impossible. Note that processes p_1, p_2 make unbounded progress while a message to q_1 is in transit here. Hence, as in the example of Fig. 2 mentioned before, the problem cannot be solved in ParSync. Clearly, such message ordering capabilities are very useful in practice, e.g., for implementing stable identifiers, bounded-message size, single source FIFOs etc.

6   Conclusions and Future Work

We have introduced a novel partially synchronous system model, the ABC model, which is completely time-free and thus rests on a causality-based synchrony condition only. We showed that it is sufficiently strong for implementing lock-step rounds and, hence, for solving any important distributed computing problem, including consensus. We also proved that algorithms designed for the Θ-Model also work correctly in the ABC model. Part of our future work is devoted to exploiting the ABC model in the chase for the weakest system model for solving consensus, and to the analysis of the ABC model's coverage in real systems, in particular, VLSI Systems-on-Chip.

Acknowledgments

We are indebted to Martin Biely, Josef Widder, Martin Hutle, Matthias Függer, Heinrich Moser, and Bernadette Charron-Bost for their contributions to the ABC model.

References

1. Aguilera, M.K., Delporte-Gallet, C., Fauconnier, H., Toueg, S.: Communication-efficient leader election and consensus with limited link synchrony. In: Proceedings of the 23rd ACM symposium on Principles of Distributed Computing (PODC 2004), St. John's, Newfoundland, Canada, pp. 328–337. ACM Press, New York (2004)
2. Alpern, B., Schneider, F.B.: Defining liveness, Tech. report, Ithaca, NY, USA (1984)
3. Attiya, H., Dwork, C., Lynch, N., Stockmeyer, L.: Bounds on the time to reach agreement in the presence of timing uncertainty. Journal of the ACM (JACM) 41(1), 122–152 (1994)
4. Biely, M., Widder, J.: Optimal message-driven implementation of omega with mute processes. In: Datta, A.K., Gradinariu, M. (eds.) SSS 2006. LNCS, vol. 4280, pp. 110–121. Springer, Heidelberg (2006)
5. Chandra, T.D., Toueg, S.: Unreliable failure detectors for reliable distributed systems. Journal of the ACM 43(2), 225–267 (1996)
6. Dolev, D., Dwork, C., Stockmeyer, L.: On the minimal synchronism needed for distributed consensus. Journal of the ACM 34(1), 77–97 (1987)
7. Dwork, C., Lynch, N., Stockmeyer, L.: Consensus in the presence of partial synchrony. Journal of the ACM 35(2), 288–323 (1988)

8. Fetzer, C., Schmid, U., Süßkraut, M.: On the possibility of consensus in asynchronous systems with finite average response times. In: Proceedings of the 25th International Conference on Distributed Computing Systems (ICDCS 2005), Washington, DC, USA, pp. 271–280. IEEE Computer Society, Los Alamitos (2005)
9. Fischer, M.J., Lynch, N.A., Paterson, M.S.: Impossibility of distributed consensus with one faulty process. Journal of the ACM 32(2), 374–382 (1985)
10. Hadzilacos, V., Toueg, S.: Fault-tolerant broadcasts and related problems. In: Mullender, S. (ed.) Distributed Systems, 2nd edn., pp. 97–145. Addison-Wesley, Reading (1993)
11. Hutle, M., Malkhi, D., Schmid, U., Zhou, L.: Brief announcement: Chasing the weakest system model for implementing omega and consensus. In: Datta, A.K., Gradinariu, M. (eds.) SSS 2006. LNCS, vol. 4280, pp. 576–577. Springer, Heidelberg (2006)
12. Lamport, L.: Time, clocks, and the ordering of events in a distributed system. Commun. ACM 21(7), 558–565 (1978)
13. Malkhi, D., Oprea, F., Zhou, L.: Ω meets paxos: Leader election and stability without eventual timely links. In: Fraigniaud, P. (ed.) DISC 2005, vol. 3724, pp. 199–213. Springer, Heidelberg (2005)
14. Mattern, F.: Virtual time and global states of distributed systems. In: Proceedings of the International Workshop on Parallel and Distributed Algorithms, pp. 215–226. Elsevier Science Publishers B.V, Amsterdam (1989)
15. Mattern, F.: On the relativistic structure of logical time in distributed systems. In: Parallel and Distributed Algorithms, pp. 215–226. Elsevier Science Publishers B.V, Amsterdam (1992)
16. Moser, H., Schmid, U.: Optimal clock synchronization revisited: Upper and lower bounds in real-time systems. In: Shvartsman, M.M.A.A. (ed.) OPODIS 2006. LNCS, vol. 4305, pp. 95–109. Springer, Heidelberg (2006)
17. Mostefaoui, A., Mourgaya, E., Raynal, M., Travers, C.: A time-free assumption to implement eventual leadership. Parallel Processing Letters 16, 189–208 (2006)
18. Ponzio, S., Strong, R.: Semisynchrony and real time. In: Segall, A., Zaks, S. (eds.) WDAG 1992. LNCS, vol. 647, pp. 120–135. Springer, Heidelberg (1992)
19. Robinson, P., Schmid, U.: The Asynchronous Bounded-Cycle Model, Research Report 24/2008, Technische Universität Wien, Institut für Technische Informatik, Treitlstr. 1-3/182-1, 1040 Vienna, Austria (2008)
20. Vitányi, P.M.B.: Distributed elections in an archimedean ring of processors. In: Proceedings of the sixteenth annual ACM symposium on Theory of computing, pp. 542–547. ACM Press, New York (1984)
21. Widder, J., Le Lann, G., Schmid, U.: Failure detection with booting in partially synchronous systems. In: Dal Cin, M., Kaâniche, M., Pataricza, A. (eds.) EDCC 2005. LNCS, vol. 3463, pp. 20–37. Springer, Heidelberg (2005)
22. Widder, J., Schmid, U.: Achieving synchrony without clocks, Research Report 49/2005, Technische Universität Wien, Institut f. Technische Informatik (submitted)

Tutorial Abstract
Virtual Infrastructure*

Shlomi Dolev

Department of Computer Science
Ben Gurion University of the Negev, Israel
dolev@cs.bgu.ac.il

Ad-hoc and mobile sensor networks are chaotic in nature. The goal of the tutorial is to present several techniques to form virtual infrastructure for such mobile ad-hoc networks. Different approaches (some of which are inherently self-stabilizing [2,3]) will be presented:

• The use of randomization to overcome the random nature of the network. In particular the use of random walks to obtain a middleware that supports group communication abstractions [11].

• The use of directed antennas to define ad-hoc virtual infrastructure. The directed antennas are used to define virtual tilling of geographic regions. The tilling definition serves as a backbone for communication procedures [7].

• The use of GPS service to define a static tilling of a geographic region. Each tile resembles a (base station free) cell in a cellular network. The mobile hosts that happen to be present at a cell implement the base station function. Whenever a mobile host arrives to a populated cell, it copies the state of the virtual base station, whenever the mobile host leaves the cell it erases the virtual state. Thus each tile is in fact a virtual automaton that may implement a router or home location server [1,4,8,9].

• One can imagine a virtual automaton deciding to move to a non mobile-host-deserted location to make sure it survives, or even move in order to collect information [5,6].

• Implementation of a virtual automaton by the moving hosts requires an investigation of security issues. One would like to avoid the possibility of an host to know or corrupt the state of the virtual automaton, reactive secret sharing techniques are suggested for this sake [10].

References

1. The virtual infrastructure project,
   http://groups.csail.mit.edu/tds/vi-project
2. Dijkstra, E.W.: Self-stabilizing systems in spite of distributed control. Commun. ACM 17 11, 643–644 (1974)
3. Dolev, S.: Self-Stabilization. MIT Press, Cambridge (2000)

* Partially supported by the Rita Altura Trust Chair in Computer Sciences.

4. Dolev, S., Gilbert, S., Lynch, N.A., Shvartsman, A.A., Welch, J.L.: Geoquorums: implementing atomic memory in mobile d hoc networks. Distributed Computing 18 2, 125–155 (2005)
5. Dolev, S., Gilbert, S., Lynch, N.A., Schiller, E., Shvartsman, A.A., Welch, J.L.: Virtual Mobile Nodes for Mobile Ad Hoc Networks. In: The 18th International Conference on Distributed Computing, DISC 2004 (2004)
6. Dolev, S., Gilbert, S., Schiller, E., Shvartsman, A.A., Welch, J.L.: Autonomous virtual mobile nodes. In: DIALM-POMC, pp. 62–69 (2005)
7. Dolev, S., Herman, T., Lahiani, L.: Polygonal broadcast, secret maturity, and the firing sensors. Ad Hoc Networks 4 4, 447–486 (2006)
8. Dolev, S., Gilbert, S., Lahiani, L., Lynch, A.L., Nolte, T.: Timed Virtual Stationary Automata for Mobile Networks. In: 9th International Conference on Principles of Distributed Systems (OPODIS 2005), pp. 96–112 (2005)
9. Dolev, S., Lahiani, L., Lynch, N., Nolte, T.: Self-stabilizing Mobile Node Location Management and Message Routing. In: Self-Stabilizing Systems (SSS 2005), pp. 96–112 (2005)
10. Dolev, S., Lahiani, L., Yung, M.: Secret swarm unitreactive k-secret sharing. In: Srinathan, K., Rangan, C.P., Yung, M. (eds.) INDOCRYPT 2007. LNCS, vol. 4859, pp. 123–137. Springer, Heidelberg (2007)
11. Dolev, S., Schiller, E., Welch, J.L.: Random walk for self-stabilizing group communication in ad hoc networks. IEEE Trans. Mob. Comput. 5 7, 893–905 (2006)

Author Index